JOURNALISM

IN

THEORY AND PRACTICE

STARDOM BOOKS

www.StardomBooks.com

STARDOM BOOKS
112 Bordeaux Ct.
Coppell, TX 75019, USA

FIRST EDITION DECEMBER 2025

STARDOM BOOKS, LLC.
112 Bordeaux Ct. Coppell, TX 75019, USA

www.stardombooks.com

Stardom Books
United States and India

JOURNALISM IN THEORY AND PRACTICE

REECH MALUAL

p. 442
cm. 13.5 X 21.5

Category : LAN008000 Language Arts & Disciplines : Journalism
BUS070060 Business & Economics : Industries - Media & Communications

ISBN : 978-1-957456-88-1

Dedication

This work is respectfully dedicated to the memory of the late Honorable Justice (Baba) Mareu D. Malual and Journalist (Mama) Audhia G. Deng.

Acknowledgments

I extend my profound and heartfelt gratitude to the myriad individuals whose unwavering support and boundless inspiration have illuminated my path, ultimately culminating in the realization of this book.

A special debt of gratitude is owed to Atem Agot Deng, whose unwavering belief in my nascent potential and the invaluable opportunity he extended to train as a Broadcast Journalist at Radio Miraya in 2012 irrevocably altered the trajectory of my career. This pivotal moment not only forged my professional identity but also profoundly shaped the foundational insights woven throughout these pages.

Furthermore, I extend my profound admiration and gratitude to my esteemed colleagues; Celia Koh, Patricia Okoed, Machrine Birungi, Sonya Demasi, Gabriel Joseph Shadar, Maal Maker Thiong, Philip Thon Aleu, David Manyang Mayar, Lucy Edward Jubara, Alfred Taban, Nhial Bol Aken, Zoran Culafic, Shelly Markoff, Kevin Bellwood, Sani Martin, Sebit Abdu, Sebit William Ker, Suzan Dokolo, and Ragina Gorle. Their collective inspiration, unwavering dedication, and unparalleled courage in braving formidable odds to report from the most challenging and often hostile environments within the Republic of South Sudan are not merely commendable but serve as a constant beacon, profoundly shaping my own understanding of journalism's indispensable and vital role.

To every one of my media colleagues across the Republic of South Sudan, I offer my deepest appreciation for your tenacious commitment to truth, integrity, and fearless reporting.

Contents

Foreword

In an era characterized by the rapid dissemination of news, the fundamental responsibilities of the press encompassing both traditional print and contemporary broadcast journalism, which necessitate rigorous observation, critical interrogation, and accountability of power are increasingly challenged. It is therefore a distinct privilege to introduce this significant publication by Reech Malual, a former colleague.

The author's journalistic career, spanning conflict zones and international legal proceedings, has underscored the inherent complexities of reporting on war, reconciliation, and delayed justice. This experience unequivocally demonstrates the critical, albeit often challenging, necessity of the journalistic role, whether navigating embedded assignments or pursuing nuanced perspectives in peace journalism, with accuracy and fairness remaining paramount.

This volume emerges at a critical juncture for journalism, a profession currently confronting significant foundational pressures. The proliferation of new media and the pervasive influence of social media have cultivated an environment where misinformation, opacity, and expedient reporting frequently supplant legitimate journalistic practices. Within this volatile context, the mechanisms of media accountability are more crucial than ever, continually challenged by the very platforms that offer unparalleled reach.

Nevertheless, this book is anchored in essential journalistic virtues: curiosity, courage, accuracy, and responsibility.

Within these pages, readers will discover a vital connection between theoretical frameworks and the practical, often chaotic, realities of journalistic practice. The text not only delineates the technical vocabulary of reporting, editing, sourcing, and framing applicable across diverse platforms from print to social media, but also articulates the moral grammar essential for every journalist: understanding the necessity of critical inquiry, pursuing narratives beyond superficial soundbites, and serving the public's right to information without bias or fear. It directly addresses rigorous fact-checking foundational to print, ethical considerations in live broadcasting, and the critical thinking requisite for navigating the information torrent in new media.

A notable aspect of the author's approach is the integration of rigorous newsroom practice with profound, reflective inquiry, a mindset characteristic of an individual who has managed deadlines under duress while contemplating the underlying purpose of journalistic endeavor. His trajectory, encompassing both local and international reporting, reinforces the global and elemental significance of journalism to human dignity. His unwavering commitment to truth serves as a crucial beacon, counteracting the incessant digital noise that often threatens to obscure essential factual information.

This book is intended as an indispensable guide and steadfast companion. For emerging journalists, it offers a definitive roadmap for careers in traditional print, digital-first newsrooms, or broadcast roles. For seasoned practitioners, it provides a vital mirror, reflecting the enduring values that must underpin their work amidst the continuous, often disorienting, evolution of media.

For all who recognize that free and fearless journalism is not merely an auxiliary function but an absolute prerequisite for a functioning democracy, this work offers a powerful reaffirmation of collective commitment to truth, transparency, and the profound, irreplaceable civic role of the press.

It is recommended to engage with this text critically and to apply its principles responsibly, thereby upholding the promise of journalism: to illuminate the unseen, to voice the unheard, and to cast light upon areas where darkness persists.

It is a profound honor to contribute this foreword to a book that is both timely, deeply grounded in integrity, and utterly committed to the highest ideals of the journalistic profession.

Zoran Ćulafić
Senior Correspondent & International Reporter
Over 40 years of Journalistic experience

Preface

As a high school student, I was thoroughly engrossed in the dream of becoming a journalist. Living with a journalist mother and a lawyer father, I often found myself drawn to the excitement of being featured in stories or appearing on screen, a prospect that profoundly captivated me.

Upon completing high school at Saint Augustine, Khartoum-Sudan, in 2009, my academic aptitude was clear, and it was widely expected that my scores would secure admission to any preferred university. However, my family envisioned a different path, believing I would be better suited to a career in law than journalism.

During the university admission process, my parents were so firm in their conviction that I was never permitted to complete my own application form, specifically to prevent me from listing journalism as an option. Consequently, law became the sole choice across all university applications. My mother, Audhia, personally accompanied me to the admission office to ensure the submission of the forms they had prepared. My subsequent admission to the University of Juba's Law School at Kadero Campus, Khartoum-Sudan, came as no surprise, given that law was the only specialty I was allowed to pursue. I bore no ill will, however, as I held immense respect for both my parents and their aspirations for my future.

Yet, the dream of becoming a journalist persisted, keeping me awake at night, contemplating how I might someday become a respected media professional. The separation of Southern Sudan from Sudan then led to a situation of force majeure, necessitating the relocation of the entire Khartoum Campus back to Juba. This resulted in an academic shutdown that lasted almost two years due to a lack of lecture halls and academic staff. While the School of Law, under the leadership of Dean, Associate Professor Deng Awur Wenyin, was undergoing construction, an invaluable opportunity arose: the Hirondelle Foundation/UNMISS Radio Miraya was seeking interns. This felt like my calling. I was accepted as one of six interns for a six-month period, from January to June 2012.

Training under seasoned colleagues such as Sonya De Masi, Gabriel Joseph Shadar, Lucy Edward Jubara, Sebit Abdu, Philip James, Sebit William, Atem Agot Deng, Celia Koh, Kevin Bellwood, Zoran, Shelly Markoff, Machrine Birungi, Patricia Okoed, and Muna Tesfay, their vast experience, among others, ignited within me a profound desire for journalistic excellence. My stories were broadcast and published on the website significantly more frequently than those of my fellow interns. Consequently, by the end of my internship, I was offered a contract as Radio Miraya Correspondent in Bentiu, Unity State, a position I was encouraged to take by my senior colleague, Atem Agot Deng, even as I continued my law studies at the University of Juba.

When I transitioned to independent journalistic work as a correspondent, Editor Atem Agot Deng accompanied me to my workstation to orient me on how to conduct myself with the independence inherent in the job. He then returned to Juba, and my new professional journey began immediately. Journalism has connected me to the full spectrum of humanity: the humble and the exalted, the impoverished and the affluent, the sorrowful and the joyous, the vulnerable and the powerful, the cruel and the compassionate.

It is, in essence, a reflection of humanity itself and the destiny of all kinds of human souls.

Being a journalist is a uniquely precious and special gift. While it may not offer immediate financial rewards, it profoundly shapes an individual, fostering all traits necessary for a life of ultimate purpose, regardless of the chosen lifestyle.

During my tenure as a correspondent for Radio Miraya, I visited some of the most volatile areas during South Sudan's civil war, often controversially described as 'tribal' by international media. Remarkably, I remained unharmed even in places like Ganyliel, Protection of Civilian sites in Bentiu, Juba, Bor, and Malakal, which served as a sanctuary for Bentiu residents displaced by the very same conflict. Today, my safety is a testament to the fairness and independence of my reporting.

Journalism is not a profession for the weak or the faint-hearted. While we universally agree that no story is worth a human life, it undeniably requires a courageous journalist to seek and report the truth under challenging circumstances.

This book aims to equip journalists and journalism students with essential field knowledge and encourage innovative, 'outside-the-box' thinking, as the profession demands. As you practice journalism, you will come to understand that nothing is more threatening than seeking and reporting the truth, not even a machine gun or a gunship. Journalism wields unmatched power because information itself is power.

In an epoch characterized by the unprecedented velocity of information dissemination and increasingly complex communication ecosystems, the salience of journalism is acutely pronounced, yet concurrently confronted by profound challenges. This treatise, "Journalism in Theory and Practice," undertakes a rigorous and exhaustive examination of this critical domain, endeavoring to reconcile the frequently divergent spheres of theoretical scholarship and pragmatic application. The objective of the book is to furnish readers with a robust conceptual framework for apprehending journalism, meticulously integrating its foundational theories, unyielding ethical imperatives, and the formidable practical impediments encountered by contemporary practitioners. From the philosophical underpinnings of objectivity and the pursuit of truth to the dynamic methodologies of reporting, editorial processes, and multimedia narrative construction, this volume addresses the dynamic and multifaceted essence of modern journalism.

This rigorous intellectual endeavor is conceived for students, academics, seasoned journalists, and indeed, any engaged citizen with a profound vested interest in the integrity and enduring future of news dissemination. We meticulously explore the historical evolution of journalistic tenets, critically scrutinize pressing contemporary discourses concerning media literacy, the proliferation of misinformation, and the transformative innovative paradigms reshaping the industry. By investigating both the underlying rationale and the practical execution, we aspire to cultivate a profound appreciation for both the meticulous craft and the evolving episteme of journalism, thereby empowering readers with the requisite knowledge and sophisticated critical instruments indispensable for navigating its increasingly intricate landscape.

Ultimately, "Journalism in Theory and Practice" functions as an authoritative compendium for those committed to buttressing the principles of a free, accountable, and indispensable press. It compels engagement with the enduring philosophical inquiries and urgent societal exigencies that fundamentally delineate journalism in the 21st century, championing a vital confluence of rigorous academic investigation and profound practical discernment.

This comprehensive account aims to proffer an indispensable framework for comprehending journalism's pivotal function in fostering informed public discourse, delivering essential shared knowledge that genuinely addresses audience requirements, and critically empowering judicious media consumption.

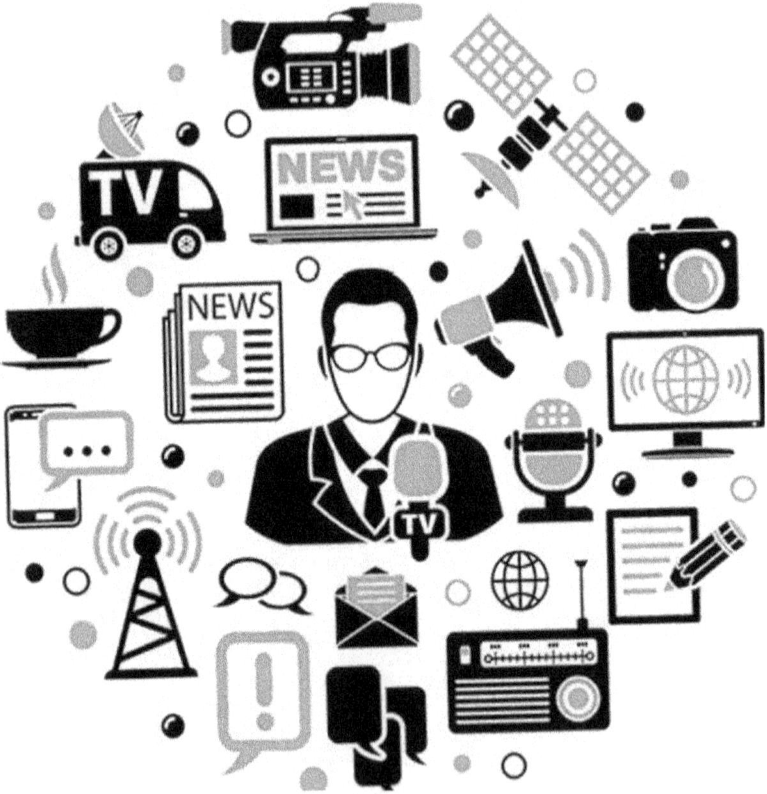
NEWS
TV
NEWS
TV

CHAPTER 1

The Evolution of Journalism

WHILE A SINGULAR, UNIVERSALLY accepted definition remains elusive, journalism is generally conceptualized as the systematic and principled process of gathering, verifying, and disseminating news, commentary, and feature content. This critical societal function, crucial for fostering informed public discourse and ensuring the accountability of power structures, is operationalized across a diverse spectrum of platforms. These encompass traditional modalities such as newspapers and magazines, established electronic media formats like radio and television, and the dynamically evolving contemporary digital ecosystem, comprising websites, blogs, webcasts, podcasts, and social media platforms. Historically, the conceptualization of journalism was predominantly confined to the dissemination of current events via print media. Nevertheless, the transformative emergence of radio, television, and the internet during the 20th century profoundly reconfigured its operational paradigms, consequently expanding its reach and purview to encompass all forms of mediated communication pertaining to current affairs, and thereby necessitating a continuous adaptation of methodologies while preserving its foundational objectives. This ongoing evolution, particularly the pervasive shift to digital formats, has ushered in a complex landscape of both unprecedented challenges, such as the proliferation of misinformation and evolving revenue models, and significant opportunities, including enhanced global reach and interactive engagement with audiences, thereby necessitating a fundamental re-evaluation of journalistic practices and ethical considerations (Forja-Pena, Orosa and García, 2024). Indeed, this digital transformation has not merely altered the media ecosystem but profoundly reshaped it, distinct from the advent of radio and television, because it infiltrates and revolutionizes every phase of the news process from content gathering and verification to production, distribution, and consumption, fundamentally redefining how information is created and consumed (Canavilhas and Fátima, 2024).

History of Journalism: From Ancient Scrolls to Digital Streams

Journalism's historical trajectory extends into antiquity. A foundational antecedent to contemporary news dissemination systems was the *Acta Diurna*, a Roman daily bulletin that is thought to have commenced prior to 59 BCE. This publication chronicled notable public events, such as speeches and governmental edicts, and was conspicuously exhibited for public inspection. This early form of public communication, despite its rudimentary nature, established a foundational precedent for public information dissemination, thereby challenging the monopolization of information by elites. The subsequent development of journalism saw significant shifts with the introduction of the printing press, which enabled unprecedentedly wider and more rapid dissemination of information, revolutionizing the scale and impact of news delivery (Canavilhas and Fátima, 2024).

Within Imperial China, during the Tang dynasty, official communications termed *bao* were disseminated among government personnel. These official gazettes underwent numerous transformations in format and nomenclature, enduring until the culmination of the Qing dynasty in 1911.

Nevertheless, the genesis of regularly published newspapers, which serve as direct precursors to modern print journalism, occurred in German urban centers and Antwerp circa 1609. A notable development in England was the advent of *The Weekly Newes* in 1622, succeeded by one of the earliest prominent daily newspapers, *The Daily Courant*, in 1702.(Weber, 2006) These early publications laid the groundwork for the establishment of journalistic practices, evolving from mere announcements to more comprehensive reporting (Nerone, 2008).

Historically, journalistic practices encountered substantial impediments, initially contending with significant governmental and ecclesiastical oversight, which included rigorous censorship, punitive fiscal measures, and stringent licensing protocols intended to restrict their impact. By the 18th century, however, the press began to experience augmented reportorial autonomy and assumed an essential public utility, underscoring the increasing acknowledgment of its pivotal role in public discourse a function it substantially maintains presently. The escalating demand for newspapers, stimulated by rising literacy levels and the introduction of steam- and electric-powered presses that facilitated unparalleled mass production, escalated daily circulation metrics from thousands to millions, signaling the definitive emergence of mass-market print journalism.

Magazines, initially conceived in the 17th century as scholarly periodicals, underwent an evolutionary process to incorporate opinion-shaping articles on contemporary issues, exemplified by publications such as *The Tatler* and *The Spectator*. The 1830s marked the proliferation of affordable, mass-circulation magazines aimed at a more extensive and less academically inclined readership, alongside specialized illustrated and women's periodicals, thereby enriching the breadth of the print media environment. The considerable financial outlay associated with extensive news collection, particularly concerning international developments, catalyzed the establishment of news agencies. These entities aggregated resources and distributed their journalistic output to a multitude of individual newspapers and magazines. Revolutionary innovations such as the telegraph, subsequently augmented by the seminal introductions of radio and television, significantly enhanced the velocity and immediacy of journalistic endeavors through the facilitation of near-instantaneous long-distance transmission. These technological advancements engendered vast new distribution channels and audiences for electronically disseminated content, thereby initiating broadcast journalism. In the late 20th century, satellites and later the internet further revolutionized the long-distance transmission of journalistic information, paving the way for new media.

Evolution of Journalistic Professionalism

Journalism witnessed a period of unprecedented professionalization throughout the 20th century, fundamentally advanced by four interdependent elements:

1. **Increased Organization:** The establishment and widespread growth of professional organizations for journalists played a crucial role in consolidating a professional identity and establishing fundamental professional standards.

2. **Specialized Education:** The development and expansion of specialized academic curricula for journalism studies elevated the field from an apprenticeship-based craft to a recognized academic discipline.

3. **Growing Literature:** A rapidly expanding corpus of scholarly and critical literature emerged, thereby promoting intellectual dialogue, facilitating critical self-reflection, and providing

theoretical underpinnings for the historical trajectory, complexities, and methodologies of mass communication.

4. **Enhanced Social Responsibility:** Journalists progressively embraced and cultivated an evolving awareness of ethical and societal obligations, which became increasingly imperative given the intricate challenges and emerging dynamics of new media and social media environments.

The formal organization of journalists began as early as 1883 with the founding of England's Chartered Institute of Journalists. Similar efforts followed, such as the American Newspaper Guild (established 1933) and the Fédération Nationale de la Presse Française. These institutes often functioned as both trade unions and professional organizations, advocating for journalists' rights, ethical standards, and fostering media accountability.

Before the latter half of the 19th century, most journalists acquired their skills through apprenticeships, typically starting as copyboys or cub reporters. This changed dramatically with the introduction of formal education. The University of Missouri offered the first university course in journalism between 1879 and 1884. By 1912, Columbia University in New York City established the first graduate program in journalism, funded by a grant from editor and publisher Joseph Pulitzer. This development recognized the increasing complexity of news reporting and newspaper operations, which necessitated specialized training. Editors also found that in-depth coverage of specialized areas like political affairs, business, economics, and science often required reporters with expertise in those fields. Furthermore, the emergence of motion pictures, radio, and television as news media demanded an ever-growing array of new skills and techniques for gathering and presenting news, directly impacting the skill sets required for **broadcast journalism**. By the 1950s, journalism or communications courses had become a common offering in colleges, preparing journalists for a diverse media landscape.

The literature surrounding journalism also experienced substantial growth. What was limited to two textbooks, a few collections of lectures, essays, and a small number of histories and biographies in 1900, became copious and varied by the late 20th century. This expanded body of work encompassed everything from historical accounts of journalism to practical guides for reporters and photographers, as well as critical discussions by journalists on the capabilities, methods, and ethics of their profession, including burgeoning discussions on **war and peace journalism**, **embedded journalism**, and the ethical dilemmas posed by rapidly evolving technologies.

A critical concern for social responsibility in journalism largely emerged in the late 19th and 20th centuries. Earlier newspapers and journals were often intensely partisan, believing their social responsibility lay in promoting their own party's agenda and critiquing the opposition. However, as the reading public grew and newspapers gained in size and wealth, the media gradually developed greater independence. Newspapers began to orchestrate their own popular and sensational 'crusades' to boost circulation, culminating in the intense competition between New York City's *World* and *Journal* in the 1890s (an era famously associated with yellow journalism).

The sense of social responsibility was significantly advanced by specialized education and widespread discussions about press responsibilities in books, periodicals, and professional association meetings. Influential reports, such as Great Britain's Royal Commission on the Press and the less extensive *A Free and Responsible Press* by an unofficial Commission on the Freedom of the Press in the

United States, greatly stimulated self-examination among practicing journalists. The rise of **new media** and **social media** has intensified this self-examination, especially concerning the spread of misinformation and the need for robust **media accountability**.

By the late 20th century, studies indicated that journalists, as a group, generally held idealistic views about their role in impartially presenting facts to the public. Various journalistic societies issued ethical statements, with the American Society of Newspaper Editors' code being particularly well-known. These ethical frameworks continue to adapt to address the unique challenges of the digital age, striving to uphold the foundational virtues of curiosity, courage, accuracy, and responsibility that define the journalistic profession, regardless of the medium.

Modern Journalism

While news has always been the fundamental core of journalism, the term "news" acquired so many broader meanings that "hard news" became a necessary distinction. This term emerged to differentiate items of clear journalistic value from those of peripheral significance. This shift was largely driven by the advent of **broadcast** journalism; radio and television which delivered news bulletins with a speed that traditional print media could not match. To maintain their audience, newspapers began offering increasing amounts of interpretive content: background articles, personality profiles, and opinion columns from writers skilled in presenting commentary engagingly. By the mid-1960s, most newspapers, particularly evening and Sunday editions, heavily adopted magazine-style techniques, reserving the traditional rule of objectivity primarily for their "hard news" content. Newsmagazines, in turn, frequently blended factual reporting with editorial commentary.

Print journalism continued to innovate through book-length reporting, which, though having a shorter history, has been notably impactful. The post-World War II proliferation of paperback books spurred the growth of journalistic literature, exemplified by works analyzing election campaigns, political scandals, and global affairs. This era also gave rise to "new journalism," pioneered by authors such as Truman Capote, Tom Wolfe, and Norman Mailer, who integrated narrative techniques traditionally found in fiction—like dialogue, scenic construction, specific points of view, and personal voice into nonfiction reporting (Jacobson, Marino and Gutsche, 2015; Krieken and Sanders, 2019)

The 20th century also witnessed a resurgence of governmental control and restrictions on the press. In communist countries, the state owned the media, with journalists and editors serving as government employees. Under such systems, the primary function of reporting news was intertwined with the duty to uphold and support the national ideology and state objectives. This often resulted in media coverage that emphasized the positive achievements of communist states while downplaying or ignoring their shortcomings. Such rigorous censorship was pervasive throughout journalism in these nations. In contrast, non-communist developing countries experienced varying degrees of press freedom, ranging from subtle, occasional self-censorship on sensitive government issues to stringent, omnipresent censorship akin to that in communist states. The highest levels of press freedom were generally observed in most English-speaking countries and Western European nations, where principles of **media accountability** were more robustly applied, allowing for a more critical and independent press.

Whereas traditional journalism emerged during a period of information scarcity and high demand, 21st-century journalism contends with an information-saturated market. Here, the sheer abundance of news, driven by **new media** and **social media**, has, to some extent, devalued it. Technological advancements like satellites, digital platforms, and the Internet have made information more plentiful and accessible, intensifying journalistic competition. To meet the growing consumer demand for real-time and highly detailed reporting, media outlets developed alternative dissemination channels, including online distribution, electronic mailings, and direct engagement with the public through forums, blogs, user-generated content, and major social media platforms such as Facebook, X (formerly Twitter), and YouTube. This transformation has also profoundly impacted specialized fields like war and peace **journalism**, where information from conflict zones can now spread instantaneously, directly influencing public perception and the ethical considerations of reporting. The practice of embedded journalism has also evolved, with social media allowing for more immediate, albeit often controlled, dispatches from the front lines.

In the second decade of the 21st century, social media platforms notably facilitated the spread of politically motivated "fake news" a form of disinformation often produced by profit-driven websites masquerading as legitimate news organizations. These sites are designed to attract and mislead specific audiences by exploiting entrenched partisan biases. The prevalence of such content highlights a critical challenge for modern journalism: upholding credibility and facts in a fragmented and often polarized information environment. The term "fake news" itself became a weapon; during and after the 2016 U.S. presidential election campaign, Donald J. Trump frequently used it to discredit news reports, even from established and reputable media organizations, that contained negative information about him, further complicating the public's trust in legitimate reporting and raising serious questions about **media accountability**. This era demands a renewed commitment from all forms of journalism print, broadcast, and new media to the core virtues of accuracy, responsibility, and fearless interrogation of power.

CHAPTER 2

Editorials

THE TERM 'EDITORIAL' TRADITIONALLY encompasses two distinct aspects: first, it refers to the comprehensive process of preparing content for publication, which involves shaping opinions and narratives within media. Second, it denotes a specific, prominent article, frequently unsigned and composed by a senior editor or publisher. This opinion-based journalistic piece articulates the publication's official position on critical public matters, reflecting the collective viewpoint of the news organization and serving as a platform for the perspectives of owners and editors on current events. Its primary aims are to influence public discourse, cultivate critical thinking, and, at times, stimulate action regarding significant public issues (Alghazo et al., 2024), while also endeavoring to interpret and assess events of particular importance (Espinosa, 2003). Editorials differentiate themselves from factual news reporting by explicitly presenting the publication's perspective, rather than merely documenting occurrences (Bolívar, 2002).

Editorial Writing

Editorial writing serves to articulate the official position of a publication or media organization concerning current affairs, often referred to as 'leading articles' or 'leaders'. These compositions explicitly convey the publication's intrinsic, opinion-driven viewpoints, aiming primarily to influence public discourse, foster critical thinking, and occasionally stimulate public engagement on salient issues (Alghazo et al., 2024). At its core, an editorial operates as an opinion-based journalistic text that not only mirrors the collective perspective of the news entity but also critically analyzes and evaluates events of considerable significance (Espinosa, 2003).

Editorial Meetings

Editorial meetings inherently assemble a multiplicity of perspectives, divergent opinions, and disparate strategic objectives from participating team members. Unmanaged, this intrinsic complexity risks engendering fragmentation, operational inefficiencies, or incongruent priorities. Consequently, the appointment of an adept leader, tasked with both facilitating the deliberative process and ensuring accountability in its strategic implementation, is indispensable for realizing cohesive results. Importantly, this leadership role extends beyond simple hierarchical standing, necessitating individuals proficient in moderating discussions, fostering consensus, and advancing strategic determinations. Within this framework, a primary duty of the presiding editor involves the strategic allocation of resources, specifically encompassing the judicious assignment and re-assignment of journalists to particular beats, stringent management of coverage directives to align with the overarching editorial vision, and precise oversight of interview execution to uphold journalistic integrity and analytical depth. Subsequently, reporters are delegated tasks and are expected to adhere to predefined deadlines throughout their investigative and reporting endeavors. This conventional process, deeply entrenched in the rigid deadlines characteristic of print journalism, is currently experiencing a significant metamorphosis. The incessant demands of digital news platforms mandate not only adaptable workflows and organizational frameworks (Hagen, Tolstad and Bygdås, 2021) but also agile leadership within editorial convenings to proactively manage these transitions and sustain operational relevance. Ultimately, effective editorial meetings, supported by comprehensive planning and proficient leadership, are crucial for achieving optimal team performance, streamlined task management, and successful adaptation within a constantly evolving media environment (Merriam et al., 2021; Rashid, 2024).

Preparation of Editorial Board Meeting Agenda

Effective structuring of an editorial board meeting agenda necessitates the initial identification and prioritization of critical items, guided by their strategic salience and contemporary relevance (Rashid, 2024). Subsequently, the precise allocation of time to each discussion point is essential for optimizing operational efficiency. Moreover, the incorporation of dedicated periods for interactive deliberation and collaborative conceptualization is paramount. Furthermore, the agenda should meticulously outline all necessary pre-meeting documentation and resources, thereby ensuring participants are thoroughly prepared to offer substantive contributions (Almeida, Ahmed and Hoek, 2023). This comprehensive approach guarantees the meeting's strategic coherence, maximizes productivity, and effectively advances the achievement of predetermined organizational objectives.

Guiding an Effective Editorial Meeting

As a lead editor, assignment editor, managing editor, or Editor-in-Chief, conducting productive editorial meetings constitutes a critical responsibility. To ensure optimal productivity and clarity, the advance preparation and distribution of a meeting agenda are essential, incorporating the following key discussion points (Rashid, 2024):

1. **Welcome and Introductions**: Initiate the session with a welcoming address and facilitate concise

introductions, integrating any pertinent member updates or acknowledgments to cultivate a collaborative environment.

2. **Review of Previous Actions**: Systematically review minutes, notes, and action items from the preceding meeting, with particular attention to previously covered news and approved story tips pending execution. This step is crucial for ensuring operational continuity, reinforcing accountability, and establishing a foundation for subsequent progress.

3. **Editor's Report**: Present a comprehensive Editor's Report, providing an incisive update on the status of ongoing news coverage. This report should strategically identify areas requiring further investigation, potential adjustments in journalistic methodology, or critical re-evaluation, thereby ensuring sustained quality and adherence to established journalistic standards (Bojić, Prodanović and Samala, 2024).

4. **Performance Report**: Disseminate a detailed Performance Report, presenting key insights derived from publication analytics and audience engagement data. This evidence-based feedback is instrumental in strategically informing and refining subsequent editorial decisions and content strategies.

5. **Story Tip Presentation**: Facilitate an interactive Story Tip Presentation session, inviting reporters and editors to propose innovative story ideas grounded in their specialized expertise or compelling emerging news narratives. This phase rigorously evaluates what constitutes 'newsworthy' content, integrating both theoretical frameworks and practical journalistic considerations (Armona et al., 2024).

6. **Assignment and Deadlines**: Systematically allocate reporters to specific news coverage, concurrently establishing explicit and achievable deadlines for story completion. This critical process not only supports journalists in crafting original, impactful, and factually accurate narratives within stringent timeframes (Lopez et al., 2022) but also underscores the editor's paramount responsibility in managing assignments and ensuring deadline adherence (Hagen, Tolstad and Bygdås, 2021).

News Tips

Leading media organizations, such as The New York Times, have established online platforms that enable the public to submit journalistic leads. Similarly, Portuguese news outlets like Observador and Público have implemented mechanisms, frequently through dedicated forms or direct email to authors, facilitating readers in reporting factual inaccuracies in articles, thereby contributing to the maintenance of accuracy (Miranda, 2023). Beyond mere error correction, certain digital-native media organizations, exemplified by eldiario.es, proactively involve their audiences in collaborative content generation processes, where public contributions can influence published narratives or be integrated into online content.

The New York Times, for instance, explicitly states on its website: "Do you have a big story? Want to share it with The New York Times? We offer several ways to get in touch with and provide materials to our journalists. No communication system is completely secure, but these tools can help protect your anonymity." This strategy highlights the media's dedication to diverse information acquisition and the safeguarding of contributors' anonymity.

This contemporary reliance on public submission channels for journalistic leads and content suggestions—accompanied by assurances of security and confidentiality represents a notable departure from traditional journalistic practices, where news leads were conventionally identified and narrative frameworks established during internal editorial meetings. This evolution signifies a shift toward a more participatory journalism model, transforming the public from passive recipients into engaged contributors in news production (Panagiotidis et al., 2020). The integration of public input not only expands the breadth of informational inputs but also fosters heightened perceptions of transparency and journalistic credibility (Lima et al., 2023). The growing deployment of AI agents to generate investigative leads for data reporting further underscores the dynamic evolution of news tip generation (Veerbeek and Diakopoulos, 2024a, 2024b). It is an ethically and professionally mandated principle of journalistic practice that media organizations are obligated to protect the confidentiality of their sources and are not bound to disclose their identities (Salvo, 2024).

A common operational protocol observed across numerous media organizations, including South Sudanese media outlets such as UN Radio Miraya where practical experience was acquired entails the convening of editorial meetings in the early morning, typically prior to 8:00 AM. This tradition serves to optimize news dissemination and adherence to daily publication schedules, underscoring the inherently rapid pace of the news cycle.

Qualities of an Effective Story Tip

A compelling news tip is characterized by several key components. Foremost, it must unequivocally be substantiated by robust documentation or unimpeachable credible evidence to warrant serious consideration by editorial management as a potential story.

Mere speculation or unsubstantiated hunches not only fail to meet the rigorous criteria for a viable tip but also risk undermining editorial credibility and wasting valuable journalistic resources. Journalistic integrity strictly requires adherence to foundational standards such as factual accuracy, verifiable relevance, and crucial timeliness when evaluating news (Bojić, Prodanović and Samala, 2024).

An effective news tip must precisely articulate a distinct issue or problem with palpable real-world consequences. It must be sufficiently specific, offering multiple substantive angles for potential narrative development. Crucially, and perhaps most importantly, a news tip must possess unquestionable inherent newsworthiness. While it might seem unfair to an individual, a professional media organization's editorial team operates under strict mandates regarding public interest and resource allocation; consequently, they will not pursue a story about, for example, a neighbor stealing cable, as such an isolated incident inherently lacks the broad public interest and significant societal implications required to meet the high threshold of newsworthy content (Armona et al., 2024). News organizations rigorously assess the prospective influence and extensive dissemination of a narrative, consequently prioritizing content that demonstrates broad audience resonance and substantially enriches public discourse (Ngoma and Adebisi, 2023).

Identifying Actionable News Tips

For a news tip to be deemed 'actionable' and warrant editorial attention, it must unequivocally demonstrate both inherent newsworthiness and a clear potential to evolve into a significant and compelling news story. Without these critical foundational elements, a mere suggestion will inevitably lack the gravitas required for serious journalistic investigation and resource allocation.

Examples of such newsworthy and actionable tips include:

- "A report on environmental pollution in South Sudan's oil fields was released yesterday."

- "We have evidence indicating this government representative is in breach of the law."

- "Here is proof that this company is engaging in unethical conduct."

- "A man was shot and killed in Munuki, Juba, Republic of South Sudan, last night; police should be contacted for details."

- "The national parliamentary session is scheduled to debate a corruption bill, according to the Assembly's Clerk."

- "The Government spokesperson is holding a news conference at 9:00 AM at their ministerial premises.

Actionable tips are critically defined by their immediate pertinence, unambiguously verifiable assertions, and substantial capacity for public impact, which fundamentally distinguishes them from generalized observations or unsubstantiated anecdotal accounts. Each provided instance reinforces the essential prerequisites of an actionable news tip, emphasizing the necessity for information that is not only clear, concise, and rigorously substantiated by robust documentation, but also inherently possesses broader public relevance. This pivotal combination frequently necessitates prompt journalistic action or deeper inquiry, thereby upholding the core journalistic tenets of factual accuracy, contextual relevance, and demonstrable societal impact (Bojić, Prodanović and Samala, 2024).

Broadcast Production and Programming: Adapting to Modern Demands

The demand for meaningful, efficient, and high-quality broadcast production and programming has intensified significantly in the contemporary media landscape. This decisive shift moves away from conventional "talking head" video conference styles towards more engaging, dynamic consumer experiences. Media leaders increasingly recognize fundamental and irreversible shifts in audience viewing and engagement behaviors, compelling the adoption of innovative techniques to robustly connect with their public. Within media organizations, particularly those with a significant presence of millennials and digital natives, there's a strong trend towards dynamic, fast-paced, entertaining, and interactive programming that deeply resonates with contemporary audiences (Ibrahim, Hidayana and Saefullah, 2024; Zhang, 2024). Based on research conducted by the Accenture Broadcast team in Chicago and published on LinkedIn in 2016, Jason Warnke outlined ten essential steps for effective broadcast video production and programming within an enterprise:

1. **Clear Vision and Leadership:** Investing in technology, equipment, and talent, while seemingly counterintuitive for organizations not primarily TV studios, is unequivocally crucial. The unmistakable trends and escalating demand in the digital broadcasting sphere emphatically underscore its necessity, mandating strategic planning and strong leadership to adapt to multi-platform environments and evolving viewer expectations (Telkmann, 2020).

2. **Knowledge of Audience:** A profound understanding of the viewing audience or readership is absolutely paramount, enabling efforts to resonate more rapidly and effectively (Luk

et al., 2020). This critically involves active experimentation, fostering interactivity, rigorously analyzing data, and directly soliciting feedback. It's imperative to find sophisticated ways to assess production effectiveness, looking beyond mere "views" to more telling metrics like "comments," "likes," and "shares," which often provide a far stronger signal of impactful content and genuine audience engagement (Nelson, 2019). News organizations increasingly rely on AI-assisted interpretation of audience feedback to meticulously refine their strategies (Brannon et al., 2024).

3. **Creating 'Snackable' Content:** Traditional long-form viewing is demonstrably effective only in highly limited cases. For the vast majority of topics, content must be rendered far more consumable, recognizing that digital audiences, particularly digital natives, often possess shorter attention spans and distinctly prefer condensed, easily shareable formats (Nguyen, Veer and Ballantine, 2025). "Snackable content" refers to shortened forms of original content meticulously focusing on a single theme or motif for quick understanding and entertainment. It's absolutely vital to think creatively about content, assiduously avoiding the trap of dismissing subject matter as "boring." Instead, the focus must be on unearthing the common thread, the compelling human element, and the most captivating way to deliver the message, thereby making the value to the viewer immediately and unequivocally apparent. While user preferences generally indicate a trend toward shorter clips, some studies suggest a preference for slightly longer snackable clips depending on the specific content (King, Zavesky and Gonzales, 2021).

4. **Streaming and Replaying Capabilities:** Proactive and meticulous planning for organizing replays within a YouTube-like video portal is absolutely essential. Effective tagging of content is critically important for ease of searching, powerfully reflecting the accelerating consumer trend for Video on Demand and the undeniable importance of comprehensive content libraries for effectively retaining viewers, especially younger demographics (Ibrahim, Hidayana and Saefullah, 2024). Radio broadcasting, too, has fundamentally transformed to meet urgent digital demands, now consistently offering on-demand content and personalized experiences (Laor, 2022).

5. **Cross-pollinate Skills:** A robust and indispensable blend of TV production expertise, core IT/infrastructure knowledge, application development skills, sharp communication acumen, and unbridled creativity is absolutely paramount. Achieving this crucial synergy undeniably takes time, as each discipline possesses its own distinct terminology and demands dedicated effort to foster mutual understanding (Mitrić, 2022). The modern media landscape unyieldingly demands professionals equipped with both traditional and cutting-edge digital skills, thereby irrevocably blurring the boundaries between journalism, PR, and marketing roles and emphasizing highly transferable professional skills (Bernhard and Rußmann, 2023). Furthermore, effective cross-functional teams are unequivocally crucial for driving innovation and ensuring success amidst complex market requirements (Koivunen, Olshannikova and Olsson, 2021).

6. **Finding Hidden Talent:** As video production capabilities expand, organizations invariably discover invaluable hidden talents among their staff: dedicated hobbyists, passionate amateur documentarians, compelling on-air personalities, skilled makeup artists, innovative graphic designers, and many more. Creating an environment that actively encourages self-expression, and fearless experimentation is the undeniable key to discovering and meticulously nurturing these individuals, thereby profoundly contributing to a diversified and dynamic talent pool essential for the evolving media industry ("International Journal of New Developments in Education," 2022).

7. **Automated Focus on Production Quality:** As these capabilities mature, diligently seeking opportunities to automate administrative and repetitive aspects of the production process becomes unequivocally critical. This strategic automation liberates personnel to exclusively concentrate on creative elements, thereby enabling more concurrent, repetitive, and industrialized broadcasts (Wright et al., 2020). Artificial intelligence is increasingly and powerfully streamlining post-production, editing, and distribution processes, optimizing media workflows, and significantly enhancing both creativity and audience interaction (Abdelraouf, 2024). For instance, AI can precisely automate scene detection, facial recognition, and subtitle generation in editing, and intelligently personalize recommendation algorithms in distribution (Benson, Okolo and Oke, 2024). This technological advancement fundamentally assists in producing high-quality content with far greater efficiency, even

for intensely demanding tasks like live sports audio mixing (Moulson et al., 2024).

8. **Track Savings from the Start:** Meticulously monitoring the substantial cost savings achieved by producing video content internally compared to outsourcing to external agencies is of paramount importance. These savings can accumulate surprisingly quickly and significantly impact budgetary allocations.

9. **Leveraging Cloud Solutions:** While early adopters might have built platforms from scratch, today's market offers a plethora of excellent Software-as-a-Service and Platform-as-a-Service options. These advanced solutions for webcasting, streaming platforms, video portals, and collaborative editing can significantly accelerate efforts, providing highly economical and flexible architectures for the production of truly high-quality broadcast content (Sharma et al., 2021).

10. **Timely Broadcast:** The demand for video broadcasts and productions has surged dramatically. Staying decisively ahead of this relentless demand is absolutely crucial for ensuring sustained success in a rapidly evolving media consumption environment.

Assignment & Reassignment of Reporters

During editorial meetings, a core responsibility of the presiding editor encompasses the strategic assignment and reassignment of journalists to specific beats, the management of coverage directives, and the oversight of interview execution. Reporters are subsequently delegated tasks and expected to adhere to stipulated deadlines throughout their reporting activities. This process, traditionally rooted in print journalism's fixed deadlines, is undergoing significant transformation due to the relentless and continuous demands of digital news, which necessitate more dynamic and adaptable workflows and organizational structures. The editor's role is pivotal in navigating this evolving landscape, ensuring journalists are supported to produce original, impactful, and factually accurate stories under increasingly tight deadlines while upholding journalistic integrity in a fast-paced environment (Lopez et al., 2022), with assignments and adherence to deadlines being a primary responsibility managed by the editor (Hagen, Tolstad and Bygdås, 2021).

Editorial Specialty

An editorial specialist is responsible for the comprehensive management of the content lifecycle, including its creation, review, editing, and systematic organization, for various publications and presentations (Carlos, 2024). This role spans diverse sectors such as technology, healthcare, and education. Key responsibilities encompass:

1. **File and text audits:** Conducting thorough content audits and developing comprehensive style guides and content strategies, which are foundational for maintaining brand consistency and overall content quality. This also involves collaborating rigorously with subject matter experts to validate accuracy and ensure the utmost relevance of content.

2. **Compiling essential documentation:** This encompasses the meticulous preparation of reports, presentations, and other vital documents, ensuring clarity and supporting informed decision-making.

3. **Strategic content planning:** Developing and implementing content plans that align with organizational objectives and target audience needs, often involving market research and analysis to identify emerging trends.

4. **Developing communications strategies:** Developing robust communications strategies that rigorously ensure all content adheres to established ethical guidelines and maintains the highest, unimpeachable standards of quality and accuracy, thereby safeguarding credibility (Hashmi, 2024).(T., 2024)

5. **Analyzing digital advertising campaigns:** Rigorously ensuring strict adherence to all legal and regulatory frameworks pertaining to digital content and advertising. This compliance is imperative not only for mitigating significant legal risks and avoiding substantial financial penalties but also for preserving an organization's reputation and maintaining public trust, particularly within highly regulated sectors.

6. **Reviewing and editing news stories:** Editors play a crucial role in enhancing the readability, accuracy, and overall quality of news stories by refining headlines, lead paragraphs, and ensuring content integrity.

7. **Orchestrating critical consultations with subject matter experts:** This involves adeptly facilitating interviews, rigorously reviewing technical drafts, and expertly integrating specialized knowledge to transform complex information into exceptionally accessible and engaging content formats.(Ekström, Ramsälv and Westlund, 2021)

This collaborative approach is instrumental in transforming intricate technical or specialized information into accessible formats for diverse audiences, thereby promoting efficient communication and the successful dissemination of knowledge while simultaneously upholding rigorous standards of precision and comprehensive detail (Hashmi, 2024). Furthermore, these specialists additionally supervise the distribution of draft articles, critically appraise and refine technical documentation to ensure its accuracy, clarity, and conformity with predefined standards, and proactively identify and integrate pertinent visual media, such as photographs and videos, to augment audience engagement and understanding. Proficiency in specialized software, such as Adobe Acrobat Professional and Interleaf desktop publishing tools, is often requisite, as it facilitates adeptness in document formatting, the creation of presentation materials, and the generation of publication-quality manuscripts, thereby guaranteeing professional presentation and cross-platform accessibility. These roles necessitate a fundamental and comprehensive grasp of complex editorial procedures and rigorous adherence to established content policies, elements critical for upholding consistency, quality, and regulatory compliance.

News Editing

In journalism, editing constitutes a critical evaluation of content by an individual or team, followed by requisite revisions to ensure adherence to established standards before publication (Azeez, 2020; Sawi and Alaa, 2024). This intricate process involves the independent scrutiny of journalistic narratives, distinct from the original authors, to identify and rectify issues such as grammar, verbosity, tone, style, fact-checking, and syntactic and semantic elements (Sawi and Alaa, 2024).

The rapid growth of online news platforms has increased the need for reliable methods to evaluate the quality and credibility of news articles (Bojić, Prodanović and Samala, 2024).

What is a News Editor?

In the dynamic landscape of modern media, a news editor assumes the pivotal responsibility for the meticulous curation and critical review of journalistic content produced by other writers, ensuring its readiness for publication across diverse media platforms, including digital and print, while upholding rigorous standards of accuracy and ethical reporting (Ekström, Ramsälv and Westlund, 2021).

These multifaceted responsibilities typically encompass comprehensive editing and meticulous proofreading, the strategic commissioning of journalistic pieces, precise coordination of writing teams, and, at times, the generation of original content to fill critical gaps (Moher et al., 2017). Possessing robust organizational capabilities and exceptional written communication skills is therefore paramount for editors, as they frequently oversee multiple articles or projects concurrently, often under considerable pressure to meet dynamic deadlines while maintaining consistent quality and adherence to editorial guidelines (Fontes and Menegon, 2021).

Furthermore, editors are often tasked with verifying factual accuracy within submitted content, thereby necessitating proficiency in research and interviewing techniques comparable to those employed by journalists and ensuring the unimpeachable credibility of published news (Audette-Longo et al., 2023).

This role increasingly demands a "new media business mind-set" with convergent skills in content production, multiplatform management, and technology utilization (Booth, Solvoll and Krumsvik, 2023), a strategic imperative reflecting the evolving requirements of the profession and crucial for navigating the complex digital news environment (Kustermann et al., 2022).

Understanding Proof-Editing

Local institutions, businesses, charities, and educational establishments frequently encounter a significant challenge: the limited availability of professionally qualified editors adept at meticulously refining their written communications. This prevalent deficiency often culminates in detrimental outcomes, including compromised clarity, eroded credibility, and an inability to effectively articulate intended messages. Moreover, documents developed collaboratively by teams are inherently susceptible to fragmented conceptualization, rendering the attainment of overarching coherence, consistency, and precision exceptionally arduous. In these widespread and high-stakes contexts, the function of proof-editing extends beyond mere utility, emerging as an imperative safeguard.

Proof-editing constitutes an intensely meticulous and rigorous process, transcending the scope of conventional proofreading. It operates as a crucial, subsequent phase to initial editorial work, specifically designed to scrutinize and perfect the editor's output. This critical stage systematically addresses latent errors and refines all on-page elements, such as headers, footers, and critical formatting matters, thereby elevating the document's professional presentation (Sawi and Alaa, 2024). Fundamentally, it encompasses a comprehensive and exhaustive review that extends beyond surface-level grammatical errors, typographical mistakes, and punctuation inaccuracies. It delves deeply into crucial aspects such as stylistic consistency, rhetorical clarity, narrative conciseness, appropriate tone, and overall textual flow, ensuring the material is not only polished but also profoundly impactful and persuasive (Azeez, 2020).

This exacting process is paramount for fostering unequivocal semantic clarity and substantially enhancing comprehension (Azeez, 2020), a necessity particularly pronounced in academic and professional contexts where content integrity, structural adherence to rigorous guidelines, and unblemished credibility are non-negotiable (Lourens, 2016).Consequently, in these profoundly impactful and high-stakes environments, professional editing and proofreading emerge not merely as beneficial, but as absolutely indispensable. They serve as foundational safeguards, rigorously upholding stringent standards of quality, ensuring unwavering credibility, and effectively preempting the detrimental consequences of miscommunication and conceptual fragmentation (Petelin, 2002).

The Critical Role of Proofreading in Document Perfection

Proofreading stands as a cornerstone for guaranteeing an impeccable document, constituting an integral and decisive stage in the content lifecycle alongside editing and review (Carlos, 2024). Its proficient execution necessitates profound expertise, unwavering diligence, and a keen eye for detail. This rigorous process entails the independent scrutiny of narratives by an individual or team, distinct from the original authors, to meticulously uncover and resolve issues such as grammar, verbosity, tone, style, fact-checking, and syntactic and semantic elements (Sawi and Alaa, 2024).

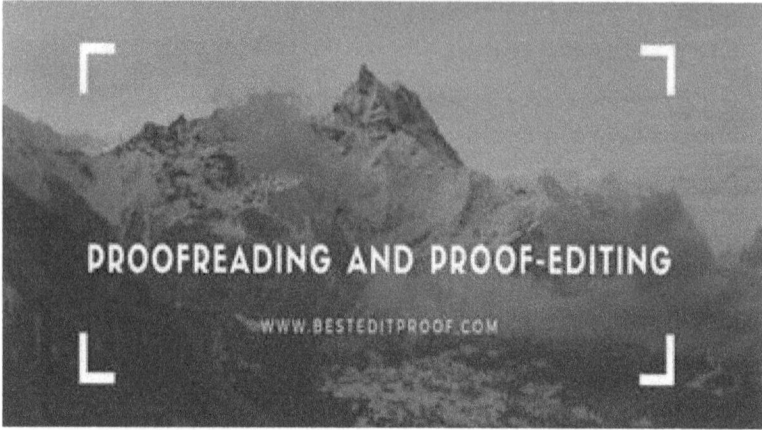

PROOFREADING AND PROOF-EDITING

WWW.BESTEDITPROOF.COM

Defining Proofreading and Proof-editing

Proofreading constitutes a rigorous and resource-intensive undertaking that transcends basic grammatical scrutiny. This process involves an exhaustive examination extending beyond conventional errors in grammar, orthography, punctuation, syntax, and spelling, to include an assessment of stylistic elements, clarity, conciseness, tone, and overall coherence, thereby ensuring the material achieves a refined and influential quality (Azeez, 2020). The fundamental aim of proofreading is to guarantee the complete absence of errors within the written discourse, meticulously verifying precision in sentence construction, appropriate usage of homonyms, capitalization, internal consistency, and numbering conventions (Azeez, 2020). Positioned as the culminating phase of the authorial process, its critical significance is irrefutable; indeed, notwithstanding its sequential placement, its impact remains paramount. Engaging a professional proofreading service guarantees that a document will be entirely divested of linguistic inaccuracies, thereby enabling the manuscript to achieve exceptional distinction.

Proof-editing, Proof-editing, though closely allied, represents a more extensive and resource-intensive endeavor than conventional proofreading or basic editorial review. This process amalgamates the meticulous examination characteristic of proofreading with the developmental and stylistic enhancements traditionally linked to copyediting, thereby yielding a refined and structurally robust final document. Such comprehensive intervention proves especially beneficial for collaboratively authored documents or texts produced by individuals lacking access to professional editorial expertise, given its capacity to resolve challenges pertaining to coherence and conceptual unity inherent in such productions. The scope of proof-editing can encompass modifications to raw text, strategic structural revisions, substantial rewriting, content condensation, or specific text styling for publication, thereby transcending the conventional parameters of basic proofreading (Azeez, 2020).

The Need for Professional Proofreading

English language experts unequivocally caution writers against the perilous trap of relying solely on self-revision. Authors, by virtue of their profound immersion in their own compositions, invariably develop a form of 'authorial blindness,' rendering them prone to overlooking critical errors and subtle inconsistencies. Consequently, following an initial round of self-correction, an independent external review becomes not merely beneficial but indispensable. A fresh, objective perspective is the sole reliable mechanism for systematically uncovering the multitude of concealed errors that invariably escape the author's gaze. Studies have shown that journalists generally hold idealistic views about their role in presenting facts impartially, but even they benefit from objective review (Ekström, Ramsälv and Westlund, 2021).

Writers frequently express profound astonishment at the sheer volume and insidious nature of errors that a professional proofreader meticulously uncovers within their manuscripts mistakes that had remained entirely invisible to the original author. Furthermore, the intervention of an experienced proofreader introduces unparalleled linguistic expertise, profoundly elevating the clarity, precision, and overall sophistication of a document's written English. This rigorous process guarantees unwavering adherence to the most stringent standards of grammar, stylistic coherence, and meticulous formatting, thereby ensuring the work not only meets but surpasses conventional expectations, truly distinguishing itself in any competitive landscape. This is especially crucial in academic and journalistic contexts where accuracy and clarity are paramount (Moher et al., 2017).

The Process and Scope of Proofreading

Proofreading involves a series of critical steps undertaken before written material reaches its intended audience. A skilled proofreader possesses a deep understanding of how to refine a manuscript, with the primary goal of ensuring it is consistently free from errors and minor imperfections. Proofreading, and its more intensive counterpart, proof-editing, generally encompass the following tasks:

1. Thorough Verification of Page Elements: Rigorously checking all page headings and numbers to ensure absolute accuracy and document integrity.

2. Precise Cross-referencing of Structural Components: Meticulously comparing the table of contents, indexes, and appendices against the main text to guarantee exact correspondence of titles and page numbers, thereby ensuring seamless navigability and internal consistency.

3. Comprehensive Error Detection: Systematically identifying and rectifying all grammatical, punctuation, syntactical, spelling, and vocabulary errors to eliminate any linguistic imperfections.

4. Rigorous Style Consistency: Ensuring and elevating the document's overall stylistic coherence to meet established academic or publication standards.

5. Unwavering Linguistic Precision: Guaranteeing the impeccable application of grammar, punctuation, syntax, and spelling to cultivate a flawless and highly polished manuscript.

6. Meticulous Structural Control: Scrupulously verifying all page numbers and titles to maintain stringent structural integrity.

7. Critical Content Layout Review: Diligently reviewing and rectifying the content's page structure to ensure optimal presentation and readability.

8. Enhanced Reader Accessibility: Ensuring with paramount importance that the content is conveyed to the reader with absolute consistency and unequivocal comprehensibility.

9. Strategic Rearrangement of Elements: Identifying and executing necessary reordering of components to achieve seamless textual flow and logical progression.

10. Proactive Clarity Enhancement: Eliminating all confusing and incomprehensible words or phrases to ensure absolute lucidity and direct communication.

11. Optimized Visual Presentation: Guaranteeing that the content is flawlessly displayed for maximum professional impact and aesthetic coherence.

12. Rigorous Adherence to Formal Tone: Strictly eliminating contractions, colloquialism, and personal pronouns to unequivocally uphold a dignified and academic tone.

13. Sophisticated Vocabulary Refinement: Strategically deploying a comprehensive and advanced vocabulary within academic manuscripts to significantly elevate the intellectual caliber and impact of the writing.

Upon the completion of the writing process, the manuscript is conventionally submitted to a designer or editor, marking the initiation of the proofreading phase. Numerous proofreading service providers observe that errors are more readily detected in a hardcopy manuscript compared to a digital display, as the dynamic nature of screen-based text can occasionally lead to omissions. Consequently, some services implement a two-stage procedure: an initial digital proofreading pass followed by a thorough hardcopy review. Furthermore, assigning distinct proofreaders to each stage can significantly enhance accuracy.

A proofreader is also instrumental in ensuring the consistency of a publication, verifying that the text, visual elements, and overarching theme are communicated to the reader in the most comprehensible and appropriate manner (Lourens, 2016). Therefore, authors should judiciously utilize professional proofreading services to guarantee the impeccability of their documents. This comprehensive approach, which often includes multiple rounds of review, is essential for identifying and rectifying issues related to grammar, style, and factual accuracy, thereby upholding the integrity and credibility of scholarly work (Sawi and Alaa, 2024).

What Proofreaders Typically Do Not Do

While a proofreader performs a crucial function, certain responsibilities typically lie beyond their purview. The extent of a proofreader's influence on a manuscript's substantive content is generally constrained, as direct content revision primarily falls within the specialized remit of editors.

1. **Content Editing:** When a proofreader identifies issues related to content, they typically flag these for the author's attention via comments rather than making direct edits. Content editing involves a broader scope, focusing on a manuscript's academic quality, analysis, referencing, and overall formatting. While editing services often incorporate an initial stage of error correction similar to proofreading, a separate proofreading pass is usually performed after editing is complete.

2. **Comprehensive Copy-editing:** Although proof-editing can overlap with some aspects of copy-editing, it does not typically cover the full extent of copy-editing, such as extensive structural rewriting or substantive content revisions. However, a proof-editor may identify and index content titles and offer recommendations, drawing on subject matter expertise where appropriate.

3. **Page Layout and Design Editing:** This specialized area requires different expertise. A proofreader may note layout or design issues but does not directly address them; instead, they comment on such concerns when necessary.

4. **Copyright Control:** Proofreaders do not assume responsibility for verifying copyright, trademark, or other intellectual property rights of the content. These legal aspects are the author's or writer's responsibility.

5. **Subject-Matter Jargon and Terminology Validation:** While editing services often ensure the appropriate use of terminology within a specific field, a proofreader's primary focus is on linguistic correctness rather than deep

subject-matter terminology validation. This is crucial for aligning manuscripts with their respective fields and facilitating understanding among specialists.

It is important to note that a proofreader's role is distinct from that of an editor; therefore, they cannot be held responsible for the author's original content or its factual accuracy, as direct content revision and subject-matter validation fall within the specialized remit of editors. Proofreaders primarily focus on linguistic correctness rather than deep subject-matter terminology or factual verification. Consequently, before engaging in a proofreading service, it is essential to understand the terms and conditions that explicitly delineate these responsibilities and the scope of services provided.This clear delineation effectively prevents misunderstandings, thereby ensuring authors can leverage these services optimally to enhance their academic output (Sawi and Alaa, 2024). Ultimately, the author bears responsibility for the accuracy of references and the originality of the work, necessitating due diligence to ensure all incorporated material is appropriately attributed and free from plagiarism (O'Sullivan, Kuper and Cleland, 2024).

Becoming a Proofreader

The path to becoming a proficient proofreader unequivocally demands the mastery of unwavering meticulous attention to detail, the development of a keen understanding of grammatical nuances, and the acquisition of profound familiarity with diverse style guides, all crucial for ensuring unparalleled textual precision across varied academic disciplines.

For motivated individuals aspiring to this specialized field, the question of "how to become a proofreader" frequently arises. A pervasive misconception suggests that proofreaders' responsibilities are limited to scrutinizing word accuracy, misspellings, and punctuation. In reality, these constitute only the most rudimentary foundational elements. Individuals who lack substantial experience or extensive knowledge in the grammar, spelling, and punctuation of the target language, or who do not possess the indispensable ability to speed-read effectively, will find themselves critically unprepared for the rigors of professional proofreading.

Indeed, effective proofreading necessitates an expansive and comprehensive general knowledge base. An aspiring proofreader must cultivate an exceptionally high level of competence in vocabulary and spelling, combined with extraordinary focus, unyielding patience, and rigorous discipline, all maintained over protracted periods. This rigorous profile precisely mirrors the core competencies demanded of scientific editors, encompassing not only linguistic and grammatical expertise but also superior effective communication skills (Moher et al., 2017).

Understanding the "Vox Pop"

"Vox pop," derived from the Latin 'Vox Populi' meaning "Voice of the People," refers to popular opinion as conveyed through informal comments from members of the public, particularly when these are broadcast or published. The core purpose of a vox pop is to gauge public sentiment on a specific question of public interest, which can range from current news and political issues to lighter topics, or those encouraging reflective thought (Nagai, 2023). This method notably excels at directly and spontaneously capturing authentic individual perspectives and immediate reactions, providing a vivid, albeit often unscientific, representation of public sentiment (Nagai, 2023). It serves as one of several methods journalists use to portray public opinion, alongside opinion polls, social media references, and covering protests (Beckers, 2020).

Vox Pop Style

A vox pop fundamentally consists of a short audio or video clip featuring direct interviews with members of the public. While prominently associated with television news as a prevalent method for journalists to represent public opinion, vox pops also find application in print media through direct quotes or summarized individual opinions (Mitrić, 2022). It is important to distinguish 'vox pop' from 'talking head'; while the latter describes a visual style featuring a framed shot of a person speaking, a vox pop's core function is to elicit and present diverse public viewpoints. This method, by directly capturing spontaneous reactions and individual perspectives on a given issue, offers an immediate, albeit inherently unscientific, representation of public sentiment. Indeed, despite ostensibly providing the "voice of people in the street" (Nagai, 2023), journalists frequently express strong criticism of vox pops, recognizing their fundamental inability to represent the broader population accurately (Beckers, 2017, 2019).

Format of a Vox Pop

Typically, vox pops comprise concise audio or video compilations featuring diverse perspectives, generally not exceeding two minutes in duration. Participants for these interviews are often randomly selected individuals encountered in public environments, including streets, educational institutions, or classrooms. To ensure a representative spectrum of opinions, an effective vox pop typically incorporates a minimum of five to ten distinct voices. Journalists frequently utilize vox pops, primarily due to their demonstrated efficacy in augmenting audience engagement.

Nevertheless, notwithstanding their widespread appeal and perceived benefits for engagement, editorial policies commonly advise against portraying vox pops as representative of the general populace, given their inherent unscientific sampling methodology (Beckers, 2019).

This intrinsic limitation suggests that although vox pops can provide anecdotal insights and humanize journalistic narratives, their capacity to accurately reflect broad public opinion is a subject of ongoing debate among journalistic professionals (Cushion, 2018).

Crafting Effective Vox Pop Questions

Open-ended questions are paramount for eliciting nuanced and comprehensive responses, preventing superficial engagement and thus providing deeper insights into public sentiment, a critical objective for vox pops. Questions must be concise and readily comprehensible; overly complex phrasing risks confusing participants, leading to irrelevant or reluctant answers. Should a question appear too intricate, it is always more effective to segment it into two smaller, more specific inquiries to ensure clarity and encourage spontaneous, authentic responses. Furthermore, the judicious use of language that genuinely resonates with the target demographic is indispensable for securing both relevant and authentic responses.

This approach not only fosters relatability but also ensures that participants feel adequately addressed, thereby encouraging more thoughtful contributions. The way questions are framed carries significant weight, as it actively shapes citizens' perceived entitlement to speak publicly, directly influencing who feels empowered to contribute and in what capacity (Baron et al., 2016).

Empowerment is key to gathering diverse perspectives for effective vox pops, though their representativeness frequently draws scrutiny (Beckers, 2017) (Beckers, 2019) (Beckers, 2021).

Purpose and Usage of Vox Pops

The principal function of a vox pop is to present a representation of public sentiment across diverse media platforms (Beckers, 2020).

Through soliciting opinions from randomly selected individuals on a specific subject, their responses furnish audiences with an immediate portrayal of popular sentiment (Beckers, 2021). Within journalistic narratives, media reports, or feature articles, a vox pop is incorporated as an audio-visual segment or a compilation of direct quotes from members of the public. These collected contributions are typically integrated into a singular audio or video compilation, frequently anonymized, to convey a collective public perspective.

Although vox pops purportedly amplify the perspectives of everyday citizens, thereby potentially challenging elite narratives, particularly within crime journalism, their political efficacy is contingent upon their contextual integration within news discourse (Higgins, 2021). Empirical evidence suggests that vox pops can significantly sway audience perceptions, given the human inclination to align with the opinions of a select group of peers (Peter, 2019). Specifically, explicitly articulated opinions within vox pops exert considerable influence on both perceived public opinion and individual attitudes (Beckers, 2019). Nevertheless, journalists frequently assess traditional vox pops as less statistically representative compared to conventional polling methods. Interestingly, vox pops disseminated via social media platforms tend to exert a more pronounced influence on journalists' perceptions of public opinion than their traditional counterparts (Blum, 2024). Despite their utility in illustrating public sentiment, critics contend that these segments often allocate insufficient exposure to diverse viewpoints and can be influenced by journalistic presuppositions rather than grounded in objective measurements of public opinion (Cushion, 2018).

Duration and Production of a Vox Pop

When conducting vox pop interviews, reporters typically do not pre-recruit participants; instead, the process relies on spontaneous engagement with individuals encountered on location. This highly efficient approach aims to gather between 12-14 interviews, each lasting approximately 10 minutes, within a single day. The rapid turnaround time for producing these segments often under a week or even within 48 hours underscores their operational expediency. Consequently, a news-focused vox pop is typically concise, ranging from 30 to 40 seconds in length. This frequent and growing practice, particularly by audiovisual journalists, is primarily motivated by vox pops demonstrated ability to significantly augment audience engagement. Nevertheless, despite their pragmatic benefits and widespread appeal, journalists consistently express profound reservations regarding the representativeness of vox pops, recognizing that these brief, randomly sampled encounters inherently fail to accurately reflect broader societal views (Beckers, 2017).

Chapter 3

Print Journalism

According to the University of London, 'Print' broadly refers to any written or pictorial communications disseminated through mechanical or electronic processes for automated replication. More specifically, it refers to 'ink and paper' formats such as books, circulars, journals, lithographs, memoranda, magazines, newspapers, pamphlets, and periodicals, thereby excluding handwritten or manually typed documents. Historically, this medium has been instrumental in facilitating communication and knowledge dissemination over several centuries (Barnett, 1998; HORIMOTO, 2011).

Print journalism, recognized for its traditional methodology, adheres strictly to established journalistic principles, operating within stringent deadlines and utilizing conventional editorial production techniques (Hagen, Tolstad and Bygdås, 2021). Notwithstanding the proliferation of digital media, print retains its critical position within the media ecosystem, significantly impacting public opinion and shaping societal discourse (Thorgeirsdóttir, 2005).

What are Print Journalists?

Print journalists are vital in informing the public, meticulously investigating newsworthy events through in-depth interviews, comprehensive investigations, and keen observations.

They uphold the pillars of democratic discourse by rigorously verifying facts, ensuring accuracy, and maintaining objectivity. They then craft compelling stories for newspapers, magazines, or journals, upholding rigorous journalistic principles and thereby contributing significantly to the enduring trustworthiness of print media and fostering an informed citizenry. Their specializations encompass roles such as Columnist, Feature Writer, Leader Writer, and Newspaper Reporter.

Key Forms of Print Media

Print media manifests in a rich tapestry of diverse forms, with several prominent examples including:

1. Newspapers, which serve as a primary source of daily news and in-depth reporting, such as The New York Times.

2. Magazines offer specialized content, lifestyle features, and niche interests, for instance, Vogue.

3. Books, which provide extensive knowledge, narrative depth, and long-form intellectual engagement, exemplified by works like Harper Lee's To Kill a Mockingbird.

4. Newsletters, delivering targeted information and updates to specific audiences, including publications like Morning Brew.

5. Flyers, often utilized for promoting local events and immediate public announcements.

Print Story Style

When crafting a print news story, authors are generally expected to produce a piece of at least five hundred words. This length is often considered essential to provide adequate detail and context for intricate narratives and comprehensive journalistic reporting. Such a story must thoroughly address the fundamental journalistic inquiries, namely, Who, What, When, Where, Why, and How, to ensure completeness and clarity, thereby delivering all crucial information to the readership without ambiguity.

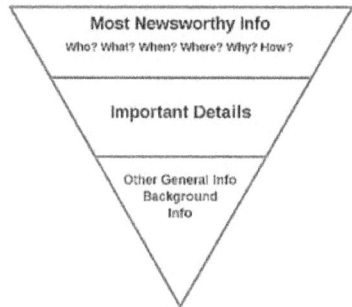

Once these questions are comprehensively addressed, editors can more readily refine the narrative, and the content will effectively meet rigorous professional journalistic standards for newsworthy information. The meticulous process of developing a print article involves critical questioning, systematic assembly, and stringent verification of facts through source interviews. This forms the cornerstone of factual accuracy and journalistic integrity.

Furthermore, this process necessitates the dissemination of truthful, unbiased information to uphold public trust, along with the proper citation and attribution of sources to confer authority and ensure ethical transparency. Finally, the content must be structured using the journalistic inverted pyramid format, which efficiently presents information and enables readers to immediately grasp the most vital details.

Opinions Columnist

A columnist consistently authors and disseminates articles, frequently as part of a recurrent series, across diverse publications, encompassing newspapers, magazines, blogs, and various digital platforms focused on news, general interest, or specialized subjects. This practice contributes to the evolution of public discourse and presents distinct viewpoints to a broad readership. These contributions primarily comprise critical analyses and subjective interpretations, often structured as concise essays aimed at informing, influencing, or stimulating critical reflection. Their professional role necessitates regular publication, typically on a weekly or bi-weekly schedule, an imperative for fostering a dedicated readership and solidifying their perceived authority. Thematic scope often spans from political endorsements to localized event narratives, demonstrating their capacity to address a wide spectrum of issues.

While some adopt a generalist methodology, engaging with an extensive range of topics, others cultivate expertise in specific domains, offering profound analysis and specialized insights.

Furthermore, numerous columnists leverage syndicates, a strategic maneuver that considerably augments their dissemination and impact through the simultaneous publication of their pertinent content across a multitude of media outlets.

Journalist Versus Columnist

It is crucial to distinguish between the distinct roles of a journalist and a columnist, as their functions, ethical frameworks, and the nature of their content diverge significantly. A journalist's primary commitment is to objective reporting of verifiable facts and events, striving for neutrality and factual accuracy to inform the public. In contrast, a columnist, while often deeply knowledgeable about a specific subject or theme, explicitly injects personal views, perspectives, opinions, anecdotes, and analysis. Their aim is not solely to inform, but also to persuade, entertain, or stimulate critical thought among readers, offering a subjective interpretation of events. Understanding this fundamental difference is vital for media consumers to critically evaluate information and discern between factual accounts and informed commentary.

Crafting a Columnist Opinion Piece

When crafting a column, the presented opinion must meticulously align with the audience's interests and expected journalistic standards. Adherence to these principles is paramount for ensuring both impact and credibility. Key considerations critically include:

1. **Providing timely and helpful information**: This ensures the column remains relevant and valuable, fostering sustained reader engagement and addressing current discourse.

2. **Developing and maintaining a consistent structural framework**: A predictable and logical structure enhances readability and comprehension, allowing readers to follow the argument effectively.

3. **Using simple, concise sentences and paragraphs**: Clarity and directness are essential to convey complex ideas without obfuscation, maximizing the column's persuasive power and accessibility.

4. **Incorporating local names and places in personal columns**: This strategy deepens relatability and resonance with the immediate readership, making the content more tangible and impactful.

5. **Leveraging credible quotes and authoritative references**: Substantiating arguments with external support lends intellectual rigor and enhances the persuasive force of the column by demonstrating thorough research and diverse perspectives.

6. **Understanding the unequivocal distinction between a column and a news story**: This differentiation is crucial to uphold journalistic integrity and prevent any misrepresentation, ensuring readers can clearly discern between factual reporting and informed commentary. In the realm of print media, opinion writing serves as a powerful conduit for authors to articulate their informed thoughts, distinct viewpoints, or deeply held convictions on a chosen topic. Such articles are integral to public discourse, capable of responding to existing narratives or initiating independent critical discussions. In contrast to the objective stance characteristic of traditional news articles, opinion pieces integrate subjectivity, thereby enabling a more expressive and rhetorically potent form of communication (Bolívar, 2002).

Functions of Print Journalism

Print media fundamentally underpins several vital societal functions, including pedagogical instruction, comprehensive informational dissemination, and enriching recreational engagement (Silva, Portillo and Fernández-Quintela, 2022). Distinguished by its unwavering and rigorous adherence to established journalistic principles (Hagen, Tolstad and Bygdås, 2021), print media has not only historically proven instrumental but continues to be a cornerstone in the credible transmission of knowledge, the cultivation of critical discourse, and the authoritative shaping of public perceptions concerning global affairs (Meier et al., 2022). This unwavering commitment to conventional standards, coupled with its intrinsic trustworthiness and enduring physical presence, unequivocally establishes print's foundational and irreplaceable role in the diffusion of ideas. Furthermore, even amidst the proliferation of digital platforms, print media maintains an indispensable and pivotal role in public health communication, effectively disseminating vital information and promoting salutary practices (Kanchan and Gaidhane, 2024). Journalism, in general, plays an indispensable and critical role in the functioning of democracy, serving as a vigilant guardian that upholds truth, accuracy, and transparency, and holds powerful institutions robustly accountable (Audette-Longo et al., 2023). Scientific journalism, in particular, makes a profound contribution to scientific instruction, crucially bridging the often-complex gap between specialized scientific discourse and broader public understanding (Alhuntushi and Lugo-Ocando, 2024).

Benefits of Print Journalism

Print media, including tangible forms such as flyers and brochures, demonstrate a higher frequency of engagement when compared to digital advertisements. This is attributed to their repeated review and dissemination among individuals, which cultivates a more sustained presence than the transient nature characteristic of digital communications. Research indicates that print advertisements lead to superior levels of cognitive encoding and engagement than digital advertisements (Venkatraman et al., 2021; Gokce, 2022). Furthermore, advertising recall rates for print media are notably 1.7 times greater (Venkatraman et al., 2021), suggesting a stronger propensity to stimulate consumer action relative to digital alternatives.

Beyond enhanced recall, print advertisements activate heightened neural activity in memory-associated brain regions, such as the hippocampus and parahippocampal areas, thereby implying deeper encoding and cognitive processing than their digital counterparts (Venkatraman et al., 2021; Gokce, 2022). The inherent physicality, multisensory experience, and contextual engagement offered by print media collectively contribute to improved comprehension compared to digital reading (Haddock et al., 2019; Spence, 2020; Froud et al., 2024).

Print Versus Digital Marketing Content

The contemporary era, frequently designated as the Computer Age, Digital Age, or New Media Age, commenced in the 1970s and continues to be characterized by immediate access to information and knowledge, profoundly influenced by the Internet of Things, heightened social mobility, and globally interconnected networks. Although digital platforms, including social media, algorithmic marketing systems, and electronic displays, continuously disseminate information, digital media effectively caters to the pervasive human propensity for instant gratification.

Digital marketing, alternatively known as online marketing, differentiates itself from traditional media by leveraging the internet and various digital communication channels, such as email, social media, web-based advertising, text messaging, and multimedia content, to promote brands and engage with prospective customers and clients (Veleva and Tsvetanova, 2020; Erwanda and Doli, 2024). This fundamental paradigm shift has significantly reshaped interpersonal interactions and commercial operations. In contrast to the considerable temporal investment required for physical travel, digital content can be disseminated and accessed almost instantaneously (Erwanda and Doli, 2024).

Empirical data indicates that over 83% of the global populace possesses a smartphone, thus representing a potential market exceeding 6.5 billion individuals accessible through digital marketing strategies. Current marketing technology trends utilize algorithms and automation to tailor content feeds based on user interests and collected data, thereby enabling highly targeted marketing initiatives directed at specific demographic segments. Digital media frequently offers a more economically efficient and rapid approach, potentially incurring lower expenditures compared to print media, contingent upon design complexities. Digital campaigns and content can be developed, deployed, and iteratively refined with greater alacrity than their print counterparts. Furthermore, digital platforms are intrinsically interactive, facilitating the acquisition of valuable consumer data.

Nevertheless, the assertion of a complete societal transition from print media to exclusively digital platforms constitute a significant subject of ongoing international academic discourse (Omar, Al-Samarraie and Wright, 2020). Industry experts acknowledge the strategic importance of both print and digital modalities, necessitating a comprehensive evaluation of their respective advantages and limitations for contemporary enterprises (Erwanda and Doli, 2024). It is noteworthy that while print media increasingly integrates a digital presence, established digital entities generally do not seek to replicate traditional print media structures. Although both print and digital media exhibit distinct benefits and drawbacks, their strategic integration can yield synergistic outcomes. For instance, the incorporation of QR codes and social media hashtags on printed materials, or the provision of digital opt-ins for print content, exemplifies how these channels can collaboratively function within a meticulously devised marketing strategy.

The State of Print

China initiated the development of printing with the woodblock method around 200 CE. Subsequently, the introduction of printing presses in Europe, including the UK, during the 1400s, heralded its own information age (O'Donnell, 2022; Li, 2023). Consequently, printed texts became more broadly accessible, extending beyond the affluent elite (Bihan et al., 2024). This newfound availability of materials significantly enhanced the lifestyles of lower social classes, profoundly empowering individuals through education and the wider dissemination of knowledge (Li, 2023).

Beyond these foundational advancements, other historical printing techniques encompassed lithography, an early printing form still utilized today; the Rotary Press; Offset printing; and Screen Printing. Indeed, print has consistently fulfilled a pivotal role throughout history, influencing societal development and fostering progress.

Presently, print media retains substantial influence, being broadly perceived as more credible and authoritative than its digital counterparts across all demographics, including Millennials (Omar, Al-Samarraie and Wright, 2020; Fotopoulos, 2023).

This perception is partly attributable to the pervasive issue of misinformation on social media platforms (Omar, Al-Samarraie and Wright, 2020). The inherent time commitment, deliberate effort, and tangible resources required for the creation and publication of printed content fundamentally cultivate a greater sense of reliability and permanence. This stands in distinct contrast to the instantaneous, often transient, and readily manipulable nature characterizing much digital content (Pinem, 2023).

Within an increasingly online business environment saturated with ephemeral information, printed content thus represents a distinct and potent marketing advantage, offering a credible and enduring impression (Mangold, Bachl and Prochazka, 2022; Ross et al., 2023; Weidmüller and Engesser, 2024).

The intrinsic physicality of print media inherently captures attention and demonstrates remarkable memorability (Spence, 2020). Its inherent durability and permanence contribute significantly to its lasting impact and recall. Furthermore, print is generally more readily comprehensible and processed than digital media, facilitating deeper engagement and allowing for a greater volume of information to be effectively conveyed on a single page, in contrast to the often-fragmented experience of social media content (Haddock et al., 2019). This translates into quantifiable benefits: advertising recall is notably 1.7 times higher with print, rendering it demonstrably more effective in stimulating action than its digital media equivalent (Venkatraman et al., 2021).

Digital media simply cannot emulate the unparalleled tactility and sensory richness inherent in print media. Print is intrinsically more engaging, and with ongoing technological advancements, print media can now stimulate all senses, fostering a truly immersive experience (Kucirkova, 2022). Factors such as paper weight, thickness, and quality are critical, as they can significantly elevate the perceived value and luxury of the products and services they detail. Specialized tactile printing methods, such as die-cutting and engraving, are readily available. Galloways has further innovated with fragranced print media, offering the ultimate sensory print experience. Ultimately, print offers a valuable and much-needed opportunity to disengage from the frantic digital world and immerse oneself fully and reflectively in the present moment (Spence, 2020; Bailey, 2022). Contrary to assumptions of obsolescence and notwithstanding the widespread adoption of digital platforms, print media retains substantial vitality, pertinence, and resilience. Within the contemporary digital landscape, printed materials demonstrate an elevated capacity for efficacy and influence. Empirical evidence indicates that print advertisements elicit superior levels of engagement and physiological arousal, subsequently leading to more robust memory encoding compared to their digital counterparts (Venkatraman et al., 2021).

The Art and Science of Editing

Indian print media editor Yogesh Chandra Pandey defines editing as the indispensable process of selecting and preparing written, visual, audible, and film media to ensure the effective and compelling conveyance of information. Fundamentally, editing involves making critical changes, particularly to a written document, to profoundly refine and elevate the finished product. Indeed, while writing lays the foundation, editing is unequivocally its indispensable counterpart. The meticulous revision of a short story through the precise cutting and strategic addition of lines serves as a compelling illustration of editing's transformative power.

Editing is a systematic and multi-faceted process that can be divided into distinct levels, including content, structure, style, format, mechanics, tone, and policy (Masse, 1985). It represents an absolutely critical step in the writing process, occurring just before publication, meticulously designed to identify, address, and rectify issues such as grammar, verbosity, tone, style, fact-checking, and syntactic and semantic elements (Sawi and Alaa, 2024). The profound importance of professional editing has been explored in various contexts, including sub-editing in news writing, which critically examines how news article text is altered (Vandendaele, Cuypere and Praet, 2015). This rigorous oversight guarantees the presentation of information with precision, veracity, and conformity to established journalistic principles, thereby bolstering the publication's credibility and ethical standing.

Types of Editing

Editing is systematically categorized into various specialized forms to address the diverse needs of content refinement and ensure a polished final product. These categories often include developmental editing, copy editing, and proofreading, each addressing different aspects of a manuscript's development and accuracy (Sawi and Alaa, 2024). Developmental editing, for instance, focuses on the overarching structure and narrative coherence, ensuring the logical flow and compelling presentation of ideas.

1. Substantive Editing : Substantive editing, also known as structural editing, focuses on the overall structure, content, and flow of a manuscript. An editor performing substantive work will suggest or implement changes to the title, language, and style, but also significant revisions to the organization of the material (Masse, 1985). Substantive editing is concerned with the core ideas, arguments, and overall organization, or what the article says (Enquist, 2000). Both "structural editing" and "substantive editing" refer to refining the core content and organization of a document.

2. Copyediting : Copyediting (also known as manuscript editing) is the process of reviewing written material ("copy") to improve its quality, readability, and to ensure it is free from errors in grammar, style, and factual accuracy. Copyediting adheres to the "five Cs": ensuring the article is clear, correct, concise, comprehensible, and consistent. This process leads to a significant number of changes between the author's version and the publisher's version, underscoring its role in ensuring accuracy for both printed and online formats (Wates and Campbell, 2007).

3. Line Editing : Line editing focuses exclusively on the flow, style, and readability of a manuscript. Unlike copyediting, it does not primarily address grammar, spelling, or punctuation errors.

The key distinction from copyediting is that line editing scrutinizes the rhythm and language at the sentence level for coherence and impact, without necessarily checking for technical accuracy or completeness of content and syntax.

4. Proofreading : Proofreading is the final stage of the writing process, involving a meticulous check for minor spelling and punctuation mistakes, typos, formatting issues, and inconsistencies before publication or sharing (Sawi and Alaa, 2024). Proofreading involves making minor changes, additions, or deletions to find and mark mistakes that need to be corrected (Azeez, 2020). While traditional proofreading concentrates on correcting grammatical, spelling, and punctuation errors, other specialized forms of proof-editing exist, including structural, technical, and academic proofreading. Artificial intelligence tools are also emerging that can assist in proofreading, offering efficiency and precision in detecting errors (Sawi and Alaa, 2024; Zhao and Liang, 2025). These tools can achieve higher recall and accuracy in detecting errors compared to human annotators, though human annotators often demonstrate higher precision (Bick et al., 2024).

5. Print Image Editing : To achieve optimal quality and ensure accurate reproduction in print images, a methodical approach involving several critical steps is essential. These steps typically encompass color correction, retouching, and resolution optimization, each contributing to the visual integrity of the final printed output. Color correction ensures that the hues and tones in the image accurately reflect the original intent, often involving calibration to specific print profiles to maintain consistency across different printing devices. Retouching, on the other hand, involves refining specific elements within the image, such as removing imperfections or enhancing details, to achieve a desired aesthetic.

More so, the following steps are crucial:

1. Calibrate your monitor for accurate color representation. This is a foundational step, as an uncalibrated monitor can lead to significant discrepancies between on-screen appearance and the final printed output, making consistent color correction impossible.

2. Select the highest-quality images. Starting with high-resolution, sharp source images is paramount, as the quality of the original directly dictates the maximum achievable print fidelity and detail.

3. Ensure the photo's color mode is set to CMYK for print. This is critical because CMYK (Cyan, Magenta, Yellow, Key/Black) is the subtractive color model used in professional printing, and the conversion from RGB to CMYK, applied during the color separation process, is essential to prevent unexpected color shifts in the final printed product (Lundström and Verikas, 2012).

4. Crop the photo to optimize composition. Thoughtful cropping enhances the visual focus and narrative of the image, eliminating distracting elements and guiding the viewer's eye for maximum impact in print.

5. Resize the image and adjust its resolution appropriately. Insufficient resolution will result in pixelation and blurriness when printed, diminishing clarity and professionalism. For JPG format, a resolution of 300 or 600 dpi (dots per inch) is typically preferred to ensure crisp detail and high print quality (Brookes, 2025).

6. Make further adjustments to suit your preferences, such as changing brightness, contrast, or color (Bevilaqua, 2020). These fine-tuning adjustments are vital for correcting exposure issues, enhancing visual appeal, and achieving the desired aesthetic impact and mood in the printed image. Techniques are presented for editing images in preparation for online submission using software like Adobe Photoshop (LaBerge and Andriole, 2003), principles of which often apply to print as well.

7. Save your work regularly. This crucial practice prevents the loss of meticulous editing efforts and ensures the preservation of progress throughout the complex image preparation process.

Defined standards and stages of control are necessary in print production to ensure efficient communication and data transfer, thereby minimizing errors and achieving consistent, high-quality output. Furthermore, a basic knowledge of print processes and the influence of paper on color reproduction is an imperative requirement for optimizing scans with color management, ensuring accurate color fidelity and visual integrity in the final printed product ("ISO 12647, GRACoL and SWOP for Separation, Proof and Print," 2008). The characteristics of the substrate, or paper, significantly influence the fidelity of color image reproduction; consequently, a robust color management system is indispensable within contemporary printing workflows to ensure consistent and accurate color output (Dharavath, 2023).

Challenges Faced by the Media

The media landscape is constantly evolving, presenting a myriad of complex and interconnected challenges that demand not only constant attention but also a commitment to rigorous professional practice. These issues are crucial for maintaining journalistic integrity, fostering public trust, and ensuring the continued relevance and efficacy of media in a rapidly changing information environment:

1. Constant Updates : Regularly updating website content is imperative for maintaining relevance and delivering superior user experience. An up-to-date and optimized website not only captivates visitors but significantly boosts search engine rankings, driving substantial web traffic. However, individuals are increasingly overwhelmed by an unprecedented deluge of information as the boundary between news creation and consumption dissolves, and a proliferation of channels and technologies become accessible for news consumption (Zhang et al., 2022). This relentless stream of news from ever-expanding sources and platforms inevitably cultivates news overload, culminating in widespread exhaustion and indifference among consumers (Zhang et al., 2022). The intense pressure to publish breaking news rapidly compels news organizations to prioritize speed over thoroughness, frequently resulting in incomplete, inaccurate, or sensationalized reporting (T., 2024).

2. Deadlines : Deadlines constitute an imperative temporal constraint within media operations, dictating the punctual submission of stories for publication or broadcast. While adhering to these strictures ideally affords reporters and producers adequate time for thorough material development, preventing rushed output, their very presence underscores a fundamental truth: without timely information and diligent research, a story's completion is rendered impossible. The journalistic adage, "A newspaper is 'made' against the clock," powerfully encapsulates the relentless urgency inherent in the profession, acknowledging news as a perishable commodity demanding daily freshness (Pilmis and Matthews, 2014).

This inherent pressure is profoundly exacerbated when journalists contend with constrained production resources, increasingly truncated deadlines, and the demand for ever-briefer news formats, a pervasive concern widely reported among reporters (Andersen, 2017). This expedited environment, often fueled by the instantaneous nature of digital platforms, frequently compels journalists to prioritize the rapid dissemination of information, a practice that critically compromises rigorous fact-checking and meticulous in-depth investigation (T., 2024).

3. Accuracy : Accuracy, defined as the precise conformity to correct values or established standards, forms the absolute bedrock of journalistic ethics. Far from being a mere objective, it is a critical responsibility; while truth suggests a report relies on factual information, accuracy demands that journalists meticulously verify the authenticity and veracity of those facts. The ramifications of inaccurate reporting extend far beyond incorrect conclusions or flawed plans, potentially eroding public trust, fueling misinformation, and undermining the credibility essential for an informed society. This fundamental principle of journalism faces relentless assault from the pervasive influence of digitalization, the rapid shifts in media landscapes, and the increasing reliance on the assertation model of journalism, which often prioritizes speed over diligent verification. Indeed, numerous studies have revealed that a substantial proportion of analyzed stories contain significant errors, primarily stemming from a dangerous over-reliance on secondary sources rather than the indispensable pursuit of primary verification (Maštrapa, John and Brautović, 2020). Consequently, journalistic practice, inherently grounded in ethical imperatives such as an unwavering dedication to truth and accuracy (Tulin et al., 2024), must prioritize rigorous verification. High-quality journalism, by its very nature, demands not only creativity but, more crucially, an unyielding commitment to verification (Lopez et al., 2022).

4. Story Impact : Impact stories serve as indispensable tools for systematically documenting real-world efficacy and illuminating the human dimension of successful initiatives, particularly in contexts where traditional monitoring, evaluation, or research capabilities may be limited. Far exceeding mere entertainment, these narratives function as potent transformative agents, profoundly shaping individual perspectives, communal values, and collective understanding. By fostering empathy, stimulating imagination, and catalyzing social change, compelling storytelling exerts a profound influence on both individuals and society. In a media landscape increasingly challenged by information overload, eroding trust, and the proliferation of misinformation, the production of stories that are not only original and impactful but also meticulously factually accurate is paramount (Lopez et al., 2022). Such narratives are vital for reinforcing credibility and engaging audiences with authentic, verifiable accounts.

5. Follow-Up : Continuous information dissemination in journalism necessitates consistent follow-up. Media entities are thus mandated to monitor and refresh narratives that have been previously reported yet remain in evolution. This presents a considerable challenge, requiring a dedicated editorial team and committed professional journalists to facilitate comprehensive and timely updates. Journalists frequently report insufficient resources for maintaining source relationships and conducting post-publication follow-ups (Andersen, 2017). Moreover, the widespread dissemination of misinformation and disinformation highlights an urgent imperative for an enhanced commitment to journalistic integrity (Borkar and Paul, 2023). Fact-checking has evolved into a fundamental journalistic practice, significantly shaping public discourse and effectively combating erroneous content across mass media and social media platforms (Suomalainen et al., 2025).

The persistent generation, circulation, and consumption of disinformation and fabricated material on social media constitute a profound and escalating concern (Shu et al., 2020), with scientific disinformation posing a particularly insidious and critical challenge (Tomassi, Falegnami and Romano, 2025). The ethical imperative for journalists not to mislead the public has attained unprecedented salience (Lopez et al., 2022). Effective mitigation of misinformation and disinformation within an evolving media landscape mandates the implementation of rigorous fact-checking methodologies (Tulin et al., 2024). This involves balancing objectivity with sensitivity, particularly when reporting on potentially detrimental events, to preclude inadvertent distress or the reinforcement of societal divisions. Furthermore, the digital era has introduced unparalleled commercial pressures upon journalists, frequently compelling a prioritization of speed and sensationalism over meticulous verification and comprehensive reporting (Lopez et al., 2022). This environment is further compounded by the erosion of traditional journalistic tenets and the pervasive influence of algorithms that prioritize engagement metrics, often directly compromising accuracy and comprehensive narrative development (T., 2024).

CHAPTER 4

Broadcast Journalism

BROADCAST JOURNALISM PERTAINS TO the systematic reporting and distribution of current events and public interest content through electronic channels, historically dominated by radio and television (Thorgeirsdóttir, 2005). Subsequently, its foundational domain has undergone substantial expansion to integrate digital platforms such as online streaming and podcasts, alongside an array of multi-platform dissemination strategies (Zhao, 2023). Key facets include:

1. Medium of Delivery: Historically, radio and television served as primary mediums, critically facilitating widespread and often immediate news transmission that profoundly influenced public discourse.

2. Purpose: Its fundamental objective is to rigorously inform, educate, and occasionally entertain the public through incisive analysis of news and current events (Auzarmi, 2024), thereby fulfilling an indispensable political function in fostering a robust democratic process, 2005).

3. Characteristics: Broadcast news is intrinsically defined by its immediacy, striving to condense and convey essential facts through compelling visual and auditory elements that powerfully evoke a "live or recent 'now'. Television, in particular, is acutely adept at capturing the "temporal structure and dynamic of the living moment" (Damgaard, 2018), offering an unparalleled sense of presence.

4. Evolution: With the advent of new media and increasing media convergence, the broadcast news industry has proactively adopted digital platforms, innovating its development by broadening information dissemination channels and substantially enhancing audience interactivity (Zhao, 2023).In essence, broadcast journalism represents a dynamic and evolving domain of news communication, delivered through engaging audible and visual modalities, continually adapting to technological shifts while steadfastly upholding its core mandate of thoroughly informing the public.

Broadcast journalism has undergone a profound transformation from its traditional roots in radio and television, evolving into an expansive digital and multi-platform ecosystem, a paradigm shift fundamentally driven and reshaped by pervasive digitalization (Cottle and Ashton, 1999; Canavilhas and Fátima, 2024). This introduction will define its core principles and evolving role in informing the public. This transformation of the media ecosystem mirrors the earlier shifts brought about by radio and television, yet with far greater intensity and continuous evolution (Canavilhas and Fátima, 2024).

Evolution of Broadcast Media

The evolution of broadcast media commenced in the early twentieth century with the advent of radio broadcasting. Since then, its scope has significantly expanded, now encompassing television and, more recently, a diverse array of digital platforms that have fundamentally redefined the media landscape by blurring the traditional boundaries between conventional and new media formats.

The Birth of Radio

early 20th Century, during World War I, the foundational advancements in radio technology and the nascent concept of broadcasting began to manifest, evidenced by experimental transmitter stations that showcased the potential of wireless communication (Mathis and Titze, 2021). This period proved instrumental in establishing the inherent connection between radio technology and mass communication (Barboutis, 2013). The discernible origins of broadcast media are inextricably tied to the emergence of radio broadcasting in the 1920s, which fundamentally instituted the "broadcasting" paradigm as a model of one-to-many communication. For instance, KDKA initiated broadcasts in 1920, and by 1950, radio access had expanded to encompass over 95% of U.S. households ("Broadcasting," 2022; Flensburg et al., 2023). This unparalleled diffusion enabled synchronous consumption of news and entertainment, thereby fostering the development of national cultures (Flensburg et al., 2023). Throughout this era, the conceptualization of broadcasting progressed to signify the widespread electronic dissemination of messages (Hamilton, 2018).

The Rise of Television

The advent of television in Mid-20th Century, subsequent to the radio era, marked a significant new phase in broadcast journalism, considerably enhancing the medium's capacity for immediacy and visual engagement throughout the 1940s and 1950s (Flensburg et al., 2023). By the 1950s, the considerable potential of television for disseminating news sparked intense discussion, facing initial skepticism concerning its ability to effectively convey intricate news narratives (Singer, Lewis and Wahl-Jorgensen, 2023). Despite these initial reservations, television's intrinsic capabilities for signal transmission and its distinctive "liveness" rapidly cemented its status as a potent and revolutionary medium (Sterne, 1999; "'Towers In The Sky': Satellites And Emerging Global Media Infrastructures," 2023). Pivotal events, such as the live transmission of Queen Elizabeth II's coronation in 1953 across numerous European nations, further accentuated its growing influence and profound transformative effect on global communication and the trajectory of television ("'Towers In The Sky': Satellites And Emerging Global Media Infrastructures," 2023).

The Age of Digital Transformation

The digital era, beginning in the late 20th century, profoundly accelerated and redefined the trajectory of broadcast media. This period witnessed a significant transformation, instigated by the rise of the internet, streaming services, and social media, which effectively transitioned broadcast journalism into a complex digital and multi-platform ecosystem (Dhiman, 2023). Such a paradigm shift fundamentally altered all facets of broadcasting, encompassing news production processes and strategies for audience interaction (Kroon and Eriksson, 2019). Characterized by continuous innovation, broadcast media evolved dramatically from its traditional analog radio and television models to widespread digital streaming and multi-platform dissemination. Although radio and television journalism considerably expanded the reach and timeliness of news delivery (Singer, Lewis and Wahl-Jorgensen, 2023), the digital age introduced both significant challenges and vast opportunities for broadcasters (Dhiman, 2023). Consequently, broadcasters have adopted a strategic approach, integrating digital platforms, leveraging sophisticated data analytics for personalized content delivery, and fostering dynamic audience engagement (Laor, 2022). Critically, digital technologies have reconstituted broadcast communication, transforming it from a largely unidirectional transmission model into an interactive and dynamic paradigm, thereby altering the relationship between content producers and their audiences. This progression has afforded unprecedented immediacy and interactivity, exemplified by the notion of ubiquitous broadcasting (Fick, 2024). Notwithstanding the clear proliferation of digital platforms in augmenting media consumption, a considerable segment of the population retains a preference for traditional terrestrial broadcasts and radio reception (Dongre and Nehulkar, 2019; Fick, 2024).

Core Principles

Despite profound technological changes, the fundamental principles guiding journalism have not only largely endured but have become even more critical in navigating the complexities of the contemporary media environment (Black, 1998). These core tenets are indispensable for maintaining integrity, fostering accountability, and sustaining public trust in broadcast journalism. Key principles include:

1. Immediacy : Broadcast media delivers news as it happens, a characteristic significantly amplified by modern digital and cellular-based live broadcast technologies (Ilan, 2021). This capability, present from early radio to satellite technologies, remains paramount in digital news, enabling real-time public awareness and rapid societal response.

2. Credibility : The public relies on broadcast journalists for accurate, verifiable, and trustworthy information. Upholding credibility is paramount, serving as the cornerstone of public confidence and safeguarding against the corrosive effects of misinformation (Shahid, 2023).

3. Objectivity : While often debated and acknowledged as an aspirational ideal rather than a perfect attainment, objectivity remains a crucial professional value. It guides journalists to strive for unbiased reporting and the transparent presentation of facts (Henkel et al., 2020). Factuality, an intrinsic component of objectivity, is vital for fostering informed public discourse in broadcasting (Kriyantono, 2020).

4. Public Service : Broadcast journalism carries a profound public service mandate, fundamentally aiming to inform, educate, and engage citizens on critical matters of public interest. This includes rigorously holding power to account, providing diverse perspectives, and facilitating robust democratic dialogue (Henkel et al., 2020).

5. Broadcast Ethics : Adherence to rigorous ethical codes is foundational, guiding journalists in making decisions that balance reporting with sensitivity, respect, and responsibility (Pepple and Acholonu, 2018). Ethical considerations extend to crucial issues such as data privacy, algorithmic biases, and transparency, especially with the accelerating integration of artificial intelligence (Gutiérrez-Caneda, Lindén and Vázquez-Herrero, 2024). Most of the time broadcast station put their focus much into breaking the biggest news which can redirect into unethical media practices.

These principles form the bedrock upon which effective, responsible, and ultimately sustainable broadcast journalism is built, navigating the complexities of a constantly evolving media landscape and reinforcing its irreplaceable role in society. Moreover, the interplay between objectivity and sensitivity poses a continuous ethical challenge for journalists, requiring careful consideration of potential harm while striving for unbiased reporting (Shahid, 2023).

Theoretical Foundations of Broadcast News

A comprehensive grasp of the theoretical foundations of broadcast news is not merely beneficial but essential for dissecting its production, consumption, and profound societal impact. These frameworks are crucial, offering incisive insights into the intricate processes by which media narratives are meticulously constructed, broadly disseminated, and ultimately interpreted, thereby profoundly molding public perception and discourse.

Crucially, these theoretical underpinnings illuminate the powerful mechanisms through which broadcast news not only mirrors but proactively *forges* social realities, directly influencing public opinion and galvanizing collective action (Chivers and Allan, 2022).

News as a Journalistic Genre

News fundamentally serves as a primary, archetypal form of journalistic discourse (Bogdanić, 2020), through which societies construct and negotiate their understanding of events and pertinent issues. It not only informs but also critically shapes public perception and discourse by means of its intrinsic structure, presentation methodology, and thematic content. The construction and subsequent dissemination of news within broadcast media adhere to specific genre conventions, which are profoundly influenced by established journalistic practices, evolving technological capabilities, and prevailing societal expectations. These conventions, in turn, play a pivotal role in influencing how audiences process information, interpret occurrences, and engage with matters of public affairs. Furthermore, the embedded ethical dimensions within these genres, encompassing concerns such as inherent bias and sensationalism, significantly impact audience interpretation and necessitate enhanced transparency and media literacy to safeguard democratic discourse (Yevdokymova et al., 2025).

Key Broadcast Communication Theories

The multifaceted dynamics and profound societal impact of broadcast news are critically illuminated by several key communication theories. These frameworks offer crucial insights into how media narratives are constructed, disseminated, and interpreted, thereby shaping public perception and discourse. The following theories are particularly pertinent in understanding these complex processes:

Agenda-Setting Theory : This influential theory posits that broadcast media significantly shapes the public agenda by strategically drawing audience attention to particular issues, thereby profoundly influencing public perception of their salience and importance (Fraile and Hernández, 2024). Despite the complexities introduced by the digital age and the proliferation of social media, broadcast news maintains an indispensable role in mediating public discourse and connecting citizens to the political sphere (Fraile and Hernández, 2024). Indeed, broadcast news persists as a primary source of news consumption for a substantial segment of the populace, notwithstanding the ascendancy of digital platforms. Its distinctive linguistic and visual presentation critically molds public perception regarding the significance of various issues (Ding, Horning and Rho, 2023). Furthermore, recent research robustly confirms the persistent intermedia agenda-setting effects across broadcast news outlets, even within highly fragmented media landscapes, as notably exemplified during events such as the COVID-19 pandemic (Budak et al., 2023).

Framing Theory : Framing theory elucidates the powerful process through which broadcast journalists meticulously select and emphasize specific facets of a story, thereby constructing a particular interpretation that profoundly influences how audiences comprehend and respond to intricate issues and policies (Tewksbury and Scheufele, 2009). These journalistic choices, whether conscious or subconscious, meticulously craft the narrative by defining responsibilities and implying courses of action via carefully selected images and words (Tewksbury and Scheufele, 2009). Within broadcast news specifically, research diligently investigates how the interplay of visual and verbal elements critically contributes to issue framing, often necessitating integrated analytical approaches to fully capture their persuasive power (Dan, 2018). For instance, comprehensive studies have analyzed the diverse and often subtle application of various frames in television news and debate programs, particularly evident during significant global events like the COVID-19 pandemic (Solvoll and Høiby, 2023).

Gatekeeping Theory : Historically, gatekeeping theory described the crucial process by which information was filtered for public dissemination, with traditional news organizations serving as authoritative central gatekeepers (Shabir et al., 2015). Editors and news personnel performed a vital "buckstopping" role, meticulously determining which information transitioned from various sources to the public (Wallace, 2017). However, rapid technological advancements and the emergence of digital media have profoundly challenged these traditional gatekeeping structures, necessitating a fundamental redefinition of what constitutes a gatekeeper and the evolving nature of their role, as the flow of information becomes inherently multidirectional (Chin-Fook and Simmonds, 2013). In this digital era, journalists now leverage social media to actively produce, publish, and distribute news stories, thereby introducing dynamic new practices and news values into the gatekeeping function (Bro and Wallberg, 2014). Concurrently, digital news divisions contend with considerable challenges related to resource constraints and the integration of news socialization practices within their evolving gatekeeping responsibilities (Scacco, Curry and Stroud, 2015).

News Value Theory : These represent the fundamental criteria consistently employed by journalists to ascertain the inherent newsworthiness of an event or story (Buschow, 2020). While core news values such as timeliness, proximity, prominence, unusualness, conflict, human interest, and impact have remarkably remained stable for over a century, their practical application can significantly vary depending on the prevailing sociocultural context (Parks, 2018). Crucially, news values also function as vital relevance indicators for audiences, directly guiding their information processing and shaping their engagement with news content (Eilders, 2006). The intricate dynamics of news selection and the often-cited "journalistic gut feeling" are profoundly influenced by the complex interplay of these enduring news values, established news practices, and the overarching framework of journalistic professionalism across diverse cultural contexts (Anastasiou, 2016). Ultimately, news values encompass material, cognitive, social, and discursive dimensions, dictating how stories are prioritized, framed, and presented within broadcast news, thereby shaping public understanding (Ilan, 2019).

Discourse Theory in Broadcast News

Discourse theory offers a critical lens through which to analyze the linguistic and structural components of broadcast narratives, thereby elucidating the complex mechanisms by which meaning is generated and propagated (Givskov, 2015). The profound influence of media discourse on public opinion is particularly pronounced within broadcast news. Specifically, within broadcast news, the deliberate application of linguistic elements, including advanced rhetorical strategies like presupposition triggers, can not only subtly guide but also definitively mold audience interpretations of facts and events, often fostering particular biases (Zare, Abbaspour and Nia, 2012).

A comprehensive understanding of these intricate dynamics necessitates the application of multimodal discourse analysis in broadcast news research. This sophisticated methodology rigorously investigates the forceful deployment of narrative strategies in audiovisual news, thereby transcending the limitations of traditional textual analysis (Bateman and Tseng, 2023). Such an integrated perspective unequivocally illustrates the intricate construction of persuasive narratives through the synergistic interplay of visual and auditory components.

Furthermore, substantial research consistently highlights the semantic polarization inherent in broadcast media language and its significant correlation with online public discourse. This scholarship meticulously reveals notable divergences in content and linguistic presentation across various broadcast stations, a disparity that is particularly evident between cable and network news organizations (Ding, M. G. Horning and Rho, 2023; Ding, M. Horning and Rho, 2023; Hosseinmardi et al., 2025). Ultimately, the strategic selection of lexicon and narrative frameworks within broadcast media plays a pivotal role in profoundly influencing political discourse and shaping public perception (Otmakhova and Frermann, 2025).

The Practice of Broadcast Journalism: Production and Technical Aspects

The production and technical dimensions constitute a foundational element of modern broadcast journalism, incorporating the operational methodologies and sophisticated instruments that have critically redefined the domain. This fundamental shift is predominantly attributable to the significant amalgamation of conventional broadcasting practices with emergent digital technologies. Consequently, this integration, marked by an escalating dependence on advanced digital platforms for content generation, dissemination, and audience interaction, mandates an ongoing adaptation of journalistic methodologies and competencies.

News Gathering and Reporting

The landscape of news gathering in broadcast journalism is now characterized by a relentless pursuit of speed, an unprecedented capacity for mobility, and an inherent design for multi-platform adaptability.

This fundamental shift is largely propelled by technological innovations that empower journalists to report from diverse locations and disseminate content instantaneously across myriad digital ecosystems.

Live Reporting Technologies

The ability to go live from virtually any location is a cornerstone of modern broadcast news. Digital, cellular-based live broadcast technologies, such as LiveU and TVU Pack systems, have revolutionized field reporting by enabling immediate transmission of high-quality video over mobile networks. These portable units encode and transmit video via bonded cellular, Wi-Fi, or satellite connections, allowing journalists to bypass traditional satellite trucks for breaking news and enabling dynamic, spontaneous coverage (Ilan, 2021). These innovations have fundamentally transformed news delivery, provided unparalleled immediacy and enabling journalists to report directly from the scene of breaking events with minimal delay. This capability not only enhances the viewer's experience by offering real-time insights but also allows news organizations to provide constant updates, thereby setting a new standard for responsiveness in news coverage.

Role of Satellite Technologies

Despite advancements in cellular broadcasting, satellite technologies maintain their enduring importance, particularly for high-bandwidth needs, remote locations without robust cellular infrastructure, or critical, uninterrupted live feeds (Bivens, 2015). Satellite uplinks facilitate the transmission of signals from remote areas to broadcast centers, playing a crucial role in international reporting and disaster coverage where terrestrial networks might be compromised. Their inherent reliability and capacity to provide high-bandwidth connectivity make them indispensable for covering major international events, natural disasters, or remote political developments where terrestrial infrastructure is nonexistent or has been severely damaged. This ensures that critical information can still be transmitted to a global audience, upholding the continuity of news reporting in challenging environments.

Multi-skilling and Multimedia Production

Modern broadcast journalists are increasingly expected to be "multi-skilled" or "backpack journalists," capable of shooting video, recording audio, writing scripts, editing footage, and publishing content across digital platforms (Cottle and Ashton, 1999). This demands a versatile skill set, combining traditional journalistic ethics with technical proficiency in digital tools, reflecting the integration of these tools and changing news production demands (Cottle and Ashton, 1999). This shift towards a "one-person band" model is driven by the imperative for efficient content creation and rapid dissemination across various digital platforms, requiring journalists to master a broader array of technical and narrative skills beyond traditional reporting. This adaptability is crucial for news organizations seeking to maintain relevance and engage diverse audiences in a fragmented media landscape. This evolution necessitates continuous professional development, as journalists must remain adept with the latest technological advancements to effectively navigate the complexities of contemporary news production and maintain audience engagement.

News Production Workflow

The news production workflow has transformed from linear, segmented processes to integrated, digital ecosystems, driven by the amalgamation of conventional broadcasting practices with emergent digital technologies. This has led to an escalating dependence on advanced digital platforms for content generation, dissemination, and audience interaction, mandating an ongoing adaptation of journalistic methodologies and competencies (Cottle and Ashton, 1999).

Digitalization and Technological Convergence

Newsrooms have experienced profound digitalization, leading to the integration of diverse technologies into streamlined production workflows (Cottle and Ashton, 1999). This technological convergence facilitates the singular creation of news content, which can then be disseminated effectively across a multitude of platforms, encompassing traditional linear broadcasts and contemporary digital-first channels, with minimal necessary modifications. This approach significantly optimizes the intrinsic value of the content while simultaneously augmenting operational efficiency and broadening audience engagement. The advent of digital transformation has fundamentally reconfigured journalistic practices, necessitating continuous adaptation to emerging methodologies, advanced tools, and requisite technical proficiencies (Canavilhas and Fátima, 2024).

Innovative Newsroom Workflows

Conceptual frameworks such as the "news engine" are designed to enhance production efficiency and broaden multi-platform dissemination capabilities by prioritizing strategic content repurposing and optimizing asset management (Bro, Hansen and Andersson, 2015). This functionality is frequently supported by centralized content management systems, which empower diverse teams to access, modify, and publish digital assets synchronously, thereby substantially accelerating publication workflows and augmenting collaborative effectiveness.

Moreover, the integration of automation within ingest, logging, and playout protocols not only rationalizes operational procedures but also minimizes human error, consequently enabling journalists to allocate their efforts towards more complex endeavors, such as investigative journalism and comprehensive analytical reporting.

Cloud-Based Solutions and Artificial Intelligence

Cloud computing is becoming progressively integral to broadcasting operations, facilitating remote production capabilities, fostering collaborative editing environments, and providing scalable infrastructure solutions (Sharma et al., 2021). This paradigm shift in technology empowers broadcasters to transcend the inherent geographical and technical constraints associated with conventional on-premises systems. It simultaneously confers exceptional agility, flexibility, and economic efficiency in the management of intricate media workflows, while also bolstering disaster recovery provisions. Concurrently, artificial intelligence is being progressively incorporated into operational workflows, undertaking tasks such as automated transcription, video logging, and the generation of metadata. These applications substantially expedite the processing and enhance the discoverability of content. Furthermore, AI's utility extends to advanced applications, including the provision of personalized content recommendations, thereby augmenting audience engagement through the delivery of customized news experiences (Chen, 2024).

Broadcasting and Distribution

The distribution landscape for broadcast journalism has undergone a profound transformation. It now operates as a dynamic hybrid model, seamlessly integrating established traditional methods with an expansive array of innovative digital delivery platforms.

This evolution enables a broader reach and more diverse consumption patterns, fundamentally reshaping how audiences access and interact with journalistic content.

Traditional Broadcast Channels

Terrestrial and satellite television, alongside radio, continue to serve as indispensable pillars for disseminating news, ensuring foundational reach across diverse demographics, particularly in areas where digital infrastructure is limited or nonexistent. These traditional channels offer a robust and consistently accessible means of news delivery, maintaining their critical role in the broader media ecosystem by guaranteeing widespread access and reliability. The sustained relevance of these traditional platforms is progressively enhanced by the widespread integration of digital approaches, which together foster a more complex and responsive media landscape, thereby expanding the breadth of journalistic dissemination.

Digital Platforms and Mobile Delivery

The significant transition towards online streaming, podcasts, and mobile-first content consumption has fundamentally reconfigured the landscape of news dissemination (Ollikainen et al., 2011). Consequently, broadcasters have strategically broadened their distribution modalities, deploying content via dedicated applications, proprietary web platforms, ubiquitous social media networks, and an expanding continuum of third-party streaming services. This multi-platform strategy is imperative for ensuring pervasive on-demand accessibility, thereby effectively serving contemporary audiences who increasingly engage with news across a heterogeneous array of devices, particularly smartphones (Sambrook and Nielsen, 2016).

Such diversification is essential for sustaining relevance and fostering engagement among younger demographics, who primarily utilize these digital channels for news consumption (Laor, 2022).

Ensuring Provenance and Authenticity

Given the widespread proliferation of deepfakes and sophisticated manipulated media, the rigorous assurance of broadcast content's provenance and authenticity has become critically important. Protocols such as C2PA are instrumental, furnishing cryptographically authenticated metadata that unequivocally verifies the origin and comprehensive history of media files. Concurrently, ATSC standards integrate robust watermarking techniques for audio and video, actively mitigating the dissemination of misinformation and consequently upholding public confidence (Simmons and Winograd, 2024). These advanced technological safeguards are essential for providing audiences with transparent and verifiable information regarding the content they consume, thereby reinforcing journalistic integrity within a complex and fragmented informational landscape.

Essential Technical Terminology

A glossary of key technical terms integral to broadcast journalism is presented below, providing foundational understanding for the concepts discussed herein:

1. LiveU/TVU Pack: These are portable cellular bonding devices engineered for the live transmission of video content across multiple mobile networks.

2. Satellite Uplink/Downlink: This refers to the procedural transmission of signals to, and subsequent reception of signals from, a communication satellite.

3. Newscast Automation: These systems are designed to automate various operational aspects of a live newscast, encompassing camera switching, graphic overlays, and content playout, typically guided by a pre-programmed production rundown.

4. Non-Linear Editing: This describes digital video editing systems that afford editors the capability to access and reorder media clips in an arbitrary sequence without altering the integrity of the original source material.

5. Codecs: These are computational algorithms employed for the compression and decompression of digital media files, facilitating their efficient storage and transmission.

6. Compression: This denotes the process of diminishing the data size of digital information, a critical function for both streaming services and data storage, often involving variable degrees of quality degradation.

7. Ingest: This process involves the systematic import of raw media footage and audio components into a broadcast system, preparing them for subsequent editing and archival procedures.

8. Playout: Constituting the terminal phase of broadcast production, this is the stage during which content is formally transmitted for public consumption via viewing or listening.

9. Multi-platform Delivery: This strategy involves the dissemination of content across a diverse array of media channels, all originating from a singular source.

10. Content Management Systems: These software applications are utilized to oversee the creation, modification, and publication of digital content, particularly within multi-platform newsroom environments.

11. Broadcast Graphics: These encompass visual elements, such as lower thirds, full-screen graphics, and animated sequences, strategically employed to augment the visual impact and informational value of news presentations.

12. Augmented Reality in Broadcast: This technology involves the real-time superimposition of computer-generated imagery onto live, real-world footage, serving to provide enriched visual information or to create immersive narrative experiences.

Ethical Considerations and Challenges in Broadcast Journalism

Broadcast journalists are confronted with ethical dilemmas that are not only distinct but also pervasive and multifaceted, inherently influenced by the medium's immediacy and extensive global reach. The rapid dissemination of information, often conducted under considerable pressure, significantly magnifies the societal implications of editorial decisions. This demanding context necessitates a steadfast adherence to ethical principles, essential for preserving public trust, upholding journalistic integrity, and mitigating the substantial risk of misinformation and societal fragmentation.

Balancing Objectivity, Sensitivity, and Public Interest : Broadcast journalists consistently face a fundamental and persistent challenge in balancing the imperative to deliver objective information with the critical need to acknowledge the significant repercussions their reporting has on individuals and communities (Shahid, 2023). This requires making difficult editorial decisions concerning content selection, narrative construction, and the judicious integration of visual and auditory elements, all while rigorously upholding factual accuracy and maintaining steadfast impartiality (Shahid, 2023). The concept of "public interest," although often serving as a principal guideline, is inherently subjective and context-dependent, frequently leading to complex ethical quandaries regarding privacy violations, potential societal detriments, and the intricate evaluation of the broader collective welfare.

Combating Misinformation and Disinformation : The digital age, characterized by relentless 24/7 news cycles, imposes immense pressure on broadcast journalists to publish information with unprecedented speed. This urgency often creates significant vulnerabilities, inadvertently facilitating the rapid spread of misinformation and disinformation across diverse platforms. Consequently, the critical role of rigorous fact-checking has become more paramount than ever, serving as a crucial bulwark against the erosion of public trust and the distortion of informed public discourse (Shahid, 2023). Journalists, operating at the vanguard of information dissemination, are tasked with meticulously verifying every piece of content before it reaches a mass audience. This formidable responsibility is further compounded by the overwhelming volume of data and the blistering pace at which it circulates, making the identification and debunking of false narratives an increasingly complex and resource-intensive endeavor.

Maintaining Impartiality in a Polarized Media Landscape : The contemporary media environment is characterized by escalating polarization, presenting significant challenges for broadcast journalists in upholding impartiality and journalistic credibility.

The proliferation of partisan news sources and the pervasive influence of echo chambers increasingly hinder audiences' capacity to distinguish between objective reporting and overt partisan commentary. This situation not only erodes public trust in media institutions but also exacerbates societal divisions.

Consequently, broadcast journalists face intensified pressure to meticulously present diverse perspectives, scrupulously avoid emotionally charged or "loaded" language, and steadfastly resist internal and external pressures that could compromise their editorial independence and neutrality (Shahid, 2023).

Ethical Frameworks and Codes : The role of professional standards and guidelines in daily journalistic practice is not Professional standards and guidelines are not merely advantageous but are, in fact, indispensable for broadcast journalists to effectively navigate the intricate and diverse ethical challenges previously outlined. Ethical frameworks and codes of conduct provide these professionals with a comprehensive, actionable set of foundational principles that critically inform their decision-making processes. These principles thoroughly address crucial aspects such as rigorous factual accuracy, equitable treatment, transparent accountability, and the imperative to minimize harm, thereby directly mitigating the inherent vulnerabilities associated with rapid news dissemination and the pressures exerted by a polarized media landscape (Steel et al., 2025). Consequently, strict and consistent adherence to these established codes is paramount, not only for re-establishing and sustaining public trust but also for actively combating the spread of misinformation and disinformation, ultimately strengthening journalistic credibility within an increasingly fragmented media ecosystem.

The Impact of Artificial Intelligence

The increasing integration of artificial intelligence into various aspects of news production introduces a complex array of new ethical considerations. These include concerns regarding the responsible collection, storage, and utilization of audience data by AI systems, which could potentially infringe upon individual privacy rights. Furthermore, there is an inherent risk of algorithmic biases inadvertently perpetuating stereotypes, marginalizing diverse perspectives, and distorting information flows through content selection and personalization algorithms. Maintaining clear transparency regarding the origin of AI-generated or AI-assisted content is crucial, especially given the prevalence of deepfakes and synthetic media, to preserve public trust and journalistic authenticity. Additionally, the significant socio-economic implications of potential job displacement among human journalists and content creators necessitate proactive strategies for workforce adaptation and upskilling (Gutiérrez-Caneda, Lindén and Vázquez-Herrero, 2024). To effectively address these challenges, journalists and news organizations are critically responsible for developing robust and comprehensive ethical guidelines for AI implementation. This proactive measure is essential to ensure that these powerful technologies unequivocally enhance core journalistic values, such as accuracy, fairness, accountability, and public trust, rather than undermine them.

The Future of Broadcast Journalism

The broadcast journalism sector is currently navigating a significant paradigm shift, primarily driven by rapid technological advancements, evolving audience consumption patterns, and the critical need for innovative strategies in content production and dissemination. This highly dynamic and complex environment mandates continuous adaptation and proactive foresight from news organizations and journalists to ensure sustained relevance and credibility.

Continuous Digital Transformation and Innovation : The future trajectory of broadcast journalism is fundamentally dependent on pervasive digital transformation. Consequently, news media organizations are necessitated to continuously adapt to emergent technologies and dynamic audience expectations, which is paramount for upholding their relevance, competitive standing, and enduring viability and impact (Canavilhas and Fátima, 2024; Chen, 2024).

This strategic imperative transcends the mere adoption of novel technological instruments, demanding a profound reconceptualization of the entire news production, dissemination, and consumption paradigm.

Digitalization, indeed, profoundly reshapes critical facets such as the professional identity of journalists and the intrinsic quality of news delivered within a multifaceted platform environment (Canavilhas and Fátima, 2024).

Therefore, successful organizational transformation is contingent upon the proactive integration of innovative methodologies across content generation, distribution, and audience interaction frameworks (Chen, 2024). This necessitates the incorporation of sophisticated analytical tools for granular audience insight, the implementation of agile content development processes, and the strategic exploitation of nascent digital platforms to engage disparate demographic segments, thereby ensuring that journalistic practices remain both technologically advanced and resonant with contemporary information consumption patterns.

Diversified Content and Personalized Recommendations : Broadcast journalism's future will be defined by a significant shift towards diverse content and highly customized news experiences.

This evolution is necessary to overcome the limitations of a uniform approach, as news organizations are now tasked with providing news journeys precisely aligned with individual audience preferences and consumption patterns (Chen, 2024). This requires developing sophisticated multi-platform content that can adapt across various channels and devices, enabling users to engage with journalistic narratives in formats that are convenient, relevant, and engaging.

This advanced personalization, driven by cutting-edge data analytics and artificial intelligence, aims not only to boost user engagement but also to strategically address information overload, ensure the delivery of highly pertinent information, and foster a deeper, more lasting connection between audiences and credible news sources (Chen, 2024).

Embracing New Formats and Social Media Platforms : Broadcast journalism is currently experiencing a significant transformation, characterized by its deliberate adoption of varied new content formats and the systematic incorporation of social media platforms into its operational framework. This profound transformation involves the investigation of novel methodologies, including short-form video content, interactive narratives, and the strategic utilization of platforms such as TikTok, to optimize news dissemination and facilitate targeted engagement, particularly with younger demographics (Gutiérrez-Caneda, Lindén and Vázquez-Herrero, 2024). These nascent digital ecosystems transcend their role as mere distribution channels, signifying fundamental alterations in audience engagement and content delivery mechanisms. Consequently, journalists are impelled to critically re-evaluate and modify their narrative strategies to leverage the unique attributes and enhance the communicative efficacy of each platform. Such adaptation is imperative for sustaining the relevance and ensuring the ongoing viability of broadcast journalism amidst a dynamic and evolving media environment.

Role of Advanced Technologies : Advanced technologies, notably artificial intelligence, big data analytics, and virtual reality, are poised to significantly reshape the landscape of broadcast journalism. AI applications encompass various stages, from news gathering through automated data analysis to discern emerging trends from extensive datasets or flag breaking news from social media feeds to content production, including the generation of initial report drafts or summarization of complex information, and personalized news delivery, by customizing content feeds to align with individual user interests and historical consumption patterns (Chen, 2024). Big data analytics offer critical insights into audience preferences and consumption behaviors, thereby facilitating more strategic content creation by optimizing topics, formats, and distribution channels. Concurrently, virtual and augmented reality are being explored for their potential in immersive storytelling, enabling the transport of audiences directly to event locations or facilitating interaction with intricate data visualizations, thus offering novel avenues for experiencing news events and complex subjects (Chen, 2024). Collectively, these technologies are expected to substantially enhance operational efficiency by automating routine tasks, achieve granular content personalization, and cultivate more engaging journalistic experiences that foster deeper understanding and retention.

Adapting to Audience Consumption Habits : Continual adaptation to evolving audience consumption patterns is paramount for the enduring viability of broadcast journalism. The increasing preference for on-demand and mobile video news signifies a departure from conventional linear broadcast schedules, moving towards flexible, user-centric access, where audiences anticipate content availability at any time, location, and on any device (Sambrook and Nielsen, 2016). This trajectory has instigated the widespread adoption of distributed content models, which involve delivering news directly to platforms where audiences are already engaged, rather than exclusively depending on proprietary broadcast channels (Sambrook and Nielsen, 2016). Moreover, immersive journalism, by harnessing technologies such as virtual and augmented reality, holds the potential to situate audiences directly within news narratives, thereby cultivating enhanced comprehension and empathy (Eskiadi and Panagiotou, 2024).

Chapter 5

Photojournalism

Introduction to Photojournalism

Photojournalism fulfills a critical function within contemporary news media, with visual elements progressively central to narrative construction (Gynnild et al., 2017). Historically, it has served as an essential method for recording events and communicating narratives via potent visuals, consistently adhering to core journalistic principles, including integrity, comprehensiveness, and authenticity (Hasemann et al., 2017). This often involves methodical practice, frequently likened to "forensic documentation," where the rigorous collection of evidential data is crucial, informed by established tenets of objectivity, impartiality, and neutrality (Kontos & Galanopoulos-Papavasileiou, 2024). Its systematic preservation of historical events and news developments, alongside its globally intelligible visual idiom, is valued for its potent communicative capacity (Mapesa, 2016).

The digital era has instigated substantial changes for photojournalism. Expedited progress in readily available technologies and the facility of immediate image dissemination through social media platforms have remarkably broadened access to photographic practices. This shift prompts significant inquiries about the changing function and unique contribution of professional photojournalists in an environment where image capture and distribution are widely accessible (Gynnild et al., 2017).

This has even engendered a perception of "professional threat" among photojournalists, given that non-professional contributors are capable of executing roles historically held by professionals (Mortensen & Keshelashvili, 2013). Nevertheless, professional photojournalism differentiates itself through its devotion to comprehensive investigation, stringent verification, and the capacity to elucidate narratives extending beyond superficial, frequently emotive, imagery (Hasemann et al., 2017). Despite these pervasive shifts, the intrinsic idealism inherent in photojournalism frequently propelled by a significant mission or an innate drive for narrative creation persists as a primary impetus for its practitioners, particularly as they contend with the ethical ramifications of digital technologies and strive to uphold the undisputed veracity of their output in an era marked by apprehension regarding image alteration (Hasemann et al., 2017).

Definition of Photojournalism

Photojournalism is a specialized field, vital to modern news, using powerful visuals to convey narratives. It is characterized by foundational values and established methodologies, adhering to core journalistic principles such as integrity, comprehensiveness, and authenticity. This often involves a stringent approach, frequently likened to "forensic documentation," where the assiduous collection of evidential material is paramount to upholding the trustworthiness and credibility of visual narratives, strictly adhering to the practical tenets of objectivity, detachment, and neutrality (Kontos & Galanopoulos-Papavasileiou, 2024). Its essential objective is to capture "pictures of the world as it is" (Hasemann et al., 2017), a pursuit that intrinsically necessitates depicting human experiences with dignity, all while being guided by stringent ethical considerations. Key attributes widely associated with professional journalism, and consequently photojournalism, include a dedication to public service, adherence to rigorous ethical guidelines, objective reporting, professional autonomy, and a sense of immediacy in news dissemination (Mäenpää, 2014).

The notion of journalistic objectivity in photojournalism is not a static ideal; rather, it represents a dynamic and contextual construct that has consistently evolved in tandem with technological advancements. This evolution can be conceptualized through the framework of "mechanical objectivity" a conviction in technological systems that purportedly generate outputs capable of transcending inherent human subjectivity. This perspective highlights how the perception and application of journalistic objectivity are intrinsically shaped by the technologies utilized for recording, creating, and distributing news content (Carlson, 2019). Consequently, the field perpetually confronts the challenge of establishing its ethical legitimacy, with robust codes of conduct playing a pivotal role in delineating the moral parameters of press photography (Lavoie, 2010).

Technicalities of Photojournalism

The technical landscape of photojournalism has undergone dramatic changes, primarily due to digitalization. The shift from analog to digital since the late 1980s has fundamentally reshaped photojournalistic work practices, not only by facilitating editing and camera usage but also by drastically accelerating the speed of image travel and dissemination, thereby revolutionizing workflows. While foundational photographic skills remain vital, modern photojournalism is deeply intertwined with digital technologies and contemporary platforms, demanding that practitioners adeptly navigate new forms of production and distribution and continuously adapt to evolving preferences for news consumption in a hybrid media environment (Mäenpää, 2023).

This necessitates a broader skillset, extending beyond traditional still photography to include areas such as video production, which has become an increasingly significant component of news photographers' responsibilities (Mäenpää, 2014). Furthermore, the widespread availability of accessible photographic technologies, such as smartphone cameras, and the ease of instant image sharing through social media, mean that the capacity to provide news images is no longer exclusively the domain of professional photojournalists, prompting significant discussions about their unique role (Beuran, 2015; Gynnild et al., 2017).

Digitalization and Workflow

The digitalization trend, which commenced in the late 1980s, has profoundly reshaped the operational practices within photojournalism. This transition from analog to digital technologies has not only streamlined editing processes and camera functionality but has also dramatically expedited the transmission and dissemination of images, thereby revolutionizing established workflows. Consequently, contemporary photojournalism now necessitates a more extensive skill set, encompassing not only traditional still photography but also emergent fields such as video production, which has become an increasingly integral responsibility for news photographers. Photojournalists are thus required to adeptly navigate these novel production and distribution paradigms, continually adapting to evolving preferences for news consumption within a hybrid media ecosystem (Mäenpää, 2014, 2023).

Accessible Technologies and Citizen Journalism

The widespread availability of accessible photographic technologies, such as smartphone cameras, and the ease of instant image sharing through social media, means that providing news images is no longer solely the domain of professional photojournalists. This democratization of photography has sparked considerable debate regarding the continued relevance and unique role of the professional photojournalist (Beuran, 2015; Gynnild et al., 2017; Mäenpää, 2014). Furthermore, this shift has fostered a "sense of professional threat" among photojournalists, as citizen journalists, equipped with mobile phones, can now undertake many tasks traditionally reserved for professionals, prompting questions about the distinct and indispensable services photojournalists provide (Mortensen & Keshelashvili, 2013).

Multimedia Integration

Modern photojournalism necessitates a broadened skillset that extends considerably beyond traditional still photography, driven by the transition to a hybrid media environment and evolving preferences for news consumption. For instance, video production has become an increasingly vital component of news photographers' responsibilities, underscoring the critical need for adaptability and proficiency across diverse digital visual mediums and platforms. This integration of multimedia elements challenges the conventional boundaries of journalistic practice, thereby requiring continuous professional development to maintain relevance in a rapidly transforming industry. This expansion of required competencies frequently generates internal divisions among photojournalists; some embrace multimedia integration to enhance their skills, while others prefer to maintain a specialization in still photography (Mäenpää, 2014, 2023).

Challenges and Ethics

Technological advancements, while presenting new opportunities, have significantly complicated the ethical terrain of photojournalism, necessitating continuous re-evaluation of established practices. The internet introduces a complex interplay of beneficial and detrimental consequences that intricately shape the photojournalist's role (Maillot, 2019). A central concern involves the urgent and ongoing discourse surrounding the ethical implications of digital tools, specifically regarding the prevention of image manipulation and the steadfast assurance of photojournalism's inherent truth value (Hasemann et al., 2017; Mäenpää, 2014; Silva & Eldridge, 2020). The historical evolution of integrity codes and ethical standards within photojournalism consistently reveals a tension between moral imperatives and actual journalistic practices, a dynamic markedly exacerbated by digital technology (Lavoie, 2010). Consequently, professional photojournalists are increasingly required to undertake comprehensive research and stringent fact-checking, tasked with uncovering the deeper narrative beyond the immediate, often emotionally charged, visuals that may be proliferated by citizen journalists (Hasemann et al., 2017). The digital era thus mandates a fundamental re-evaluation of photojournalism ethics, with a particular emphasis on the intricate relationships among images, photographers, and the subjects they portray (Silva & Eldridge, 2020). This demanding ethical environment, combined with the complex effects of the internet, frequently exacts substantial personal tolls on photojournalists (Maillot, 2019).

The Essentials of Photojournalism

At its core, photojournalism operates as a vital and dynamic discipline, continually navigating profound technological shifts and societal changes. Its integrity and enduring relevance in this rapidly evolving media landscape are sustained by a foundation of critical principles, clearly defined objectives, and an ever-evolving skillset.

Foundational Principles & Ethical Considerations of Photojournalism

In an era of profound technological shifts and evolving media landscapes, the enduring credibility and unique role of photojournalism are fundamentally sustained by its unwavering commitment to truth and rigorous ethical practice. These foundational principles are critical for navigating the complexities of digital media and maintaining public trust. Key principles include:

Veracity and Objectivity : Photojournalism is fundamentally dedicated to the pursuit of truth, aiming to depict "pictures of the world as it is" (Hasemann et al., 2017) to furnish reliable public information. This commitment necessitates a rigorous methodology, often compared to "forensic documentation," where the primary emphasis lies in collecting objective, evidentiary material. Adherence to principles of objectivity, detachment, and neutrality is paramount in this process (Kontos & Galanopoulos-Papavasileiou, 2024). Nevertheless, the concept of objectivity itself is dynamic and has been significantly influenced by technological advancements. For instance, "mechanical objectivity" arose from the conviction that technology could inherently generate unbiased outputs, a viewpoint that continues to shape discussions regarding technology's impact on journalistic truth (Carlson, 2019).

Public Service and Ethics : Core values such as public service, ethics, autonomy, and immediacy are central to professional journalism and, by extension, photojournalism. The defense of professional autonomy, in particular, is critical for photojournalists navigating evolving technological landscapes and maintaining control over their craft (Mäenpää, 2014). Ethical legitimacy remains a continuous concern, reflecting historical tensions between moral imperatives and journalistic practices, a dynamic further complicated by digital technology.

In this context, codes of conduct play a crucial role in defining the moral boundaries of press photography (Lavoie, 2010), guiding the intricate relationships among images, photographers, and the subjects they portray, particularly in the digital era (Silva & Eldridge, 2020). This ethical framework mandates respecting human dignity, especially when depicting pain and suffering (Barcelos, 2014).

Integrity and non-manipulation : Maintaining integrity is paramount, forming the bedrock of public trust and the fundamental mission of photojournalism as a pursuit of truth, akin to "forensic documentation".

The historical development of ethical codes consistently reveals a persistent tension between moral imperatives and journalistic practices, a dynamic markedly exacerbated by digital technology, which necessitates continuous re-evaluation of ethical frameworks (Lavoie, 2010a, 2010b; Silva & Eldridge, 2020).

Photojournalists must rigorously resist manipulating images, recognizing that any alteration fundamentally undermines the credibility and truth value essential to their work and the public trust it aims to uphold (Kontos & Galanopoulos-Papavasileiou, 2024).

This commitment to non-manipulation is a cornerstone of ethical practice, especially in the digital era where technological advancements have intensified the historical tension between moral imperatives and journalistic practices, demanding a continuous re-evaluation of ethical frameworks (Lavoie, 2010a, 2010b).

Core Objectives and Role of Photojournalism

Anchored in its foundational principles of truth, integrity, and public service, photojournalism's primary goal is to inform the public through compelling and ethically sound visual storytelling.

This critical mission is achieved through several essential objectives, which include:

Informing the Public Accurately : Photojournalists are tasked with providing accurate and thorough information, fundamentally dedicated to the pursuit of truth and delivering reliable public information. This commitment to veracity and integrity, often seen as akin to "forensic documentation," emphasizes informing the public, which is crucial for a functioning democracy and forms the bedrock of public trust (Kontos & Galanopoulos-Papavasileiou, 2024; Mäenpää, 2023).

Documenting Reality and Storytelling : The fundamental purpose of photojournalism is to meticulously document reality and narrate significant stories through compelling and insightful images, ultimately serving as a crucial pursuit of truth (Hasemann et al., 2017). This commitment not only creates a vital archive for history and news but also fosters a universally understood visual language, essential for public understanding and trust (Kontos & Galanopoulos-Papavasileiou, 2024; Mapesa, 2016). Furthermore, photojournalists commit to capturing reality as simple witnesses to inform with honesty, transparency, and veracity, thereby creating irrefutable and lasting documents that serve as the initial historical record (Mraz, 2018). This dedication to capturing reality without embellishment underscores the photojournalist's role in providing an authentic visual chronicle of events (Rodal & Segarra, 2017).

Providing Context and Depth : In an age characterized by the proliferation of instant and often superficial imagery from diverse sources, particularly amplified by accessible technologies and social media (Gynnild et al., 2017), professional photojournalists distinguish themselves by rigorously prioritizing in-depth research, thorough fact-checking, and the pursuit of deeper narratives that extend beyond immediate emotional reactions. This commitment reflects photojournalism's foundational dedication to truth and public service, enabling them to contextualize events and contribute to a comprehensive understanding of news, thus preserving public trust (Kontos & Galanopoulos-Papavasileiou, 2024; Mäenpää, 2023). This often involves employing 'slow and intimate photography' techniques, emphasizing relationship-building and empathy to encourage subjects to relax and open up, thereby capturing more authentic and nuanced stories (Hasemann et al., 2017).

Navigating the Digital Landscape : Amidst a landscape where accessible technologies and social media have democratized image dissemination, enabling anyone to capture and share news images (Gynnild et al., 2017), professional photojournalists assert their enduring relevance. They do so by rigorously upholding core journalistic values such as objectivity, ethical legitimacy, and public service (Kontos & Galanopoulos-Papavasileiou, 2024; Mäenpää, 2014), distinguishing their work from the ubiquitous stream of amateur content. Photojournalists define their professional ambitions by actively negotiating these changes, striving to go deeper into narratives, get closer to human experience, and depict the world with fresh, insightful originality, thereby maintaining their critical function in informing the public and preserving journalistic integrity (Hasemann et al., 2017).

Evolving Skills and Technical Proficiency Photojournalism

The technical demands on photojournalists have significantly evolved with digitalization, requiring a diverse and adaptable skillset that encompasses not only traditional photographic expertise but also proficiency in digital workflows, multimedia integration, and critical engagement with advanced technologies. This evolution necessitates continuous adaptation to new forms of production and distribution in a hybrid media environment, as digitalization has fundamentally reshaped photojournalistic practices since the late 1980s (Mäenpää, 2023; Thomson & Sternberg, 2021). Photojournalists must now be proficient in digital editing and camera usage, knowledgeable about current digital technology and smartphone photography applications, and capable of producing video content alongside still images. Furthermore, this expanded skillset includes the ability to critically engage with the ethical implications of digital tools, particularly concerning image manipulation, to uphold the truth value inherent in their work (Silva & Eldridge, 2020), and to navigate the personal tolls introduced by the complex interplay of technology (Maillot, 2019).

Digital Proficiency and Workflow Adaptation : Since the late 1980s, digitalization has fundamentally reshaped photojournalistic practices, necessitating a diverse and adaptable skillset that extends beyond traditional photographic expertise. Photojournalists must now be proficient in digital editing and camera usage, deeply knowledgeable about current digital technology, and adept at utilizing smartphone photography applications. Furthermore, this evolution demands continuous adaptation to new forms of production and distribution in a hybrid media environment. Modern photojournalism increasingly requires proficiency in multimedia integration, including the ability to produce video content alongside still images, and even to write their own stories and possess strong organizational skills to meet employer demands (Mäenpää, 2014; Thomson & Sternberg, 2021).

Multimedia Integration : Modern photojournalism increasingly requires proficiency in multimedia integration, extending beyond traditional still photography to encompass video production as a significant part of news photographers' work (Mäenpää, 2014). This necessitates proficiency across various visual mediums and an adaptable skillset, including the ability to utilize smartphone photography applications (Prestianta, 2022). Employers now seek candidates who can not only tell stories through images but also write their own stories and possess strong organizational skills to meet these evolving demands (Thomson & Sternberg, 2021).

Critical Engagement with Technology : Digital technology, despite enhancing operational efficiency and expediting image distribution, presents substantial obstacles to preserving journalistic integrity. Consequently, photojournalists are obligated to critically assess the ethical ramifications of digital instruments, especially concerning image manipulation, and to meticulously uphold the veracity of their output by ensuring events are represented accurately and without alteration (Mäenpää, 2014; Silva & Eldridge, 2020). Furthermore, they are required to skillfully manage the intricate balance of both advantageous and disadvantageous impacts that the internet imposes on their arduous profession, while also recognizing the potential personal costs associated with these pressures (Maillot, 2019).

Specific Technicalities of Photo Capturing

The act of taking a photograph in photojournalism transcends the simple act of pressing a shutter button; it embodies a sophisticated integration of technical expertise, profound ethical judgment, critical engagement with evolving technologies, and an unwavering commitment to the journalistic objective. These demands informed, deliberate decisions often made under immensely challenging and rapidly evolving circumstances, distinguishing professional photojournalism from mere image capture. This necessitates a profound understanding and precise application of photographic principles, such as lighting, composition, and exposure, allowing for accurate visual representation and an unwavering commitment to the journalistic objective.

Photojournalists must wield precise control over aperture, shutter speed, ISO, and focus to capture diverse scenarios effectively and make rapid, informed decisions in dynamic, often challenging environments (Ramos & Marocco, 2017).

Equipment and Tools for Image Capture

While professional-grade digital single-lens reflex and mirrorless cameras remain fundamental for their image quality, versatility, and range of interchangeable lenses, the overall array of tools for capturing images in photojournalism has diversified significantly, now also encompassing advanced mobile devices, which are increasingly viable for breaking news and citizen journalism. For example, a photojournalist's toolkit often includes multiple high-end camera bodies, various lenses, and specialized transmission equipment to facilitate rapid content delivery. Beyond these essential devices, photojournalists also rely on an assortment of lighting equipment, specialized filters, and robust storage solutions to manage vast quantities of high-resolution imagery efficiently (Mortensen & Keshelashvili, 2013; Palomo & Guerrero-García, 1970; Prestianta, 2022) .

Digital Cameras : Professional-grade digital single-lens reflex and mirrorless cameras remain fundamental for their superior image quality, unparalleled versatility, and extensive range of interchangeable lenses. These advanced systems provide photojournalists with precise control over critical photographic parameters such as aperture, shutter speed, ISO, and focus, which is essential for accurately capturing diverse and often rapidly evolving journalistic scenarios (Ramos & Marocco, 2017). This level of control and technical fidelity ensures accurate visual representation and unwavering commitment to the journalistic objective required in professional news gathering. For instance, a typical photojournalist's toolkit often includes multiple high-end camera bodies and a wide array of specialized lenses to adapt to various situations, from wide-angle to telephoto (Palomo & Guerrero-García, 1970). Photographers' choices profoundly affect how reality is perceived, given that diverse focal lengths can significantly modify the presentation of a scene, thereby underscoring the photographer's influence in constructing visual narratives (Rehman, 2018).

Mobile Devices : The ubiquity and advanced capabilities of smartphones have positioned them as increasingly viable and indispensable tools for photojournalism, particularly for breaking news and citizen journalism, given their immediate accessibility and ease of dissemination (Mortensen & Keshelashvili, 2013).

Consequently, photojournalists are now expected to be proficient in using these devices, recognizing their unique strengths for immediacy and accessibility, and integrating them into their broader multimedia skillset, a proficiency increasingly sought after by employers (Prestianta, 2022; Thomson & Sternberg, 2021). However, the integration of mobile devices, especially features like photo filters, has ignited significant debates within the journalistic community concerning professionalism, authenticity, and the potential for de-professionalization (Alper, 2013; Mortensen & Keshelashvili, 2013).

Critics argue that such features can compromise journalistic integrity by altering reality or depicting sensitive events in a 'stylishly vintage' manner, thereby blurring the lines between reporting and editorializing, and raising ethical questions about image manipulation (Alper, 2013; Silva & Eldridge, 2020). Such practices, alongside the daily visual saturation and lack of respect for privacy, are seen by some as devaluing photojournalism and eroding public trust.

Despite these concerns, professionals acknowledge that while mobile devices cannot entirely supplant traditional photographic cameras, they serve as valuable tools, particularly in urgent situations, and enable a broader public to document events, contributing to what some term "citizen journalism" (Palomo & Guerrero-García, 1970).

Lenses : A variety of lenses are employed to suit different situations, from wide-angle lenses for establishing shots to telephoto lenses for capturing distant subjects or intimate details without intrusion. While focal length does not alter perspective from a single viewpoint, different lenses merely change magnification, making subjects appear smaller with wide-angle lenses and larger with telephoto lenses (Ganapathy-Doré et al., 2013). However, these choices profoundly influence how reality is perceived and can significantly modify the presentation of a scene, thereby underscoring the photographer's influence in constructing visual narratives (Rehman, 2018).

On-Field Photographic Techniques and Considerations

The actual process of photo-taking in photojournalism is a complex and demanding endeavor, meticulously guided by stringent journalistic principles, advanced technical skill, and an acute awareness of the prevailing conditions, particularly when operating in fast-paced, unpredictable, or highly sensitive environments. This necessitates not only precise control over photographic parameters like aperture, shutter speed, ISO, and focus to ensure accurate visual representation, but also the constant exercise of ethical judgment to uphold truthfulness and avoid manipulation, even amidst the pressures of real-time reporting (Iqbal & Badar, 2022; Mäenpää, 2014; Ramos & Marocco, 2017). This ethical imperative extends to carefully navigating the boundaries of image alteration, as permissible adjustments such as limited cropping or tonal corrections must never compromise the emotional truthfulness or integrity of the photographic content (Urbonavičiūtė, 2015).

Composition : Composition, a crucial technicality, involves arranging visual elements within the frame to create a compelling and clear narrative, thereby profoundly influencing how reality is perceived and ensuring accurate visual representation (Iqbal & Badar, 2022; Rehman, 2018). This process demands adherence to principles such as the rule of thirds, leading lines, and framing, all while rigorously upholding journalistic integrity and truthfully reflecting reality. Photojournalists aim for compositions that not only contain journalistic elements and offer more value than ordinary photos but also scrupulously avoid misrepresenting the scene through framing or other compositional choices that could alter reality or mislead viewers (Iqbal & Badar, 2022; Mäenpää, 2014). These ethical imperatives underscore the critical role of composition in maintaining the veracity of the visual narrative.

Lighting : Managing available light, whether natural or artificial, is a key technical skill, fundamental not only for achieving proper exposure but also for upholding the visual accuracy and ethical representation inherent in photojournalism.

Photojournalists must quickly and critically assess lighting conditions, making conscious adjustments to camera settings to ensure the accurate depiction of a scene without altering its authenticity or emotional truthfulness (Rehman, 2018; Urbonavičiūtė, 2015). The choices made regarding lighting profoundly influence how reality is perceived, underscoring the photographer's role in constructing a truthful visual narrative.

Consequently, artificial lighting is typically used minimally, if at all, to maintain the documentary nature of the image and prevent any misrepresentation, aligning with the overarching ethical imperative to avoid manipulation (Iqbal & Badar, 2022; Mäenpää, 2014; Rehman, 2018).

Focus and Depth of Field : Accurately focusing on the subject is paramount not only to convey clarity and draw the viewer's eye but also to ensure a truthful visual representation (Iqbal & Badar, 2022). Similarly, controlling depth of field allows photojournalists to ethically isolate subjects or show them within their environment, depending on the story's needs, thereby influencing how reality is perceived and contributing to the construction of a truthful visual narrative without misrepresentation (Rehman, 2018; Urbonavičiūtė, 2015). While these technical decisions may appear individually nuanced, they collectively and profoundly influence how audiences interpret and perceive events, thereby rendering meticulous application and stringent ethical considerations paramount in photojournalism (Urbonavičiūtė, 2015).

Establishing Relations and Empathy : Beyond purely technical settings, "slow and intimate photography" represents a qualitative approach centered on building profound relationships and fostering empathy with subjects. This methodology is crucial for photojournalists to not only gain trust and encourage sources to relax and open up, particularly in vulnerable situations, but also to capture narratives with greater depth and emotional truthfulness (Hasemann et al., 2017). By prioritizing a nuanced understanding over superficial documentation, this approach directly contributes to upholding the ethical imperative of authentic representation, ensuring the integrity and veracity of the visual story (Iqbal & Badar, 2022; Urbonavičiūtė, 2015).

"Forensic Documentation" Approach : The photo-taking process often resembles "forensic documentation," where the gathering of evidentiary material is paramount to ensure images serve as credible and truthful records of events. This approach mandates capturing details with uncompromising objectivity, detachment, and neutrality, reflecting the core ethical imperative of photojournalism to uphold truthfulness and avoid manipulation (Mäenpää, 2014; Urbonavičiūtė, 2015).

This entails a deliberate commitment to capturing events as they naturally transpire, thereby minimizing any artificial intervention or manipulation to uphold the scene's authenticity and integrity. Often, media reports, including videos and photos, become evidence in judicial processes, serving as crucial components for objective assessment (Kontos & Galanopoulos-Papavasileiou, 2024). This rigorous adherence to objectivity transforms photographic evidence into a reliable foundation for analysis, contributing significantly to a comprehensive understanding of complex situations (Mäenpää, 2014).

Navigating Challenges During Image Capture

The act of taking photos in a news context is a multifaceted endeavor, fraught with inherent complexities and a distinct set of challenges that distinguish it from other photographic practices. Photojournalists are often seen as "transparent windows on the world, capturing the reality of the camera lens" (Hrib, 2023), yet they must continuously navigate the paradox of presenting neutral records while consciously selecting and crafting compelling images for public dissemination.

Limited Control over Variables : Photojournalists operate with significant constraints, having complete control over only two of the 22 variables that influence how images look, sharing partial control over 13 others, and possessing no control over the remaining seven, which include aspects such as subject behavior or ambient conditions. This inherent lack of full control over crucial elements, such as subject behavior or unpredictable ambient conditions (Thomson & Greenwood, 2016), necessitates rapid adaptation and decision-making under pressure.

This significantly complicates the ethical imperative to maintain objectivity and truthfulness in visual reporting, as every quick decision must still uphold the integrity of the narrative (Kontos & Galanopoulos-Papavasileiou, 2024).

Ethical Constraints in Real-time : While capturing images, photojournalists constantly navigate ethical dilemmas, ensuring they do not exploit vulnerable individuals or situations, and adhering to journalistic photography ethics (Iqbal & Badar, 2022). The inherent unpredictability of live news situations, coupled with the imperative for rapid dissemination, places immense pressure on photojournalists to make instantaneous ethical judgments that uphold the integrity of the narrative despite limited control over variables. This often involves navigating a delicate balance between the imperative to document events as they unfold and an ethics of care that prioritizes the dignity and privacy of subjects, recognizing the inherent dilemma in balancing information provision with respecting human dignity (Kontos & Galanopoulos-Papavasileiou, 2024; Mäenpää, 2023; Thomson & Greenwood, 2016).

Speed vs. Deliberation : Digital technology has drastically accelerated the speed at which images can be captured and disseminated, creating a significant tension between the incessant demand for immediacy and the critical need for careful, considered photographic choices that uphold journalistic standards. This rapid environment places immense pressure on photojournalists to make instantaneous ethical judgments (Kontos & Galanopoulos-Papavasileiou, 2024) while maintaining truthfulness and objectivity, thereby complicating the meticulous application of ethical principles essential for preserving the integrity of the visual narrative (Thomson & Greenwood, 2016). Consequently, photojournalists must often make swift decisions under pressure, balancing the urgency of real-time reporting with the ethical obligation to avoid staging or manipulating situations to preserve the authenticity of the visual record (Mäenpää, 2023).

Avoiding Manipulation : The inherent ease of digital manipulation underscores the critical necessity for a stringent ethical code governing the entire photographic process, both during capture and throughout post-production. Photojournalists are ethically obligated to ensure that the images they produce are an unvarnished and accurate representation of events as they unfolded, steadfastly resisting any inclination to alter reality. This commitment extends to eschewing deceptive practices such as manipulative framing, staging, or the use of in-camera effects that could distort or misrepresent the authentic scene, thereby safeguarding the integrity and veracity of the visual narrative (Iqbal & Badar, 2022; Mäenpää, 2014; Urbonavičiūtė, 2015). This commitment to authenticity is a foundational tenet of photojournalism, as the integrity of a photograph relies on its faithful representation of reality (Barber, 2020; Urbonavičiūtė, 2015), making its authority unquestionable (Barber, 2020). This rigorous adherence reinforces public trust in the media's capacity to deliver objective accounts of events, especially in an era where digital manipulation can easily undermine the credibility of visual information (Mäenpää, 2014).

In conclusion, the technicalities of photo-taking in photojournalism extend beyond merely mastering camera functions; they demand a sophisticated integration of technical expertise, situational awareness, ethical judgment, and an unwavering commitment to truthful visual storytelling, all performed under the demanding conditions of news gathering.

The essential photojournalist today is not just a photographer but a visual storyteller, an ethical gatekeeper, and a technologically adept communicator who upholds foundational journalistic values while continuously adapting to new tools and challenges in the pursuit of truth.

This comprehensive understanding positions them to effectively navigate the complexities of contemporary media landscapes and maintain the integrity of visual news reporting (Mäenpää, 2014). In summary, while the core mission of honest, objective, and dignified storytelling remains the bedrock of photojournalism, the technical landscape has vastly expanded. It now encompasses sophisticated digital tools, demands comprehensive multimedia content creation, and requires a heightened and continually evolving awareness of ethical responsibilities in an increasingly visual, interconnected, and challenging global environment.

Chapter 6

Journalistic Correspondence

THIS JOURNALISTIC GENRE IS primarily distinguished by its singular ability to provide direct, eyewitness accounts. These narratives are not only significant but are essential for cultivating an authentic understanding, offering audiences insights into occurrences and cultures that might otherwise remain ambiguous, unattainable, and susceptible to considerable misinterpretation (Østergaard, 2021). The physical presence of correspondents at the scene facilitates a more profound and intricate analysis of societal structures and contemporary issues, thereby promoting a broader comprehension for the readership (Kabel, 2016).

Correspondent

A correspondent is a reporter who specializes in covering a particular topic or geographic region. For example, a radio station's financial correspondent would conduct extensive research on economic matters, while a television station might employ a Middle East correspondent, or a newspaper an education correspondent. This specialization provides correspondents with a deep understanding of their chosen field, enabling them to delve into the intricacies of events, uncover less obvious connections, and contextualize developments within a broader framework. Such expertise facilitates in-depth reporting and nuanced analysis, which is crucial for delivering comprehensive and authoritative news by enhancing its reliability and depth (Kabel, 2016).

Reporter

A reporter is an individual primarily employed to gather and report news or conduct interviews for newspapers or broadcasts. Media organizations typically maintain a team of reporters responsible for collecting news for their broadcasts and publications. This crucial role often involves extensive "legwork" and "firsthand witnessing," directly contributing to the authenticity and reliability of news reports from the field (Reich and Godler, 2017). A reporter's unwavering dedication to on-the-ground investigation is paramount, as it critically ensures the public receives meticulously verified and profoundly impactful information. This fundamental emphasis on direct experience, widely known as "shoe-leather reporting," serves as an indispensable pillar of journalistic integrity, particularly vital amidst the pervasive influence of digital media. It guarantees that news narratives are firmly anchored in tangible reality, thereby safeguarding against the proliferation of unsubstantiated or speculative accounts (Reich and Godler, 2017).

Stringer

In journalism, a stringer is a freelance journalist, photographer, or videographer who contributes reports, photos, or videos to a news organization on an ongoing basis. Crucially, stringers are compensated individually for each piece of work that is published or broadcast, rather than receiving a regular salary. Freelance journalists and stringers often engage in ad-hoc collaborations with media houses, especially for events not significant enough to deploy in-house reporters (Kabel, 2016; Sparre, 2017). This model offers media organizations significant flexibility and cost-effectiveness, enabling broader coverage of diverse topics and geographical areas without the overhead associated with full-time staff, particularly for stories that do not warrant deploying salaried reporters.

The concept of freelancers in journalism has evolved, with an increasing number of self-identified freelance journalists navigating precarious employment situations (Himma-Kadakas and Mõttus, 2021; Rosenmeier et al., 2021; Josephi and O'Donnell, 2022). This compensation structure, while offering flexibility, often results in unstable income, lack of benefits, and intense competition, contributing to the increasingly precarious employment conditions faced by many independent journalists in a rapidly changing media landscape characterized by declining revenues and evolving staffing models.

Freelancer

A freelancer is an independent contractor who undertakes work on a per-job or per-task basis, typically for short-term projects. The advantages of freelancing often include the flexibility to work remotely, a customizable schedule, and an improved work-life balance. However, this flexibility is frequently counterbalanced by the absence of job security, comprehensive benefits, and the relentless necessity for continuous self-promotion and client acquisition. These factors culminate in significant, often precarious, challenges in establishing and sustaining a stable career, particularly within the dynamic and competitive media landscape (Matthews and Onyemaobi, 2024). Freelancers, commonly identified as independent professionals, contractors, or 'solopreneurs,' play a critical and increasingly prominent role across various creative and media sectors, including journalism, television, and publishing (Clifton, Füzi and Loudon, 2019). Their growing presence reflects evolving industry structures, yet also underscores the heightened individual responsibility for career management and financial stability.

Pathways and Values of Correspondence

Within journalistic correspondence, the distinct roles and operational modalities ranging from specialized correspondents and versatile reporters to the increasingly prevalent figures of stringers and independent freelancers collectively highlight the diverse yet interconnected mechanisms of news gathering and dissemination. Each of these roles navigates a unique constellation of professional challenges and opportunities, reflecting the evolving landscape of media employment and the imperative for journalistic integrity (Matthews and Onyemaobi, 2024).

Becoming a correspondent is an exceptionally competitive and rigorous endeavor. Aspiring correspondents are typically required to obtain a degree in a relevant field, such as journalism or English, and acquire extensive practical experience, often through campus publications or internships. Furthermore, an indispensable portfolio of published work is essential, effectively demonstrating a candidate's proven proficiency in reporting, writing, and independently analyzing complex issues. The development of acute observational skills and a consistent capacity for critically evaluating information from diverse sources are also paramount for achieving sustained success in this challenging profession.

Historically, foreign correspondents often progressed their careers by rising through the ranks of newspaper staff, commencing with general reporting assignments prior to potential deployment to a foreign bureau, contingent on the media organization's maintenance of such offices. Nevertheless, significant recent transformations within the news industry have led to the closure or substantial reduction of foreign bureaus by numerous newspapers, consequently intensifying competition for available roles. Despite these changes, news agencies such as the Associated Press and Reuters continue their operations;

however, obtaining a position within these organizations typically demands substantial prior experience and a proven professional record. Comparable stringent career trajectories are observed in broadcast media and online publications, underscoring that these roles are not acquired solely through digital means but fundamentally necessitate extensive practical, on-the-ground experience and direct engagement. This substantial industry evolution has, as a result, prompted many journalists to pursue opportunities outside traditional media, frequently transitioning into institutional communication roles where compensation may be more advantageous (Aguar-Torres, 2025) and employment stability greater.

Independence and Self-Reliance in Journalism

Independent journalists operate autonomously, often with minimal supervision from editors. This independence necessitates a strong sense of responsibility and a high degree of self-discipline, requiring them to rigorously self-edit and adhere strictly to established journalistic values and ethics. This operational freedom is critical, as it empowers independent journalists to fearlessly investigate and report on sensitive and often 'forbidden' themes, such as official corruption, human rights abuses, and electoral fraud. By bringing these issues to light, they actively challenge dominant narratives and official secrecy, thereby contributing to the erosion of legitimacy for regimes or institutions that rely on suppressing such information. The Cambridge Dictionary posits that the increasing assertiveness of the press has empowered independent journalists to tackle previously forbidden themes, such as official corruption and electoral fraud, further eroding the legitimacy of regimes. The critical function of independent journalism in exposing societal ills becomes indispensable, especially in contexts where traditional media outlets face compromise or constraint due to political or economic pressures. By fearlessly investigating sensitive issues and challenging dominant narratives, independent journalists amplify the voices of the marginalized and rigorously hold power accountable (Buschow, 2020).

Individual Editorial Responsibility

Correspondents, freelancers, stringers, and citizen journalists are frequently expected to self-edit their work, often with limited or no direct supervision from professional media editors. This autonomy necessitates that they assume significant individual editorial responsibility, requiring them to critically evaluate information, reconcile diverse viewpoints, and offer balanced analysis of events. This inherent independence, while granting unparalleled freedom to report on critical issues, simultaneously imposes an even greater imperative for rigorous ethical standards and factual accuracy. Operating without the institutional safeguards of traditional newsroom structures, independent journalists face a heightened personal accountability. This underscores the critical importance of unwavering journalistic integrity and absolute adherence to truthfulness, especially given their direct capacity to shape public perception in the absence of conventional editorial checks and balances (Skana and Gjerazi, 2024).

Journalistic Responsibility

At its core, a journalist's fundamental duty is to serve the public interest by rigorously upholding journalistic ends: actively seeking truth and providing a fair, comprehensive, and unbiased account of events and issues (Almirón, 2020). Conscientious journalists, irrespective of their medium or specialization, are *obligated* to serve the public with uncompromising thoroughness and honesty. This necessitates not merely practicing but *embodying* the core values of responsible journalism, which inherently demands ethical reporting entirely free from manipulation and biases. By consistently delivering true and fair news, journalists profoundly influence contemporary issues, playing a critical role in shaping informed public discourse and holding institutions accountable (Syahri, 2020; Cohen-Almagor, 2023). Indeed, professional and quality journalists are bound by stringent ethical codes that not only guide their understanding and competence but also unequivocally define what constitutes "good work," thereby separating verifiable truth from conjecture or error (Syahri, 2020; Oso, Adeniran and Arowolo, 2024). These foundational professional values including truth, impartiality, and originality are absolutely crucial in shaping responsible journalistic practice (Komatsu et al., 2020). The indispensable importance of high-quality, ethically sound journalism for sustaining a healthy democratic public sphere cannot be overstated. However, this vital role is increasingly challenged by persistent declines in public trust in journalism, making unwavering adherence to these principles more critical than ever (Steel et al., 2025).

The ABCD of Journalism

Effective journalistic writing is characterized by its economy of style, employing succinct, clear, and direct prose within brief, focused paragraphs. This methodology, fundamental to journalistic practice, is vital for public enlightenment, maintaining professional credibility, and optimizing readability and comprehension (Damgaard, 2018; Jaakkola, 2018). This commitment to precision and clarity is encapsulated by the "ABCD principle": Accuracy, Brevity, Conciseness, and Directness. Adherence to this principle ensures that information is presented with optimal clarity and efficiency, enabling audiences to rapidly assimilate complex topics without ambiguity and thereby fostering informed public discourse (Sonni, Putri and Irwanto, 2024).

1. **Accuracy**: refers to providing information that conforms to established facts and truth. In journalism, accuracy is a cornerstone ethical guideline, demanding meticulous verification of facts (Maštrapa, John and Brautović, 2020). It is central to the newswriting style (Jaakkola, 2018), serving as the bedrock upon which all credible reporting rests. Without unwavering accuracy, journalistic integrity is compromised, and public trust, once eroded, is exceptionally difficult to regain.

2. **Brevity**: denotes shortness in duration or writing, expressing much in few words; as famously noted by Polonius in Shakespeare's Hamlet, "brevity is the soul of wit." Succinctness is a key characteristic of effective writing (Sword, 2009), crucial for maintaining reader engagement and ensuring that essential information is conveyed efficiently in an increasingly saturated media landscape. It respects the reader's time and attention.

3. **Conciseness:** in common usage and linguistics, is a communication principle that eliminates redundancy by using as few words as possible while preserving meaning. This principle enhances clarity and impact, preventing diluted messages and ensuring that every word serves a deliberate purpose. By distilling complex ideas to their core, conciseness facilitates rapid comprehension and reduces the likelihood of misinterpretation.

4. **Directness:** is the quality of being plain, straightforward, or proceeding in a straight line without deviation. This involves expressing complex ideas clearly and avoiding excessive jargon (Andersen, 2017), thereby ensuring accessibility for a broad

audience. A direct approach cuts through ambiguity, allowing readers to grasp the central message without unnecessary effort or confusion, thereby maximizing the communicative effectiveness of journalistic content.

CHAPTER 7

War & Peace Journalism

WAR JOURNALISM PREDOMINANTLY FOCUSES on violence and violent actors, inherently fostering a militaristic mindset among audiences. This often leads audiences to overvalue violent responses to conflict while overlooking non-violent alternatives, a phenomenon understood to result from established news reporting conventions concerning warfare. This conventional reporting frequently frames conflicts as zero-sum games, severely simplifying complex situations into binaries where only two parties contend for a single objective. This simplification often obscures the root causes, diverse stakeholders, and potential non-military solutions, thereby predisposing news towards a form of war journalism that critically lacks fairness and accuracy.

In contrast, peace journalism analysis critically suggests that conventional conflict news, with its pervasive emphasis on violence and reliance on official sources, profoundly impacts the parties involved in a conflict. At critiques war journalism for its often uncritical acceptance of official narratives, which can provide insufficient or deliberately inaccurate information and make media unwitting conduits for state or factional propaganda, as starkly illustrated in the coverage of the Araq War, such approach is normally seen to elevate the visibility of violent actors, thereby reinforcing a cycle where violence becomes the primary lens through which conflict is understood and reported, frequently overlooking opportunities for de-escalation and peaceful resolution (Olivera, Thomas and Kilby, 2020).

War Versus Peace Journalism

Peace journalism is both a style and a theory of reporting that aims to present stories about war and conflict with balance, directly contrasting with war journalism, which fundamentally entrenches a bias towards violence. Peace journalism actively and ethically strives to minimize the division between opposing parties by conscientiously avoiding the repetition of facts that demonize one side, thereby actively working to de-escalate conflict. Conversely, war or violence journalism exclusively reports on the conflict arena, obsessively focusing on which side gains the upper hand in hostilities. This perniciously simplifies complex conflicts into a dangerously reductive binary framework of "us vs. them" and consistently emphasizes victory for one side, thereby perpetuating antagonism and hindering resolution.

Peace journalism distinguishes itself by adopting an approach that meticulously scrutinizes the profound effects framing has on public perception, thereby ensuring that news selection and dissemination offer comprehensive context and background from all involved parties. This stands in stark contrast to war journalism's superficial focus on visible effects of violence, which systematically overlooks the underlying causes, diverse stakeholders, and long-term consequences, consequently impeding a holistic understanding of conflict. It focuses on analyzing the structure of conflict, exploring the visible and invisible effects of violence, and offering solutions and prevention strategies, in stark contrast to conventional journalism which often exacerbates conflict through sensationalized coverage (Tayeebwa, 2017) (Guo, Duan and Yang, 2025).

The Role of the War Correspondent

A war correspondent is a journalist who covers stories directly from a battlefield or active war zone. This form of journalism is widely regarded as singularly important and impactful, as it uniquely provides an unfiltered, eyewitness perspective that builds profound audience trust. By delivering direct, factual accounts from the front lines, these journalists play a critical and often unparalleled role in informing the public about the grim realities of conflict, frequently at immense personal risk. Their immediate and authentic reports possess the power to significantly shape public perception and understanding of global events, making them indispensable conduits between the theater of war and the civilian populace. Furthermore, war correspondents often operate under immense pressure from news outlets and deadlines to deliver immediate, impactful, and visually dramatic stories. This pervasive drive for sensationalism and graphic accounts of conflict can inadvertently lead to a superficial focus on visible events, rather than a deeper examination of the underlying complexities, root causes, and potential pathways for peaceful resolution. This journalistic imperative for immediate, dramatic narratives thus critically aligns with the tenets of war journalism, prioritizing conflict escalation, simplifying intricate situations into reductive binaries, and reinforcing division over comprehensive, nuanced reporting that could foster understanding and facilitate de-escalation (Olivera, Thomas and Kilby, 2020).

Where War Correspondents Operate

War correspondents are specialized journalists authorized by armed forces to be present during times of war or armed conflict. They operate in the most conflict-ridden parts of the world, attempting to get close enough to the action to provide written accounts, photos, or film footage. While this is widely considered the most dangerous form of journalism, providing eyewitness accounts from the front lines, these journalists often operate under immense pressure from news outlets and deadlines to deliver immediate, impactful, and visually dramatic stories. This pervasive drive for sensationalism and graphic accounts of conflict can inadvertently lead to a superficial focus on visible events, rather than a deeper examination of the underlying complexities, root causes, and potential pathways for peaceful resolution. This journalistic imperative for immediate, dramatic narratives thus critically aligns with the tenets of war journalism, prioritizing conflict escalation, simplifying intricate situations into reductive binaries, and reinforcing division over comprehensive, nuanced reporting that could foster understanding and facilitate de-escalation (Olivera, Thomas and Kilby, 2020).

Safety of Journalists in Active Warfare

War correspondents should only enter a war zone with permission from all warring parties involved in the conflict. If only one side grants permission, the journalist's safety primarily rests with themself and the permitting armed party. However, international humanitarian law unequivocally mandates the protection of journalists, provided they do not actively participate in hostilities. This protected status is maintained precisely when journalists refrain from direct involvement in armed conflict. News media, regardless of whether they are perceived to be used for propaganda, are explicitly immune from attack, unless definitively proven to be employed for military purposes or to incite egregious acts such as war crimes, genocide, or violence. The deliberate targeting of journalists in armed conflict is not merely a violation but a grave international war crime, underscoring the severe legal repercussions for those who disregard these fundamental protections. Despite these established legal frameworks, the adequacy and implementation of available protection mechanisms for journalists in conflict zones are frequently undermined, as deliberate attacks, assaults, and arrests upon journalistic professionals frequently occurring (Dahal, 2021).

Peace Journalism: A Responsible Approach to Conflict Reporting

Journalism, particularly in conflict zones, is far more than a mere transmission of "facts"; it is an intricate process that encompasses critical decisions about "what" to report and "how" to report it. This intricate process inherently demands rigorous selection, profound responsibility, and unwavering adherence to the highest ethical standards and principles, especially when confronting the complexities of conflict. The critical imperative to accurately and ethically portray conflicts gained profound momentum with the emergence of peace and conflict studies in the twentieth century. This seminal discipline furnished invaluable evaluative criteria, sophisticated analytical tools, and innovative approaches for dissecting conflicts, thereby charting more effective pathways for their management and resolution. Building upon these foundational insights, peace journalism critically re-evaluates and refines traditional news reporting paradigms, challenging conventional notions of balance, fairness, and accuracy. Its core aim is to foster a deeper, more nuanced understanding of conflicts and actively contribute to the enduring pursuit of world peace.

This transformative approach to reporting was formally conceptualized as "peace journalism" by the renowned Norwegian scholar Johan Galtung, widely acclaimed as the father of peace studies. His pivotal introduction of a comprehensive model for peace reporting occurred during a seminal summer school in Taplow Court, UK, in August 1997, an event meticulously organized by former BBC journalist Jake Lynch, who has since emerged as an indispensable, pioneering figure in the global advancement and implementation of peace journalism.

Lynch, alongside Annabel McGoldrick, significantly advanced the popularization of peace journalism, powerfully articulating its essence as a deliberate editorial choice designed to encourage society to actively value and pursue non-violent responses to conflict. This seminal definition, drawing directly from their extensive collective experiences as seasoned reporters and dedicated trainers, rapidly became a crucial cornerstone, profoundly shaping subsequent academic discourse and guiding practical applications within the evolving field (Lynch, 2015).

Defining Peace Journalism

Peace journalism is precisely defined as "when editors and reporters make choices of what to report, and how to report it that create opportunities for society at large to consider and value non-violent responses to conflict" (Olivera, Thomas and Kilby, 2020). This approach functions as a comprehensive "road map that traces the connections between journalists, their sources and the consequences of their reporting," offering a critical lens through which to evaluate media's profound influence on conflict narratives. Operating as a vital "remedial strategy," it actively endeavors to "supplement the news conventions to give peace a chance," directly addressing and counteracting the often conflict-reinforcing biases inherent in traditional war reporting. Crucially, this robust approach is not a form of advocacy journalism but stands as a rigorously ethical framework, deeply rooted in established journalistic principles, aiming to cultivate a more nuanced, holistic, and peace-oriented understanding of complex conflicts.

Characteristics of Peace Journalism

Building upon this robust ethical framework, peace journalism operates on five core principles. These principles rigorously guide journalists in making informed decisions about content selection and framing, thereby proactively fostering constructive societal engagement with conflict resolution rather than merely sensationalizing violence. These foundational principles include:

1. **Comprehensive Contextualization:** Exploring the backgrounds and contexts of conflict formation from the perspectives of all involved sides, not just the often-portrayed two-sided narrative common in mainstream media. This includes examining the historical roots, cultural factors, and underlying grievances of all parties involved.

2. **Inclusive Voice:** Giving voice to the views of all rival parties across all levels of society, moving beyond elite voices to include ordinary citizens, victims, and peacebuilders.

3. **Solution-Oriented Approaches:** Actively seeking and reporting on creative ideas for conflict resolution, development, peacemaking, and peacekeeping. This necessitates a focus on peace initiatives, reconciliation efforts, and potential solutions, rather than an exclusive preoccupation with violence and destruction.

4. **Transparency and Accountability:** Rigorously exposing lies, cover-up attempts, and culprits across all factions, while also transparently revealing excesses committed by, and suffering inflicted upon, peoples of all parties. This ensures a truly balanced and comprehensive portrayal of responsibility and suffering.

5. **Focus on Post-Conflict Development:** Paying diligent attention to peace stories and post-war developments, including reconstruction, reconciliation, and the long-term impacts of conflict.

The peace journalism model fundamentally differentiates itself from conventional violence, war, or victory-oriented reporting. While traditional war journalism predominantly concentrates on the dramatic depiction of violence, often serving as a conduit for propaganda, promoting elite interests, and fixating on notions of triumph, peace journalism is intentionally structured around comprehensive conflict analysis, rigorous truth-seeking, the integration of diverse human perspectives, and solution-focused reporting. It places significant emphasis on comprehending the root causes and extensive ramifications of conflict, actively cultivating empathy, and thoroughly investigating tangible pathways to sustainable peace, rather than solely documenting the destructive dimensions of warfare.

Since its emergence in the mid-1990s, peace journalism has garnered considerable interest from both practitioners and academics globally, as well as from other stakeholders engaged with the intersection of media, peace, and conflict. It has evolved into a prominent, globally distributed reform movement comprising journalists, scholars, and activists.

Notwithstanding its expanding influence across various continents, peace journalism continues to attract scholarly debate and critique. Discussions persist regarding both the intrinsic necessity and practical feasibility of its conceptual framework. Similar to any novel concept seeking to refine established practices, peace journalism occasionally encounters resistance, particularly from professionals who are disinclined to challenge the conventional paradigms of mainstream media reporting, which they often characterize as "war reporting." Some critics contend that this approach may compromise journalistic objectivity or merely rearticulate existing journalistic principles.

Conversely, proponents assert that its heightened emphasis on specific elements, particularly framing and a solutions-oriented methodology, provides an indispensable framework for more ethical and effective reporting. This perspective holds that peace journalism, rather than rejecting the principle of objectivity, seeks to broaden its scope by intentionally presenting facts from a standpoint that acknowledges and prioritizes non-violent responses to conflict, thereby fostering a more comprehensive understanding of intricate situations (Valdez et al., 2023).

Necessity for Peace Journalism

The assertion that news reporting frequently prioritizes agreement and negative events underscores a fundamental flaw within contemporary journalistic practices. This problem profoundly distorts reality, particularly during conflicts, a situation exacerbated by an over-reliance on official sources that often provide biased or incomplete information (McLeod, 2009). This critical deficiency in news coverage emphatically highlights the necessity for peace journalism. War journalism's inherent bias towards official sources renders it acutely susceptible to propaganda, which can be defined as a deliberate attempt to "shape perceptions, manipulate cognitions, and direct behavior" (Mohi-ud-Din, Rasul and Munir, 2021).

Galtung and Ruge's seminal 1965 research aimed to identify the determinants of newsworthiness during the Cold War, a period characterized by intense geopolitical tensions and a bipolar global structure (Galtung and Ruge, 1965; Harcup and O'Neill, 2016). Despite the subsequent evolution of the global landscape into a new world order, the question of "what makes the news" remains a central and urgent inquiry for contemporary researchers (Joye, Heinrich and Wöhlert, 2016).

In their influential paper, Galtung and Ruge identified twelve key factors influencing foreign news selection among Norwegian journalists: frequency, threshold, unambiguity, meaningfulness, consonance, unexpectedness, continuity, composition, reference to elite nations, reference to elite individuals, reference to persons, and reference to negative aspects (Galtung and Ruge, 1965; Thomas, Alhassan and Lie, 2020). This publication was long regarded as the "most influential explanation" of news values, establishing a foundational framework that subsequent studies rigorously revisited, reconsidered, or expanded upon with alternative criteria (Harcup and O'Neill, 2001; Joye, Heinrich and Wöhlert, 2016). These pioneering Norwegian researchers observed that specific factors, particularly those emphasizing official sources, systematically influenced inclusion patterns in conflict reporting. This resulted in news largely dictated by conventional representational norms, thereby revealing a critical systemic limitation of traditional journalism (Harcup and O'Neill, 2016).

Peace journalism directly addresses and critiques these entrenched patterns, vigorously advocating for people-centered narratives over official pronouncements, process-oriented reporting over mere event coverage, and the pursuit of peace-focused angles rather than an exclusive preoccupation with violence (Lynch, 2015). Conventional reporting often frames conflicts as zero-sum games, reducing complex situations to binaries where only two parties contend for a single objective (Entman, 2010). Consequently, news unequivocally requires substantial remedial measures to truly "give peace a chance," as these inherent conventions predispose it towards a form of war journalism that is demonstrably skewed and incomplete (Lynch and Freear, 2023).

Numerous instances of conflict reporting demonstrate how media can become unwitting or willing conduits for propaganda, thereby actively shaping public perception through manipulation.

The international coverage of the Iraq War serves as a stark and troubling example of how media narratives can be controlled by political sources (Kull, Ramsay and Lewis, 2003; İnceoğlu, Cinarli and Aral, 2006). Western media, without critically verifying the accuracy of information, prominently amplified the Bush administration's assertions regarding "weapons of mass destruction," which subsequently proved entirely false. This highlights a damning indictment of journalistic integrity and due diligence (Kull, Ramsay and Lewis, 2003; Mosdell et al., 2006; McLeod, 2009).

Mainstream journalistic practices frequently emphasize violent aspects of conflicts, while often neglecting their underlying causes, consequences, and potential resolutions (Joseph, 2014).

Compounding these critical observations, practitioners themselves openly acknowledge the deep-seated systemic flaws of inaccuracy, unfairness, and imbalance that pervade mainstream media reporting, further underscoring the urgent need for a corrective approach like peace journalism. As BBC journalist David Lyon articulated in his concluding remarks following a critique of peace journalism:

"This is not to say that everything in journalism is fine. In a world where Fox News, with its ridiculously partisan comic-book view of foreign news, can try to patent the notion of being "Fair and Balanced", and where most British newspapers take a strong "line" one way or another on conflicts, there are problems. Seeing the "Sun" trying to find good news from Iraq has had a sort of black humor in recent months. The affair of Iraq's missing weapons of mass destruction raised searching questions in newsrooms on both sides of the Atlantic as it should have. Research findings showing that most of the British television audience believe it is the Palestinians who are "occupying" territory, not Israelis, should set alarm bells ringing."

Lyon's frank assessment serves as a powerful indictment, unequivocally highlighting the profound systemic problems and urgent critical self-reflection demanded within the industry. While peace journalism builds upon many existing journalistic principles, leading some to perceive it as merely "reinventing the wheel," its crucial and distinctive contribution lies fundamentally in its transformative emphasis on specific elements of news reporting, most notably, framing (Olivera, Thomas and Kilby, 2020).

While framing is an indispensable aspect of news dissemination, peace journalism distinguishes itself through an approach that critically examines the profound effects these frames exert on the public (Samsudin, 2019; Lam, 2020). Established journalism studies, such as those by McQuail, have consistently affirmed media's significant role in constructing social reality (McQuail, 2000; Solnet et al., 2022). The frames, whether consciously or unconsciously chosen by journalists, fundamentally determine how this reality is constructed, thereby shaping public understanding (Zaklama, 2025). As Gitlin pertinently observes, frames are often "largely unspoken, unacknowledged, organize the world both for journalists who report it and, in some important degree, for us who rely on their reports" (Bishop, 2006). This inherent power of framing is central to peace journalism's analytical framework (Entman, 2010).

A compelling demonstration of propaganda and manipulation, manifested through politically motivated conflict representation, can be observed in media coverage of conflicts in Eastern Europe, which was often framed to serve the interests of media controllers (Husband, 2017). This phenomenon contrasts sharply with the portrayal of conflicts in Africa, such as those in Sudan, South Sudan, and Nigeria, or the Israeli Palestinian conflict, where similar manipulative framing frequently occurs.

During the Kosovo War, for instance, media played a pivotal role in fostering an environment that compelled the international community to address prior inaction, particularly in the aftermath of the Bosnian War (Robinson, 2000; Auerbach and Bloch-Elkon, 2004). Western newspapers, for example, characterized the air strikes as humanitarian intervention for Albanians, purportedly aimed at halting 'ethnic cleansing' attributed to the Serbs (Bilder, 2010; Ristić and Satjukow, 2022).

The Rwandan genocide similarly underscored the inaccuracies and problematic reliance on non-African sources in reporting African conflicts, often fitting the narrative into a reductive framework of "African tribalism versus Western racism" (Newbury, 1995). The role of radio and newspapers in inciting ethnic hatred and violence during the 1994 Rwandan genocide has been extensively documented (Kellow and Steeves, 1998; Ntete, 2022). This historical pattern highlights a persistent failure to adequately represent complex realities.

Irrespective of whether frames are analyzed from the media's or the public's perspective, or as dependent or independent variables, peace journalism warrants recognition for elevating the "frame feature" of news to an essential element of consideration in journalistic practice (Provencher, 2000). The imperative for a critical and forward-looking press necessitates that media outlets possess the capacity to scrutinize deeply ingrained beliefs and assumptions. The distinct frames proposed by peace journalism significantly facilitate this crucial task, offering journalists robust tools for more nuanced and responsible reporting (Givskov, 2015).

While some critics argue that peace journalism introduces nothing fundamentally new, expecting "invention" from a social science discipline be it communication or peace and conflict studies—is unrealistic. Social sciences aim not to invent but to examine existing phenomena through diverse approaches, perspectives, and analytical levels, which is precisely what peace journalism achieves within the established field of journalism. Moreover, both communication and peace and conflict are inherently multidisciplinary fields, reflecting their profound complexities (Shaw, Lynch and Hackett, 2012). Any concept derived from these fields, such as peace journalism, therefore strives to understand and illuminate the intricate dynamics that characterize them, offering a vital framework for more ethical and effective reporting. This approach extends beyond merely reporting visible conflict effects to exploring invisible impacts, identifying areas of agreement, and presenting solution-oriented narratives, thereby shifting from war journalism to a more proactive, people-oriented, and constructive form of reporting (Olivera, Thomas and Kilby, 2020; Valdez et al., 2023). This distinction underscores peace journalism's commitment to presenting a holistic and less biased account of conflicts, moving beyond the traditional sensationalism often associated with war reporting (Jamaluddin, Khan and Shahzad, 2020). This transformative perspective, integral to peace journalism, transcends mere conflict description to actively seek avenues for resolution and understanding, emphasizing reconciliation over the perpetuation of adversarial narratives (Valdez et al., 2023). Indeed, peace journalism actively endeavors to provide a deeper and more contextualized perspective of conflicts, moving beyond the reporting of violent events to understanding underlying causes and facilitating peacebuilding efforts (Jamaluddin, Khan and Shahzad, 2020; Valdez et al., 2023).

Desirability for Peace Journalism

Peace journalism has profoundly reshaped scholarly discourse concerning the societal role of journalists, particularly within conflict contexts, by critically interrogating established norms of news reporting and raising fundamental questions about the principle of objectivity (Andersen, 2017; Olivera, Thomas and Kilby, 2020).

Mass media are widely acknowledged to frequently reinforce prevailing worldviews, rather than initiating societal transformation (Reid, Giles and Abrams, 2004; Gavin, 2018; Glogger et al., 2022). This phenomenon has been extensively examined through diverse theoretical frameworks, such as the reinforcing spirals model, which elucidates the contribution of media exposure to the genesis and perpetuation of social identities and ideologies (Slater, 2014). Consequently, a perspective maintains that the primary role of journalism does not encompass instigating societal change, advocating for journalists to "preserve their position as observers not players" (Andersen, 2017; sager, 2022). Nevertheless, scholarly discourse highlights ongoing debates concerning the feasibility of journalists maintaining a purely observational stance, particularly considering historical precedents where influential journalistic accounts demonstrably incorporated participatory elements and distinct personal perspectives (Andersen, 2017).

Journalists, as the "Fourth Estate" in democratic systems, undeniably perform a pivotal societal function (Szabo, 2013; Damissah et al., 2025). This designation acknowledges the media's capacity to scrutinize governmental actions and influence public discourse (Damissah et al., 2025). Although they may not directly instigate events, their reportorial methods profoundly shape public understanding. Thus, owing to the inherent responsibilities of their profession, journalists operate as active participants rather than passive observers, irrespective of political affiliations (Shultziner, 2025).

This intrinsic professional responsibility is precisely what peace journalism foregrounds. It is conceptualized as a normative mode of media coverage during conflict, characterized by its responsible and conscientious nature, with the overarching aim of contributing to the establishment and preservation of peace.

This framework encourages journalists to recognize their role in constructing societal realities and to uphold their ethical obligation to "give peace a chance" (Olivera, Thomas and Kilby, 2020). Rooted in journalistic ethics, peace journalism advocates for an elevated awareness of reporting's impact on both the audience and evolving news developments (Ajetunmobi, 2023). This voluntary approach encourages journalists, editors, and media outlets to consciously move beyond the traditional "regime of objectivity," aiming instead to actively "be part of the solution and not the problem" (Valdez et al., 2023).

Addressing the misconceptions often raised by its detractors, peace journalism unequivocally rejects the notion of being a universal panacea or a form of advocacy journalism, with its originators and proponents explicitly eschewing partisan reporting (Lynch, 2015; Prager and Hameleers, 2018). Instead, peace journalism, as articulated by Lynch and McGoldrick, centers on deliberate editorial choices designed to cultivate societal consideration and appreciation for non-violent conflict resolution (Lynch, 2015). This transformative approach fundamentally redefines conflict coverage by actively challenging conventional news values and championing a profound focus on peace, truth, the human element, and actionable solutions (Tayeebwa, 2017; Olivera, Thomas and Kilby, 2020). Crucially, neither Galtung's "ten points for a peace-oriented newspaper" nor Lynch and McGoldrick's "17-point plan for practical Peace Journalism" incorporate any elements of advocacy (Lynch, 2015). Rather, these influential frameworks systematically prioritize core principles that ensure comprehensive, ethical, and insightful reporting: they demand equitable representation for all parties involved in a conflict; insist on articulating the underlying intellectual and systemic perspectives; deliberately de-emphasize "elite nations, elite persons, personification and negative events" to broaden the narrative scope; unequivocally respect the public's intelligence; vividly depict the tangible benefits of peace; thoroughly examine developmental issues beyond narrow political confines; and, significantly, move beyond exclusive reporting of violent acts or mere sensationalized descriptions of "the horror," opting instead to meticulously illustrate how everyday frustrations, systemic blockages, or chronic deprivations fundamentally contribute to the conditions that generate violence (Lynch, 2015).

Consequently, the adoption of peace journalism does not equate to transforming journalistic practice into advocacy (Prager and Hameleers, 2018). Furthermore, by advocating for an active and responsible approach to reporting complex issues through contextualization, rather than a passive and superficial one, peace journalism ought not to be conflated with "journalism of attachment." This latter concept originated during the Bosnian War, a period characterized by certain journalists openly aligning themselves with the Bosnian government against Serbian forces. Martin Bell, a former BBC correspondent, characterizes journalism of attachment as a practice that "will not stand neutrally between good and evil, right and wrong, the victim and the oppressor."

Peace journalists maintain a professional distance from the subjects they report on, unequivocally rejecting advocacy journalism and partisan reporting (Lynch, 2015; Prager and Hameleers, 2018). Their objective is to cover all perspectives of a conflict by providing necessary contexts, ensuring equitable representation for all parties involved, and articulating underlying intellectual and systemic perspectives (Lynch, 2015). This approach, which prioritizes a profound focus on peace, truth, the human element, and actionable solutions, thereby precludes personal engagement with any single side and systematically avoids the pitfalls of activism (Lynch, 2015; Tayeebwa, 2017; Olivera, Thomas and Kilby, 2020). Consequently, their journalistic practice is neither activism nor a form of "journalism of attachment," which, as exemplified during the Bosnian War, involves openly aligning with one side and eschewing neutrality between conflicting parties (Lynch, 2015).

While often perceived as challenging traditional journalistic norms, peace journalism does not inherently conflict with a nuanced understanding of journalistic objectivity. Indeed, the notion of objectivity itself, far from being a monolithic or universally accepted standard, has been a subject of vigorous debate within academia and media practice long before the advent of peace journalism (Szabo, 2013; Konieczna and Maria, 2023). Critics contend that a purely detached, value-free reporting is often unattainable or even undesirable, given the inherent biases in framing, selection of facts, and the constructed nature of news. In this context, peace journalism offers an alternative framework that, rather than abandoning objectivity, redefines it through a commitment to comprehensive truth-seeking and contextual depth.

t moves beyond a superficial neutrality to provide a more holistic understanding of conflict, thereby striving for a deeper form of journalistic accuracy. For instance, some journalists advocate for a revised approach to objectivity when reporting on marginalized or minority groups, emphasizing context and substantive truth over a detached, potentially exclusionary, presentation of facts (Konieczna and Maria, 2023). This perspective aligns with peace journalism's emphasis on diverse voices and underlying systemic issues. Furthermore, the socio-economic transformations brought about by globalization have profoundly reshaped the journalistic landscape, shifting the industry from a traditional focus on "public service and objectivity" towards models driven by "consumerism and commercialism." In this evolving environment, the call for peace journalism gains added urgency, advocating for a return to ethical considerations and public welfare that transcend market-driven imperatives.

The preceding discussion highlights how peace journalism redefines objectivity, moving beyond superficial neutrality towards comprehensive truth-seeking and contextual depth. If, as many scholars and practitioners contend, absolute journalistic objectivity is inherently elusive, then peace journalism's deliberate commitment to highlighting pathways to peace, truth, the human element, and actionable solutions, while maintaining professional distance from actors, is not a 'bias' in the pejorative sense. Rather, it represents a principled, ethical stance that prioritizes the mitigation of harm and the promotion of constructive conflict resolution over a detached, potentially incomplete, portrayal of events. This approach starkly differentiates from partisan reporting or 'journalism of attachment,' by fostering an environment conducive to dialogue and understanding without aligning with any specific party.

Peace journalism offers a superior methodological approach, providing a more intricate depiction of conflicts through the elucidation of their historical antecedents, contextual factors, and systemic processes elements often neglected by conventional media outlets. This approach prioritizes the inclusion of diverse perspectives, stating that "It does not promote particular accounts and perspectives, but where they are unjustly excluded, it should enable them to be seen and heard." Consequently, this framework aligns with the principles of equity, diversity, and equality by ensuring an exhaustive and unbiased presentation of various viewpoints within a conflict, thereby enhancing public comprehension and fostering a more equitable and peaceful societal environment (Valdez et al., 2023).

Practicability of Peace Journalism

Journalistic practice is not an isolated endeavor but is profoundly shaped by a complex interplay of political, economic, organizational factors, and ingrained newsroom structures and routines.

These pervasive influences present significant challenges to any journalistic approach, extending beyond superficial political considerations to encompass deep-seated economic, organizational, and institutional determinants.

To systematically comprehend these multifaceted pressures, Shoemaker and Reese's established hierarchy of influences on media content offers a comprehensive analytical framework. This model posits that individual perspectives form the foundational level of influence, progressively extending to encompass media routines, organizational elements, the extra-media context, and overarching ideological considerations (Reese and Shoemaker, 2016; Paasch-Colberg and Strippel, 2021). A significant implication of this framework is that the formation of journalistic output necessitates analysis across diverse theoretical perspectives and analytical levels, acknowledging the intricate interdependencies between influences at each tier (Paasch-Colberg and Strippel, 2021; Alcântara and Simões, 2023). Its persistent relevance derives from its capacity to meticulously structure and synthesize observations across these varied levels, thereby elucidating the profound and complex multifactorial dynamics intrinsic to journalistic production (Salaudeen, 2021; Alcântara and Simões, 2023). Within this analytical construct, the integration of peace journalism principles thus demands a deliberate endeavor to overcome individual journalistic biases and to reconfigure ingrained journalistic practices that often privilege conflict-centric narratives over approaches fostering constructive discourse (Valdez et al., 2023).

To systematically understand these multifaceted pressures on journalistic practice, particularly in the context of implementing alternative frameworks like peace journalism, a comprehensive 2010 international survey proved instrumental. This study, involving 1700 journalists from 17 countries, meticulously investigated perceived sources of influence on their work, categorizing them into six distinct domains (Hanitzsch et al., 2010):

1. **Political Influence:** Deriving from the political environment, government officials, and political figures, this influence can manifest through direct pressure, legislative frameworks, and the strategic control or dissemination of information, shaping journalists' access and narratives to align with political agendas or state interests.

2. **Economic Influence:** Pertaining to journalists' profit expectations from their news organizations, advertisers, and market forces, this influence often drives editorial decisions towards sensationalism, conflict-centric narratives, or stories that attract larger audiences, potentially at the expense of in-depth, nuanced reporting that might not generate immediate profit.

3. **Procedural Influence:** Encompassing constraints such as limited space and time, alongside established standards and routines within news production, these influences dictate how stories are framed and presented. They can lead to simplified narratives, a focus on easily verifiable facts, and reduced contextual depth, often prioritizing speed and accessibility over comprehensive analysis.

4. **Organizational Influence:** Relating to supervisors, senior editors, managers, and the proprietors of news organizations, this influence shapes newsroom culture, resource allocation, and editorial policies, directly impacting the themes and approaches deemed permissible or prioritized in reporting.

5. **Professional Influence:** Involving policies, conventions, legal frameworks, and ethical principles of journalistic practice, this influence dictates what is considered 'good' or acceptable journalism, shaping reporting norms, sourcing practices, and the professional identity of journalists, thereby either supporting or challenging the integration of new ethical frameworks like peace journalism.

6. **Reference Groups' Influence:** Including colleagues, rival news organizations, audiences, family, and social circles, this influence encompasses peer pressure, competitive dynamics, audience expectations, and personal values, collectively shaping how journalists perceive their role and responsibilities, and influencing their reporting choices.

n contrast to prevailing perceptions regarding the primary influence of economic and political determinants, research revealed that journalists frequently overrate the significance of these two factors. Instead, the most salient factors influencing journalistic practice were identified as originating from organizational, professional, and procedural spheres (Hanitzsch et al., 2010). Further investigations, extending from this initial study, have illustrated the relative and context-dependent nature of these influences, demonstrating their variability across different national settings. Specifically, political influences are perceived to exert greater force in less democratic nations and those characterized by diminished press freedom (Hanitzsch and Mellado, 2011; Hamada, 2021). This indicates that the dynamic interaction of these elements contributes to the global diversity of journalistic cultures (Hanitzsch, 2007; Hanitzsch et al., 2010).

Although these studies imply that journalists do not consider political factors to be the paramount influences in their professional work, a conclusion that diverges from common assertions within media and communication research that the existence of political influence is not thereby disproven. Nonetheless, considering that journalists are the ultimate agents responsible for the adoption or rejection of peace journalism, comprehending their perceived impediments is both advantageous and imperative.

This chapter explored the potential practicability of war and peace journalism, drawing upon the author's extensive journalistic experiences arguing that while external and internal pressures often define journalistic 'heads-up,' this influence is not inherently negative; rather, it can be harnessed constructively. For transformative changes to occur across the previously identified, most influential levels, organizational, professional, and procedural peace journalism must be actively embedded within journalistic processes as a deliberate editorial decision driven by sustained editorial resolve. This perspective is strongly corroborated by the work of Vanessa Bassil, whose research further elucidates several factors contributing to these dynamics, which are subsequently expounded upon.(Mont'Alverne, Athanásio and Marques, 2018) Bassil contends that the effective integration of peace journalism is contingent upon a sophisticated comprehension of distinct socio-cultural contexts, thereby implying that a universal methodology proves insufficient across heterogeneous media landscapes(Mitra, 2016).

1. Organizational Influence : Given the survey's classification of organizational influence into "within the newsroom" and "within the media organization" concerning editorial and managerial decision-makers, the strategic integration of peace journalism into a news organization's core editorial and managerial directives is paramount, directly influencing every working journalist.

As organizational influence inherently stems from leaders defining employees' work trajectories, embedding peace journalism principles within managerial decisions necessitates a profound reshaping of the organizational structure, leading to systemic adjustments in personnel roles and responsibilities. Consequently, for peace journalism to truly succeed, a fundamental transformation of individual and institutional norms and culture is indispensable, unequivocally mandating a decisive top-down approach within organizations (Olivera, Thomas and Kilby, 2020). This decisive top-down organizational mandate, therefore, necessitates that journalists and editors, as integral agents within their respective organizations, proactively and consistently adopt and implement peace journalism principles. (Valdez et al., 2023).

2. Professional Influence : Professional policies and conventions, unlike immutable doctrines, are inherently dynamic and subject to evolution; a principle vividly demonstrated within the field of journalism. The imperative to integrate a conflict-sensitive approach into journalistic professional conventions has become increasingly evident, particularly considering its prior neglect or insufficient attention before the advent of peace and conflict studies (Nohrstedt and Ottosen, 2015). This integration necessitates a continuous process of re-evaluating and strengthening ethical obligations, especially in light of contemporary challenges such as disinformation and hate speech (Gómez, Sáez and Álvarez-Villa, 2024). It is notable that some media organizations are already implicitly implementing the tenets of peace journalism, even without explicitly labeling them as such (Harrison and Pukallus, 2022). This observation indicates that the ethical framework provided by peace journalism for conflict reporting possesses considerable potential for broader adoption by media outlets committed to stringent standards of professionalism and ethics. Consequently, the widespread integration of this framework would profoundly influence editors across organizations, thereby cultivating a more accountable approach to conflict reporting (Stupart, 2021; Steel et al., 2025).

3. Procedural Influence : Procedural aspects represent a profoundly practical consideration within journalism. As with any professional discipline, journalism is governed by established procedures, which are delineated by prevailing standards and routines. rrespective of the specific media platform utilized, journalists consistently face limitations concerning spatial and temporal parameters (Olivera, Thomas and Kilby, 2020). Nevertheless, such constraints should not be perceived as a justification for diminished quality in journalistic output. Core tenets, including accuracy, impartiality, and equipoise in reporting, constitute foundational professional standards, and peace journalism emphatically reinforces their significance. Moreover, it evolves these principles by positing itself as a conceptual framework that modernizes them via the incorporation of conflict analysis and transformation methodologies. Although these procedural limitations can present considerable challenges, they do not impede the implementation of peace journalism, which endeavors to elevate the caliber of reporting despite these constraints (Tayeebwa, 2017). Such an approach facilitates the production of more nuanced journalistic accounts, transcending simplistic narratives, even in the context of profound conflicts (Kotišová, 2023). This overarching conceptual framework provides journalists with a mechanism not only to uphold conventional ethical benchmarks but also to proactively foster de-escalation and mutual comprehension within conflict-affected regions (Mitrić, 2022).

Conclusive Sentiments on Peace Journalism

In conclusion, the Lebanese Peace Journalism expert, Vanessa Bassil, Peace Journalism stands as a critical and constructive response to the pervasive issues in contemporary news reporting. Such reporting often relies heavily on elite sources, unduly highlights violent acts, employs inflammatory language, and exhibits unexamined biases, leading to profound societal implications by misrepresenting reality and facts, thereby undermining public understanding and perpetuating conflict dynamics. Peace Journalism thus emerges from an urgent need for high-quality, responsible reporting, possessing the transformative potential to effect change at personal, professional, and structural levels (Valdez et al., 2023; Thomas, 2024). This framework encourages journalists to provide a deeper and contextualized perspective of conflicts, focusing on peacebuilding and understanding the factors that lead to violence (Valdez et al., 2023).

The essential objective of peace journalism is to comprehensively inform the audience by providing extensive context and background, alongside the nuanced perspectives of all parties involved. This empowers the audience to evaluate "non-violent responses to conflict"; the media's responsibility is to rigorously select and present information, considering its profound consequences for public discourse and societal stability. By presenting stories with balance and avoiding the demonization of one side, peace journalism aims to minimize division and foster understanding.

Debating the necessity of Peace Journalism is unproductive, as myriad examples of problematic reporting consistently affirm its importance, a fact supported by both practice and research. The prevailing frame in conflict coverage often remains war journalism, even in regions with significant conflict, highlighting the persistent need for alternative approaches (Olivera, Thomas and Kilby, 2020; Rawan and Rahman, 2020). Such discussions detract from the imperative task of addressing systemic problems in media content and focusing on actionable solutions within academia, newsrooms, and civil society.

Criticizing the terminology or the inherent desirability of "Peace Journalism" offers no tangible improvement to reporting quality or media performance. Therefore, it is paramount to transition from the 'why change is needed' debate to a proactive exploration of 'how change can be achieved'. This transition, however, necessitates a collective and candid acknowledgment of deficiencies in media performance when reporting conflicts. A key challenge in this transition is the disconnect between academic theory and journalistic practice, which needs to be bridged for peace journalism to become more flexible and applicable in mainstream newsrooms (Tayeebwa, 2017; Olivera, Thomas and Kilby, 2020).

Peace Journalism offers a compelling answer, representing a vital reform addressing proven problems in news coverage and inaugurating a new paradigm in media, communication, and journalism research. It is thus not merely a "better application of known methods" but rather a sophisticated toolkit of techniques and conceptual frameworks adapted from the fields of peace and conflict. It provides journalists with a framework to actively contribute to conflict resolution and highlight positive factors, even though negative news often satisfies traditional newsworthiness criteria (Galtung and Fischer, 2013; Valdez et al., 2023).

If media practitioners and theorists perceive Peace Journalism as 'good to have but hard to apply,' then it becomes an imperative to dedicate robust research, rigorous experimentation, and thoughtful strategic planning towards making it more widespread, feasible, and convincing to individuals who currently struggle to accept, understand, or effectively implement it. Studies have shown that peace journalism is not a one-size-fits-all approach and requires adaptation and transformation in cooperation between journalists and academics (Olivera, Thomas and Kilby, 2020).

For instance, experienced journalists who are proponents of peace journalism are more likely to produce reports reflecting its indicators (Abunales, 2016). Should Peace Journalism not be embraced as a viable solution, then the considerable efforts currently expended on criticizing or debating would be far more efficiently invested in urgently seeking and developing credible alternatives to address the destructive impact of "war journalism"(Shah, 2022).

Finally, Peace Journalism crucially offers practitioners an indispensable ethical framework for producing reports and stories that transcend mere factual relay. It instills hope and fosters positivity within communities in conflict zones, where media often mirrors the polarization of their lived reality. This hope also extends to journalists themselves, many of whom grapple with upholding their professional principles, operating free from political and commercial agendas, and maintaining their integrity without risking their livelihoods. Peace Journalism unequivocally reminds them that they are engaged in intrinsically "good" work, thereby playing a profound and positive role in their societies by adhering to ethical, responsible, and unbiased reporting.

The critical roles of editors, journalists, reporters, and their managers, the primary producers of news deserve a more profound and systematic analysis, which both journalism and peace and conflict fields must collaboratively undertake to elevate the role of media in societies, and consequently, to improve societies themselves. This underscores an urgent and critical need for a collaborative approach involving universities, training institutes, and international organizations to facilitate the global adoption and refinement of peace journalism practices (Nohrstedt and Ottosen, 2015).

Such a concerted effort is essential for journalism to effectively contribute to international norm-setting and to elevate the profession's ethical standards concerning violent conflicts (Nohrstedt and Ottosen, 2015; Harrison and Pukallus, 2022). This proactive engagement aims to bridge the current disconnect between academic discourse and practical journalistic application, transforming theoretical constructs into actionable strategies for media professionals (Olivera, Thomas and Kilby, 2020; Lynch and Tiripelli, 2022).

CHAPTER 8

Democratic Journalism

DEMOCRATIC JOURNALISM PROFOUNDLY REDEFINES news dissemination, fundamentally empowering readers to directly influence story prominence through collective voting, a pivotal, seismic shift largely ignited by the advent of social media. This approach unequivocally champions content driven by the undeniable "wisdom of the crowd," forcefully challenging the entrenched gatekeeping of traditional media where editorial fiat once unquestionably dictated public narratives. This transformative evolution is particularly evident in citizen journalism, which utilizes "produsage" characterized by collaborative content production and open editing practices, thereby cultivating greater inclusivity and representation of diverse perspectives and catalyzing democratic participation in news production (Bruns, 2009).

Democratic journalism is not merely a practice, but a fundamental pillar predicated upon essential democratic rights, free speech, assembly, human rights, and the rule of law. It functions as an indispensable bulwark against abuse of power, profoundly integrating with civic consciousness and societal cohesion to sustain a healthy public sphere.

This unbreakable bond with democracy not only defines its core mission but also protects it from the corrosive forces of rampant commercialism, sensationalism, and the manipulative control exerted by media elites, thereby ensuring its integrity and its capacity to serve the public good, though its specific manifestations naturally vary across global contexts.

In his seminal 1984 publication, *Journalism*, Norman B. Moise conceptualized communication as a foundational human imperative, emphasizing its omnipresence across virtually all biological organisms. He postulated that its most rudimentary form likely involved unicellular entities exchanging chemical cues for reproductive processes, contrasting this with its most sophisticated expression in humanity, which incorporates intricate global information networks spanning from interpersonal exchanges to widespread media dissemination. This inherent drive for communication forms the bedrock of journalism's primary function: enabling societies to interpret their surroundings and undertake rigorous analysis of unfolding events. Furthermore, this pivotal journalistic role in informing the citizenry and cultivating public discourse is deemed indispensable for the robust operation of a democracy, thereby promoting individual liberties and autonomous governance (Scherman, Fierro and Shan, 2025). Correspondingly, as highlighted by McNair, journalism serves to challenge conventional wisdom through its incisive and impactful critique of influential groups, simultaneously enhancing public accessibility and augmenting the thoroughness of its political process coverage (McNair, 2010). The democratic functions of journalism in the digital age require new alliances and a reconsideration of how these functions can be sustained and enhanced amidst evolving technological landscapes (Esser and Neuberger, 2018).

As Norman B. Moise articulates in his 1984 work, Journalism (pp. 3-4): "The art of communicating is a complicated process, for it implies both the ability to express and to understand. Early human beings gestured, made noises, and used elaborate systems of sound symbols to transmit their feelings and thoughts to one another.

Today we have developed a system of communicating that includes not only gestures and signs but also oral and written messages. "

The Indispensable Role of Journalism in a Democratic Society

Journalism serves two fundamental purposes in a democratic society. Firstly, it empowers citizens to make responsible, informed choices, thereby safeguarding against decisions based on ignorance or misinformation [Current Document]. Secondly, the provision of information acts as a crucial "checking function," ensuring that elected representatives uphold their oaths of office and fulfill the mandate of their constituents [Current Document]. This monitorial or "watchdog" role is a widely discussed normative function of the press, essential for holding power accountable and informing citizens (Hanitzsch and Vos, 2016; Kalogeropoulos, Toff and Fletcher, 2022; Ots, Berglez and Nord, 2023).

Normative Roles of Media in Democracy

The media provides essential information, enabling individuals to make their own decisions [Current Document]. Its monitorial role involves practices such as publishing reports, identifying agendas and potential threats, reporting on political, social, and economic decisions, and illuminating public opinion [Current Document]. The media is pivotal in holding public officials accountable for malpractices and guarding against corruption and other malevolent dealings within government by informing the public with facts and truth, assessing whether institutions operate within legal boundaries [Current Document]. Studies suggest that different models of democracy have different implications for public discourse and media performance, thus shaping how journalists should understand their work to play a functional role within each model (Riedl, 2018).

Challenges of Democratic Journalism

A persistent challenge for democratic journalism is the potential unreliability and bias within the news ecosystem itself, which may not always accurately reflect public opinion [Current Document]. Many platforms facilitating democratic journalism grapple with issues like manipulation, inherent biases, censorship, and a lack of professional review [Current Document]. While alternative approaches exist, they often encounter similar problems [Current Document]. Ultimately, selecting and ranking news stories necessitates criteria, and altering the selection method merely shifts the source of potential bias [Current Document]. Press freedom in democratic countries is severely challenged and in certain cases steadily declining, with common factors influencing this decline across different media systems (Maniou, 2022). Furthermore, media owners' political affiliations can significantly influence editorial decisions, pressuring journalists to align their reporting with owners' interests (Danso, 2025).

Journalism and Politics

The intricate and often interdependent relationship between journalism and politics is fundamental to a functioning democracy, crucially empowering citizens, holding political power accountable, shaping public discourse, influencing political outcomes, and reinforcing the system of checks and balances essential for democratic governance (Amodu, Usaini and Ige, 2016; Hanitzsch and Vos, 2016; Nielsen, Cornia and Kalogeropoulos, 2016; Kalogeropoulos, Toff and Fletcher, 2022; Ots, Berglez and Nord, 2023; Damissah et al., 2025; Scherman, Fierro and Shan, 2025). The relationship between politicians and journalists is intrinsically symbiotic; politicians seek media platforms for publicity, while journalists depend on political figures and events as a primary source of news.

However, journalists wield substantial power, capable of profoundly influencing public perception and shaping electoral outcomes, sometimes with devastating consequences. Conversely, governments perceived as weak or failing in their public duty often struggle to maintain a favorable relationship with the media, frequently resorting to coercive tactics, inducements, or financial pressures that fundamentally undermine journalistic ethics, integrity, and its independent role as a democratic watchdog.

Indeed, research consistently demonstrates that political influences are significantly more potent in less democratic countries, particularly those with lower levels of press freedom and higher degrees of political parallelism, thereby exacerbating the risks to independent journalism and democratic accountability (Hanitzsch and Mellado, 2011; Hamada, 2021). This dynamic can lead to a divergence between journalistic values and algorithmic values, especially in the context of digital platforms where news selection is increasingly influenced by algorithms rather than human editors (Vestergaard, 2022).

Citizen Journalism's Role in Democracy

The active engagement of citizens in political commentary and the articulation of their democratic concerns constitute a cornerstone of democratic vitality. This critical involvement often manifests through citizen journalism, also known by various terms such as collaborative media, participatory journalism, democratic journalism, guerrilla journalism, or street journalism. This form of journalism empowers community members to actively participate in the process of collecting, reporting, analyzing, and disseminating news and information, thereby democratizing the information ecosystem. Social media platforms, in particular, have emerged as indispensable tools for fostering political engagement and amplifying citizen voices. Indeed, research consistently suggests that heightened engagement with participatory media, when integrated with traditional journalistic efforts, significantly enhances positive assessments of democratic processes and boosts political system efficacy (Bucy and Groshek, 2017). The recent Sudanese uprising vividly demonstrated the transformative power of citizen journalism in shaping democratic narratives and mobilizing public action. Consequently, authoritarian and dictatorial governments across Africa, acutely aware of the threat posed by informed citizenry, have frequently resorted to shutting down social media platforms to suppress dissent. These online spaces invariably become crucial outlets for opposition messaging and collective action, particularly when traditional offline political avenues are curtailed or suppressed. This deliberate suppression underscores the inherent and profound threat that unmediated public discourse poses to regimes seeking to maintain control through information monopolies, as it directly challenges their authority and narrative.(Ajaegbu and Ajaegbu, 2024) (Chitanana and Mutsvairo, 2019).

The Fourth Estate

The "Fourth Estate" concept defines the media's essential role as an independent monitor of power, crucial for ensuring checks and balances within democratic systems (Nielsen, Cornia and Kalogeropoulos, 2016). This role inherently involves the media's responsibility to disseminate vital information and alert the public to significant events, thus acting as a crucial conduit between the government and the governed (Ajaegbu and Ajaegbu, 2024).

Journalism, or the media fraternity, is widely considered the "fourth wing," or "fourth estate," of government. This concept positions media as an unofficial, yet essential, branch that functions distinctly from the formal governmental powers—the Executive, Legislature, and Judiciary to scrutinize government actions and shape public discourse.

Its crucial role lies in reinforcing the system of checks and balances, thereby serving as a critical oversight mechanism, even if not formally institutionalized within government structures (Amodu, Usaini and Ige, 2016; Damissah et al., 2025).

The term "Fourth Estate," also known as the fourth power, designates the press and news media, recognizing its explicit capacity for advocacy and its implicit influence in framing political narratives (Damissah et al., 2025). This concept traces its origins to the traditional European hierarchy of the three estates of the realm: the clergy, the nobility, and the commoners. Historically, within governmental structures, these were often conceptualized as the Executive, Legislature, and Judiciary in modern democratic systems.

Initially, society's first estate comprised the clergy, followed by the nobility, with the third estate encompassing commoners and the bourgeoisie. The press subsequently emerged as the "fourth estate," a designation first coined in the early to mid-19th century, building upon governmental frameworks established during pivotal events such as the French Revolution (Szabo, 2013). The media's role in reinforcing the system of checks and balances within government underpins its conceptualization as the fourth power of government (Amodu, Usaini and Ige, 2016). Nevertheless, scholars generally concur that journalism does not wield power in the same authoritative sense as the legislative, executive, and judicial branches (Østergaard, 2021). The concept of the Fourth Estate positions media as an unofficial yet essential branch alongside formal governmental powers, acknowledging its critical capacity to scrutinize government actions and shape public discourse. This classification underscores the historical understanding that an independent press functions as a crucial oversight mechanism, operating distinctly from the three traditional branches of government (Damissah et al., 2025).

The Enduring Power of Media

The press holds significant power in shaping public will, and given the adage that "information is power," media inherently serves as an indispensable cornerstone in democratic settings. This enduring influence thus solidifies its indispensable role in cultivating informed public discourse and ensuring governmental accountability (Damissah et al., 2025). A seminal historical event illustrating this power occurred in 1734, amidst growing public resentment against British Authority in the colonies. More than three decades after the establishment of the first American newspaper, a courageous New York printer, John Peter Zenger, was compelled to print a scathing critique against the corrupt practices of the British Governor-General. Zenger was subsequently sued and tried for seditious libel, a high-count charge. However, he was acquitted, following the compelling defense by his attorney, Andrew Hamilton, who argued that "Falsehood makes the libel." This landmark case established a crucial precedent in legal history: proving the truth of a statement should not constitute defamation.

This acquittal significantly bolstered the nascent concept of press freedom, enabling future challenges to authority. This landmark acquittal unequivocally demonstrated the indispensable power of the press to serve as a vital check against governmental overreach and potential tyranny, thereby solidifying its foundational role as an essential guardian of public interest and an undeniable catalyst for democratic progress and social change. The profound and enduring legacy of Zenger's case continues to resonate deeply within contemporary legal and journalistic discourse, shaping discussions on media accountability, the critical importance of press freedom, and the imperative protections afforded to journalists who courageously report on powerful figures. (Damissah et al., 2025).

Despite intense censorship, with copies of John Peter Zenger's Weekly Journal confiscated and publicly burned on Wall Street on November 6, 1734, the colonial media began to openly criticize English authority. This daring stance proved instrumental in fostering and promoting the ideals of American independence. British authorities of the time even labeled the Colonial American press as "Propaganda press" due to its significant role in galvanizing opposition against British rule and promoting revolutionary sentiment. This initial historical phase unequivocally demonstrated the media's profound ability to shape public sentiment and drive substantial political transformation, thereby establishing fundamental tenets for its acknowledged function within contemporary democratic frameworks (Marsili, 2021).

CHAPTER 9

Investigative Journalism

INVESTIGATIVE JOURNALISM REPRESENTS A crucial and distinct journalistic practice, characterized by methodical, stringent, and independent investigation designed to uncover concealed information and address entrenched systemic issues (Ismail, Ahmad and Mustaffa, 2014; Cancela, Gerber and Dubied, 2021). Despite varying conceptualizations, a general agreement exists regarding its core principles, highlighting the critical need for journalists to thoroughly investigate matters of substantial public interest, including criminal activities, racial inequities, political corruption, and corporate misconduct (Carson, 2019).

This arduous discipline, distinctively motivated by the commitment to reveal malfeasance and enforce accountability among powerful figures or organizations, frequently necessitate prolonged durations, occasionally extending over several months or years, for exhaustive research and precise development. It is fundamentally differentiated from daily news reporting by its comprehensive analytical depth, wider thematic coverage, and specialized data collection approaches (Ismail, Ahmad and Mustaffa, 2014).

Crucially, investigative journalism distinguishes itself by a resolute dedication to unearthing information that influential parties, such as corporations, government agencies, or individuals, actively seek to suppress, thus serving a crucial societal role by diligently exposing detrimental practices that affect the public good (Biscop and Décary-Hétu, 2022). This diverse domain is additionally recognized by several appellations, such as exposé journalism, adversarial journalism, in-depth journalism, muckraking journalism, advocacy journalism, public service journalism, and watchdog journalism, each term denoting a distinct conceptualization or emphasis (Ismail, Ahmad and Mustaffa, 2014).

Purpose of Investigative Reporting

Investigative journalism serves as a critical democratic function by exposing social injustice and it equally considered as one of the most vital public functions of the press. This is achieved through rigorous fact-checking of sources and, at times, by going undercover to reveal hidden corruption, violence, and unethical abuses of power. Such work often requires deep local knowledge and significant newsroom investment (Turkel et al., 2021), with its proactive scrutiny aiming to hold political and business leaders accountable (Mills, 2018; Kibarabara, Cheruiyot and Muindi, 2022). As journalism has evolved and adapted to 21st century technological standards, its methods of gathering information have transformed. While the core duties of gathering, recording, verifying, and reporting on public information have remained consistent, the journalistic process has changed significantly, especially in how information is collected, disseminated, and consumed. This evolution has culminated in the prominence of investigative journalism, enabling it to overcome challenges like information hoarding.

Importance of Investigative Journalism

Investigative writing, a potent form of communication, thoroughly examines a subject and substantiates a central argument by comprehensively presenting its findings to the reader.

An investigative report serves a pivotal function, as its official conclusions can precipitate significant actions, such as employment termination, the implementation of corrective measures or training, or counseling. The dynamic interplay between investigative reporting and public relations, for example, frequently catalyzes tangible societal and corporate changes (NeCastro, 2014). Despite facing economic pressures and declining audiences, investigative journalism is concurrently regarded as both an imperiled and promising endeavor, exerting a transformative influence on mainstream journalism (Birnbauer, 2017; Wuergler et al., 2023). This journalistic practice is fundamental to a robust democracy, as it ensures the accountability of those in positions of authority and generates fresh perspectives and actionable solutions for societal challenges (Şen, 2021).

Elements of Effective Investigative Writing

The integrity and clarity of an investigative report are significantly enhanced by a well-organized structure, which ensures consistency across reports and minimizes preparation and drafting overhead. Ideally, investigative reports necessitate the utilization of tools that support seamless collaboration, robust documentation, and dynamic report generation.

The Executive Summary is often considered the most crucial and widely disseminated section, offering a complete yet concise overview of the complaint or allegation, the scope of investigative activities, a summary of findings, and a definitive conclusion. Journalists are expected to produce conclusive and comprehensive reports by meticulously addressing these elements. Extensive research, encompassing interviews and data analysis, constitutes the foundational element of investigative reporting.

Furthermore, the development of a compelling narrative structure, augmented by effective storytelling, is vital for sustaining reader engagement, complementing the application of specialized investigative methodologies designed to reveal concealed information and ascertain factual accuracy. The efficacy of report writing hinges on adherence to principles of accuracy, conciseness, comprehensiveness, objectivity, and a methodical presentation of events (Yisrael, 2010; Lovell et al., 2023). To ensure its resilience against critical examination, the narrative must be factual, chronologically structured, readily comprehensible, and exhaustive (Sennewald and Tsukayama, 2015).

Investigative Report

An investigative report constitutes a formal document that articulates the findings derived from an inquiry initiated by a formal complaint or specific incident. This document functions as a comprehensive record wherein investigators delineate identified issues, meticulously analyze pertinent evidence, and establish an objective conclusion predicated exclusively on empirical data, rather than on the subjective perspectives of the investigator or other implicated parties. The standard methodology encompasses the collection and analysis of information to ascertain causal factors, the meticulous documentation of research outcomes, and the systematic preparation of a report that delineates factual observations, investigative findings, and actionable recommendations (Zákopčanová et al., 2020; Hutchinson, Dekker and Rae, 2024). Novice investigators, often daunted by the complex demands of synthesizing extensive findings and adhering to rigorous structural and evidentiary standards, frequently expedite the drafting of their final investigative reports (Horsman, 2019). Such precipitancy can result in reports characterized by excessive verbosity, imprecision, or incompleteness, thereby omitting crucial information.

Conversely, seasoned investigative journalists recognize the final report as a pivotal opportunity to demonstrate the rigor and comprehensiveness of their inquiry. They present factual data to relevant stakeholders in a manner that elucidates the investigative conclusion and substantially reduces the necessity for subsequent inquiries, by ensuring comprehensive coverage of the journalistic "five Ws and single H." A meticulously prepared report optimizes efficiency by clearly and accurately presenting all requisite facts within its executive summary or introductory and concluding sections.

Nevertheless, even experienced investigative journalists, driven by the imperative to progress to subsequent assignments or disseminate news rapidly, occasionally undervalue the profound significance of the final report. Such oversight can potentially undermine the veracity of their endeavors and impede the efficacious dissemination of pivotal findings to pertinent stakeholders (Sennewald and Tsukayama, 2015).

Core Principles of Investigative Journalism

At its essence, investigative journalism is characterized by systematic, rigorous, and original inquiry, primarily aimed at uncovering concealed truths and exposing systemic issues (Ismail, Ahmad and Mustaffa, 2014; Cancela, Gerber and Dubied, 2021). It meticulously addresses critical concerns of significant public interest, encompassing criminal activities, social inequalities, widespread corruption, and corporate misconduct (Carson, 2019). This demanding endeavor frequently necessitates exhaustive research, often spanning several months or even years, with the overarching objective of not only revealing wrongdoing but also rigorously holding powerful entities accountable. This commitment to truth and accountability demands considerable perseverance, often exposing journalists to substantial risks, thereby underscoring the vital role of personal courage and resilience in their pursuit of the public interest (Shah, 2021).

Report Writing Protocols

A well-defined structure and meticulous presentation are critical for upholding the clarity and integrity of any investigative report follows the writing protocols mentioned hereunder:

1. **Structural Integrity and Clarity**: A rigorously organized structure is paramount for ensuring consistency, minimizing preparation time, and bolstering the overall credibility of an investigative report. Essential tools should facilitate seamless collaboration, robust documentation, and dynamic report generation to uphold these standards.

2. **Executive Summary**: This section stands as the most critical and widely disseminated component, serving as a comprehensive yet concise overview that must encapsulate the allegations, investigative scope, key findings, and definitive conclusions.

3. **Compelling Narrative Structure**: Beyond factual accuracy, a robust narrative structure and captivating storytelling are crucial. These elements not only sustain reader engagement but also effectively translate complex findings, augmenting the impact of specialized investigative methodologies designed to reveal concealed information.

4. **Unwavering Accuracy and Comprehensiveness**: Effective report writing is anchored in uncompromising accuracy, conciseness, comprehensiveness, and objectivity. The narrative must be factual, chronologically structured, readily comprehensible, and exhaustive to rigorously withstand critical examination and validate its conclusions (Yisrael, 2010).

5. **Fact checking**: Investigative journalists must always meticulously verify facts, assessing the credibility and significance of their information sources. Informed by these principles, investigative journalism necessitates the comprehensive collection, analysis, and rigorous fact-checking of extensive data to uncover truths and influence public discourse.

Steps in Investigative Report Writing

These meticulously designed steps are crucial for systematically guiding the investigator through evidence collection, analysis, and the synthesis of findings into a coherent, verifiable, and ultimately persuasive narrative, thereby ensuring thoroughness and impartiality in the investigative process. The rigorous process of conducting and documenting an investigative report demands a structured approach to unconditionally ensure thoroughness and impartiality. This document delineates five essential steps for investigative journalists:

1. **Specifying the Allegations:** Articulate with utmost precision the specific claims, incidents, or suspected wrongdoings that form the basis of the investigation. This initial clarity is paramount for establishing a focused scope, guiding subsequent evidence collection, and preventing investigative drift.

2. **Providing Subject Information:** Beyond basic identification, journalists must meticulously gather comprehensive details about the individuals or entities involved, including their backgrounds, affiliations, and potential motivations, to establish context, identify conflicts of interest, and anticipate potential challenges in the investigation.

3. **Summarizing Interviews:** Systematically document and meticulously summarize all interviews, including dates, locations, participants, and key statements. This rigorous approach ensures an accurate and verifiable record, facilitates cross-referencing with other evidence, and critically identifies discrepancies or corroborations essential for the investigation's thoroughness and impartiality.

4. **Outlining and Analyzing Evidence:** Critically analyze and systematically present all collected evidence, rigorously assessing its validity, relevance, and interconnections to construct a coherent and incontrovertible foundation for the investigative findings.

5. **Making Recommendations Based on Findings:** An investigative journalist must rigorously formulate impartial conclusions and develop concrete, actionable recommendations, ensuring they are unequivocally supported by the assembled evidence. This critical step translates findings into practical guidance, facilitating accountability and driving necessary changes.

The investigation process defines scope, plans the inquiry, collects and analyzes evidence, and documents findings (Zákopčanová et al., 2020; Hutchinson, Dekker and Rae, 2024). Experienced journalists recognize the final report as an opportunity to present facts thoroughly, addressing all journalistic "five Ws and single H" and minimizing follow-up questions. This robust methodology ensures reports are not only accurate and complete but also powerfully persuasive, profoundly differentiating investigative journalism through its commitment to depth, precision, and the public interest above fleeting speed or superficial sensationalism.

Technicalities of Investigative Journalism

The technical aspects of investigative journalism have evolved significantly with the advent of digital technologies, moving beyond traditional approaches to integrate advanced analytical tools and open-source intelligence.

While the core duties of gathering, recording, verifying, and reporting information remain consistent, the methodologies and techniques employed have undergone a profound transformation, now leveraging sophisticated data analysis platforms and digital forensics to uncover truths and manage complex information environments.

Methodology and Techniques

Contemporary investigative journalists are progressively leveraging advanced digital instrumentation and methodological approaches, such as sophisticated data analysis platforms and open-source intelligence techniques, to effectively manage the intricate challenges posed by modern information environments.

These critical technological advancements facilitate the systematic analysis of extensive and heterogeneous data collections, thereby uncovering complex correlations, discerning latent patterns, and meticulously validating information that would otherwise prove inaccessible.

Systematic and Rigorous Inquiry

Investigative journalism is fundamentally predicated on a rigorous commitment to thorough fact-checking, meticulously validated through in-depth interviews and extensive data analysis (Lovell et al., 2023). Furthermore, it strategically employs unconventional investigative methods, such as undercover operations, to systematically expose concealed corruption or systemic abuses of power. Indeed, this unwavering commitment to methodical inquiry, meticulous fact-checking, and rigorous verification is paramount for establishing the irrefutable credibility and transformative impact of investigative reports, especially when confronting and exposing powerful interests that often resist scrutiny and accountability (Carson, 2019).

Data Journalism and Analytics

The exponential proliferation of available data presents both considerable challenges and substantial opportunities for investigative journalism. Journalists are increasingly employing data science methodologies to derive unprecedented knowledge and profound insights from structured datasets (Bravo and Tellería, 2020; Dean et al., 2024; Veerbeek and Diakopoulos, 2024). The integration of automation and artificial intelligence is crucial for processing extensive datasets, thereby uncovering vital correlations and revealing previously undetected patterns that might otherwise remain obscure (Stray, 2019; Cifliku and Heuer, 2025). Specialized tools, such as SociaLens, enhance journalistic capabilities by autonomously identifying and extracting query-specific data from online sources, offering deeply nuanced insights with notable efficiency and without necessitating extensive coding expertise (Jamil and Rubaiat, 2024). Furthermore, Generative AI significantly optimizes newsgathering processes by effectively prioritizing documents based on newsworthiness and producing concise, accurate summaries.

Digital Forensics and OSINT

In the contemporary digital landscape, journalists leverage digital forensics to authenticate user-generated content, scrutinize metadata, analyze geolocation data, interpret satellite imagery, and examine closed-circuit television footage (Chouliaraki and Al-Ghazzi, 2021; Khan et al., 2023). This methodological approach is pivotal for substantiating the factual accuracy of journalistic narratives, particularly within conflict-affected regions (Chouliaraki and Al-Ghazzi, 2021).

Furthermore, digital forensics finds application in cybercrime investigations and for reconstructing the chronological sequence of digital activities (Bartliff et al., 2020; Horan and Saiedian, 2021; Pandey et al., 2024). Open-source intelligence analysis represents a related methodology employed for the systematic acquisition of information from publicly accessible sources (Hauter, 2021). This includes exploiting social media platforms, public records, and online databases to gather crucial intelligence, thereby augmenting the scope and depth of journalistic inquiry (Nurhadiyati, 2024).

Investigative Report Structure and Clarity

The efficacy of investigative writing is predicated upon its adherence to principles of precision, conciseness, thoroughness, and impartiality (Yisrael, 2010; Sennewald and Tsukayama, 2015). A meticulously structured report is instrumental in guaranteeing coherence and perspicuity, typically featuring an executive summary that succinctly delineates the allegations, scope, findings, and ultimate conclusions. Furthermore, the narrative must be verifiably factual, chronologically ordered, and exhaustive to withstand rigorous examination.

Ethical Protocols and Professional Standards

Ethical considerations are paramount in investigative journalism, particularly with new digital tools. The increasing reliance on advanced digital instrumentation, such as sophisticated data analysis platforms, open-source intelligence, and digital forensics, introduces complex ethical dilemmas (Chouliaraki and Al-Ghazzi, 2021). For instance, a significant challenge in digital open-source investigations involves balancing the journalistic ideal of transparency with the crucial duty to protect the privacy and security of data subjects (Woude, Dodds and Torres, 2024). As ethical guidelines for OSINT are still emerging, practitioners often rely on personal assessments and dialogues with colleagues to navigate these complex privacy-related editorial choices (Woude, Dodds and Torres, 2024). Therefore, strict adherence to ethical protocols and professional standards is essential not only for ensuring the integrity of the investigative process but also for maintaining public trust and the credibility of journalistic findings in an increasingly data-driven information environment (Steel et al., 2025). The proliferation of readily accessible online data, while offering considerable advantages for open-source intelligence methodologies, simultaneously mandates rigorous ethical deliberation concerning its acquisition, analytical processing, and subsequent dissemination (Woude, Dodds and Torres, 2024).

Transparency vs. Privacy : A principal ethical dilemma, particularly evident in digital open-source investigations, lies in reconciling the journalistic imperative for transparency with the fundamental obligation to safeguard the privacy and security of data subjects. As comprehensive ethical guidelines for Open-Source Intelligence are still in their formative stages, practitioners frequently depend on individual judgment and peer consultation to navigate complex privacy-related editorial decisions (Woude, Dodds and Torres, 2024).

Source Criticism : Upholding the credibility of journalistic output necessitates a stringent protocol for evaluating both sources and source materials. This critical assessment is paramount for verifying the factual accuracy and reliability of all assertions made. Furthermore, such an approach demands a prudent skepticism regarding truth-claims, the transparent articulation of interpretive frameworks, and the active integration of self-reflection in information validation (Steensen et al., 2022).

Professional Conduct : Adherence to professional standards is not merely advisable but *imperative* for practitioners in investigative journalism, as these standards delineate the rigorous scope and evaluative criteria essential for maintaining the integrity and credibility of the field (Bjerknes, 2020; Cancela, Gerber and Dubied, 2021; Steel et al., 2025). Within journalistic institutions, ethical codes function as indispensable instruments, serving to uphold accountability and safeguard public trust. This commitment to high-quality, ethically informed journalism is, moreover, fundamentally consequential for fostering a robust and informed democratic discourse (Steel et al., 2025).

Accountability : Investigative journalism functions as an indispensable mechanism for holding public officials and powerful entities accountable for malpractice and corruption. Rigorous adherence to established protocols and professional standards is paramount, guaranteeing that reported findings are not merely impartial but are exclusively substantiated by verifiable evidence, thereby precluding reliance on subjective opinions. This unwavering commitment to factual verification is fundamental to establishing the enduring credibility of investigative reports and, critically, amplifying their profound impact on fostering an informed and robust democratic public discourse.

The rigorous application of methodologies and adherence to ethical principles inherent in investigative journalism are crucial for enhancing transparency and accountability within systems of governance. This function becomes particularly critical in contexts where governmental actions or inactions, often obscured from public view, significantly impact public welfare and the equitable distribution of resources, thereby necessitating rigorous journalistic scrutiny to ensure transparency and accountability (Bhatti, 2025).

Perils of Investigative Journalism : Investigative journalists often confront substantial threats and challenges, an inherent vulnerability stemming from their primary function of scrutinizing and holding powerful entities accountable. These perils manifest as diverse forms of oppression, encompassing legal actions such as defamation lawsuits and Strategic Lawsuits Against Public Participation, as well as physical dangers including violence, intimidation, and even assassination, particularly in regions characterized by restricted press freedom or pervasive corruption (Biscop and Décary-Hétu, 2022). This adversarial landscape underscores the imperative for robust legal protections and international solidarity to safeguard journalists, thereby sustaining their crucial function within democratic societies (Audette-Longo et al., 2023).

Legal Threats : Strategic Lawsuits Against Public Participation represent a pervasive threat to journalistic integrity and press freedom. These lawsuits are inherently vexatious and frivolous, meticulously designed not to win on merit, but to exhaust the financial and emotional resources of critics, notably investigative journalists. The exorbitant legal costs associated with defending against SLAPPs impose an immense burden, often forcing journalists to abandon critical investigations or face devastating professional and personal repercussions.

This calculated legal harassment severely curtails press freedom by fostering an environment of fear, ultimately driving self-censorship and undermining the public's right to information (Papadopoulou and Maniou, 2024).

Physical and Psychological Dangers : Beyond legal ramifications, journalists frequently face severe threats to their physical safety and well-being. These dangers encompass outright violence, pervasive harassment, and even targeted assassinations, particularly when reporting on highly sensitive topics such as organized crime, profound political corruption, or human rights abuses (Shah, 2021). Journalists, especially those intrepidly covering precarious areas like environmental crimes, illicit activities, or systemic corruption, contend with an alarmingly heightened risk of murder, arbitrary arrest, brutal assault, persistent threats, and relentless harassment (Verhovnik, 2018; Freedman, 2020; Danso, 2025). The cumulative psychological toll of consistently reporting on traumatic events or confronting imminent personal danger is also a profound peril, frequently manifesting as chronic stress, anxiety, and even post-traumatic stress disorder, significantly impacting their mental health and sustained ability to operate (Verhovnik, 2018). Such threats not only jeopardize the safety of individual journalists but also foster a climate of apprehension across the wider media landscape, thereby impeding the capacity for independent and effective investigative reporting (Danso, 2025).

Internet Surveillance : Investigative reporters, by virtue of their critical reliance on confidential sources and their fundamental watchdog role, face acute and escalating vulnerability to sophisticated internet surveillance tactics.

The pervasive increase in both digital and physical threats, extending even to established democratic nations, compels journalists to operate under the constant and justifiable assumption that their communication channels and devices are compromised (Salvo, 2021). This environment of persistent digital intrusion severely jeopardizes source protection, stifles critical investigations, and ultimately undermines press freedom. The enduring threat posed by state-sponsored digital espionage, combined with the capacity of malicious non-state actors to exploit systemic vulnerabilities, mandates the perpetual and anticipatory refinement of cybersecurity protocols and digital hygiene practices within the journalistic profession (Walulya and Nassanga, 2020).

Media Capture and External Influence : The autonomy of investigative journalism faces significant compromise due to diverse and pervasive forms of media capture. These include overt or subtle governmental interests that shape editorial content, partisan influences originating from media proprietors with distinct political allegiances, and potent external pressures such as advertising boycotts, monetary incentives (e.g., bribes), or direct acts of aggression against journalists (Louis-Sidois and Mougin, 2020; Danso, 2025). Such external influences consistently impair editorial independence and inhibit critical reporting, consequently subverting the fundamental mission of journalism. Moreover, the existence of internal corruption within media entities poses a substantial impediment, fostering intrinsic conflicts of interest that significantly diminish their ability to undertake unbiased and efficacious investigations (Maniou and Ketteni, 2020). Collectively, these multifaceted challenges significantly compromise the pivotal function of journalism as a societal watchdog, consequently fostering a chilling effect on critical reporting. (Salvo, 2021).

Information Hoarding : Investigative journalists frequently encounter significant impediments to accessing vital information, primarily due to the deliberate opacity of governmental bodies and corporate entities. This opacity often stems from a desire to conceal misconduct, protect financial interests, or avoid public scrutiny.

Such practices, which constitute information hoarding by powerful institutions, manifest as denied freedom of information requests, the classification of documents, or the use of non-disclosure agreements, thereby directly obstructing comprehensive investigations and impeding the ability of journalists to hold power accountable (Danso, 2025). Governments frequently engage in aggressive information suppression, employing both legal and extralegal tactics, which severely exacerbate the formidable challenges journalists face in their pursuit of truth (Chandel, 2024). This calculated obstructionism compels journalists to dedicate excessive resources to information acquisition, thereby siphoning invaluable time and funding away from critical analysis and dissemination. Governments often weaponize the concept of "classified information" to hoard vital public interest data, effectively curtailing transparency and accountability.

Breaking The News : The pervasive pressure within the journalistic landscape to disseminate news rapidly can lead even seasoned journalists to prematurely conclude investigations or underestimate the critical importance of thoroughly developed and meticulously verified final reports. This expediency risks profoundly compromising the depth and integrity of their work, potentially resulting in incomplete narratives, unsubstantiated claims, or even the unwitting propagation of misinformation. Such shortcuts not only undermine the credibility of individual journalists and media outlets but also erode public trust in the journalistic process, ultimately hindering its vital role as a societal watchdog. This phenomenon is profoundly exacerbated by the intensely competitive nature of digital platforms, which, driven by algorithms and audience metrics, relentlessly prioritize immediate dissemination and viral engagement over meticulous verification and in-depth analysis. This constant pressure compels journalists to accelerate news cycles, often at the expense of comprehensive fact-checking and nuanced context, leading to a proliferation of sensationalized, incomplete, or even inaccurate reporting. Such an environment not only compromises journalistic integrity but also significantly impedes the sustained, painstaking efforts required for robust investigative journalism. (T., 2024).

Lack of Resources : A pervasive and systemic lack of resources, characterized by insufficient funding for in-depth investigations and inadequate remuneration for journalists, profoundly compromises the capacity for rigorous and independent reporting. These critical financial constraints within media organizations not only severely restrict the scope and depth of essential investigations (Fierens et al., 2023) but also necessitate drastic measures such as staff reductions and an unfortunate reliance on superficial, less resource-intensive reporting models. This vicious cycle ultimately diminishes the quality and impact of journalistic output, eroding public trust and undermining journalism's vital role as a societal watchdog.

Opportunities in Investigative Journalism

Yet, amidst these significant perils, the field of investigative journalism is demonstrating remarkable resilience, actively embracing new opportunities fostered by technological advancements, collaborative models, and evolving funding structures.

Collaborative Journalism : The traditional "lone wolf" paradigm in investigative journalism is proving increasingly inadequate to confront the escalating complexities and transnational scope of contemporary corruption and organized crime, thereby necessitating a transition towards integrated cross-border collaborations and networked approaches. Entities such as the International Consortium of Investigative Journalists serve as prime illustrations of this evolving paradigm, with their methodology underscoring how the amalgamation of diverse resources, specialized expertise, and extended jurisdictional capabilities facilitate unparalleled large-scale, comprehensive investigations. Seminal projects, exemplified by the Panama Papers, which engaged hundreds of journalists worldwide, would be logistically and economically prohibitive for singular news organizations to execute, given their extensive scale, substantial financial requisites, and demand for highly specialized proficiencies (Konow-Lund, 2020; Buschow and Suhr, 2023). Beyond streamlining intricate investigative processes, this collaborative methodology also encompasses crucial aspects such as joint fundraising endeavors and unified audience engagement strategies, thereby bolstering the long-term viability and influence of essential journalistic undertakings (Audette-Longo et al., 2023).

Technological Enhancements : Digital tools and artificial intelligence present substantial opportunities to profoundly augment investigative processes. AI and automation, for example, can significantly mitigate the time devoted to laborious data analysis, thereby empowering journalists to process extensive, often unstructured datasets and discern critical insights with unparalleled efficiency. This encompasses the automation of repetitive tasks, the identification of intricate patterns, and the detection of anomalies within massive information volumes (Jamil and Rubaiat, 2024; Cifliku and Heuer, 2025). Moreover, Generative AI now transcends basic summarization, actively aiding in the prioritization of newsworthy content, the preliminary drafting of reports, and even the identification of complex interconnections across disparate sources to formulate hypotheses for more in-depth inquiry (Dean et al., 2024; Veerbeek and Diakopoulos, 2024). Complementing these advancements, data journalism emerges as a pivotal innovation, systematically employing scientific methodologies to extract actionable knowledge from structured data, consequently fostering more evidence-based narratives and uncovering systemic issues that might otherwise remain concealed (Bravo and Tellería, 2020; Meier et al., 2022).

New Funding Models and Sustainability : In response to declining traditional revenue streams, innovative business models prioritizing user needs and public service are emerging as viable solutions. Foundations and non-profit organizations, exemplified by ProPublica, play a crucial role in sustaining investigative journalism. Their support not only covers significant operational expenses, such as travel and research time, but also, critically, shields journalists from commercial pressures, thereby robustly safeguarding editorial independence (Leimbach et al., 2015; Medina, Sánchez-Tabernero and Breiner, 2021). This diversified funding approach enables independent organizations to steadfastly maintain their editorial autonomy, mitigating undue influence from any singular patron or commercial interest (Leimbach et al., 2015).

Increased Public Engagement : Importantly, collaborative and participatory frameworks substantially augment public engagement in investigative journalism, strategically utilizing civic involvement to bolster accountability concerning influential institutions and individuals (Konow-Lund, 2020). This proactive participation is integral to the democratic function of citizen journalism, empowering community members to actively contribute to the gathering, reporting, analysis, and dissemination of news, thereby intensifying public scrutiny and reinforcing the journalistic mandate. This evolution towards participatory methodologies not only expands the scope and profundity of journalistic inquiry but also cultivates a more knowledgeable and civically active populace (Konow-Lund, 2020).

Impact and Accountability : Investigative journalism serves as a crucial catalyst for social change, systematically exposing injustice, rigorously holding political and business leaders accountable, and actively instigating concrete actions based on its findings, which often include significant consequences such as employment termination or comprehensive corrective measures. Crucially, the societal impact of such reporting extends beyond mere exposure, actively driving tangible policy reforms and profoundly shaping public discourse. This process unequivocally reinforces democratic principles and fosters vital transparency in governance, serving as a cornerstone of societal accountability. (Bhatti, 2025).

In conclusion, despite the formidable challenges and severe perils that continually threaten investigative journalism, ranging from pervasive legal threats and state surveillance to media capture, the field is undergoing a profound transformation. This resurgence is powerfully fueled by collaborative approaches, sophisticated digital tools, and innovative funding strategies. These pivotal developments are not merely enabling but actively solidifying investigative journalism's indispensable and impactful role in rigorously upholding transparency and accountability, which are foundational pillars of democratic societies. The relentless evolution of artificial intelligence, while introducing novel challenges, simultaneously unlocks unprecedented opportunities for journalistic inquiry, thereby demanding a critical and nuanced understanding of its profound capabilities and ethical implications for its responsible and effective integration.

CHAPTER 10

Sensitive Reporting and Ethical Media Practice

REPORTING ON SENSITIVE TOPICS inevitably involves navigating the personal domains of individuals. Journalists must approach this aspect of their profession with a deep sense of responsibility, acutely aware of the potential harm their reporting can inflict. Beyond merely conveying information, the reporter's role encompasses the delicate task of handling sensitive subjects with the highest ethical considerations. Whether exploring matters of crime, tragedy, or personal struggles, journalists play a pivotal role in shaping public perceptions. This section delves into the ethical guidelines that should direct reporters when engaging with such intricate subjects.

To meet the standard of sensitive reporting in media practice, a journalist must precisely unveil truth, respect privacy and dignity, adhere to a journalistic imperative, avoid sensationalism and stereotypes, practice cultural sensitivity, infuse empathy into storytelling, and provide support and resources to individuals, often referred to as subjects or survivors (rather than just victims).

Unveiling Truth with Precision

At the heart of ethical reporting lies an unwavering commitment to truth and accuracy, aligning with the Accuracy principle of the ABCD of Journalism discussed previously. When navigating the landscape of sensitive topics, journalists must proceed with utmost care, relying on verifiable sources and rigorous fact-checking processes. Presenting a balanced and unbiased narrative ensures that all parties involved have an opportunity to voice their perspectives, fostering a comprehensive and fair understanding of events.

Respecting Privacy and Dignity

Reporting on sensitive topics frequently involves delving into individual's private lives. Journalists must approach this with a profound sense of responsibility, recognizing the potential for harm. Obtaining informed consent for interviews and upholding the privacy and dignity of those involved are paramount. This requires careful balance, meticulously navigating the line between public interest and personal sensitivity.

The Journalistic Imperative

The term 'imperative' signifies something of utmost importance or necessity, or something commanding. In journalism, this translates to duties that are profoundly imperative. A cornerstone ethical principle in journalism is the imperative to minimize harm. When unraveling sensitive stories, journalists must be acutely aware of the potential impact on the lives of those in the spotlight. Exercising caution and sensitivity in the selection and presentation of information ensures that the story genuinely serves the public interest without gratuitously causing undue harm or distress.

Avoiding Sensationalism and Stereotyping

In the pursuit of audience attention, journalists often face the temptation of sensationalism. Reporting on sensitive topics demands a conscious departure from the allure of sensational headlines. Instead, the focus should remain on providing accurate and balanced coverage, actively steering clear of stereotypes and biases. The narrative ought to be a mirror reflecting truth, rather than a distorted lens fueling sensationalism, reinforcing the need for 'Directness' in reporting.

Cultural Sensitivity in Reporting

Sensitivity to diverse cultural backgrounds is paramount when reporting on topics intersecting with various traditions. Journalists must proceed cautiously, avoiding assumptions and generalizations that might perpetuate stereotypes or offend specific communities. Delving into the intricacies of cultural nuances leads to a more informed and accurate portrayal of the subjects, fostering deeper understanding among readers.

Providing Support and Resources

The impact of reporting on sensitive topics extends beyond the newsroom. Journalists bear the responsibility of not just transmitting information, but also of providing support and resources to those directly affected by their stories. This can include offering access to counseling services, helplines, or support groups. Journalists can serve as conduits for positive change, guiding readers to avenues where they can seek further assistance or find relevant resources.

Transparency and Accountability in Sensitive Reporting

Maintaining public trust is integral to journalistic ethics and particularly to sensitive reporting. Transparency and accountability are the foundations upon which this trust is built. Journalists should openly disclose their sources, methods, and any potential conflicts of interest when tackling sensitive topics. This not only strengthens the journalist's credibility but also invites scrutiny and ensures accountability to the audience.

Empathy in Storytelling

Beyond facts and figures, reporting on sensitive topics demands a human touch. Journalists should strive to infuse empathy into their storytelling, recognizing the profound emotional weight these narratives carry. By connecting with human experience, reporters can bridge the gap between mere information and genuine understanding, fostering a sense of shared humanity.

Long-Term Impact Assessment

Ethical reporting extends beyond immediate publication. Journalists should consider the potential long-term impact of their work on individuals and communities. This involves reflecting on the consequences of the narrative and taking proactive steps to mitigate any adverse effects, ensuring that the story contributes positively to societal discourse.

Collaboration with Experts

When addressing intricate and sensitive subjects, journalists should collaborate with field experts. This ensures a more comprehensive and accurate understanding of the topic. Engaging with professionals such as psychologists, sociologists, or legal experts can provide invaluable insights that enhance the quality and ethical standing of the reporting.

Continuous Ethical Education

Journalism is an ever-evolving field, and ethical standards may shift over time. Reporters should engage in continuous ethical education to stay abreast of changes and challenges. This involves attending workshops, participating in discussions, and staying informed about evolving ethical guidelines to uphold the highest standards of journalistic integrity.

Public Engagement and Feedback

Ethical reporting involves an ongoing dialogue with the audience. Journalists should actively seek and engage with public feedback, fostering a sense of accountability to the community. This open communication channel allows reporters to address concerns, correct inaccuracies, and demonstrate a commitment to transparency.

The landscape of reporting on sensitive topics requires a delicate balance between the pursuit of truth and the protection of individual's well-being. By adhering to principles of truth and accuracy, respecting privacy, minimizing harm, avoiding sensationalism, cultivating cultural sensitivity, providing support, maintaining transparency, infusing empathy, considering long-term impact, collaborating with experts, engaging in continuous ethical education, and embracing public feedback, journalists can navigate this complex terrain with integrity. Ethical reporting is not merely a professional obligation; it is a catalyst for a more informed and empathetic society, where the power of the press is wielded with profound responsibility.

Ethnic & Racial Reporting

Ethnic reporting is a challenging yet crucial aspect of journalistic practice. Since the early 20th century, the issue of how conflict is instigated along tribal and racial lines has become a pressing concern. Ethnic, racial, and religious conflicts were particularly significant after World War II and during the Cold War, as decolonization led to various ethnic groups vying for control of postcolonial nation-states. The Rwandan Genocide, one of the worst ethnic conflicts in recent history towards the end of the 20th century, stands as a stark example of such violence. Ethnic conflicts invariably bring forth numerous negative consequences, including the erosion of social cohesion.

The code of ethics for journalists generally prohibits delving into the tribal or racial backgrounds of an accused or perpetrators of a crime, including those involved in communal conflicts.

Gender Media Reporting

Gender-sensitive reporting actively avoids stereotypes that limit and trivialize women and men, striving instead to present an accurate and comprehensive portrait of the world and its possibilities. According to Free Press Unlimited, gender media reporting is a sensitive practice aimed at producing media content that is mindful of gender inequalities and portrays women and men fairly. Gendered media refers to media that influences gender issues and mobilizes citizens regarding prevalent cultural and societal norms related to gender equality. Such media highlights gender-specific issues, such as ongoing discrimination against women, sexual abuse against women and girls, or concerns affecting any other gender, including LGBTQIA+ individuals and emerging gender minorities.

Forms of Gender Based Violence

It is imperative for journalists covering gender-based violence to possess a comprehensive understanding of its four distinct forms. This knowledge is crucial to ensure that their professional reporting extends beyond familiar manifestations of violence, encompassing all relevant issues and dynamics within each specific locality.

Physical violence is defined as any action that inflicts bodily injury through illicit physical force. Sexual violence encompasses any sexual act perpetrated against an individual without their explicit consent. Psychological violence refers to any conduct that causes significant emotional or mental harm to an individual. Economic violence manifests as the systematic denial of fundamental economic rights, such as land ownership or equitable remuneration, to individuals based on their gender.

Cruciality of GBV Reporting

It can never be better argued that the pervasive nature of gender-based violence, affecting individuals across all demographics, necessitates rigorous reporting to shed light on its multifaceted impact. Ethical reporting of gender-based violence and sexual and gender-based violence is paramount to fostering recovery and preventing further detrimental and enduring effects on survivors. These adverse consequences are frequently intensified when survivors abstain from reporting or seeking assistance, thereby perpetuating a cycle of silence and suffering. Reporting facilitates survivors' access to essential medical, psychosocial, and legal services, which are critical for mitigating the profound health impacts of such violence. Furthermore, it holds perpetrators accountable, highlighting the media's ethical imperative to investigate and report on GBV in all contexts, adhering to the fundamental journalistic principle of humanity and contributing to broader justice. (Stevens et al., 2024)

In an article published on Medium, Jemimah Njuki asserted that several Kenyan media outlets have recently disseminated narratives that disempower women and girls. For example, following a male perpetrator's rape of a female student, one newspaper characterized the incident as 'stranger than fiction,' citing the absence of screams or alarms from two other assaulted girls. Another report concentrated on male teachers' apprehensions about instructing in girls' schools, driven by concerns of false accusations of rape. The author of this article controversially suggested that female students might provoke teachers through behaviors such as sitting with uncrossed legs or not wearing undergarments.

During a live television interview, a journalist interrogated a female victim of robbery and rape, querying whether her actions, statements, or attire might have instigated the perpetrators.

These examples illustrate a systemic failure by the media to conceptualize the rape of women and girls as a manifestation of male power dynamics or to acknowledge men's agency and their sole responsibility for such actions. Such media portrayals demonstrate a recurring pattern wherein rape and other forms of violence against women are trivialized, presented humorously, and survivors are subjected to victim-blaming, which actively discourages reporting and reinforces a culture of impunity. This phenomenon is not geographically limited to Kenya. In the United Kingdom, researchers identified 12 newspaper articles within a single day that employed victim-blaming rhetoric, extending even to the blaming of child victims of sexual violence. Correspondingly, a 2016 report from Australia revealed that up to 15 percent of articles concerning domestic violence contained implicit elements of victim-blaming.

Such journalistic coverage is deeply problematic and constitutes a significant regression, particularly given the media's profound influence in shaping societal perceptions on critical issues and mobilizing action. A salient illustration is the climate change discourse, where studies indicated that media's construction of uncertainty around the issue correlated with reduced public willingness to alter personal behaviors. When media reports attribute blame for rape to women and girls, society risks disengaging, failing to recognize it as a broader societal issue, and consequently abrogating responsibility for individual or collective action to effect change, thereby undermining efforts toward justice and equality.

Therefore, it is critically important for journalists to report on sexual violence with informed insight, possessing a robust theoretical understanding of the root causes of gender inequality and the necessary societal transformations. Otherwise, they risk inflicting further harm by perpetuating myths and falsehoods, thereby obstructing justice. For instance, an undue focus on a woman's or girl's attire during a rape incident can lead to 'reverse criminalization,' where victims are unjustly held accountable for their own assault, a profound perversion of justice that reinforces patriarchal norms. Njuki highlights three crucial strategies journalists can adopt to enhance their reporting on Gender-Based ViolenceHandbook on Gender-responsive Police Services for Women and Girls Subject to Violence, 2021)

1. **Seek expert insights**: Media organizations must consult specialists to contextualize GBV issues effectively and offer theoretical insights. These experts, from non-governmental organizations, research institutions, universities, and other relevant bodies, provide credible, evidence-based narratives that challenge misconceptions and foster accurate, nuanced reporting.[1]

2. **Provide foundational training**: Journalists covering GBV and gender issues require a fundamental understanding of ethical considerations and best practices for addressing these sensitive topics. Mandatory basic training for journalists on concepts such as gender inequality, gender-based violence, patriarchy, and its manifestations should be integrated into university-level journalism curricula. Such

---

1. The Pulitzer Center has documented how gender and social justice activists can influence GBV reporting, leveraging social media and multimedia projects as part of its broader work on gender and inequality. In Kenya, Dr. Wandia Njoya, a feminist and social justice activist, exemplifies an individual who publicly contextualizes violence against women through her blog.

training builds critical awareness and equips journalists with the ethical framework needed to avoid harmful portrayals and uphold survivor dignity. Unfortunately, specialized centers for journalist training on GBV reporting are rare; a notable initiative was a call during Australia's National Family Violence summit for comprehensive domestic violence training for all news centers in the country.[2]

3. **Adhere to existing guidelines:** Media institutions must comply with established guidelines for reporting gender and sexual-based violence. For example, in 2013, a global protection cluster of humanitarian organizations developed guidelines for reporting gender and sexual-based violence in humanitarian contexts. Most principles within these guidelines, such as employing non-judgmental language, avoiding information or images that could jeopardize survivors, and consulting experts familiar with the topic and context, represent fundamental ethical and safety principles applicable beyond humanitarian settings. Adhering to these best practices is essential for protecting survivors, ensuring ethical reporting, and maintaining journalistic integrity.[3]

In her conclusion, Jemimah Njuki emphasized that while media cannot be held solely accountable for societal perceptions of rape and other forms of Gender-Based Violence, it is imperative that media is not complicit in reinforcing them. The media possesses a unique and

---

2. In 2011, Canada's International Development Research Centre implemented a program to train journalists in Africa and the Middle East to improve the quality of science reporting. At a 2014 conference in Nairobi, Kenya, science journalists from across Africa acknowledged that such training significantly enhanced media reporting on science, environment, agriculture, and health

3. Another valuable resource is the Sonke for Gender Justice Guidelines for Journalists and Editors.

powerful opportunity to leverage its platform to actively transform these communal perceptions for the common good and serve as a catalyst for positive social change.

GBV Effects & Consequences

Journalists, reporters, and editors reporting on Gender-Based Violence bear a critical responsibility to understand that its effects and consequences are often profoundly long-lasting. While inappropriate reporting can inadvertently exacerbate trauma and perpetuate harm, it is only through rigorous professional and ethical practices that these severe physical and psychosocial impacts can be effectively minimized and survivor's healing supported.

Physical Effects

The physical repercussions may manifest as a diverse array of conditions, potentially including transient or enduring incapacitation, nutritional deficiencies, the exacerbation of pre-existing chronic illnesses, and persistent pain. Furthermore, victims of gender-based violence may experience reproductive health issues, sexually transmitted infections, and severe injuries requiring extensive medical intervention (Breaking the Cycle of Gender-based Violence, 2023). These health consequences can range from physical injury to unwanted pregnancies, exposure to sexually transmitted infections, and fertility problems (Daalen et al., 2022).

Psychosocial or Mental Effects

Psychosocial or mental consequences often encompass a range of emotional and psychological disturbances, such as anger, anxiety, fear, shame, self-loathing, self-blame, post-traumatic stress disorder, and depression, among other potential manifestations.

These mental health impacts can be particularly devastating and long-lasting, frequently leading to diminished functioning and a lower quality of life for survivors (Bibi, Mallal and Ali, 2025) (Koutra et al., 2022).

Writing a GBV Story

A common challenge for journalists new to Gender-Based Violence reporting is grasping how to effectively construct a narrative. To support reporters venturing into the GBV beat, the following are crucial considerations for crafting such stories:

1. Ensure accuracy and employ appropriate, non-judgmental terminology.

2. Prioritize the survivor's perspective and avoid any form of victim-blaming.

3. Engage with and seek insights from experts in the field.

4. Inform the public about the complexities and realities of GBV.

. Provide details regarding available support and assistance resources for survivors.

Covering Children's Stories

Media houses, editors, and reporters are ethically obligated to uphold the dignity and rights of every child in all reporting circumstances. When interviewing children and covering their concerns, particular care must be taken to respect each child's right to privacy and confidentiality, ensure their views are heard so they can participate in decisions affecting them, and guarantee their equal protection.

Media often portrays children through various archetypes, predominantly positive, though some representations can be negative, particularly concerning specific demographics. Children are frequently represented in terms of age, lifestyle, and identity. While news coverage of this group can sometimes be negative, other media forms positively represent and cater to children and other demographics.

Impact of Media Programming on Children

Media organizations should implement cautious practices, such as isolating programs intended for children. Concurrently, parents bear the responsibility of protecting their children from potentially harmful media content. Studies indicate that exposure to on-screen violence can lead to behavioral problems, nightmares, and sleep disturbances. Such imagery can also distress older children, and parents are encouraged to discuss accidental exposures with their children to provide comfort and explanations, alleviating fears.

Furthermore, media demonstrably influences the health and lifestyle decisions of pre-teens and teenagers. For instance, media messages can normalize or glamorize unhealthy behaviors like consuming junk food, smoking, vaping, drinking alcohol, and using other drugs. Media holds a substantial responsibility towards children in this regard, whether consciously acknowledged by families or not. Therefore, media professionals must adhere to stringent ethical guidelines when creating content, particularly regarding vulnerable populations like children, to mitigate negative influences and uphold social responsibility (Skana and Gjerazi, 2024) (Kiasalar et al., 2022).

The Deceased and Journalism

The erroneous notion that an individual's rights terminate upon death, with protection and respect reserved exclusively for the living, fundamentally misinterprets the concept of post-mortem dignity. Since rights are actively asserted rather than passively granted, and the deceased are inherently unable to self-advocate, a significant ethical responsibility falls upon their next of kin. They must articulate concerns regarding the dignified treatment, respectful representation, and preservation of their loved one's remains and legacy. The profound impact of media representations, whether through graphic imagery, serene portrayals, or dramatic interpretations in television programs, cannot be overstated in shaping societal perceptions of death and mortality. Recognizing this powerful influence is not merely important but imperative for promoting a nuanced, respectful, and accurate public understanding of dying and remembrance. In the complex and rapidly evolving contemporary digital landscape, upholding journalistic ethics presents increasing challenges, especially for citizen journalists who often operate without formal professional training. However, this complexity does not absolve established media outlets, which, regrettably, sometimes fall short of optimal ethical practices when reporting on deceased individuals. Therefore, it is an unequivocal ethical imperative that media organizations refrain from disseminating images or sensitive information concerning the deceased without the explicit and informed consent of surviving family members. This practice underscores a fundamental respect for privacy and post-mortem dignity.

Public Communication of Deceased Individuals by Media Outlets

Contemporary photographic depictions of deceased individuals should generally not be disseminated without explicit authorization (Nwabueze, 2024). However, pre-existing, appropriate photographs of the deceased may be shared, typically with the consent and facilitation of a surviving family member.

A standard obituary or death announcement characteristically includes the decedent's name, the date of death, and relevant details concerning commemorative services. Alternatively, a more profound media tribute might integrate personal narratives and an image of the deceased. This methodology endeavors to reconcile the public's right to information with critical ethical considerations regarding post-mortem dignity, particularly in light of the ubiquitous online dissemination of imagery.

Reasons Why Media Reports Deaths

Media organizations bear a societal obligation to report fatalities for several fundamental reasons:

1. To ensure public understanding of the circumstances and causal factors surrounding an individual's death, thereby contributing to broader public health and safety initiatives.

2. To uphold transparency and prevent the concealment or obfuscation of deaths, particularly those involving public figures, ensuring accountability and maintaining public trust.

3. To highlight systemic issues, hazardous conditions, or events that pose a risk of further fatalities or injuries, thus serving as a vital preventative measure and informing policy decisions.

4. To provide accurate information, counter misinformation, and address speculation surrounding deaths, thereby preserving factual integrity and preventing undue distress or manipulation.

CHAPTER 11

Ethics of Journalism

THE SOCIETY OF PROFESSIONAL Journalists asserts in its preamble that public enlightenment is the precursor to justice and the bedrock of democracy. Ethical journalism aims to facilitate the free exchange of accurate, fair, and thorough information, always with the intention to do no harm. An ethical journalist consistently acts with integrity. The SPJ identifies four core principles as the foundation of ethical journalism, encouraging their adoption by all media professionals.[1]

Professional integrity serves as the cornerstone of a journalist's credibility. For instance, the Radio, Television, and Digital News Association, an organization dedicated solely to electronic journalism, bases its code of ethics on principles such as public trust, truthfulness, fairness, integrity, independence, and accountability.

Ethics, in this context, involves rational justification for journalistic moral judgments, affirming or rejecting what is considered morally right

---

1. The SPJ Code of Ethics is a statement of abiding principles supported by explanations and position papers that address changing journalistic practices. It is not a set of rules, rather a guide that encourages all who engage in journalism to take responsibility for the information they provide, regardless of medium. The code should be read as a whole; individual principles should not be taken out of context. It is not, nor can it be under the First Amendment, legally enforceable. Countries have own code of ethics and conduct for Journalists. South Sudan is one example amongst others.

or wrong, just or unjust. More broadly, ethics reflects on human beings and their interactions with nature and other individuals, encompassing concepts of freedom, responsibility, and justice. Media ethics specifically promotes and upholds values like universal respect for life, the rule of law, and legality. It addresses ethical considerations regarding how media should utilize texts and images provided by citizens for public consumption. While journalists routinely research, write, edit, and file news stories, features, and articles for television, radio, and print (magazines, journals, newspapers, often in both print and online formats), they are expected to be guided by journalistic ethics. Their primary role is to create and assemble news stories that genuinely interest their audience, underscoring the critical need for ethical guidance.

Core Values of Journalism

On a global scale, journalism is underpinned by five broadly acknowledged foundational values: accuracy, independence, impartiality, humanity, and accountability. These tenets function as universally accepted frameworks guiding ethical journalistic conduct, and they are elucidated as follows:

Accuracy : Accuracy in journalism is a crucial ethical guideline. While truth signifies that a report is based on verifiable facts, accuracy further demands that a journalist meticulously verifies the veracity of those facts. This ethical imperative requires journalists to be precise in their daily duties and reporting, making accuracy an integral part of their professional lives as they report stories of public significance. News stories necessitate the diligent assembly and publication or broadcast of information that has been thoroughly fact-checked to ensure its factual correctness.

Importance of Accurate Reporting in Journalism

Accurate journalistic reporting fosters informed decision-making within media organizations and cultivates public trust. Conversely, the dissemination of inaccurate information in news stories, features, inquiries, or reports can lead to erroneous conclusions. The utilization of misinformation in the construction of content for publication or strategic marketing purposes carries a substantial risk of negative audience reception and detrimental outcomes, thereby compromising the fundamental 'ABCD of Journalism' principle of Accuracy.(Domenico and Visentin, 2020) Moreover, upholding accuracy is critical for maintaining journalistic integrity and ensuring that the public receives reliable information necessary for civic engagement and informed judgments (Shahid, 2023).

Elements of Accuracy in the News

Facts presented in a news item must be unequivocally true and factual, forming the bedrock of journalistic credibility. This stringent requirement means that every statement, name, date, age, quotation, and every definitive word, expression, or sentence must be precise and faithfully reflect reality without embellishment or distortion. Ethical journalism mandates the unwavering pursuit of truth and truthfulness, considering these as proto-norms essential for establishing trust among individuals, organizations, and institutions (Harro-Loit and Eberwein, 2023).

Accuracy and Standards for Factual Reporting : Events reported solely by a single eyewitness necessitate explicit attribution to that source. Conversely, information corroborated by two or more independent eyewitnesses may be presented as established facts. Disputed factual claims similarly require clear attribution to their respective sources.

To further ensure accuracy, independent verification by another employee of the publishing entity is highly recommended. This diligent approach minimizes misreporting, which can otherwise escalate social tensions, especially when complex issues like biodiversity loss or conflicts are involved (Borkar and Paul, 2023). Furthermore, the rapid dissemination of digital content and the influence of social media have exacerbated the challenge of maintaining accuracy, necessitating advanced verification tools to detect misinformation (Agunlejika, 2025).

Accuracy in Writing : Journalists are expected to possess strong linguistic proficiency, and their writing is therefore anticipated to meet high grammatical and stylistic standards. Accuracy in writing refers to the correctness and precision of the language used in written communication. This entails ensuring that the content is grammatically correct, utilizes appropriate vocabulary and spelling, and adheres to the rules of syntax and punctuation.

Independence

The ethical framework governing journalism necessitates that media professionals operate autonomously, unencumbered by external pressures. The preeminent duty of ethical journalism is to uphold and serve the public's interest. Operating independently requires journalists to adhere to the following principles:

1. **Mitigate Conflicts of Interest:** Journalists are obligated to prevent both actual and perceived conflicts of interest. Should unavoidable conflicts emerge, transparent disclosure is imperative.

2. **Decline Inducements and Undue Influence:** Media practitioners should refrain from accepting gifts, favors, fees, complimentary travel, and preferential treatment.

They must also abstain from political or other external activities that could compromise their integrity, impartiality, or professional credibility.

3. **Exercise Critical Scrutiny Regarding Remunerated Information:** Journalists ought to approach sources offering information in exchange for favors or financial compensation with skepticism and must never pay for access to news. Content originating from external providers, regardless of whether it is compensated, must be explicitly identified.

4. **Withstand Pressure:** Journalists must resist offering preferential treatment to advertisers, donors, or any other vested interests, and withstand internal and external pressures seeking to influence news coverage.

5. **Differentiate Editorial Content from Advertising:** It is crucial to clearly delineate editorial content from advertising material. Journalists should avoid hybrid formats that obscure these boundaries and ensure all sponsored content is prominently labeled

Challenges to Journalistic Independence

Journalistic independence has long been a paramount value, remaining one of the four core principles of the Society of Professional Journalist's Code of Ethics. However, the rapidly evolving media landscape presents numerous challenges to this traditional notion of independence. Today, numerous individuals and organizations operate within contexts that inherently compromise traditional impartiality. Examples include sports enthusiasts blogging about their favorite teams, "mommy bloggers" chronicling their family's lives, activists reporting on issues where they possess direct involvement, and journalists whose work is underwritten by specific companies or non-profit organizations. These scenarios fundamentally challenge the tenets of disinterest and objectivity. Consequently, individuals engaged in journalistic acts often grapple with categorizing their roles, vacillating between descriptors such as journalism, blogging, citizen journalism, or brand journalism. This definitional ambiguity underscores deeper ethical quandaries regarding accountability and transparency.

Crucially, this discussion does not aim to re-litigate past debates regarding the professional status of bloggers or to adjudicate emerging ambiguities between traditional journalism and public relations. Rather, its imperative is to critically examine the evolving role of independence within news organizations and to propose robust strategies for safeguarding journalistic integrity, especially in environments where strict independence may no longer be a viable or realistic aspiration.

Journalistic Independence Versus Involvement

The traditional business models that have historically sustained journalism are eroding, while digital tools have democratized publishing, making it accessible to virtually everyone. Consequently, individuals and organizations with direct involvement in the communities and issues they cover are increasingly engaging in journalistic practices. This often occurs to expand coverage in areas where they possess economic interests or personal passions. While some may argue that their expertise mitigates any drawbacks of their involvement, or that their passion and engagement offer unique knowledge and value that compensate for a lack of independence, these situations still warrant careful consideration.

Journalists and Politics

Many news organizations typically prohibit staff members from engaging in political activities beyond casting a vote, a measure primarily implemented to safeguard journalistic impartiality and maintain public trust in their reporting. Established ethical codes frequently proscribe various actions, such as seeking public office, volunteering for or contributing financially to political campaigns, addressing governmental bodies on policy matters, and even displaying campaign paraphernalia like yard signs, bumper stickers, or buttons on personal property or attire, all of which could compromise the perception of objectivity.

Journalists and Community Affairs

News organizations committed to upholding independence typically avoid heavily restricting staff involvement in community life. Their approach prioritizes managing potential conflicts effectively through a combination of thoughtful assignment allocation, transparent disclosure, and sound judgment, rather than outright prohibition.

Personal Passion

Contemporary journalistic practice frequently integrates factual reporting, analytical commentary, and personal narratives, particularly when addressing subjects of significant personal interest to the content creators. In these instances, the traditional emphasis on strict objectivity may be re-evaluated, as the journalist's passion and direct experience often contribute substantially to their expertise and content development. Nevertheless, transparent disclosure of these personal affiliations is crucial for audience comprehension.

Furthermore, core journalistic standards, such as accuracy and error correction, remain paramount, and personal involvement does not absolve practitioners from upholding these fundamental principles.

Combining Activism and Journalism

Niche organizations, ranging from neighborhood activist groups covering hyperlocal news to entities reporting on environmental, criminal justice, and social issues, are increasingly providing journalistic content and commentary in domains where they possess direct involvement. These organizations may include established activist groups that produce journalism to address information gaps or to exert influence, or they could be emergent journalistic startups that deliberately prioritize a degree of involvement over traditional notions of independence. The organizational structure of the news entity largely determines the extent to which editorial content can be insulated from funding sources. For instance, if an organization funds a newsletter or blog directly from its operational budget, achieving strict separation can be challenging and may appear disingenuous. In such scenarios, the emphasis should be on delivering high-quality journalism while transparently disclosing that funding originates from member contributions, donors, or other sources. Conversely, when activists initiate their own news operations, they must strategically consider mechanisms to safeguard editorial content from undue influence by funders, a concern frequently debated within broader media ethics discussions.

For these types of journalistic endeavors, comprehensive disclosure is often paramount. For example, a journalist residing in a specific neighborhood who refrains from membership or leadership roles in local groups offers a distinct perspective compared to one who serves as president of a homeowner's association.

Funding by an Interested Organization

The growing trend of companies and non-profit organizations establishing newsrooms to report on topics pertinent to their operations has forged a novel domain, merging conventional journalistic methodologies with public relations strategies (Comfort, 2020). This hybrid approach necessitates a comprehensive re-evaluation of established ethical frameworks, particularly concerning transparency and the inherent potential for conflicts of interest stemming from these organization's dual objectives. The emergence of such entities, including nascent venture-backed news organizations and philanthropic foundations supporting citizen journalists, introduces considerable complexities, as their foundational objectives and organizational paradigms can significantly influence editorial autonomy (Westlund, Krumsvik and Lewis, 2020). This issue is particularly acute for patient advocacy groups that disseminate health-related news, where potential financial entanglements with industry benefactors may compromise reporting integrity (Ehrlich et al., 2019). Consequently, it is imperative that editorial policies be revised to mandate comprehensive disclosure of funding sources, detailing the specific research stage to which funding is allocated, its nature, and its monetary value (Daou et al., 2018).

Journalistic Independence Versus Impartiality

While closely related, independence and impartiality are distinct journalistic values. Often, these two principles are pursued together, and many organizations define their stance on point-of-view and involvement alongside independence and impartiality. However, it is crucial to assess each value separately. An organization can, for example, adopt a point-of-view approach to journalism while still prioritizing independence over direct involvement. For instance, a news outlet might transparently commit to covering climate change issues with a clear preference for measures to combat it. Yet, it could still mandate that its staff members refrain from joining environmental groups, donating to environmental causes, or endorsing political candidates. Despite its acknowledged editorial position, the organization would maintain that such independence better equips its journalists to objectively evaluate the effectiveness of environmental groups, politicians, and other stakeholders.

Impartiality

Impartiality signifies the quality of being unbiased and unprejudiced, upholding a standard of fairness. It is a principle of justice dictating that decisions should be based on objective criteria, rather than being influenced by bias, prejudice, or improper favoritism. To be impartial means to approach a situation objectively, without a predetermined preference for any particular outcome. For example, jurors must demonstrate impartiality when reaching a verdict, preventing biases and preconceptions from influencing their judgment.

Example of the Principle of Impartiality

Achieving impartiality can be challenging, as it often requires setting aside personal egos and emotions. An extreme illustration of this principle would be a scenario where multiple individuals are injured in an attack; impartiality would suggest prioritizing aid for the combatant most in need of help, irrespective of their role in the conflict. Similarly, covering a story where an acquaintance, relative, or even the journalist themselves is indirectly involved demands unwavering impartiality.

Benefits of Impartiality : Media organizations and professionals greatly benefit from practicing impartiality, as it fosters fairness in decision-making processes, ensuring equitable treatment for all individuals and freedom from bias.

Impartiality also cultivates trust and credibility among stakeholders, demonstrating a commitment to ethical practices and transparency.

Fairness versus Impartiality : Fairness, in many contexts, can be understood as the appropriate application of impartiality, especially when evaluating concern for other's interests. In essence, fairness is a broader concept that can apply to systems, ideas, or individuals and their decisions (e.g., 'democracy provides fair outcomes,' or 'that's a fair decision'). It can denote equality or bear a meaning similar to impartiality. Impartiality, however, is more specific to judgments or decisions (one would typically not say 'capitalism is not an impartial system,' though 'fair' could apply). It implies consciously setting aside personal biases during a decision-making process, ensuring both sides receive a legitimate opportunity.

Humanity : The concept of humanity encompasses the entire human race, embodying the qualities that define us as human, such as the capacity for love and compassion. This idea underscores the inherent value of helping others. The dictionary defines humanity as all human beings collectively (the human race, humankind), and it also refers to the quality or condition of being human, including kindness and benevolence. To act humanely, journalists are expected to demonstrate compassion in their reporting, adhering to the fundamental principle of ·'do no harm'.

Humanity can be characterized by our unique capacity to feel, reason, evoke emotional responses, or form relationships. It also refers to compassion, benevolence, or the state of being human. C. G. Bowers noted that showing compassion for an enemy during a bloody struggle is an indication of humanity. The value of humanity mandates that journalists be kind, helpful, and empathetic towards others, irrespective of their differences or backgrounds.

Minimization of Harm

Often referred to as the 'Do No Harm' principle, ethical journalism strives to treat sources, subjects, colleagues, and members of the public as human beings deserving of respect. To minimize harm in their reporting, journalists must:

1. **Balance Information Needs with Potential Harm:** Weigh the public's need for information against the potential for harm or discomfort. The pursuit of news does not grant license for arrogance or undue intrusiveness.

2. **Show Compassion:** Exercise compassion for those who may be affected by news coverage. Employ heightened sensitivity when dealing with minors, victims of sex crimes, and sources or subjects who are inexperienced or unable to give consent. Consider cultural differences in approach and treatment.

3. **Distinguish Legal Access from Ethical Justification:** Recognize that legal access to information does not automatically confer ethical justification to publish or broadcast it.

4. **Protect Private Individuals:** Understand that private individuals possess a greater right to control information about themselves than public figures or those seeking power, influence, or attention. Carefully weigh the consequences of publishing or broadcasting personal information.

5. **Avoid Sensationalism:** Resist pandering to lurid curiosity, even if others do.

6. **Balance Rights:** Balance a suspect's right to a fair trial with the public's right to know. Consider the implications of identifying criminal suspects before formal charges are laid.

7. **Assess Long-Term Impact:** Consider the long-term implications of the extended reach and permanence of publication. Provide updated and more complete information as appropriate.

Accountability

In media ethics, accountability is synonymous with answerability, culpability, liability, and the expectation of providing explanations and taking responsibility for one's duties and reports. As a critical aspect of journalistic responsibility in reporting, accountability has been central to discussions concerning issues within the mass media sector, whether at the organizational or individual journalist level.

Accountability and Transparency

Ethical journalism inherently means taking responsibility for one's work and openly explaining decisions to the public. Journalists are therefore urged and obligated to act accountably and transparently as presented hereunder:

1. **Explain Ethical Choices:** Articulate ethical choices and processes to audiences, fostering a civil dialogue with the public about journalistic practices, coverage, and content.

2. **Respond Promptly:** Respond quickly to questions concerning accuracy, clarity, and fairness.

3. **Correct Mistakes:** Acknowledge and correct mistakes promptly and prominently. Explain corrections and clarifications carefully and clearly.

4. **Expose Unethical Conduct:** Expose unethical conduct within journalism, including within their own organizations.

5. **Uphold High Standards:** Adhere to the same high standards they expect of others.

Seeking and Reporting Truth

Ethical journalism must be accurate and fair. Journalists are expected to be honest and courageous in gathering, reporting, and interpreting information. The process of seeking and reporting the truth requires journalists to consistently:

1. **Take Responsibility for Accuracy:** Assume responsibility for the accuracy of their work. Verify information before releasing it, utilizing original sources whenever possible.

2. **Prioritize Accuracy Over Speed:** Remember that neither speed nor format excuses inaccuracy.

3. **Provide Context:** Offer sufficient context. Exercise special care not to misrepresent or oversimplify when promoting, previewing, or summarizing a story.

4. **Update Information:** Gather, update, and correct information throughout the lifespan of a news story.

5. **Keep Promises:** Be cautious when making promises but steadfast in keeping them.

6. **Identify Sources Clearly:** Identify sources clearly, providing the public with as much information as possible to judge their reliability and motivations.

7. **Evaluate Source Motives for Anonymity:** Carefully consider source's motives before promising anonymity. Reserve anonymity for sources who face danger, retribution, or other harm, and who possess information unobtainable elsewhere. Clearly explain why anonymity was granted.

8. **Seek Responses from Subjects:** Diligently seek out subjects of news coverage to allow them to respond to criticism or allegations of wrongdoing.

9. **Limit Undercover Methods:** Avoid undercover or other surreptitious methods of gathering information unless traditional, open methods will not yield information vital to the public.

10. **Hold Power Accountable:** Be vigilant and courageous in holding those in power accountable. Give voice to the voiceless.

11. **Support Open Exchange of Views:** Support the open and civil exchange of views, even those they find objectionable.

12. **Serve as Watchdogs:** Recognize a special obligation to serve as watchdogs over public affairs and government, striving to ensure that public business is conducted openly and that public records are accessible to all.

13. **Provide Access to Source Material:** Provide access to source material when it is relevant and appropriate.

14. **Portray Diverse Experiences:** Boldly tell the story of the diversity and magnitude of the human experience. Actively seek sources whose voices are seldom heard.

15. **Avoid Stereotyping:** Avoid stereotyping. Journalists should examine how their own values and experiences may shape their reporting.

16. **Label Advocacy and Commentary:** Clearly label advocacy and commentary.

17. **Never Distort:** Never deliberately distort facts or context, including visual information. Clearly label illustrations and re-enactments.

18. **Never Plagiarize:** Never plagiarize. Always attribute sources.

CHAPTER 12

Embedded Journalism

EMBEDDED JOURNALISM, ALSO KNOWN as Military journalism, encompasses the reporting and documentation of military operations and activities. Practitioners within this field typically operate under Public Affairs or Information Commands, with primary responsibilities including public information dissemination, fostering morale, and cultivating community relations within military contexts. Their work is directed towards both internal military audiences and external publics, with the strategic aim of managing public relations and defense communication for armed forces.

Embedded journalism describes a practice where war correspondents are integrated into military units during periods of armed conflict. While the underlying concept has historical precedents, the specific term gained prominence during media coverage of the 2003 invasion of Iraq. This strategy was adopted by the U.S. military in response to dissatisfaction expressed by domestic news organizations regarding the restricted access they experienced during the 1991 Gulf War and the 2001 U.S. invasion of Afghanistan.[1]

Journalists covering the war on the battlefield independently of any military force were known as 'unilateral'.

---

1. Center, Pew Research (2003-04-03). "Embedded Reporters". Pew Research Center's Journalism Project. Retrieved 2023-11-03.

They deliberately chose this approach to circumvent stringent military restrictions, such as those mandating embedded journalists to remain strictly with assigned units, thereby seeking unfettered access and greater editorial control. Crucially, many feared that constant protection and proximity to troops on the battlefield would inevitably bias their judgment, compromising objectivity toward coalition forces. Consequently, the military frequently viewed unilateral journalists with deep suspicion, considering them highly problematic on the battlefield. This often manifested in a refusal to communicate with them or to acknowledge their status as legitimate 'official' media, effectively marginalizing their presence and reporting. (Paul and Kim, 2005; Cover and Reid, 2010). An imbedded civilian journalist taking picture of American soldiers in Pana Afghanistan (Photo source: internet, http//en.wikipedia.org/

An imbedded civilian journalist taking picture of American soldiers in Pana Afghanistan (Photo source: internet, http//en.wikipedia.org/

The methodology faces significant critique due to its perceived role in propaganda, with embedded journalists accompanying military operations frequently portrayed as de facto advocates or public relations representatives for military forces.[2] During the initial phase of the 2003 Iraq War, an estimated 775 journalists, comprising reporters and photographers, were embedded with US military units. These media professionals entered into contractual agreements with US military authorities, stipulating that they would refrain from disseminating information deemed sensitive, such as troop positions, future operational plans, or classified weaponry. While this unparalleled integration of media personnel into military operations offered immediate access to frontline experiences, it simultaneously sparked intense debate, raising significant concerns about potential biased reporting, compromised journalistic objectivity, and the implicit censorship of critical information (Mooney, 2004).[3] Joint training for war correspondents started in November 2002 in advance of start of the war.[4] When asked why the military decided to embed journalists with the troops, Lt. Col. Rick Long of the U.S. Marine Corps replied, *"Frankly, our job is to win the war. Part of that is information warfare. So, we are going to attempt to dominate the information environment."*[5]

---

2. Cockburn, Patrick (23 November 2010). "Embedded journalism: A distorted view of war". The Independent. Retrieved 3 September 2020.

3. Pros and Cons of Embedded Journalism. PBS. Archived from the original on 2003-04-21.

4. Borger, Julian (1 November 2002). "Flabby journalists sent to boot camp". The Guardian – via www.theguardian.com

5. Postmortem: Iraq war media coverage both dazzled and obscured. (www.berkeley.edu).

Military Media Censorship

Military media censorship was starkly evident during the initial phase of South Sudan's first civil war in early 2014. A significant incident highlighted this censorship: during a press briefing with spokespersons from the SPLA and the Presidential office, Al Jazeera journalist Mohammed Adow was officially declared 'persona non grata' This action directly resulted from his report that rebel forces were positioned approximately fifteen miles from Juba, the capital of the Republic of South Sudan. Ethically, journalistic reports on military setbacks that are not officially acknowledged by armed forces are generally considered inappropriate. Furthermore, disseminating specific details about operational strategies, troop deployments, or armament is typically deemed impermissible for the media during such periods. While belligerent parties often rationalize this stringent information control as indispensable for national security, it can paradoxically transform ethical codes for wartime journalists into instruments of political communication, rather than remaining mere instructional guidelines (Serrano, 2014). This inherent tension between ethical journalistic practice and state-imposed censorship is further complicated by the evolving professional roles of journalists in conflict zones. These journalists are often compelled to acquire new technical proficiencies while simultaneously facing potential targeting by combatants (Blum, 2024).[6]

---

6. In a press briefing by Col. Philip Aguer Panyang the then Sudan People's Liberation Army's (SPLA) Spokesperson, and Hon. Ateny Wek Ateny the then presidential spokesperson conducted at the office of the president at the Ministries' Complex, Juba, The Republic of South Sudan in January 2014.

In 2003, Philip Smucker, an independent correspondent for *The Christian Science Monitor* accompanying the 1st Marine Division, became the first journalist to contravene U.S. military guidelines in Iraq, marking the United States' initial disciplinary action against media personnel for violating military reporting regulations. This incident occurred within the context of the Pentagon's newly instituted embedding program for Operation Iraqi Freedom, which, while providing journalists direct access to military units, also imposed stringent rules to maintain operational security and control information flow (Mooney, 2004; Clonan, 2008; Lindner, 2009). Although not officially embedded, all reporters in the operational theater were subject to Pentagon oversight, reflecting the military's robust information control strategies during the conflict (Eilders, 2005). His unauthorized disclosure of a Marine unit's location during a CNN interview on March 26, 2003, constituted a direct contravention of these critical guidelines designed to protect troop movements and safety, resulting in his immediate expulsion. This expulsion underscored the inherent tension between journalistic independence and military information control, highlighting the challenges faced by war correspondents operating under such restrictive conditions[7] (Lindner, 2009) (Mooney, 2004).

Four days after this, Fox News Channel correspondent Geraldo Rivera compromised operational security by publicly disclosing sensitive information regarding U.S. troop deployments and future tactical objectives from Iraq. During a televised segment, Rivera explicitly detailed troop movements, stating, *"Let me draw a few lines here for you. First, I want to make some emphasis here that these hash marks here, this is us. We own that territory.*

---

7. Silha Center: University of Minnesota. www.silha.umn.edu.

It's 40%, maybe even a little more than that." A CENTCOM[8] spokesperson later criticized Rivera's actions, specifically noting that he 'actually revealed the time of an attack prior to its occurrence,' which constituted a severe compromise of military operations. Consistent with the case of Philip Smucker, Rivera operated without official embed status and was consequently removed from the operational theater and repatriated to Kuwait[9]. This incident underscored the critical importance of information control in wartime and the potential risks posed by unauthorized journalistic activities (Eilders, 2005).

A week later, Rivera apologized. *"I'm sorry that it happened,"* he said on Fox News Channel, *"and I assure you that it was inadvertent. Nobody was hurt by what I said. No mission was compromised."* However, a network review, he admitted, *"showed that I did indeed break one of the rules related to embedment."*[10]

In December 2005, the U.S. Coalition Forces Land Component Command in Kuwait rescinded the accreditation of two embedded journalists affiliated with the Virginian-Pilot newspaper. This action, impacting a two-week assignment, stemmed from their purported contravention of a directive prohibiting the photographic

---

8. The United States Central Command is one of the eleven unified combatant commands of the U.S. Department of Defense. It was established in 1983, taking over the previous responsibilities of the Rapid Deployment Joint Task Force. Its area of responsibility includes the Middle East, Central Asia and parts of South Asia.

9. Carr, David (1 April 2003). "A NATION AT WAR: COVERAGE; Pentagon Says Geraldo Rivera Will Be Removed from Iraq". The New York Times.

10. Direct quotation of the apology by Journalists Geraldo Revira to the US People and the Army: I Messed Up, but 'Nobody Was Hurt"

documentation of damaged military assets.[11] Such incidents highlight ongoing tensions in military-media relations, where journalistic access is often contingent on adherence to military-imposed restrictions on information dissemination and visual content (Brandenburg, 2007; Clonan, 2008).

Ethics of Embedded Journalism

The ethics of embedded journalism are considered controversial.[12] The practice has been criticized as being part of a propaganda campaign and an effort to keep reporters away from civilian populations and sympathetic to invading forces; for example, by the documentary films *War Made Easy: How Presidents & Pundits Keep Spinning us to Death* and *The War You Don't See.*

Embed critics objected that the level of military oversight is too strict and that embedded journalists would make reports that were too sympathetic to the side they are travelling with during the war, leading to use of the alternate term 'imbedded journalist,' or 'imbeds'. *"Such correspondents drive around in armored military tanks and armored personnel carriers,"* said journalist Gay Talese in an interview, *"who are spoon-fed what the military gives them, and they become mascots for the military, these journalists. I wouldn't have journalists embedded if I had any power! There are stories you can do that aren't done. I've said that many times.[13] "*

---

11. "MRE Criticizes Expelling of Embeds Over Pix of Shot-Up Humvee – Editor & Publisher". www.editorandpublisher.com. 15 December 2005.

12. Knightley, Phillip. The First Casualty, 1975. p. 333

13. Interview with Gay Talese, David Shankbone, Wikinews, October 27, 2007.

On June 14, 2014, The New York Times published an opinion piece critical of embedded journalism during both the U.S. military occupation of Iraq and the war in Afghanistan. It was written by PVT Chelsea Manning, the former U.S. Army intelligence analyst known for leaking the largest set of classified documents in American history. At no point during her 2009–10 deployment in Iraq, Manning noted, were there more than a dozen American journalists covering military operations in a country of 31 million people and 117,000 U.S. troops.

She charged that the military deliberately vetted reporters to screen out those judged likely to produce critical coverage, leading embedded journalists to avoid controversial reporting that could raise red flags for fear of losing access.

This deliberate control, Manning contended, ultimately gutted the American public's access to unfiltered facts, hindering their ability to adequately evaluate the conduct of American officials. Manning further illustrated the military's institutional control by citing a 2013 court challenge by freelance reporter Wayne Anderson.

Anderson, terminated after publishing adverse reports despite claiming adherence to his agreement, saw the ruling uphold the military's stance that there is no constitutionally protected right to be an embedded journalist. This legal precedent effectively legitimizes the military's power to dictate terms of access and reporting, affirming the control Manning critiqued.

Even Gina Cavallaro, a reporter for the Army Times, inadvertently supported this critique, observing that journalists' increased reliance on the military for access meant the military is getting smarter about getting its own story told.

While Cavallaro qualified her statement by adding, "*I don't necessarily consider that a bad thing,*" her observation nonetheless affirmed the military's strategic cultivation of its own narrative through embedded programs, echoing Manning's concerns about information control.[14]

Embedded journalism often lacks ethical independence, as military directives dictate operations. This frequently creates conflict with journalists' desire to uphold their values and ethics, often resulting in their expulsion. This inherent conflict underscores the challenge of maintaining journalistic independence while operating within a framework designed to control information dissemination (Brandenburg, 2007).

---

14. Embed Cavallaro sees war from the inside". 6 April 2005. Archived from the original on 6 April 2005.

CHAPTER 13

Unethical and Illegitimate Journalism

A FUNDAMENTAL UNDERSTANDING OF unethical and illegitimate journalistic practices begins with recognizing the bedrock principles that underpin credible reporting, including truth,' 'accuracy,' and 'objectivity.' These are not merely abstract ideals; they are the indispensable cornerstones upon which public trust, the integrity of information, and ultimately, a functioning democracy depends. Journalists are critically enjoined to maintain an unwavering detachment from all personal affiliations whether religious, social, or national and from acquaintances. This imperative detachment is paramount for effectively mitigating inherent biases that could irrevocably compromise the impartiality and fidelity of their reporting. Consequently, any failure to rigorously adhere to the core values of truth, accuracy, objectivity, and accountability inevitably and severely erodes journalistic integrity, culminating in practices that are not only unethical and illegitimate but profoundly detrimental to informed public discourse and the very fabric of democratic processes.

Misinformation

Misinformation is characterized as information that is erroneous or deceptive, disseminated without the express purpose of misleading. This category includes data that is factually incorrect, incomplete, or conveyed through partial or selective truths, thereby differentiating it from disinformation, which involves the intentional spread of false information to deceive. While misinformation is typically an "honest mistake," its impact nonetheless remains profoundly significant, actively shaping public perception and frequently leading to undesirable outcomes.(Zeng and Brennen, 2023).

Disinformation

Disinformation, defined as the deliberate dissemination of false information with the explicit intent to deceive, represents a concerted and adversarial effort. It involves actors employing sophisticated strategic deceptions and manipulative media tactics to advance specific political, military, or commercial objectives. This deliberate creation and spread of falsehoods can manifest in various forms, including fabricated news, conspiracy theories, propaganda, and manipulated media such as deepfake videos (Nault and Ruhi, 2023).

Misinformation Versus Disinformation: The Key Distinction

The critical distinction between misinformation and disinformation lies in the intent behind their dissemination, as misinformation typically lacks a malicious objective, whereas disinformation is purposefully crafted to mislead (Gondwe, 2025).

A common question is: what is the difference between misinformation and disinformation? While they sound similar, a key distinction exists: Disinformation involves the intentional practice of providing information that has been deliberately falsified. Misinformation, conversely, is the practice of communicating false or inaccurate information, regardless of any intention to deceive. However, both misinformation and disinformation can manifest through various forms of hoaxing or scamming.

The primary difference between misinformation and disinformation is **intentionality** (Søe, 2016; Calo et al., 2021; Hameleers, 2022; Bastos and Tuters, 2023; Jahn, 2023; López, Pastor-Galindo and Ruipérez-Valiente, 2024).

Feature	Misinformation	Disinformation
Intent	Unintentional; no deliberate intent to deceive or harm	Intentional; deliberately created and spread to deceive or manipulate
Origin	Can arise from error, misunderstanding, or negligence	Orchestrated, strategic, and often for specific objectives (political, financial)
Accuracy	False, inaccurate, misleading, incomplete, or partial truth	False, manipulated, or fabricated
Examples	Sharing an incorrect news article without checking, accidental factual errors	Propaganda, fabricated stories to advance political goals, hoaxes (Puska, Baroni and Pereira, 2024)

While the intent differentiates them, some academic discussions use "misinformation" as an umbrella term for any false information, including that which is intentionally spread, because the psychological and cognitive consequences can be similar regardless of intent (Pantazi, Hale and Klein, 2021; Altay et al., 2023; Lasser et al., 2023). However, it's crucial for analysis and mitigation strategies to acknowledge the underlying intent.

Information Disorder

Beyond misinformation and disinformation, the complex landscape of false information encompasses several other related terms, each with distinct characteristics and implications. To adequately address the pervasive challenges posed by these phenomena, this broader context is often referred to as "information disorder," a comprehensive framework that acknowledges the multifaceted nature of problematic information flows in contemporary digital environments. This broader framework includes concepts such as mal-information, which refers to truthful information shared with malicious intent to cause harm, and fake news, often characterized by its sensationalist nature and fabricated content.

Lying

Whether in digital, print, or broadcast media, journalists are not permitted to publish information that is wholly or partially untrue. Such actions are considered unethical and erode public trust in the media.

A notable instance involves Brian Williams, a former NBC Nightly News anchor, who falsely claimed during a broadcast that he was a passenger on a helicopter hit by a rocket-propelled grenade in Iraq in 2003. In 2015, NBC suspended him for six months without pay, significantly impacting his career.

While adherence to ethical principles can be challenging, there is no ethical alternative to upholding impartiality, objectivity, balance, guarding against bias, respecting privacy, and consistently prioritizing the public interest. Media organizations can only gain and maintain credibility by consistently publishing and broadcasting the truth.

Fake News

This contemporary term gained prominence, notably used by the American President Donald J. Trump, to describe media outlets that published information critical of him without, in his view, adequately presenting his perspective, contrary to journalistic codes of ethics and conduct. 'Fake news, 'or information disorder, refers to false or misleading information presented as news, often with the deliberate aim of damaging an individual's or entity's reputation. The question arises whether prominent media organizations like the BBC, CNN, or NBC might ever engage in unethical practices.

Indeed, such situations can occur if editors, for any reason, decide to introduce bias, leading to inaccurate reports and other ethical transgressions. Fake news is characterized as information deliberately constructed to emulate conventional journalistic outputs, with the express purpose of misleading recipients. This intentional replication, coupled with an inherent absence of established organizational protocols and adherence to editorial standards, erodes public confidence and intrinsically compromises the accuracy and credibility of the content, thereby facilitating its deceptive efficacy (Lazer et al., 2018; Jahn, 2023). Furthermore, these manufactured narratives often exploit emotional appeals and cognitive predispositions to accelerate their dissemination and firmly embed their erroneous propositions within societal discourse (Antunes et al., 2023).

Mal-information

Mal-information is characterized by the presentation of factually accurate information in a distorted or decontextualized manner, with the explicit intent to inflict harm, manipulate judgment, erode trust, or incite discord (Tomassi, Falegnami and Romano, 2024). This process involves the strategic instrumentalization of truthful, yet sensitive, information, often through its decontextualization, selective emphasis, or the exploitation of emotional vulnerabilities, to achieve a specific, frequently detrimental, agenda (Calo et al., 2021).

Impact and Consequences

The insidious proliferation of misinformation, disinformation, and mal-information carries far-reaching and detrimental societal implications, fundamentally eroding democratic processes and destabilizing public health initiatives. Regardless of intent, the widespread dissemination of false information poses an urgent and complex challenge in the digital age, demanding concerted attention.

The pervasive manipulation of information ecosystems, encompassing both deliberate disinformation and unintentional misinformation, as well as mal-information, precipitates profound and multifaceted adverse implications for individual well-being, democratic processes, and collective societal functionality (Kauk et al., 2024).

Societal Harm : Both misinformation and disinformation exert profound and widespread influences on individuals, communities, and broader society (Tomassi, Falegnami and Romano, 2024).

Specifically, misinformation contributes to the formation of detrimental misconceptions concerning real-world events, thereby significantly shaping individual behaviors and decisions, which can precipitate extensive and often irreversible societal repercussions (Puska, Baroni and Pereira, 2024).

Threat to Democracy : Disinformation represents a significant and subtle peril to democratic systems, as it actively corrupts public discourse, exacerbates societal polarization, fragments collective consensus, and systematically undermines confidence in governmental bodies, electoral procedures, and verifiable information, thereby impeding judicious civic participation (Schaewitz et al., 2020).

Disinformation campaigns, characterized by the deliberate fabrication and widespread dissemination of false narratives, aggressively seek to undermine political processes, coercively shape public opinion, and critically erode the foundational trust indispensable for a robust and functioning democracy (Mouratidis, Kanavos and Kermanidis, 2025).

Economic and Health Risks : The pervasive dissemination of misinformation, disinformation, and mal-information poses an existential threat to economic stability, manifesting as market volatility, consumer panic, and significant financial losses, and engenders devastating public health emergencies, strikingly exemplified by the perilous rise of vaccine skepticism (Puska, Baroni and Pereira, 2024).

For instance, during the unprecedented COVID-19 pandemic, the torrent of misleading narratives catastrophically undermined public health and safety by inciting populations to defy essential scientific guidelines and adopt perilous behaviors (Zhang et al., 2023). This phenomenon profoundly compromised critical health choices, from vaccination adherence to nutritional practices, directly contributing to severe public health crises and exacerbating societal vulnerabilities (Kauk et al., 2024).

Erosion of Trust : The relentless proliferation of false information precipitates a profound and perilous erosion of public trust across institutions, media, and interpersonal communication (Ripoll and Matos, 2020). Such a systemic breakdown in credibility not only severely compromises collective decision-making but also engenders an environment of profound skepticism, thereby hindering the public's capacity to discern verifiable information. Exacerbating this challenge, the blurring distinctions among journalism, advertising, and entertainment critically impede the public's ability to distinguish factual reporting from deceptive narratives (Jaidka et al., 2024).

A comprehensive understanding of these concepts and their critical distinctions is imperative for effectively navigating the contemporary information environment and for developing robust strategies to mitigate their pervasive societal harms and safeguard democratic processes (Calo et al., 2021). The growing sophistication of misinformation techniques, particularly with the advent of advanced generative artificial intelligence models, renders this understanding even more critical. These AI models are capable of producing highly convincing and scalable deceptive content, thereby further blurring the distinction between fact and fiction and accelerating the erosion of public trust (Ferrara, 2024). The capacity of artificial intelligence to produce deceptive or synthetic content, frequently referred to as "hallucinations," presents a substantial obstacle to maintaining information integrity (Bhatti, 2025).

Hoaxing : A hoax is a form of disinformation, representing a deliberate act of deception where false information is intentionally shared to mislead and trick others into believing something untrue. Hoaxes are fabricated stories that masquerade as truth, meticulously designed to convince an audience of a falsehood (Rahmanian, 2022). These deliberate untruths are concocted to appear genuine, often with the explicit intention to deceive and exploit cognitive biases and emotional responses, thereby making individuals susceptible to manipulation (Zubiaga and Jiang, 2020; Aissing, 2024). While they can manifest in various forms, such as fabricated news stories or deceptive messages, hoaxes are typically complex fabrications that extend beyond simple pranks, capable of causing significant societal disruption. Their impact can range from shaping public opinion and undermining trust in institutions to disrupting democratic processes and influencing critical events like elections and public health crises (Rahmanian, 2022; Aissing, 2024; Surjatmodjo et al., 2024). Hoaxing primarily manifests in four key ways: fabricated or false news, viral messaging, deep-faking, and memes.

Fabricated or False News : Fabricated or false news, often broadly termed 'fake news,' consists of stories presented as current events designed to deceive (Berrondo-Otermin and Cabezuelo, 2023).

Specifically, fabricated news lacks any factual basis, yet it is meticulously crafted to mimic the style and structure of credible journalistic content, thereby creating an illusion of legitimacy (Rahmanian, 2022). Crucially, unlike parody, there is no implied understanding between the creator and the audience that the information is fictional; instead, the intent is deliberate deception (Rahmanian, 2022). These inaccurate narratives are often produced to achieve monetary gain or political advantage, effectively replicating the form of news media but entirely devoid of its organizational processes or ethical intent (Rahmanian, 2022; Alghamdi, Luo and Lin, 2023). This intentional presentation of false or misleading information, sometimes incorporating doctored images or legitimate news taken out of context, aims to influence public opinion, generate clicks, or outright deceive (Berrondo-Otermin and Cabezuelo, 2023). Such deliberate manipulation is particularly effective because it frequently exploits individuals' cognitive biases and emotional responses, increasing their susceptibility to believing and subsequently disseminating these false narratives (Aissing, 2024), thereby making them highly effective tools for influencing public opinion.

Viral Messaging : False information can disseminate rapidly across messaging platforms such as WhatsApp and Messenger. Such information gains increased credibility when propagated by trusted individuals. The intrinsic openness of social media, facilitating the unrestricted dissemination of unverified content, renders these platforms highly susceptible to the rapid propagation of false information via fraudulent accounts and malicious campaigns, often augmented by automated software programs (Akhtar et al., 2023). Messaging platforms, particularly WhatsApp, with their public group functionalities and forwarding mechanisms, have emerged as pivotal channels for the proliferation of misinformation campaigns, leading to the implementation of countermeasures like restrictions on simultaneous message forwards and the identification of viral content (Melo et al., 2024). Analogously, fringe communities operating on platforms such as Telegram exploit these channels for swift information propagation, encompassing the distribution of false content (Hoseini et al., 2024). The dissemination of false rumors frequently exhibits characteristics of herding behavior, wherein misinformation expands through deeper cascades, thereby influencing collective behavior rather than fostering collective intelligence (Pröllochs and Feuerriegel, 2023).

Deep-faking : Deepfaking entails the manipulation of video content to falsely depict individuals engaging in actions or uttering statements they did not perform or articulate. These synthetic media are autonomously generated by machine-learning systems, marking a significant advancement in the manipulation of reality (Farid, 2022). Essentially, deepfakes constitute digitally altered synthetic media portraying individuals undertaking actions or making statements that lack any real-world basis (Mustak et al., 2022). Their creation relies on generative artificial intelligence tools, leveraging machine learning and complex multi-layered neural networks (Lundberg and Mozelius, 2024). The escalating realism and accessibility of deepfake content frequently impedes individuals' ability to identify manipulated media, thereby facilitating numerous scams and deceptive practices (Croitoru et al., 2024). Although initially conceived for entertainment purposes, deepfakes have progressively transformed into instruments for propagating misinformation, engaging in blackmail, perpetrating fraud, and orchestrating political manipulation, notably exemplified by fabricated videos of global leaders (Singh, 2025). A prominent example includes a deepfake video of Ukrainian President Volodymyr Zelenskyy, which emerged in early 2022, purportedly urging his country's surrender (Cavedon-Taylor, 2024). Consequently, deepfakes present substantial risks, encompassing the manipulation of public opinion, exacerbation of geopolitical tensions, destabilization of financial markets, various forms of scams, defamation, and identity theft (Gambín et al., 2024).

Memes : Memes, conceptualized as self-replicating units of cultural information, possess the capacity to disseminate unverified assertions. Internet memes have emerged as pervasive instruments of communication, frequently comprising visual elements augmented by textual content (Alam et al., 2024).

Although their primary function often pertains to comedic expression, memes are also capable of subtly transmitting persuasive narratives or potentially deceptive content to their recipients (Alam et al., 2024). Furthermore, they serve as potent conduits for the propagation of propaganda and unsubstantiated information (Alam et al., 2024). Empirical studies indicate that memes exert an influence on the subsequent dissemination of misinformation, exemplified by instances related to vaccine hesitancy (Kapoor and Behl, 2024). The digital landscape is frequently saturated with memes and other forms of entertaining content, which can occasionally eclipse the prevalence of factual news or even overt misinformation, thereby underscoring their substantial contribution to online discourse (Altay, Berriche and Acerbi, 2021). The rapid dissemination of hoaxes is often attributed to the inherent difficulty in discerning their deceptive nature. The sophisticated characteristics of numerous hoaxes, exemplified by deepfakes generating highly realistic synthetic media (Mustak et al., 2022; Croitoru et al., 2024) and fabricated news emulating credible journalistic forms (Rahmanian, 2022), render their differentiation from factual information particularly challenging. Moreover, social media platforms significantly contribute to their propagation by facilitating swift dissemination, wherein unverified messages readily spread via viral communication and established networks (Akhtar et al., 2023; Melo et al., 2024). Individuals may consume content they perceive as truthful, particularly when it originates from trusted sources or is presented in compelling formats such as memes conveying persuasive narratives, leading to subsequent re-sharing. Such swift and frequently uncritical sharing substantially extends the reach of hoaxes, escalating isolated deceptions into extensive misinformation campaigns, thereby posing a significant threat to information integrity (Surjatmodjo et al., 2024; Wu et al., 2024).[1]

Media Scamming : Online scams involve perpetrators leveraging digital platforms to coerce individuals into revealing confidential data, including login credentials or financial specifics, or to exploit their trust and susceptibilities for unlawful profit. Distinguished from hoaxing, which predominantly involves deception via misinformation, scamming encompasses a wider spectrum of fraudulent endeavors. These commonly present in five main categories: phishing, deceptive advertising, catfishing, fraudulent competitions/quizzes, and identity theft, all predominantly aimed at achieving financial enrichment or personal exploitation (Kipngetich, 2025). The widespread expansion of the digital era has not only reshaped social and commercial engagements but has simultaneously created an environment conducive to a significant rise in online scams and financial fraudulent activities, thereby posing considerable difficulties for individuals, entities, and financial establishments alike (Kipngetich, 2025).

Phishing : Phishing, a form of cybercrime, involves perpetrators disseminating electronic communications, such as messages or emails, to individuals' personal devices. These communications are meticulously crafted to appear credible, frequently impersonating reputable organizations or businesses, with the deceitful intention of acquiring sensitive information or engaging in blackmail (Ghazi-Tehrani and Pontell, 2021). Such attacks skillfully exploit principles of human psychology, employing social engineering tactics to compel victims into divulging confidential data or executing actions that compromise their security (Schmitt and Fléchais, 2024).

---

1. If you see something that concerns or confuses you, it's important to not share it further as this can help draw more attention to them. Instead report to the app, game, or site that you've seen it on. https://www.nspcc.org.uk/

These deceptive practices are a pervasive threat within the broader landscape of online financial fraud, which encompasses a diverse array of schemes, including identity theft, online payment fraud, and cryptocurrency-related scams (Kipngetich, 2025).

The nature of phishing has progressed significantly, transforming from widespread, unsophisticated endeavors into advanced attacks, including spear phishing, which are specifically aimed at high-value targets (Ghazi-Tehrani and Pontell, 2021).

The principal aims of these illicit activities encompass the infiltration of devices with malware, the illicit acquisition of sensitive personal data, the unauthorized takeover of digital accounts, and the direct inducement of financial transactions from the victims.

Extensive phishing operations illustrate the dual exploitation of technological weaknesses and human behavioral characteristics by attackers, thereby highlighting the complex methodologies utilized and the psychological elements contributing to victim susceptibility (Chrysanthou, Pantis and Patsakis, 2023).

These schemes often leverage principles of human psychology and complex methodologies, employing sophisticated social engineering tactics to coerce victims into trusting fraudulent communications and revealing confidential data. This ultimately leads to detrimental outcomes such as device infiltration with malware, illicit acquisition of sensitive personal data, unauthorized takeover of digital accounts, or direct inducement of financial transactions from the victims (Schmitt and Fléchais, 2024).

False Advertising : False advertising, also known as the promotion of products with untrue claims, involves publishing or circulating advertisements with intentionally false statements to promote the sale of property, goods, or services. This can include fake competitions or products claiming capabilities they lack, often leading to negative experiences for online consumers.

In the digital era, false advertising has become a critical issue impacting consumer purchasing behavior online, as some businesses incorporate deceptive practices into their marketing strategies (Ahmed and Othman, 2024a, 2024b). These deceptive strategies often involve unethical advertising, misleading information, and outright deception (Ahmed and Othman, 2024). Firms may use false or misleading claims to exaggerate product benefits, sometimes even employing tactics where truth is used to tell lies by omitting crucial details. For instance, a mobile phone manufacturer might display professional photographs to showcase its camera's quality without disclosing that these were taken by professional photographers using specialized equipment (Wu and Geylani, 2020). Regulating deceptive advertising is an ongoing challenge for consumer protection (Zulham, 2023). Debunking messages from regulators, media, or competing firms can reduce the impact of misinformation in advertising, either by changing consumer misbeliefs or reinforcing correct ones (Fong, Guo and Rao, 2021). Crucially, the effectiveness of such debunking messages is profoundly influenced by critical factors such as source credibility, the framing of the message, and the cognitive biases inherent in the target audience.

Catfishing : Catfishing entails the creation of a fictitious persona by an individual, leveraging another person's personal data and imagery, sometimes even fabricating a complete identity inclusive of visual representation, birthdate, and geographic location, to manipulate others.

This form of online deceit involves the perpetrator assuming an identity that is not their own (Ryan and Taylor, 2024), distinguishing it from mere impersonation by its explicit aim to cultivate an online relationship with the victim (Lauder and March, 2022).

The motivations for catfishing are diverse, encompassing desires for amusement, the presentation of an idealized self, the pursuit of meaningful interactions, or financial exploitation (Ryan and Taylor, 2024). Victims frequently experience a spectrum of emotional responses, including distrust, affection, despair, indignation, shame, and feelings of foolishness (Ryan and Taylor, 2024). Although certain jurisdictions have legislative frameworks addressing online fraud and the unauthorized use of fabricated identities, the identification of catfishing perpetrators and the enforcement of these statutes remain challenging due to their deliberate efforts to obscure their true identities in the digital realm (Hasibuan and Syam, 2023). A contemporary development, termed the "cyber-industrialization of catfishing and romance fraud," underscores the increasing organizational sophistication of these scams through established business models and software platforms (Wang and Topalli, 2024).

Competitions or Quizzing Scams : These scams leverage the allure of significant rewards, luring individuals with promises of valuable prizes or substantial monetary gains. The Internet's inherent characteristics—low communication costs, global reach, and functional anonymity—have allowed such online schemes to proliferate and escalate dramatically, facilitating the swindling of vast sums from victims (Liu et al., 2024). A prominent example is cryptocurrency giveaway scams, which deceitfully persuade victims to make irreversible fund transfers under the false pretense of receiving even greater returns (Liu et al., 2024). Beyond direct financial scams, the 'quizzing' aspect can also manifest as fraudulent participation in online qualitative studies, where individuals provide intentionally false responses for monetary incentives, thereby compromising data quality and research integrity (Mistry et al., 2024). The emergence and widespread accessibility of generative AI tools, such as voice cloning and high-fidelity image manipulation, further exacerbate these threats by making scams far more sophisticated, believable, and challenging for victims to discern, significantly increasing the likelihood of successful victimization (Houtti et al., 2024).

Identity Theft : Identity theft involves deceiving individuals into divulging personal information, which is subsequently exploited for unauthorized access to social media or other accounts. More precisely, online identity theft constitutes a widespread crime where perpetrators intentionally utilize another person's account, primarily to secure financial advantages, obtain credit, or acquire other benefits (Wang, Zhu and Yang, 2021). This criminal activity is pervasive within the digital sphere, and although emerging AI technologies have significantly accelerated its speed and expanded its scale, they also present novel opportunities for detection and prevention (Gorichanaz, 2025).

As personally identifiable information becomes increasingly valuable for malicious actors, victimization rates from identity theft continue to escalate (Kayser, Back and Toro-Alvarez, 2024). Cybercriminals employ diverse tactics to compromise accounts, turning them into gateways for further illicit activities such as blackmail, fraud, and spam. Academic research, frequently drawing upon theories like Routine Activity Theory, delves into the factors influencing both victimization and the fear associated with online identity theft (Guedes, Martins and Cardoso, 2022). The repercussions of identity theft are far-reaching, extending beyond monetary losses to include substantial cybersecurity threats and a critical demand for enhanced real-time online identity authentication (Virmani, 2020; Wang, Zhu and Yang, 2021).

The imperative for advanced authentication mechanisms is underscored by the escalating sophistication of contemporary online fraud, which increasingly exploits artificial intelligence to fabricate highly realistic deceptive content and to amplify the scale of malicious activities (Houtti et al., 2024; Gorichanaz, 2025).

These five forms of media scamming underscore the increasingly sophisticated and diverse tactics criminals employ, leveraging both technological vulnerabilities and human psychology to exploit online users. As digital interactions become inextricably linked to daily life, a comprehensive understanding of these evolving schemes is paramount for safeguarding personal information and financial well-being. The rapid advancements in tools like generative AI and the industrialization of fraudulent operations (Houtti et al., 2024; Wang and Topalli, 2024) accelerate the pace and scale of online fraud (Gorichanaz, 2025), necessitating not only ongoing vigilance but also highly adaptive and proactive security measures to effectively protect individuals and institutions from severe financial and psychological harm (Kipngetich, 2025).

Inaccuracy : The dissemination of false or misleading information, whether unintentional or deliberate, constitutes a significant hallmark of unethical journalistic practices. Such inaccuracies may manifest as factual errors, misquotations, or erroneous statistical data. A particularly egregious instance of inaccuracy, and a profound violation of international journalistic ethics and professional standards, involves the publication of a photograph depicting an individual unrelated to the subject matter of the accompanying report. This misrepresentation, whether accidental or intentional, undermines the credibility of the publication and distorts public perception (Fiki and Idi, 2025).

Unethical Communication : Ethical communication seeks and shares truth, whether partial or complete, striving for balance if not complete unbiasedness. Unethical communication cultivates ignorance or prejudice, exploits the audience through misinformation, or silences relevant matters. Unethical communication consists of six forms: coercion, destructiveness, deceptiveness, intrusiveness, secretiveness, and manipulation. Engaging in any of these forms constitutes unethical behavior. If a media house commits such unethical acts, it could lead to the withdrawal of accreditation by a government. This could also result in significant financial penalties and a severe loss of public trust, potentially jeopardizing the media entity's operational viability and reputation (Rahman, 2023).

Media Censorship

Censorship, as delineated by a media and communication dictionary, pertains to any system or environment wherein publicly disseminated content whether expressed, exhibited, published, broadcast, or distributed is subjected to deliberate restriction, suppression, or control. This systematic control over the circulation of information is often exercised through prior restraint, post-publication penalties, or gatekeeping mechanisms. At a national level, the stated rationales for such control frequently involve political stability, moral order, social cohesion, or religious doctrine.[2] These directives often aim to shape public opinion, limit dissent, or preserve specific societal norms, with some measures primarily serving to preclude public embarrassment or protect the ruling establishment (Real and Menjívar, 2024).

Censorship can be defined as a regulatory system designed to vet, edit, and prohibit certain forms of public expression.

---

2. The National security Services of the Republic of South Sudan removes articles of interests from News Papers and sometimes newspapers sell with a missing cutout page/s. (Author's Notes and public obervation).

This process is overseen by a censor, an official mandated by a governmental, legislative, or commercial body to review specific materials against predefined criteria. These criteria, especially those related to public attitudes on taste and decency, can quickly become outdated.

More broadly, censorship involves the practice and process of suppressing, either partially or totally, any text, or the entire output of an individual or organization, on a limited or permanent basis. It represents the suppression or prohibition of speech or writing deemed subversive to the common good. While censorship occurs to some degree across all manifestations of authority, in modern times, its relationship with government and the rule of law has become particularly significant.

In essence, censorship is the suppression of speech, public communication, or other information based on the belief that such material is objectionable, harmful, sensitive, or inconvenient. This control can be exercised by governments, private institutions, and other controlling bodies.

Self-Censorship

According to Oxford Learner's Dictionaries, self-censorship is the act of self-regulation undertaken by an individual Journalist, author, publisher, columnist, or even an entire industry. Media industries frequently warn their members that a failure to self-regulate may lead to state intervention. At an individual level, self-censorship involves internally regulating what one chooses to express publicly, often driven by a desire for conformity.

A concerning example from the Republic of South Sudan illustrates this in a manner that National security agents are reportedly stationed at printing presses to remove articles deemed against their interests from newspapers.

The media fraternity, therefore, sometimes refers to these agents as true editors, as they disregard the work of professional editors within media houses. Lacking journalistic experience or training, these security officers may remove any article mentioning word; 'Security' or touching upon a general they support. This constitutes an abuse of power and a disrespect for the national security service itself, which should ideally intervene only when articles genuinely threaten the country's existence.

Influenced Editorials

Editorials are intended to operate free from any external influence. Their purpose is to shape public opinion, foster critical thinking, and at times, galvanize action on matters of public interest or national significance. Consequently, an editorial swayed by undue influence possesses the capacity to mislead an entire nation in a detrimental direction, given media's profound impact on culture, religion, economics, and politics.

Paid Editorial

Journalists are ethically prohibited from paying sources for information, and similarly, they should not accept payment for coverage. While paying for coverage is not uncommon in some media houses, and financial incentives are generally considered an inappropriate basis for selecting news stories, there's also an argument that paid editorial helps sustain some publications, without which many news outlets might cease to exist. The question of whether the good outweighs the bad is complex and often left to practicing journalists to reconcile based on their direct experience.

Modern Paid Editorial

Various arguments support publications and media institutions accepting payment for editorial content. However, the validity of these arguments hinges on questions of journalistic integrity and adherence to core values. In certain instances, accepting payment might be deemed reasonable and justifiable for coverage.

Undeniably, the income generated from small payments for editorial coverage can be substantial, often amounting to thousands of pounds monthly. Publishing is a challenging industry, and mainstream media has struggled to maintain its market position, with many sister institutions going out of business. It is therefore clear that, without income from these placement charges, some publications might disappear entirely. The existence of a broader range of publications is often viewed as a genuine public good, fostering competition and increasing the diversity of information available to consumers. Historically, agencies have advised clients to shift advertising budgets to Public Relations, which is often more profitable for the agency. While this strategy might benefit clients, it does little to ensure the survival of publications.

More recently, some media houses have been established specifically on the basis of paid editorial, such as local institutions like Liberty Media, Talkline Media, Pesahiko Media, and Zoom Media. These entities thrive on providing coverage in exchange for payment, proving particularly useful for community affairs and social events. Thus, paid editorial is emerging as an efficient and increasingly popular avenue in the modern media landscape.[3]

---

3. These are local media house in the Republic of South Sudan that are basically on social media and charge for every live streaming per hour or service.

Segregated Media Action

To foster equity for smaller companies and businesses, paid editorial offers an alternative, ensuring they too can secure editorial coverage. Without it, advertisers with larger budgets might monopolize editorial space. While this link between coverage and advertising spend might be less direct for many business-to-business publications, the risk exists that publications could reduce coverage of non-advertisers if they lose payments for coverage. This could lead to a situation where only the largest companies, capable of affording extensive display campaigns, have access to editorial. Such a scenario would not only diminish the diversity of content within publications but also potentially limit access for companies with smaller marketing budgets.

Conversely, established companies often leverage their financial resources to dominate paid editorial services, gaining a monopolistic advantage. While this disadvantages smaller businesses by limiting their chances of publication, it simultaneously provides a revenue stream for media outlets.

Paid Editorial's Future

Paid editorial, also known as native advertising in digital contexts, is experiencing rapid growth. This trend may be inevitable, with only older industry professionals clinging to past models. The question arises: why not embrace this change? Younger audiences, it is argued, are far less concerned about this distinction than their older counterparts.

Israel, a technology hub, is cited as an example where publications directly link paid media spend to editorial coverage more than any other European country. If this model works there, its broader applicability warrants consideration. In Africa, South Sudan is reportedly leading in the adoption of paid editorials; the national SSBC is allegedly hesitant to broadcast news unless financially 'facilitated.'

Many local media outlets now offer streaming, photoshoot, and YouTube services primarily on a paid basis.

Measuring Paid Editorial Against Ethics

The concept of paying for editorial coverage is largely detested by most journalists, for several compelling reasons. These reasons include, but are not limited to, diverting media practice from its core values and ethics, and allowing financial contributions rather than newsworthiness to dictate content. It suggests that paid editorial could reduce journalism to a 'pay-to-play' model.

Perhaps the most potent argument against paid editorial is its potential illegality. The UK's Business Protection from Misleading Marketing Regulations 2008, though less explicit than consumer legislation, strongly imply that passing off advertising as editorial is a breach of the Advertising Standards Authority guidelines, specifically the CAP Code. While the ASA's sanctions are limited, it can prohibit advertising that fails to meet these standards.

Paid Editorial's Value in PR

One significant aspect of Public Relations is that editorial coverage is perceived as far more convincing than traditional advertising. Studies indicate that an article written by a journalist can be four or more times as effective as a similarly sized advertisement. This efficacy stems from the public perception that advertising originates from a company trying to sell a product, whereas a journalist is seen as an independent third party, writing from an unbiased perspective. Consequently, journalistic views carry substantial weight with the public. However, if journalists are influenced by payments, this crucial element of third-party endorsement vanishes, diminishing PR's effectiveness. While PR firms might pay journalists to produce extensive articles about their clients, if the readership remains unaware of this financial arrangement, the impact of this endorsement remains unchanged.

Paid Editorial Coverage

When editorial content is subjected to commercial influence, the focus of publications tends to shift from prioritizing editorial merit and significant entities to featuring those possessing substantial financial resources and a willingness to fund coverage. This compromises the inherent value of publications, resulting in audience disengagement and potentially leading to the withdrawal of financial support from funders, thus undermining their economic viability and risking their eventual cessation. Furthermore, this practice presents considerable professional and ethical dilemmas for journalists, restricting their capacity to pursue stories based on journalistic principles and effectively reducing them to content producers for commercially motivated interests. This shift blurs the critical distinction between independent journalistic reporting and paid promotional material. This phenomenon, increasingly prevalent with the rise of "native advertising" and sponsored content, challenges the traditional firewall between journalistic integrity and business objectives by subordinating reporting to revenue generation (Levi, 2015; Christensen, 2017; Wang and Sparks, 2018).

This convergence of advertising and editorial content, frequently termed native advertising or sponsored content, presents substantial ethical quandaries for journalistic integrity and audience trust (Hagelstein, Einwiller and Zerfaß, 2021; Beckert, 2022). Native advertising, which integrates promotional messages within journalistic frameworks to achieve persuasive objectives discreetly, elicits ethical scrutiny owing to its intrinsically misleading character (Naderer et al., 2020; Beckert, 2022). The imperative for transparency is paramount, with journalistic guidelines advocating for explicit identification of sponsored content to differentiate it from independent editorial; however, consumers frequently misinterpret such content as non-promotional, despite explicit disclosure mechanisms (Krouwer, Poels and Paulussen, 2019; Hagelstein, Einwiller and Zerfaß, 2021). This insufficient transparency can diminish public confidence in media organizations, as audiences perceive a breach of trust when content presented as objective editorial is, in reality, commercially driven (Aribarg and Schwartz, 2019).

While the comprehensive ramifications of this trajectory are challenging to ascertain, partly given the historical presence of financially supported editorial content, it is broadly anticipated that this trend will persist and likely expand considerably. Although this might contribute to the economic sustainability of a greater number of publications, audiences exhibit acuity in identifying publications that uphold stringent editorial standards, conferring greater credibility upon them compared to those whose content is influenced by financial considerations. This discernment is also evident among advertisers, suggesting a similar perceptive capacity in the general readership.

The long-term impact on the media landscape is a significant concern, as economic pressures on traditional journalism frequently compel organizations to adopt sponsored content models for revenue generation (Poutanen, Luoma-aho and Suhanko, 2016). While this may offer short-term financial stability, it risks alienating audiences who value independent reporting and unbiased information (Levi, 2015). The integration of artificial intelligence in digital journalism further poses ethical challenges for sponsored editorial content, particularly concerning its potential for covert governmental propaganda (Forja-Pena, Orosa and García, 2024).

Journalistic Bias

Media bias constitutes a fundamental challenge to journalistic integrity, emerging when journalists and news producers exhibit partiality in their reporting and coverage. This partiality, often a pervasive or widespread inclination, contravenes established journalistic standards, thereby eroding the objectivity and fairness crucial for maintaining public trust (Patil et al., 2021; Pansanella et al., 2023). Such bias extends beyond individual viewpoints or isolated articles, reflecting deeply systemic issues within news production, often driven by factors like media ownership, the political leanings of journalists, and economic pressures to align content with audience interests or revenue models (Patil et al., 2021; Pansanella et al., 2023; T., 2024). These systemic biases manifest through selective reporting, strategic framing, and nuanced linguistic choices, which inadvertently yet profoundly shape public perception. Consequently, this practice not only compromises editorial independence but also exacerbates a growing crisis of trust in media institutions and significantly contributes to the proliferation of misinformation (Gutiérrez-Caneda, Lindén and Vázquez-Herrero, 2024; T., 2024).

Types and Manifestations of Bias

Editorial biases encompass publication bias, wherein research outcomes impact editorial decisions, and author-related bias, characterized by external factors pertaining to authors or their circumstances influencing editorial selections. For example, an article exhibiting a bias favoring motorcycle riding might underscore attributes such as fuel efficiency, experiential enjoyment, and maneuverability. Conversely, content demonstrating an opposing bias could exclusively highlight associated risks like injury and noise, while neglecting any affirmative characteristics.

Beyond these specific instances, media bias can manifest through a multitude of forms (Spinde et al., 2023). Scholarly research frequently categorizes bias into distinct subtypes, including visibility bias, tonality bias, and agenda bias (Eberl, Boomgaarden and Wagner, 2015). Additional manifestations include gatekeeping bias, defined by selective inclusion or exclusion of information, coverage bias, relating to the prominence afforded to a given narrative, and statement bias, which utilizes specific linguistic choices or evaluative terms to privilege certain perspectives (Spinde et al., 2023). Furthermore, media bias can originate from factors such as media ownership structures, the political orientations of journalists, or the preferences of the target audience (Patil et al., 2021; Pansanella et al., 2023).

Impact on Perception and Behavior

Previous research indicates that media bias influences both individual and public perceptions of news events. Given that media serves as a primary conduit for citizens' political information, such bias can potentially impact audience political beliefs, party affiliations (Singh, 2025), and even alter voting patterns (Spinde et al., 2023). The profound influence of media bias on how individuals and groups interpret news can shape attitudes toward political candidates, policies, and social issues, potentially leading to a less informed or more polarized citizenry (Pansanella et al., 2023; Yang, 2023).

The ubiquitous nature of bias often results in news consumers encountering skewed media narratives without conscious recognition of the underlying partiality, highlighting a widespread lack of awareness regarding this phenomenon. This presents an ongoing challenge for developing effective communication strategies to counteract its potential adverse impacts. Moreover, media bias exacerbates the issue of filter bubbles or echo chambers, wherein readers predominantly engage with news that aligns with their pre-existing beliefs, fostering a narrow and circumscribed perspective (Spinde et al., 2023).

Strategies for Detection and Mitigation

Addressing media bias and cultivating critical awareness necessitates the implementation of diverse methodologies. This imperative is particularly heightened by the pervasive dissemination of personalized algorithms across search engines and social media platforms, which demonstrably exacerbate extant biases. These algorithms operate by curating information based on prior consumption patterns and cognitive confirmation biases, thereby solidifying pre-existing convictions and potentially fostering a more atomized perception of reality. the strategies included the following:

Forewarning messages : Implementing explicit *forewarning messages* directly *within news content* can proactively inform readers about potential biases, thereby fostering critical evaluation of information and encouraging the consideration of diverse perspectives. This approach leverages metacognitive awareness to mitigate the impact of confirmation bias, encouraging a more deliberative processing of news (Rodrigo-Ginés, Carrillo-de-Albornoz and Plaza, 2023).

Text annotations : Providing contextual notes or highlighting biased language directly within the text serves as a direct educational tool, empowering readers to critically analyze content, explicitly identify subtle forms of partiality, and thus foster a more informed and discerning engagement with news narratives.

Political classifiers : The Political classifiers are analytical tools or algorithms designed to categorize news content based on its political leanings, providing objective assessments that empower consumers to recognize inherent biases, critically evaluate information, and actively diversify their news consumption across a broader ideological spectrum.

Visualizations : Visualizations can generally contribute to cultivating this awareness and encourage more balanced news intake by alerting individuals to potential biases, highlighting specific instances of bias, or enabling content comparisons (Hanitzsch and Vos, 2016). These visual aids make complex bias patterns more accessible, promoting a deeper understanding of media landscapes.

Other strategies include promoting media literacy and critical thinking among news consumers (Rodrigo-Ginés, Carrillo-de-Albornoz and Plaza, 2023), equipping them with the cognitive tools to discern and resist biased narratives. Highlighting instances of media bias can also mitigate its negative effects (Spinde et al., 2023) by bringing specific examples to public attention. Furthermore, understanding the mechanisms through which media bias operates, such as personalized algorithms on search engines and social networks, is crucial, as these can reinforce existing biases by filtering information based on past history and confirmatory tendencies (Antunes et al., 2023).

Beyond these direct interventions, fostering robust media literacy and critical thinking among news consumers is paramount (Rodrigo-Ginés, Carrillo-de-Albornoz and Plaza, 2023), empowering individuals with the cognitive tools necessary to actively discern, resist, and ultimately navigate the pervasive landscape of biased narratives and filter bubbles. Crucially, highlighting specific instances of media bias can also mitigate its negative effects (Spinde et al., 2023) by bringing concrete examples to public attention. Furthermore, understanding the underlying mechanisms through which media bias operates, such as personalized algorithms on search engines and social networks, is vital, as these can reinforce existing biases by filtering information based on past history and confirmatory tendencies (Antunes et al., 2023).

Communicating Media Bias Effectively

Despite the recognized importance of effectively communicating about media bias, scholarly inquiry has scarcely delved into the contribution of visualizations and augmented perception in comprehending this phenomenon, consequently leaving numerous potential avenues unexplored. Accordingly, this study investigates the effectiveness of various strategies in fostering media bias awareness, potentially shedding light on prevalent impediments to discerning media consumption. From extant literature, three salient methodologies were chosen for comprehensive examination: forewarning messages, textual annotations, and political classifications. Presently, theoretical underpinnings for bias messaging and visualizations are limited, with both visualization and bias theories having conducted scant rigorous testing of appropriate strategies within this specific research area.

Forewarning Messages : Drawing upon socio-psychological inoculation theory, it is possible to build psychological resistance against persuasive attempts by preemptively exposing individuals to a warning message. This process is analogous to immunizing against a virus by administering a weakened dose. An 'inoculation message' is thus expected to protect individuals from a persuasive attack by presenting them with weakened forms of impending persuasion. The perceived threat of such a forewarning inoculation message tends to prompt individuals to strengthen their own positions, making them more resistant to subsequent persuasive influences. Consequently, one strategy to aid in detecting bias involves preparing people ahead of media consumption by alerting them to the potential occurrence of media bias, thereby forewarning them against biased language influences. Such warnings are well-established in persuasion research and have demonstrated effectiveness across various applied contexts.

Furthermore, these warnings not only protect attitudes against influence but also assist in evaluating the quality of information and communicating that information appropriately. For biased language, this approach might specifically work by directing a reader's attention to the universal motive of evaluating information accuracy, while relying on their individual capacity to detect bias when encountered.

Annotations : In contrast to pre-emptive notifications regarding the presence of bias, an alternative approach entails informing individuals during the reading process itself, thereby directly enhancing their awareness of biased language and offering immediate assistance in detecting it within an article. Recent scholarly works in information science concerning media bias has largely concentrated on its identification and detection. While some studies investigating the effects of visualizing media bias in news articles to aid detection have demonstrated promising outcomes, others have not found comparable effects, a discrepancy potentially attributable to technical challenges in accurately annotating individual articles. Nevertheless, annotations present significant potential for fostering greater media bias awareness and promoting more balanced news consumption.

Political Classification : Another strategy to enhance media bias awareness involves the political classification of biased material after readers have engaged with it. This approach functions as a post-consumption intervention, providing readers with a critical lens for re-evaluating the content. Colleagues could propose an ideological left-right map where media sources are politically classified. The authors suggest that revealing a source's political leaning serves as a crucial prompt, encouraging readers to actively question their own interpretations, critically assess the presented information, and proactively seek out diverse perspectives to form a more comprehensive understanding.

Similarly, several other studies indicate that feedback on the political orientation of an article or source can lead to increased media bias awareness and, consequently, more balanced news consumption. This critical engagement with source classification can also implicitly expose users to diverse viewpoints on controversial topics, thereby fostering the development of more nuanced and balanced perspectives. A study by Munson and colleagues further suggests that a feedback element indicating a user's history of biased news consumption modestly contributes to more balanced news consumption. Building on these findings, we will investigate whether the mere representation of a source's leaning helps raise bias awareness among users, particularly when an article is classified as politically skewed.

Partisan Media Bias Awareness : Attempts to enhance media bias awareness can be complicated by the fact that bias detection and news evaluation often depend on the beholder's political ideology. This partisan effect manifests as individuals perceiving content aligning with their opinions as less biased and content contradicting their viewpoints as more biased; this incongruence between a reader's position and an article's position may heighten the perception of media bias, whereas congruence may diminish it. Thus, partisan media consumers may engage in motivated reasoning to overcome the cognitive dissonance experienced when encountering media bias in articles that generally align with their views. According to Festinger, cognitive dissonance arises when two cognitive elements are inconsistent, leading to mental discomfort, and individuals experiencing dissonance are motivated to reduce this inconsistency to alleviate the negative emotion.

Consequently, increasing media bias awareness might intensify experienced cognitive dissonance, potentially leading to even more partisan ratings of bias.

Alternatively, varying norms about what constitutes appropriate media coverage, depending on one's political identity, or inattention to news quality and the motive to support only truthful news, offer other explanations for partisan bias ratings.

These latter approaches lead to contrasting expectations for how increased awareness, particularly through visualizations, might affect the partisanship of media bias ratings: either decreasing it as people are reminded of broader norms and accuracy motives, or increasing it. This highlights a critical challenge in designing interventions to mitigate media bias: the potential for such interventions to either exacerbate or alleviate partisan divisions, depending on the specific cognitive mechanisms engaged.

Therefore, it is crucial to consider how the design of propaganda detection tools, especially those leveraging AI, can navigate these partisan complexities to genuinely foster critical thinking rather than reinforcing existing biases (Zavolokina et al., 2025) (Hamborg et al., 2021). Such tools must contend with the fact that users, even those with high media literacy, may struggle to correct for biases when information aligns with their pre-existing beliefs, a phenomenon observed even when individuals are motivated to process information thoughtfully (Sude, Sharon and Dvir-Gvirsman, 2023).

This challenge is further complicated by cognitive biases such as naive realism and confirmation bias, which predispose individuals to interpret information in ways that reinforce their existing worldviews, making them more susceptible to disinformation and less likely to identify bias in congruent content (Rodrigo-Ginés, Carrillo-de-Albornoz and Plaza, 2023) (Ordaz, 2023).

Journalistic Favoritism

Journalistic favoritism, a significant source of media bias, can manifest in several ways. One prevalent form is 'paid journalism,' often a 'pay-to-play' dynamic where financial incentives dictate coverage.

This can involve sources compensating journalists or media outlets for publication, or conversely, outlets paying for information, thereby creating a conflict of interest that can lead to biased or suppressed reporting. Favoritism also arises from personal connections, such as a journalist having relationships with individuals involved in a story, which can compromise objectivity and introduce conflicts of interest. When journalists unethically favor one side due to these relationships, presenting it positively even if its position is not entirely justified, it severely undermines journalistic integrity and erodes public trust. A fundamental ethical principle of journalism demands a balanced story, compelling journalists to diligently seek out and present multiple, diverse perspectives before disseminating information. Failure to uphold this principle not only distorts public understanding but also contributes to a broader landscape of media bias.(Temmerman et al., 2018) Moreover, partisan bias can lead fact-checkers themselves to disproportionately label information aligning with their beliefs as true and contradictory information as false, further exacerbating the problem of misinformation and necessitating methods to mitigate such influences (Tomassi, Falegnami and Romano, 2024).

CHAPTER 14

Journalism and Public Relations

JOURNALISM AND PUBLIC RELATIONS operate within the same media landscape yet fundamentally diverge in their core purposes. While journalism is rigorously dedicated to delivering unbiased news and informing the public with objective facts, public relations primarily aim to cultivate a positive image and manage perceptions for its clients through strategic persuasion.

This foundational divergence invariably creates an inherent tension, as one seeks impartial truth and the other advocates specific interests. Nevertheless, both professions are inextricably intertwined in the dissemination of information and the powerful shaping of public discourse, a relationship often fraught with ethical considerations. This intricate dynamic, characterized by a sometimes-contentious reliance, has led many journalists to view public relations as the "dark side" of information dissemination, often accusing practitioners of "spin" (White and Hobsbawm, 2007).

Journalism

Journalism primarily serves a broad public, focusing on information vital for societal well-being and democratic function. Its fundamental role involves objective informing and scrutiny, serving the collective public interest rather than specific demographics. As a cornerstone of democratic societies, journalism provides essential, verifiable information critical for informed decision-making and robust public discourse. Journalists are professionally obligated to report facts accurately, verify information from diverse sources, and present a comprehensive, nuanced understanding of events. Journalism's credibility and public trust depend intrinsically on its unwavering independence from undue political or commercial influence, alongside a steadfast commitment to the public interest. This commitment demands adherence to ethical guidelines and a continuous pursuit of truth, even when challenging established narratives or powerful entities. Such dedication to impartiality and accuracy is vital for maintaining public trust and ensuring citizens receive reliable information essential for a functioning democracy (Shahid, 2023).

Public Relations

Public Relations is a pivotal and strategic communication discipline purposefully designed to manage reputation, foster understanding, and proactively influence public opinion and behavior. This involves a meticulously planned and sustained effort to establish, cultivate, and maintain goodwill and mutual understanding between an organization and its diverse publics. At its core, PR strategically seeks to influence, engage, and build enduring relationships with key stakeholders across diverse platforms, ultimately shaping and managing public perception to achieve specific organizational objectives. Essentially, PR is the art and science of communication that not only fosters positive relationships but also ensures sustained engagement with an organization's publics. Key objectives of PR encompass the strategic dissemination of important company news or events, the proactive maintenance of a positive brand image, and the effective mitigation of negative events, thereby safeguarding an organization's credibility and market position.

TPR activities are multifaceted and can be manifested through various channels, such as press releases, news conferences, interviews with journalists, and social media engagement, each tailored to reach specific audiences and achieve distinct communication goals. Public relations professionals function as crucial strategic communicators and mediators between their organizations and various publics, including employees, investors, customers, and communities, ensuring transparent and effective dialogue. The integral aim of public relations is, therefore, to initiate and preserve reciprocally advantageous relationships between an organization and its constituent publics, as its ultimate success or failure is predicated upon their sustained engagement (Chukwu, 2023).

Interdependence of PR and Journalism

While distinct, public relations strategically leverage journalistic platforms to enhance the public perception of its clients. Conversely, media organizations frequently accrue substantial financial gains from PR services, primarily through advertising revenue or sponsored content. This intrinsic interdependence signifies a considerable reliance of public relations on journalism, a dependency that is progressively becoming reciprocal. Public relations critically relies on journalists for broad information dissemination and essential media exposure, meticulously constructing narratives that advance client interests. Concurrently, journalists, often operating under increased pressure, routinely engage PR professionals as vital sources for breaking news, contextual information, and expert analysis. This foundational reliance establishes a profound mutual dependence, frequently termed "media subsidy." This intricate dynamic inherently produces considerable tension and substantial ethical challenges, as PR's core objective of strategic persuasion directly contradicts journalism's fundamental commitment to objective reporting.

The extensive reliance of journalists on PR-generated content, particularly evident in local news outlets with limited resources, inevitably fosters a notable convergence, where PR professionals frequently exert significant influence over the news agenda. This influence arises from the strategic communication efforts of public relations, aimed at shaping perceptions and promoting understanding, often utilizing various communication tools such as media relations and content creation to convey messages effectively (Chukwu, 2023; Farhi et al., 2023).

Qualities of a PR Expert

Successful PR professionals possess a range of essential qualities, including exceptional communication skills encompassing compelling written, verbal, and interpersonal abilities strategic thinking, adaptability, and strong relationships with media contacts and stakeholders. These communication proficiencies are fundamental for articulating complex messages clearly and persuasively across diverse platforms, fostering understanding and engagement. Public relations can be a powerful tool, particularly when integrated with other promotional efforts like advertising, personal selling, sales promotions, and direct marketing, ensuring a clear and consistent message across all strategies.

Other crucial competencies include ethical decision-making, paramount for maintaining trust and credibility; crisis management, essential for navigating unforeseen challenges and protecting organizational reputation; digital literacy, vital for leveraging modern communication channels; and a deep understanding of public opinion, which informs effective communication strategies. Strategic thinking allows PR experts to anticipate issues, develop proactive communication plans, and align PR efforts with overarching organizational goals, ensuring that communication efforts are not merely reactive but forward-looking and impactful. Furthermore, emotional intelligence and creativity are paramount for PR experts to craft persuasive messages, elicit favorable feedback, and cultivate positive, mutually beneficial relationships with diverse audiences (Hadeed et al., 2024). These attributes enable professionals to connect authentically and tailor communications that resonate deeply with their intended publics.

The Publicist Role

The publicist, a pivotal role within public relations, frequently serves as the quintessential representation of the profession in the public imagination. Operating within either an agency or an in-house team, publicists engage in direct, strategic collaboration with clients to meticulously develop and rigorously implement their brand strategies. In this capacity, publicists are indispensable figures in media relations, functioning as critical intermediaries between clients and the media. Their foremost responsibility is to strategically secure positive media coverage, a complex endeavor that necessitates crafting compelling narratives, expertly distributing targeted press materials, and skillfully pitching stories to journalists to shape public perception and enhance credibility. This strategic outreach is crucial for managing perceptions and fostering understanding between an organization and its public (Dike, 2025). Moreover, they are adept at identifying and analyzing stakeholder communication needs and developing mutually beneficial engagement strategies (Gregory and Fawkes, 2019).

PR's Target Audience

While public relations campaigns occasionally address the general population, their efficacy is overwhelmingly contingent upon a strategic focus on specific, well-defined target audiences (Farhi et al., 2023).

This deliberate approach is paramount for maximizing the impact of communication, ensuring that messages reach and resonate with those most likely to respond favorably. For commercial entities, this precision involves identifying consumers predisposed to purchasing a particular product or service, based on their interests, purchasing power, and behavioral patterns. Conversely, for advocacy or membership organizations, the focus shifts to potential members, activists, key supporters, or influential figures who possess decision-making authority. A target audience in PR and communications is thus not merely a general recipient but specifically defined as the segment of individuals most inherently interested in, or affected by, the messaging pertaining to a product, service, charity, or cause. It fundamentally encompasses the precise publics an organization aims to engage and build mutually beneficial relationships with (Gregory and Fawkes, 2019; Chukwu, 2023). Consequently, effective PR necessitates meticulous audience analysis to meticulously tailor messages that are not only relevant but also persuasive, aligning with specific demographics, psychographics, and behaviors. This strategic segmentation is critical for optimizing communication efficiency and achieving desired outcomes, ranging from influencing purchasing decisions and fostering community engagement to shaping public policy and reputation. This targeted approach ensures that public relations efforts are not diffused across a broad, undifferentiated audience but rather concentrated on those segments where they can yield the most significant strategic advantage (Chukwu, 2023) (Farhi et al., 2023).

Essential Tools for Public Relations

Effectively executing public relations strategies necessitates a diverse and comprehensive toolkit, integrating both traditional and contemporary communication channels.

These tools are indispensable for managing an organization's public image, building stakeholder trust, and ultimately achieving strategic communication objectives (Dike, 2025). Reputation management, in particular, relies heavily on credible information disseminated through various public relations activities to foster favorable perceptions (Ugoani, 2020). Among these, media relations encompassing press releases, media kits, and direct outreach to journalists remains fundamental for securing earned media coverage and shaping public discourse (Chukwu, 2023).

Media Kits

Media kits are indispensable tools in public relations, designed for the strategic dissemination of information to key media outlets and journalists. These comprehensive packages typically furnish journalists with essential resources, including backgrounders, fact sheets, executive biographies, and high-resolution images, thereby enabling the development of accurate, consistent, and engaging stories. A meticulously assembled media kit serves as a foundational resource, critical for maintaining message integrity and facilitating swift, unified communication, particularly during pivotal or challenging periods. With the evolution of digital platforms, electronic press kits have become standard, offering instant global access to these vital resources and enhancing efficiency. Increasingly, modern public relations extend beyond these traditional kits, integrating social media platforms, influencer collaborations, and search engine optimization to strategically broaden reach and foster real-time engagement with diverse online communities (Søilen, 2024).

Media Database

Media databases serve as meticulously curated, structured repositories containing comprehensive contact details for journalists, influential individuals, and key media outlets. They are indispensable tools, empowering public relations practitioners to precisely identify and strategically engage pertinent media contacts to secure valuable earned media coverage. These databases are critical for maximizing the impact of communication by ensuring that press releases, media kits, and other strategic communications are delivered to the most appropriate and influential outlets and journalists. This precision targeting not only optimizes outreach efforts but also significantly increases the likelihood of securing valuable earned media coverage, thereby enhancing an organization's credibility and public perception. Consequently, media databases are essential for cultivating and sustaining robust relationships with key media figures, thought leaders, and digital influencers. Furthermore, the strategic integration of these databases with broader digital public relations strategies, particularly through social media engagement and influencer collaborations, significantly amplifies an organization's capacity for dynamic, real-time interaction and proactive reputation management (Søilen, 2024; Dike, 2025).

Press Release

A press release serves as a formal, authoritative declaration, strategically disseminated to news media to unveil crucial information, announce significant developments, or articulate a public stance. These documents are meticulously crafted official statements, crucial for directly shaping public perception and establishing an organization's credibility. Their meticulous crafting ensures they function as foundational sources, informing journalists about newsworthy events, products, or corporate milestones.

This strategic approach aims to compel comprehensive media coverage that accurately reflects the organization's narrative and enhances its reputation. As a fundamental tool for information dissemination, press releases provide a standardized format, ensuring consistent messaging. Their effectiveness is critically dependent on their inherent news value and unequivocal clarity, which dictate their uptake by media outlets and their capacity to attract public attention. In the contemporary digital landscape, the efficacy of press releases is significantly amplified. Online distribution channels, including new media platforms and social media, not only facilitate broader dissemination and immediate public access but also enhance search engine visibility and enable direct engagement with diverse audiences, extending their reach beyond traditional media (Hadeed et al., 2024).

Press Release Distribution

This entails the methodical dissemination of press releases to relevant stakeholders, encompassing both traditional journalists at national and local publications and digital opinion leaders such as niche bloggers and influencers. Crucially, the strategic distribution of these communiqués can profoundly shape public perception and augment an organization's reputational standing, as managers maintain significant control over the framing and emphasis of information to influence audience perceptions and foster favorable impressions (Gottschalk, 2024). This strategic dissemination is vital for ensuring that key messages reach the intended audience effectively, thereby enhancing visibility and credibility. Furthermore, effective distribution channels are integral for maximizing the reach and impact of an organization's narrative, ensuring that its message resonates across diverse media landscapes. Modern distribution increasingly leverages digital platforms and services, accelerating content production and dissemination to reach a broader, more targeted audience, and fostering immediate public engagement and direct interaction with target demographics (Elrod and Fortenberry, 2020; Gottschalk, 2024; Hadeed et al., 2024). While organizations can distribute press releases themselves, many opt for professional distribution services. These services, often provided by formal public relations offices, prove invaluable by acting as communication liaisons with external entities and significantly increasing the chances of content being picked up by news outlets through established networks and optimized delivery methods (Aronoff, 1976; Elrod and Fortenberry, 2020).

Social Media Management

Social Media Management encompasses the dynamic and continuous process of strategically creating, curating, and scheduling content designed to expand and engage a targeted audience across various social media platforms. These strategies are meticulously modeled to proactively influence public perception, significantly contributing to improved word-of-mouth advocacy and fostering deep attitudinal loyalty among stakeholders. Integral tools and strategies are employed for managing an organization's holistic online presence and communication, which includes developing robust social media content strategies and actively managing online reputation. Indeed, effective social media communication strategies are pivotal, directly impacting corporate reputation and underscoring the critical importance of strategic online engagement for contemporary businesses.

This function is also indispensable in crisis communication, where social media serves as an essential and immediate tool for rapidly disseminating information and proactively managing stakeholder relationships during critical periods. Effective social media managers are typically equipped with excellent copywriting skills, a demonstrated ability to produce creative and compelling content, and a solid understanding of SEO principles, keyword research, and analytics platforms like Google Analytics, all of which are crucial for optimizing reach and impact. They expertly leverage social media's inherently interactive nature to cultivate meaningful relationships and strengthen brand connections with customers and broader publics. By consistently creating engaging and relevant content, organizations can strategically differentiate themselves from competitors and assiduously cultivate a positive and resilient brand image.

Furthermore, consistent and authentic interaction with audiences on social media platforms is fundamental for fostering stronger relationships, building enduring trust, directly influencing public perception, and thereby maintaining a robust and favorable brand image. The strategic application of social media analytics is also increasingly vital for evidence-based decision-making and for advancing public relations efforts by providing actionable insights. Consequently, social media management is no longer merely a transient trend but has emerged as an essential and critical component of strategic public relations, facilitating direct engagement, fostering community building, and enabling real-time reputation monitoring and management. This integration ensures that organizational messaging is consistently aligned across all platforms, reinforcing overall communication objectives and amplifying the strategic impact of public relations initiatives (Anuar et al., 2025). This proactive management of an organization's online presence, utilizing tools such as social listening and sentiment analysis, is critical for maintaining a positive brand image and mitigating potential reputational risks (Gasana, 2024).

Content Creation

Content creation constitutes the systematic development of diverse media formats, including but not limited to textual articles, video productions, and graphical infographics. These outputs are meticulously designed and tailored to specific target audiences, serving as a cornerstone for reputation building, thought leadership, and direct stakeholder engagement, thereby advancing overarching public relations objectives. This comprehensive process typically involves multiple phases, commencing with initial conceptualization and extending through to the promotion of the finalized product, frequently necessitating interdisciplinary collaboration among specialized experts. Within the domain of PR, content generation is recognized not merely as a pivotal instrument, but as fundamental for shaping public perception, building brand authority, and driving strategic communication goals. It frequently adheres to a systematic, multi-stage methodology to maximize impact and ensure message consistency, thereby guaranteeing strategic alignment and effectiveness. While specific frameworks may vary, a common approach often encompasses the following sequential phases: information acquisition, thematic analysis and topic identification, strategic planning, content actualization, optimization and dissemination, strategic promotion, and comprehensive performance evaluation with iterative refinement.

Public relations practices are intrinsically linked to content creation, leveraging compelling narratives to foster and sustain positive relationships with clients and stakeholders through effective communication processes. Content creation in PR extends beyond traditional press releases to include blog posts, videos, podcasts, and interactive media, all strategically designed to tell an organization's story, build its brand narrative, and deeply engage its target audience across various platforms.

This multifaceted approach ensures that public relations experts can craft persuasive and constructive messages, acquire favorable feedback and reinforcing their importance within organizations (Hadeed et al., 2024).

Media outreach

Media outreach involves proactively engaging with journalists and media outlets to secure favorable coverage, thereby enhancing an organization's visibility and reputation. This strategic function is crucial for controlling narratives, shaping public discourse, and ensuring key messages reach target audiences effectively. It often involves cultivating long-term relationships with key media contacts, understanding their editorial needs, and meticulously crafting and pitching relevant stories that align with their audience interests, ultimately contributing to broader communication objectives and mitigating reputational risks (Gasana, 2024; Søilen, 2024; Anuar et al., 2025).

Media Monitoring

Tracking media coverage to assess campaign effectiveness and public sentiment is a critical component of effective public relations. Media monitoring allows strategic communications and marketing teams to stay informed about public perceptions of their company, products, services, or competitors, enabling more effective and proactive responses to feedback (Cullerton and Patay, 2024). It is an indispensable tool for enhancing organizational reputation management by integrating media and PR strategies to create cohesive narratives and foster stakeholder trust (Awoyemi et al., 2023).

A media monitoring specialist is responsible for tracking and analyzing media coverage relevant to a company, its competitors, and its industry.

In PR practices, media monitoring helps businesses understand competitor strategies and behaviors, assess audience reactions to their messages, and gain a competitive advantage by informing differentiated strategies and more effective communication plans (Taherdoost and Madanchian, 2023; Nsibande, Dinath and Niemand, 2025). Furthermore, the integration of data science and artificial intelligence into media monitoring tools allows for advanced analytics, including sentiment analysis, which helps identify public sentiment, emerging trends, and potential issues before they escalate (Madupati, 2022; Mohamed and Bayraktar, 2022; Olukemi, Broklyn and Bell, 2024). This capability is particularly vital for real-time, context-sensitive analysis of public sentiment during crisis communication and for brand reputation management (Umezurike et al., 2025). Ultimately, media monitoring provides essential data for the quantitative and qualitative analysis of information campaign outcomes, contributing to enhanced decision-making and strategic insights in PR (Захарченко, 2022; Vasudevan, 2025).

PR Analytics and Reporting

In the dynamic landscape of modern public relations, robust analytics and reporting are not merely beneficial but *indispensable* for rigorously evaluating the efficacy of PR efforts and unequivocally demonstrating their tangible impact through comprehensive data presentation. Analytics, through the systematic examination of data, uncovers critical patterns, trends, and actionable insights, transforming raw information into strategic intelligence. Reporting then translates this intelligence into structured, often visual, presentations typically through graphs and tables enabling clear and compelling communication of performance. By leveraging predefined Key Performance Indicators and other pertinent metrics,

PR professionals gain a profound and nuanced comprehension of their initiatives' effectiveness, moving beyond anecdotal evidence to data-backed certainty. This rigorous, data-driven methodology is paramount for informing agile and strategic decision-making, ensuring PR efforts are consistently optimized for maximum efficacy and organizational goal alignment. Businesses commonly utilize three types of analytics, each offering distinct value:

Descriptive Analytics

This foundational type of analysis retrospectively examines past data to meticulously document and interpret events, thereby providing PR professionals with a clear and comprehensive understanding of *what has already occurred*. It is indispensable for evaluating the efficacy of past campaigns, assessing media coverage, and gaining insights into audience engagement. By scrutinizing historical data, PR teams can accurately describe and summarize previous outcomes, revealing critical patterns, successes, and areas for improvement. For instance, descriptive analytics enables PR professionals to precisely track media mentions over defined periods, conduct detailed sentiment analysis for specific campaigns, and identify optimal timings for audience interaction on social media platforms. This retrospective insight is crucial for demonstrating accountability, learning from prior initiatives, and establishing a robust baseline for future strategic planning and optimization.

Predictive Analytics

Predictive Analytics is a forward-looking analytical approach that leverages statistical models and machine learning algorithms to forecast future trends and outcomes based on historical data (Rijmenam et al., 2018).

This enables PR strategists to anticipate potential crises, identify emerging opportunities, and strategically plan proactive communication initiatives.

By harnessBy identifying intricate patterns in past data, predictive analytics empower PR professionals to not only predict what *could* happen, but also to proactively adjust their strategies, mitigate potential reputational damage, and capitalize on nascent opportunities before they fully materialize, thereby shifting PR efforts from reactive to strategically anticipatory.

Prescriptive Analytics

Representing the most advanced stage of analytics, prescriptive analytics moves beyond merely understanding past events or predicting future outcomes to explicitly recommending specific actions to be taken (Rijmenam et al., 2018). This critical capability guides PR professionals in proactively optimizing strategies for maximum effectiveness and achieving specific objectives. Building upon descriptive and predictive insights, prescriptive analytics not only suggests what will happen, but crucially, also *what should be done* to achieve desired results, thereby transforming organizations' ability to act strategically (Rijmenam et al., 2018). This includes recommending optimal messaging, ideal timing for content release, or the most effective channels for reaching specific target audiences to maximize campaign impact and drive measurable outcomes.

These analytical approaches empower PR professionals to move decisively beyond intuition, facilitating data-driven decisions that are not only more precise, efficient, and effective in shaping public perception but also instrumental in robustly achieving strategic communication goals. The increasing reliance on data analytics within PR is further evidenced by the integration of data science into public relations software development, enhancing capabilities for advanced analytics, sentiment analysis, media monitoring, and campaign optimization through sophisticated techniques like machine learning and natural language processing (Madupati, 2022).

By harnessing these profound analytical insights, public relations professionals can transition definitively from merely reacting to events to proactively shaping narratives and achieving strategic objectives with unparalleled precision and foresight, thereby securing a critical competitive advantage and ensuring sustained organizational success.

Ultimately, PR specialists leverage business analytics and reporting to translate high-level public relations objectives into measurable requirements, develop data-driven solutions, and validate the strategic contributions of PR to organizational success. This methodical approach ensures that public relations initiatives are not only aligned with overarching business goals but also continuously refined through empirical evidence (Vasudevan, 2025).

Key Elements of Public Relations

The successful execution of Public Relations campaigns is predicated on a clear, systematic understanding and application of four interdependent core elements: goals, objectives, strategies, and tactics. Differentiating these components is fundamental for effectively structuring, coordinating, and evaluating any PR initiative. This framework ensures that PR efforts are not only meticulously planned but also directly aligned with overarching organizational aims, moving beyond isolated activities to integrated, purpose-driven communication.

Goals : Broad, long-term outcomes that PR efforts aim to achieve, providing a foundational direction and overarching purpose for all communication activities. These are typically aspirational, qualitative statements that articulate the desired ultimate impact on public perception, reputation, or stakeholder relationships, ensuring PR initiatives are intrinsically linked to the organization's strategic vision.

Objectives : Objectives are precise, quantifiable, and time-bound statements that operationalize broader PR goals, establishing specific, measurable outcomes required for successful campaign execution and serving as indispensable benchmarks for evaluating efficacy and demonstrating return on investment. They translate aspirational goals into actionable targets, thereby directly guiding strategic planning and tactical implementation.

Strategies : The overarching plans or comprehensive approaches meticulously designed to achieve the defined objectives and, by extension, the broader goals of a public relations campaign. Strategies articulate the fundamental "how" the chosen pathways and methods – through which an organization intends to leverage its resources and communicate effectively to shape public perception, influence stakeholder behavior, and fulfill its strategic communication aims. They serve as the critical link between aspirational objectives and concrete tactical execution, providing a coherent framework for action.

Tactics : PR Tactics, within the domain of Public Relations, refer to the precise activities, instruments, and communication deliverables deliberately employed to implement overarching strategies.

These constitute the practical, measurable actions formulated to translate strategic blueprints into tangible outcomes, thereby facilitating direct engagement with target audiences and the attainment of stipulated objectives. Such applications encompass a diverse range of practical initiatives, including the composition of press releases, oversight of social media content, coordination of events, execution of media outreach, and the development of digital campaigns.

Fundamentally, tactics delineate the operational methodologies and specific components of a campaign's day-to-day execution, ensuring the practical realization of broader strategic frameworks. The effective integration of these elements is crucial for establishing a cohesive and impactful public relations campaign, as each tactic directly contributes to a strategic objective, which, in turn, supports a broader organizational goal (Wojciechowski and Skrzypek-Ahmed, 2022).

Stages of PR Strategy Development

The strategic development of Public Relations campaigns is systematically structured around three meticulously defined and interdependent stages. These stages guide the process from initial conceptualization and high-level decision-making to precise, tangible implementation, thereby ensuring a comprehensive and iterative approach to reputation management and stakeholder engagement:

Grand Strategy : This initial phase represents the foundational, *policy-level stratum* of decision-making, critically orienting Public Relations efforts toward overarching long-term objectives, rigorous ethical standards, and the cultivation of enduring stakeholder relationships. During this stage, PR professionals meticulously integrate the organization's broader mission and strategic vision, thereby ensuring that all communication initiatives are intrinsically aligned with fundamental values and designed to foster sustainable engagement and trust with key stakeholders. It systematically addresses the fundamental "why" and "what for" behind PR activities, establishing a strategic imperative that underpins all subsequent campaign development and execution.

Strategy : This stage involves campaign-level decisions, meticulously outlining the comprehensive approach and strategic allocation of resources. It serves as the critical juncture where the grand strategy is translated into actionable plans for specific campaigns, defining the overarching direction and the methodical pathways required to achieve particular objectives. This stage fundamentally focuses on orchestrating resources and developing a cohesive framework that bridges aspirational goals with tangible tactical execution.

Tactics : This stage, focuses on implementation, represents the meticulous operationalization of chosen strategies through precise, tangible activities. Tactics are the concrete, measurable actions and communication deliverables that translate strategic blueprints into direct engagement with target audiences, ultimately achieving specific objectives. This encompasses a diverse range of practical initiatives, including but not limited to, the composition of press releases, diligent oversight of social media content, strategic coordination of events, robust execution of media outreach, and the development of digital campaigns. Fundamentally, this stage delineates the operational methodologies and specific components of a campaign's day-to-day execution, ensuring the practical realization of broader strategic frameworks and desired communication outcomes.

This hierarchical framework, with its distinct yet intrinsically interconnected stages from overarching grand strategy to specific tactical implementation is instrumental in ensuring that PR initiatives are not only meticulously planned but also deeply integrated and strategically aligned with the organization's overarching mission and objectives. This structured, cascading approach guarantees that resources are optimally allocated, and execution is carried out with precision, directly contributing to demonstrable and measurable outcomes. Furthermore, the clear delineation of responsibilities across these stages facilitates a robust and multi-faceted evaluation framework, enabling continuous assessment of public relations effectiveness at every level and fostering accountability (Gregory and Macnamara, 2019).

Public Relations Campaign Planning

A PR campaign is designed to introduce an organization, share its narrative, and foster positive relationships with various publics, including internal employees, media journalists, and customers. Such campaigns typically consist of defined goals, overarching strategies, and specific tactics.

Planning a public relations campaign, while requiring expertise, follows a structured process. Here's a breakdown of the key steps:

Steps	What is it about?	Sources/Remarks
Business Goal	A summary of the challenges being addressed and how they align with overall business objectives.	Relates to business objectives
Communications Objectives	What needs to be achieved through communication and how its success will be measured.	What and why
Strategies and Key Message/s	The chosen methods to convey the organization's story and the overarching narrative.	Overall story
Target Audience/s	The specific groups of people to reach, such as customers or regulators.	Customers, regulations
Tactics and Ideas	How the message will be delivered, often developed through brainstorming and research.	Brainstorming, research
Channels/Media	Specific publications, programs, or platforms chosen based on demographics or geography.	Demographics or geographic
Execution Details	Timelines for implementation and allocation of resources.	

Characteristics of a Public Relations Campaign

The efficacy and ultimate success of any public relations campaign are intrinsically linked to the embodiment of three fundamental and interconnected characteristics, which serve as the strategic pillars guiding its development and execution:

Identifying a clear objective : A strong public relations campaign is built on a clear objective. While this could be as broad as raising awareness for a product, service, or brand, ideally it should be more specific, for instance, increasing sales for a company or influencing public or government behavior for an advocacy group. Such specific objectives are not merely beneficial but essential, as they provide a definitive roadmap for tactical execution, ensure optimal resource allocation, and, crucially, enable the rigorous measurement of campaign efficacy against predefined benchmarks. This specificity directly underpins the ability to demonstrate tangible outcomes that align with broader organizational and business objectives (Wojciechowski and Skrzypek-Ahmed, 2022).

Formulating the message that will help achieve that objective : Public Relations campaigns necessitate a message that is not only clear and concise but also strategically formulated to resonate with the target audience. This message should precisely and unambiguously articulate the organization's core values, mission, or objective, effectively informing the audience while simultaneously motivating them towards a specific desired action. Such a focused approach ensures that communication initiatives are intrinsically aligned with broader organizational goals and address the specific needs and concerns of the target demographics (Wojciechowski and Skrzypek-Ahmed, 2022). This careful crafting of messages, alongside the broader communication efforts, contexts, and systems, acts as a driving force for success, while obstacles and distractions can function as constraining forces that must be meticulously managed (Abed, 2025).

Communicating that message to the appropriate audience : Effective public relations hinges on the precise delivery of formulated messages to specific target audiences, most likely to be receptive and influenced by communication. This necessitates meticulous audience identification, which involves comprehensively understanding their needs, concerns, and potential problems (Wojciechowski and Skrzypek-Ahmed, 2022). By tailoring messages to address these specific demographic insights, PR professionals can ensure maximum resonance and persuasive impact. Concurrently, strategic channel selection becomes paramount, as the chosen platforms must optimally facilitate message reception and minimize potential communication obstacles (Abed, 2025). This dual focus on audience understanding and appropriate dissemination channels is critical for translating strategic blueprints into direct engagement that achieves desired objectives.

This strategic approach ensures that communication efforts are not only heard but also acted upon, fostering desired behavioral changes and strengthening relationships between the organization and its publics (Gregory and Macnamara, 2019).

Elements Beyond the Conventional in PR

Beyond these fundamental characteristics, a constellation of other indispensable factors profoundly influences the ultimate success and efficacy of any public relations campaign. Overlooking these nuanced considerations can significantly undermine strategic objectives and impede the achievement of desired outcomes. These additional elements often involve a deep understanding of audience psychology, the prevailing socio-political climate, and the dynamic interplay of various communication channels as explained hereafter:

Strategic Resource Allocation : Effective budgeting extends beyond mere financial allocation, encompassing the strategic deployment of both financial and human resources to maximize campaign impact and achieve predefined objectives. This ensures that resources are optimally leveraged to realize broader strategic frameworks and desired communication outcomes (Gregory and Macnamara, 2019).

Ethical and Regulatory Adherence : Strict adherence to legal and ethical guidelines is imperative, functioning not merely as a means to avoid pitfalls but as a proactive measure to safeguard organizational reputation, maintain credibility, and mitigate significant "constraining forces" (Abed, 2025) arising from issues such as defamation or conflicts of interest related to incentives for public figures.

Precision in Messaging : Meticulously crafted, unambiguous messages are a strategic imperative for public relations professionals. Such precision is essential for ensuring accurate audience reception, preventing misinterpretation or unintended offense, and directly contributing to desired behavioral changes and communication outcomes, thereby averting "obstacles and distractions" (Abed, 2025). Furthermore, consistent recognition of an organization's audience needs and interests enables PR professionals to construct more persuasive and impactful messages (Santos, 2022).

Creating a PR Action Plan : To ensure the strategic efficacy and ultimate success of a public relations campaign, professionals must rigorously integrate several critical considerations into their planning and strategizing, extending beyond fundamental characteristics to address the multifaceted dynamics of communication and engagement. This involves developing a detailed and adaptable communication plan that accounts for both internal and external factors, aligning campaign goals with broader organizational objectives (Abed, 2025).

Understanding the Company : A profound comprehension of the company's vision, mission, objectives, business priorities, strategies, and culture is not merely fundamental, but absolutely critical for ensuring that public relations efforts are strategically aligned with and effectively contribute to broader organizational goals (Gregory and Macnamara, 2019; Wojciechowski and Skrzypek-Ahmed, 2022). This deep understanding allows PR professionals to craft messages and strategies that genuinely resonate with the organization's identity and strategic direction, thereby mitigating potential misalignments or reputational risks.

Market Environment : A thorough analysis of the market in which the company operates, encompassing market expectations and its current competitive position, is not merely foundational but crucial for shaping effective public relations strategies. This comprehensive understanding ensures that PR efforts are precisely aligned with market realities, enabling the formulation of targeted messages that resonate with the audience and proactively address potential challenges (Wojciechowski and Skrzypek-Ahmed, 2022).

Executive Expectations : Knowing the PR expectations of the executive team is crucial for ensuring alignment with leadership goals and overall organizational objectives (Gregory and Macnamara, 2019; Wojciechowski and Skrzypek-Ahmed, 2022). This proactive understanding and alignment are vital not only for securing essential executive buy-in and optimizing resource allocation but also for elevating public relations from a purely tactical function to a strategic imperative. This strategic integration directly supports corporate success by mitigating potential misalignments and ensuring PR efforts contribute effectively to broader strategic frameworks and desired communication outcomes.

Competitive Landscape : Understanding competing companies and anticipating their actions and strategies, through detailed competitor analysis, is not merely advantageous but essential. This comprehensive analysis allows PR professionals to effectively identify market gaps, craft unique value propositions, and develop proactive communication strategies that lead to more effective positioning and differentiation, thereby enabling a company to stand out in a crowded marketplace and mitigate potential competitive threats (Wojciechowski and Skrzypek-Ahmed, 2022).

Alignment with Business Objectives : Ensuring PR outcomes are directly aligned with and demonstrably contribute to overarching business goals is paramount. This alignment is critical not only for substantiating the value of public relations as a strategic function but also for realizing overall organizational objectives and maximizing strategic efficacy by integrating PR efforts with broader corporate frameworks. This integration also allows for the effective measurement of PR's impact on key performance indicators, thereby validating its strategic importance and contribution to business success (Gregory and Macnamara, 2019) (Bentele, 2008).

Target Audience Insight : A thorough understanding of the precise target audience encompassing their needs, concerns, and interests is paramount for the effective development of tailored and impactful communication strategies (Santos, 2022; Wojciechowski and Skrzypek-Ahmed, 2022). This deep insight enables public relations professionals to craft messages that resonate authentically, fostering stronger connections and driving desired behavioral responses within the intended demographics.

Consumer Behavior : Knowledge of the underlying motivations and reasons behind customer or buyer actions is paramount Public Relations. This insight is essential for not only informing highly persuasive messaging and effective engagement strategies by understanding audience perceptions, but also for accurately predicting audience responses and proactively shaping public opinion and behavior (Ugoani, 2020; Santos, 2022; Abed, 2025). Ultimately, these diverse elements and meticulous planning considerations form the indispensable foundation for constructing comprehensive and successful public relations campaigns, directly contributing to their strategic efficacy and the achievement of desired organizational outcomes. This strategic integration elevates public relations from a purely tactical function to a strategic imperative, ensuring alignment with leadership goals and broader business objectives (Gregory and Macnamara, 2019; Wojciechowski and Skrzypek-Ahmed, 2022). Consequently, public relations functions as a critical management function, integrating participative management and action, which not only drives strategy effectiveness by shaping public opinion and behavior but also validates its strategic importance through measurable contributions to key performance indicators (Bentele, 2008; Gregory and Macnamara, 2019; Ugoani, 2020; Abed, 2025).

Forms of Public Relations

Public relations encompass various forms, each serving distinct purposes: Media Relations, Strategic Communications, Community Relations, Public Affairs, Internal Communications, Online and Social Media Communications, Crisis Communications, and Social Responsibility Management. These forms are integral to comprehensive public relations practices.

Media Relations : Media relations, a strategic management of communication between an organization and media professionals aimed at building and maintaining a positive reputation and fostering mutually beneficial relationships with the public (Awoyemi et al., 2023). This is achieved by informing the public about the organization's mission, policies, and practices in a positive, consistent, and credible manner (Turk, 1985). Effective media relations leverage planned and sustained efforts to disseminate information through various channels, utilizing both traditional and contemporary media platforms to reach diverse audiences (Chukwu, 2023).[1]

---

1. Media relations is a form of public relations. The goal of media relations is to educate the media (newspapers, radio, television, and other forms of journalism) to report on a company's objectives, accomplishments, and management accomplishments. See: https://www.indeed.com/ and https://www.pr.co/media-relations.

Strategic Communications : Strategic communication management is precisely defined as the systematic planning and execution of information flow, communication initiatives, media development, and reputation management within a long-term strategic framework. Its primary function is to purposefully convey deliberate messages through the most suitable media channels to designated audiences at opportune times, thereby directly contributing to and achieving desired long-term organizational objectives. This holistic approach positions communication management as a dynamic process that necessitates a delicate balance between three crucial factors: the message, the media channel, and the audience.[2]

Strategic communication puts audience understanding at the heart of policy and service design, resulting in better decision-making and improved delivery. The three levels of analysis macro, meso, and micro that comprise successful strategic communication are explained in detail. This chapter teaches students and experts how to apply these levels in professional practice and identifies their important elements.

Communication is strategic when it aligns with an organization's mission, vision, and values, enhancing its strategic positioning and competitiveness against rivals. Understanding communication strategy requires viewing it solely from the organization's perspective. As defined, *"The nature of organisational communication in general, and strategic communication in particular, is the purposeful use of communication by an organisation to fulfill its mission".*(Hallahan et al., 2007; Thomas and Stephens, 2014; Zerfaß et al., 2018)

---

2. Bockstette, Carsten (December 2008). "Jihadist Terrorist Use of Strategic Communication Management Techniques" (PDF). George C. Marshall Center for European Security Studies. Archived from the original (PDF) on 2011-07-19. Retrieved 2015-09-08.

Therefore, a Strategic Communications Framework should be laid out to achieve communication objectives with the audience or organization. The deliberate application of specific content will help clearly achieve business goals.[3] Even though communication is something that does happen in the organization, businesses that take steps to implement sound strategies impacting the effectiveness of their business communications can achieve measurable results.[4]

Community Relations : Community relations serve as a pivotal strategic imperative for businesses, cultivating mutually beneficial partnerships within their operational spheres. This goes beyond mere philanthropy, embedding social, environmental, and ethical considerations directly into core business practices. By doing so, organizations forge deep, meaningful relationships and foster invaluable goodwill. Through financial contributions, direct donations of time or products, and various community-centric initiatives, companies can establish robust relationships and build profound trust with local populations. Frequently integrated within comprehensive Corporate Social Responsibility frameworks, effective community relations stand as an indispensable link between corporations and the communities they operate within (Thyagaraju, 2020).

Such initiatives are critical for addressing complex societal challenges, significantly enhancing corporate reputation, solidifying stakeholder trust, and securing a business's vital social license to operate. This, in turn, directly contributes to long-term sustainability and

---

3. Knudsen, G. H., & Lemmergaard, g. (2014). Strategic serendipity: How one organization planned for and took advantage of unexpected communicative opportunities. Culture & Organization. 20(5), 392–409.

4. See: Mulhern (2009)

generates profound positive impact (Abdullah et al., 2017). These actions encompass a wide array of efforts meticulously designed to alleviate social concerns, including impactful charitable activities, unwavering adherence to fair labor standards, proactive support for community development, and vigorous promotion of health and safety (Singh, 2024). Furthermore, often recognized as 'neighborhood PR' or 'community outreach,' community relations function as an essential strategic communication management instrument for both businesses and governmental entities, adeptly facilitating engagement with their broader operational environment. This multifaceted approach ensures that organizations are perceived as exemplary corporate citizens, actively and demonstrably contributing to the well-being and economic prosperity of the areas in which they proudly operate.[5]

Public Affairs : According to Public Affairs Networking, public affairs is precisely defined as integrating crucial elements such as government relations, media communications, issue management, corporate and social responsibility, information dissemination, and strategic communications advice. Fundamentally, it involves strategic engagement efforts between organizations, specifically designed to cultivate and maintain essential business and governmental relationships. The field has undergone significant transformation in recent years, reflecting its dynamic nature, and is now firmly established as a specialized and critical sub-discipline of public relations. This specialization encompasses various functions such as lobbying, government affairs, and community relations, all vital for effective

---

5. Community relations is considered a two-way benefit to its society. It positions businesses as civically and ethically responsible in their local communities, fosters goodwill among the locals–your potential customers, and helps the community to thrive. See: https://maclyngroup.com/.

communication management within the public sector (Gawroński et al., 2021) (Dong, Zheng and Morehouse, 2023).[6]

Internal Communications : The Local Government Association of the UK defines internal communications as encompassing strategic narrative development, managerial dialogue, employee participation incentives, and transparent communication practices. The multifaceted nature of these activities frequently leads to the conflation of employee engagement with internal communication. Nevertheless, despite internal communication's undeniable role as a principal driver of engagement, it is imperative to distinguish internal communication as an active function, a mechanism utilizing information and dialogue to inform, motivate, and inspire. Employee engagement, conversely, represents a responsive outcome, the anticipated consequence of strategic investments in staff communication and the cultivation of a constructive organizational culture.[7]

Online & Social Media Communications : This critical area of public relations encompasses the dynamic exchange of information and ideas across digital channels, including the internet, social media platforms, and messaging applications. Social media, as defined by Tufts University, provides interactive platforms where individuals actively create, share, and exchange information and ideas within virtual communities and networks. This inherent interactivity makes these platforms indispensable for fostering direct engagement and building relationships with diverse stakeholders.

---

6. See: http://www.publicaffairsnetworking.com/

7. Internal communications is the function responsible for effective communications among participants within an organization. https://www.local.gov.uk/

The widespread adoption of these channels is evident, with numerous organizations, such as Tufts' Office of Communications and Marketing, actively managing official accounts across major platforms like Facebook, X/Twitter, Instagram, LinkedIn, and YouTube. This ubiquitous presence underscores the profoundly pervasive and strategically vital role of online and social media communications in shaping contemporary public relations efforts, enabling real-time dialogue, reputation management, and the agile dissemination of key messages to target audiences.This digital evolution, marked by the 24/7 online world and interactive platforms, necessitates a comprehensive shift from traditional PR practices to dynamic strategies that fully leverage digital tools. This is crucial not only for continuous, real-time engagement and reputation management but also for fostering direct stakeholder relationships, enabling agile message dissemination, and ensuring PR remains strategically vital in contemporary communication landscapes (Søilen, 2024).

Crisis Communications : Crisis communication constitutes a critical and strategic approach designed to guide organizations and engage stakeholders through disruptive events, thereby safeguarding organizational resilience and reputation (Søilen, 2024). In these volatile situations, the capacity for proactive, swift, and transparent communication is not merely crucial but imperative for mitigating potential damage and preserving public trust. The absence of a robust crisis communication strategy, coupled with inadequate planning and specialized tools, can lead to irreparable damage to an organization's credibility, stakeholder relationships, and long-term viability (Gregory and Macnamara, 2019; Wojciechowski and Skrzypek-Ahmed, 2022). Therefore, a well-developed crisis communication framework is essential, not only for ensuring effective and timely information dissemination during a crisis but also for strategically managing perceptions and protecting an organization's standing in a 24/7 online world (Søilen, 2024). This proactive engagement allows an organization to strategically share information, manage crises impacting its customers and reputation, and uphold its role as a responsible entity. The underlying principle is that a company's reputation is continuously evaluated by stakeholders, irrespective of active management efforts (Bentele, 2008). A highly effective crisis communication model typically integrates five key elements: communication, coordination, collaboration, cooperation, and control.

Social Responsibility Management

Social responsibility management, within the realm of Public Relations, involves orchestrating and supervising initiatives designed to benefit the community and tackle social challenges. Leaders significantly amplify their impact by prioritizing accountability to society and the broader community, as this is crucial for an organization to gain and sustain its 'licence to operate' and maintain a positive standing in public opinion (Gregory and Macnamara, 2019). While both Corporate Social Responsibility and PR endeavor to cultivate strong stakeholder relationships, CSR focuses on tangible contributions to community well-being, whereas PR strategically manages the organization's public image and reputation by communicating these efforts and ensuring alignment with societal expectations. This integrated approach elevates PR's role from mere communication to a vital strategic function that underpins organizational legitimacy and sustains success (Gregory and Macnamara, 2019).

PR Versus Advertising

Public Relations is primarily oriented towards cultivating public awareness and strengthening overall organizational reputation by leveraging earned media channels and fostering enduring stakeholder relationships. In contrast, advertising endeavors to stimulate immediate sales and revenue generation via meticulously controlled, paid promotional efforts (Søilen, 2024). This foundational divergence highlights public relations' capacity to engender trust and credibility through independent third-party validation, starkly differing from advertising's direct, commercially driven promotional communications (Dike, 2025). Although both public relations and advertising function as strategic promotional instruments, their overarching strategic objectives exhibit considerable divergence:

Feature	Public Relations	Advertising
Primary Goal	Build awareness and enhance overall reputation [Current Document]	Generate profit and revenue through direct sales [Current Document]
Approach	Networking and various communication methods [Current Document]	Specific, paid campaigns [Current Document]
Control	Less direct control over message placement and interpretation	High control over message, placement, and frequency
Credibility	Earned media often perceived as more credible	Paid media may be perceived as less credible

Corporate Advertising Controversy

Corporate advertising has historically been considered a controversial practice within the marketing industry. Unlike traditional advertisements that promote a specific product or service, corporate advertising focuses on enhancing the overall image of the firm, making its purpose notably similar to public relations (Søilen, 2024). However, this similarity in objective often blurs the lines between genuine corporate communication and promotional content. The controversy arises precisely because corporate advertising, by its nature, employs *paid media* channels to cultivate a favorable public image.

While public relations strives for credibility through *earned media* and independent third-party validation, corporate advertising, despite its image-building aims, maintains significant control over its message and placement due to its commercial nature. This inherent characteristic often leads stakeholders to perceive such paid image-shaping efforts with skepticism, questioning their authenticity compared to the more independently validated messages sought by PR, thus contributing to its controversial status. This skepticism often stems from the perception that corporate advertising, despite its sophisticated messaging, inherently lacks the unbiased endorsement associated with earned media, thereby potentially undermining its intended impact on corporate reputation (Cowan and Guzmán, 2018).

Public Relations in Theatre

In the theatre industry, PR responsibilities include planning and executing tailored publicity campaigns for a diverse range of clients, from individual artists to production companies, theatres, and specific shows. The goal extends beyond mere exposure; it involves strategically securing appropriate and credible media coverage across diverse platforms including print, online publications, broadcast media, and specialist press to cultivate public awareness, enhance reputation, and foster trust for artists, productions, and theatre companies. This strategic leverage of earned media, distinct from paid advertising, is vital for independent third-party validation, which significantly underpins artistic legitimacy and sustained audience engagement in the cultural sector (Søilen, 2024; Dike, 2025).

Disadvantages of Public Relations

Despite its numerous advantages in fostering credibility and managing reputation, public relations also presents distinct disadvantages. For instance, PR practitioners frequently encounter ethical dilemmas, such as conflicts of interest between serving public good and representing client interests (Mitrić, 2022). Public relations inherently faces several significant challenges:

1. No Direct Control : Organizations often lack direct control over how their message is interpreted or presented by the media. This can lead to misrepresentation or unintended framing of the message, potentially distorting the intended communication and even damaging the organization's reputation, as PR relies on third-party validation which is inherently outside direct organizational influence (Dike, 2025).

2. Lack of Guaranteed Results : There is no guarantee that PR efforts will result in media coverage or achieve desired outcomes. Earned media depends heavily on the news value of the content and the subjective editorial decisions of media outlets. This inherent unpredictability means that significant investments in PR can sometimes yield no visible coverage, making it a high-risk strategy compared to paid advertising where placement is guaranteed (Søilen, 2024).

3. Difficulty in Evaluating Effectiveness : Measuring the precise impact and return on investment of PR campaigns can be challenging. While various metrics exist, attributing specific, quantifiable business outcomes directly to PR efforts is complex due to the often long-term and intangible nature of reputation building and stakeholder relationship management. This contrasts with advertising, where direct sales or lead generation can be more readily tracked, making PR's contribution harder to isolate and justify in purely financial terms (Søilen, 2024).

Generally, public relations initiatives are inherently precarious due to their reliance on external media for message dissemination. Content can be readily overshadowed by emerging news or deemed insufficiently newsworthy, potentially leading to its rejection or marginalization. This significantly compromises its intended reach and efficacy. Consequently, public relations offers no assurance that crucial messages will consistently reach their target audiences, as news organizations maintain ultimate discretion over content dissemination, thereby introducing an undeniable element of transmission uncertainty and rendering the eventual impact highly unpredictable (Elrod and Fortenberry, 2020).

CHAPTER 15

Journalistic Accountability

BEYOND HOLDING GOVERNMENTS ACCOUNTABLE to the people, journalists themselves are subject to legal and regulatory frameworks, with ethical conduct being paramount. Media contributes to domestic accountability by elevating issues of public and institutional concern onto public and political agendas. However, this function does not justify disregarding ethical practices, as the principle of respecting other's rights forms a cornerstone of journalistic accountability.

Specifically, media accountability, defined as a relationship between an actor and a forum where the actor justifies their conduct and faces judgment, is indispensable for rigorously upholding journalistic standards and thereby cultivating and sustaining public trust, as it compels transparency and responsiveness from media organizations. (Rozgonyi, 2023).[1]

---

1. Communicators and journalists have rights, responsibilities, and accountabilities to exercise and live by and which must provide guarantees against censorship and protection of freedom of expression, safeguarding the confidentiality of journalistic sources, and ensuring that information held by the government can be timely and easily accessed by the public.

Journalistic Accreditation

The National Council for the Training of Journalists states that accreditation is highly valued by employers, serving as a recognized benchmark of best practice. This benchmark is predicated on stringent performance standards designed to ensure excellence in journalism education and training. These standards encompass a comprehensive set of professional values and competencies that students must demonstrate prior to graduation, reflecting a commitment to both craft and academic rigor (Henderson and Christ, 2014) (Solkin, 2020).[2]

Government Regulations and Journalism

In many countries, national governments establish media authorities to regulate journalistic practices. These authorities assess journalists and media organizations based on government-approved standards, granting or denying accreditation accordingly.[3]

Accreditation is essential for media houses to legally conduct coverage and be recognized as professionals within a country. However, the primary reason for issuing such licenses is to retain the power to withdraw them if journalists or media houses fail to conform to national standards or ethical guidelines as defined by media laws and regulations.

To maintain their operational licenses and avoid discreditation, journalists and media organizations are compelled to adhere to specific rules.

---

2. https://www.nctj.com/work-with-nctj/become-an-accredited-course

3. In the Republic of South Sudan, the Media is regulated with the Media Authority Act, 2013, Access to Information Act 20213 and South Sudan Broadcasting Corporation Act 2013 in addition to policies as the accreditation of Journalists and code of ethics.

This system functions as a form of accountability, often leading to indirect self-censorship to ensure compliance.[4]

Propaganda

Propaganda is a message intrinsically designed to serve the self-interests of its messenger. It relies on the calculated dissemination of information to sway public opinion and control beliefs (Ahmad, Shah and Lee, 2025). This strategic communication systematically exploits emotions over rational thought, relentlessly advancing a specific point of view or agenda (Krishnamurthy, Gupta and Yang, 2020; Martino et al., 2020).

Propaganda is a pervasive and transhistorical phenomenon, intrinsically linked to the consistent pursuit of dominance by power entities (Toursinov, 2024). The discourse surrounding media manipulation and propaganda has significantly intensified in recent years, particularly exacerbated by the pervasive spread of disinformation and fake news through digital channels. Digital propaganda has emerged as an exceptionally potent instrument, especially within geopolitical arenas, where sophisticated, bot-driven campaigns actively shape narratives and systematically erode public trust in democratic institutions (Marigliano, Ng and Carley, 2024). The resurgence of propaganda as a critical analytical concept, frequently juxtaposed with terms such as "fake news" and "post-truth," underscores the imperative for an updated theoretical framework to precisely delineate

---

4. Accreditation' means recognition of news media representatives by the Government for purpose of access to sources of information in the Government and to news materials, written or pictorial, released by the Press Information Bureau and/or other agencies of the Government. In return any media house whose staff is not accredited is not supposed have the privilege of performing journalistic works in a given locale.

its technical parameters and comprehend its function in reinforcing ideological objectives and managing public sentiment. Despite recent scholarly scrutiny of related terminology, propaganda itself, as a technical construct, has received comparatively less focused attention, thereby necessitating a revised analytical-theoretical framework to enhance conceptual and terminological precision (Mitrić, 2022).

Forms of Propaganda

In its endeavor to influence public opinion and modify behavior, propaganda strategically employs diverse forms, each designed to leverage specific psychological and rhetorical techniques. Propaganda techniques frequently exploit human vulnerabilities, employing tactics such as flag-waving, appeals to national sentiments, and loaded language to evoke strong emotional responses and circumvent critical thinking (Krishnamurthy, Gupta and Yang, 2020; Martino et al., 2020). The various forms of propaganda are explained hereinafter:

Bandwagon Propaganda : This technique compels an audience to adopt a belief or action by asserting that "everyone else is doing it," thereby creating a fear of exclusion or isolation for those who do not conform. It capitalizes on the fundamental human desire for social conformity and belonging, leveraging principles of social proof and in-group bias to create a sense of urgency and avoid isolation (Mosiichuk, 2024). By strategically appealing to these innate psychological mechanisms and the perceived social credibility of a widespread trend, it systematically undermines critical thinking and drives the uncritical adoption of the promoted idea or behavior (Guarino et al., 2020; Martino et al., 2020). This approach is particularly effective in social media environments, where the visibility of trends and rapid dissemination of content can amplify its impact, even leading to the unwitting spread of disinformation among susceptible individuals (Antunes et al., 2023).

Testimonial Propaganda : Testimonial propaganda employs the endorsement of esteemed individuals, such as prominent personalities, experts, or public figures, to advocate for a concept, product, or political candidate. This method capitalizes on the 'appeal to authority' and the perceived 'social credibility' of the endorser (Guarino et al., 2020; Martino et al., 2020), with the objective of influencing the audience by bestowing legitimacy upon the promoted entity and circumventing a thorough, critical assessment of the underlying facts.

Plain Folks Propaganda : The Plain Folks technique entails a communicator adopting the persona of an ordinary individual, aiming to forge a sense of shared identity and immediate relatability with the audience. By portraying themselves as "one of us," they cultivate trust and suggest a deep understanding of common struggles and aspirations, thereby making their message, product, or candidate appear more credible and appealing without critical scrutiny. This strategy often relies on simplistic language and everyday scenarios to obscure underlying agendas, thereby fostering an uncritical acceptance of the propagandist's message.

Name-calling or Labeling Propaganda : Name-calling or labeling is a propaganda technique employed to discredit an opponent by associating them with disparaging, emotionally charged language or pre-existing biases, thereby circumventing rational discourse and eliciting strong, negative reactions from the target audience (Pandiani, Sang and Ceolin, 2024). This tactic often involves the use of derogatory labels or loaded language, which are designed to evoke strong emotional responses and bypass logical evaluation, thus shaping perceptions through emotional manipulation rather than factual debate (Pandiani, Sang and Ceolin, 2024) (Martino et al., 2020).

Transfer Propaganda : Also known as association, this technique projects positive or negative qualities from one person, entity, object, or value onto another, aiming to make the latter more acceptable or to discredit it. It often utilizes symbols, images, or concepts to evoke specific emotional responses and link them to the target, thereby bypassing rational assessment and influencing perception (Pandiani, Sang and Ceolin, 2024). This technique avoids rational thought by using established emotional connections to symbols or ideas, thereby manipulating the audience's perception of the target without direct argument (Martino et al., 2020).

Fear Propaganda : Fear propaganda deliberately instills anxiety or panic, leveraging perceived threats or negative consequences to compel an audience to adopt a particular viewpoint or action (Pandiani, Sang and Ceolin, 2024). This technique exploits innate psychological mechanisms and in-group bias, skillfully manipulating human cognition and emotion to foster support for a particular agenda or to coerce specific behaviors (Mosiichuk, 2024). It circumvents rational thought by tapping into primal fears, making the audience more susceptible to the propagandist's desired message. This form of manipulation, often leveraging emotionally charged language and psychological or rhetorical tricks, functions as a powerful tool within propagandistic discourses, political campaigns, and advertising (Krishnamurthy, Gupta and Yang, 2020; Martino et al., 2020; Toursinov, 2024). It shapes public opinion by exploiting innate psychological mechanisms and emotional vulnerabilities, thereby circumventing critical assessment and subtly coercing audiences towards a desired viewpoint or action (Mosiichuk, 2024; Pandiani, Sang and Ceolin, 2024).

Logical Fallacies Propaganda : This form Propaganda employs flawed reasoning to persuade, presenting arguments that appear sound but are built on incorrect premises or assumptions, often leveraging specific logical fallacies to circumvent critical analysis. Examples include the appeal to ignorance, which asserts something is true because it hasn't been disproven, or substituting emotional appeals for logical thought (Martino et al., 2020). Other common fallacies include the straw man, which misrepresents an opponent's argument to make it easier to attack; red herring, which introduces irrelevant data to distract from the main issue; black-and-white fallacy, which presents only two extreme alternatives as the only possibilities; whataboutism, which discredits an opponent's argument by charging them with hypocrisy; and causal oversimplification, which assumes a single cause for a complex issue (Martino et al., 2020; Pandiani, Sang and Ceolin, 2024). These techniques manipulate audiences by exploiting cognitive biases, thereby hindering rational deliberation and fostering uncritical acceptance of the promoted message.

Soap Propaganda : Soft soap propaganda is a technique that often relies on flattery or insincere compliments, aims to disarm an audience by appealing to their ego or desire for affirmation, thereby making them more receptive to a message (Pandiani, Sang and Ceolin, 2024). By skillfully cultivating a sense of personal connection or appreciation, this method exploits innate psychological mechanisms and emotional vulnerabilities, effectively bypassing critical scrutiny and hindering rational deliberation (Martino et al., 2020; Mosiichuk, 2024). Ultimately, this psychological and rhetorical trick leads to an uncritical acceptance of the propagandist's agenda (Krishnamurthy, Gupta and Yang, 2020). This subtle form of manipulation can be particularly effective in political and marketing campaigns, where it serves to establish a perceived rapport with the audience.

Glittering Generalities Propaganda : This technique employs emotionally appealing words and phrases that, while carrying positive connotations, are deliberately vague and lack concrete evidence or specific meaning. These "slogans" or "clichés" (Martino et al., 2020) are designed to evoke strong emotional responses and associations with concepts like freedom, honor, or prosperity without providing any verifiable details, thereby precluding rational assessment and fostering uncritical acceptance of the promoted idea or product (Pandiani, Sang and Ceolin, 2024). For instance, advertisers claiming their product is "the best" without defining specific criteria exemplify this approach.

Negative Propaganda : Negative propaganda specifically targets an opponent's character, record, or views with the intention of discrediting them, sowing doubt, or generating public distrust. This technique often employs disparaging or emotionally charged language, aligning with strategies like name-calling or labeling, and can involve questioning an opponent's credibility (Pandiani, Sang and Ceolin, 2024). Such propaganda frequently bypasses rational discourse by eliciting strong negative reactions, thereby influencing perception without engaging in substantive debate. Common manifestations include "attack ads," which exclusively highlight perceived negative aspects, and "contrast ads," which strategically compare the propagandist favorably against the opponent by emphasizing the latter's flaws. It is widely observed in political campaigning, where its goal is to undermine public support for rivals. Propaganda, particularly in the digital age, can be more effective than ever due to the ability to influence public opinion through social media, potentially altering election outcomes (Guarino et al., 2020). The technologies and tactics used in internet-based "influence operations" are constantly changing, employing both automated bots and anonymous human accounts to amplify and suppress information (Chang et al., 2021; Woolley, 2022). Detecting propaganda is tricky because it doesn't necessarily lie; instead, it adeptly appeals to emotions or selectively presents facts to bypass rational assessment.

Moreover, propaganda techniques frequently utilize loaded language, name-calling, and repetition, deliberately manipulating perceptions and hindering critical analysis to influence public discourse

(Martino et al., 2020; Mosiichuk, 2024; Pandiani, Sang and Ceolin, 2024).

Techniques and Dissemination of Propaganda

In 1939, social scientists Alfred and Elizabeth Lee classified seven common propaganda techniques in their book *The Fine Art of Propaganda*: name-calling, glittering generalities, transfer, testimonial, plain-folk, card-stacking, and bandwagon. Today, propaganda is disseminated through a vast array of modern media, including radio, television, films, and digital platforms like social media and smartphones. One particularly potent form of digital propaganda is the 'toxic meme,' which leverages emotionally charged words, name-calling, doubt, exaggeration, and appeals to fear or prejudice to influence audiences (Pandiani, Sang and Ceolin, 2024).

Characteristics of Propaganda

In the contemporary information landscape of the 21st century, the rise of the internet and social media has led to challenges associated with the devaluation of information, exacerbated by the proliferation of manipulative communication strategies. Renée Hobbs highlights that propaganda now leverages algorithmic personalization to filter digital content, target advertising, and differentiate product pricing by using data from user behaviors, beliefs, interests, and emotions (Hobbs, 2020). This personalization intensifies the effects of propaganda by creating echo chambers and reinforcing pre-existing biases, making individuals more susceptible to its influence.

Understanding this function of propaganda can lead to a deeper consideration of how texts activate emotion and tap into audience values for various purposes.

This form of communication often operates by activating strong emotions through techniques such as loaded language and emotional appeals, simplifying complex information, appealing to the hopes, fears, and dreams of a target audience, and attacking opponents through logical fallacies like straw man arguments or whataboutism (Martino et al., 2020; Тенева, 2023; Pandiani, Sang and Ceolin, 2024). Propaganda, in this context, does not always rely on outright falsehoods but can achieve its aims by selectively presenting facts or manipulating affective responses (Martino et al., 2020).

Colored Propaganda in Politics

In politics, propaganda is often categorized by its 'color,' indicating the perceived source and truthfulness (Norén, 2018). This categorization provides a framework for understanding how different propaganda strategies are deployed, often manipulating perceptions of truth and source credibility to achieve specific political gains, particularly during elections or in furtherance of political agendas (Vlăduțescu, 2014; Mitrić, 2022).

These techniques involve specific rhetorical and psychological tactics, ranging from using emotionally charged language and appeals to authority to employing logical fallacies such as red herrings and black-and-white fallacies (Martino et al., 2020).

Black Propaganda : This form aims to deceive by making it appear as though the message originates from an opposing or discreditable source, effectively concealing its true origin. It often involves international social media disinformation campaigns, employing deliberate falsehoods, "fake news," or misdirection to discredit an adversary. This tactic is inherently coercive, functioning as a weaponization of information that abuses power to negatively influence the target audience by undermining trust in legitimate sources (Becker, 1949; DeDominicis, 2019; Mitrić, 2022; Fernández, 2023; Toursinov, 2024).

Grey Propaganda : The source of grey propaganda is deliberately concealed, making it difficult for audiences to ascertain its true origin or intent. Unlike black propaganda, its content might not be entirely false, but the lack of transparency about its source, often achieved by creating platforms that mimic legitimate news sources, is a key characteristic This deliberate ambiguity means that both the sender and the message's veracity are obscured, creating uncertainty and undermining trust without resorting to overt lies.

White Propaganda : White propaganda transparently identifies its source and typically conveys information that is accurate or not intentionally deceptive, though its presentation remains biased (Norén, 2018). It serves the sender's interests by carefully selecting and framing information, including valid claims, to subtly influence perceptions and opinions. The ultimate goal is to persuade audiences through a message that appears credible and transparent. This approach often leverages selective communication and framing to sway public opinion while maintaining an appearance of objectivity (Yu et al., 2021; Pandiani, Sang and Ceolin, 2024). Even with transparent sourcing, the strategic selection and emphasis of certain facts can still subtly steer public discourse and opinion toward a predetermined agenda. Thus, white propaganda, while seemingly benign, functions through carefully curated narratives and emphasis, illustrating how strategic communication for political ends can employ non-consensual persuasion using verifiable information (Mitrić, 2022).

Hate Speech

Hate speech is defined as communication that offends, threatens, or insults groups based on characteristics such as race, color, religion, national origin, sexual orientation, disability, or other traits (Hassan et al., 2022; Fino, 2023). There is no universal consensus on its precise meaning, as definitions can vary depending on context and legal frameworks (Anttila and Domínguez-Armas, 2025). However, it generally refers to expressions that spread, incite, promote, or justify hatred based on intolerance, such as racial hatred, xenophobia, or discrimination against minorities (Gajardo and Mata, 2023). These expressions often involve targeting individuals or groups based on their membership, conveying messages of racial inferiority, and are persecutory, hateful, and degrading in nature (Anttila and Domínguez-Armas, 2025).

Hate speech, a virulent form of discrimination, can manifest in written, verbal, audio-visual, or mass communication, aiming to subject certain groups to hatred and dehumanization (Guyatt et al., 2012; Pérez et al., 2023). Its increasing intensity and prevalence, particularly on social media, have been linked to stress and depression in victims, and the creation of a hostile environment for vulnerable groups (Pérez et al., 2023). Historically, hate speech has often preceded public incitement to violence and specific criminal acts, including genocide, functioning as a component of organized systems of persecution (Schweppe and Perry, 2021). Such communication often fosters a climate of violence through the demonization and dehumanization of opponents portraying outgroups as fundamentally different, inferior, and even existential threats violating their human dignity and effectively marginalizing the victim group from the human community. The direct relationship between hate speech and violent acts, such as the "Unite the Right" attacks in Charlottesville or the Rohingya genocide, underscores its severe consequences (Pérez et al., 2023). Due to its violation of human rights and its potential to drive violence, hate speech frequently warrants legal and social interventions to counter its spread. For example, the International Convention on the Elimination of All Forms of Racial Discrimination views hate speech as a disregard for human dignity and fundamental human rights, aiming to undermine both individuals and societies (Hassan et al., 2022).

Elements of Hate Speech

Grasping the profound and destructive impact of hate speech, which is intrinsically linked to psychological harm, the creation of hostile environments, and the incitement of violence and even genocide (Guyatt et al., 2012; Schweppe and Perry, 2021; Pérez et al., 2023), necessitates a thorough examination of its fundamental constitutive elements. These elements demonstrably contribute to its pervasive harm and typically include:

Targeting an individual or group : Hate speech specifically directs animosity and expresses denigration or vilification towards individuals or groups based on a broad spectrum of identity factors, including race, ethnicity, religion, sexual orientation, gender, disability, nationality, or other protected characteristics (Hassan et al., 2022; Fino, 2023; Anttila and Domínguez-Armas, 2025). This targeting differentiates it from general offensive language by conveying messages that are often rooted in ideologies of intolerance and are persecutory, hateful, and degrading in nature (Mchangama and Alkiviadou, 2022).

Dehumanization : Dehumanization is a form of hate speech that aims to strip target groups of their humanity, reinforcing a sense of an "in-group" and validating shared negative views. This process often involves the creation of an "enemy image," attributing negative characteristics to the target group, denying their individuality, and portraying them as a homogeneous collective (Gajardo et al., 2022; Gajardo and Mata, 2023). By systematically 'othering' and depicting outgroups as fundamentally different, inferior, or even existential threats, hate speech erodes empathy and legitimizes their exclusion and potential violence. This serves to marginalize the victim group from the human community. This rhetorical strategy not only reduces the targeted individuals to mere objects but also primes an audience for discriminatory actions by portraying them as unworthy of ethical consideration or protection (Schweppe and Perry, 2021).

Tension Amplification : Hate speech actively exploits existing societal tensions, seeking to reproduce and intensify them (Baumgarten et al., 2019) by promoting social division and polarization. This is often achieved through blaming target groups for present and past events and portraying them as fundamentally different, inferior, and even existential threats to the in-group (Gajardo et al., 2022). Such rhetoric, frequently amplified by emotionally charged language and logical fallacies, correlates with the escalation of violence by framing outgroups as adversaries. Moreover, hate speech often employs incitement to discrimination, hostility, or violence, urging audiences to act against the targeted group, thereby directly contributing to real-world harm and conflict (Hassan et al., 2022).

Unification and Division : Hate speech constructs a stark 'us versus them' dynamic, which not only fosters strong unity within the in-group by establishing a shared enemy but also actively demonizes and dehumanizes the out-group. This process systematically legitimizes exclusion and animosity, acting as a potent catalyst for amplifying societal tensions and polarization, thereby paving the way for increased discrimination and potential violence (Baumgarten et al., 2019; Hassan et al., 2022).

Hate speech serves as a critical precursor to extreme discrimination and violence, actively cultivating a fertile ground for "othering" by depicting targeted communities as outside the bounds of normal societal protections (Schweppe and Perry, 2021). This deliberate process of demonization and denial of their fundamental humanity systematically erodes empathy, thereby lowering inhibitions against discrimination and violence. Moreover, the systematic nature of hate speech systematically intensifies social tensions and polarization, especially when amplified by influential figures or groups, contributing to the dynamics of atrocity crimes (Jacob and Morada, 2023). Such rhetoric is directly linked to escalating levels of violence and crime, including the potential for wars and genocidal persecutions, and has prompted international bodies like the United Nations to develop strategies for combating these discourses while upholding freedom of expression (Pérez et al., 2023; Rodríguez-Peral, Franco and Bustos, 2025).

Hate Speech in Mass Violence & Genocides

Hate speech is a critical component of state-organized persecution, psychologically preparing a population for planned atrocities. In the years following the Rwandan Genocide, there has been increasing recognition that the presence of hate propaganda can signal impending genocide or widespread violence and conflict. This recognition has led to a greater focus on early detection and prevention of such rhetoric.

The presence of hate speech serves as an indicator of increasing social tension and polarization when employed in an orchestrated and strategic manner. In many cases of genocide and mass atrocity, hate speech has been present just before their onset, leading researchers to conclude a close correlation between political or religious campaigns of hate speech aimed at minority groups and the likelihood of violence escalation.

When voiced through leaders with a sympathetic audience, hate speech contributes to the dynamics of atrocity crimes by identifying and labeling a homogenous group (Jacob and Morada, 2023). This "othering" is a necessary step in identifying the targeted community as not being protected by the usual rules of social behavior (Schweppe and Perry, 2021).

Hate speech is deeply intertwined with psychological processes that erode empathy and justify aggression. Frequent exposure to derogatory language about immigrant and minority groups can lead to political radicalization and deteriorate intergroup relations. It can replace empathy with intergroup contempt, acting as both a motivator and a consequence of such language (Bilewicz et al., 2020). Dehumanization, a common element of hate speech, increases the risk of conflict and violence and makes it harder to resolve existing conflicts (Deffenbaugh, 2024). While dehumanization has often been considered an alarming early warning sign for mass systematic killing, some research suggests "toxification" may be a more precise indicator (Neilsen, 2015). Blatant forms of dehumanization are surprisingly prevalent and potent, uniquely predicting aggressive intergroup attitudes and behavior beyond subtle forms of dehumanization and outgroup dislike, thereby promoting vicious cycles of conflict (Kteily and Bruneau, 2017). Research also indicates that exposure to hate speech deteriorates neurocognitive mechanisms related to understanding others' pain, further hindering empathy (Pluta et al., 2023).

Historically, hate speech has often been a precursor to violence. In Rwanda, for example, a radio station broadcast incitements for Hutus to slaughter their Tutsi neighbors (Schweppe and Perry, 2021). Similarly, the use of hate speech and incitement against the Rohingya community in Myanmar directly correlated with the escalation of violent attacks (Morada, 2023).

Falsehoods, ranging from selective reporting to deliberate mischaracterization of events and adversaries, or even plain fabrication and lies, create a breeding ground for incitement to commit violence (Holvoet, 2022).

Consequently, the United Nations Committee on the Elimination of Racial Discrimination developed early-warning procedures, including a "special set of indicators related to genocide," to detect and prevent developments in racial discrimination that could lead to violent conflict and genocide at the earliest possible stage. These indicators allow the committee to assess factors known to be significant components of situations that escalate to conflict and genocide.

The UN has also introduced a strategy and plan of action on hate speech to support states in their efforts to combat these discourses while simultaneously respecting freedom of expression (Rodríguez-Peral, Franco and Bustos, 2025).

The international legal framework recognizes incitement to genocide as an international crime (Fino, 2023). This proactive approach by international bodies underscores the severe ramifications of hate speech and the imperative to address it not merely as an expression of opinion, but as a potential precursor to egregious human rights violations (Bilewicz et al., 2020; Schweppe and Perry, 2021). The extensive nature of this framework underscores the international community's dedication to the surveillance and reduction of hate speech dissemination, acknowledging its profound impact on social equilibrium and the prevention of widespread atrocities (Timmermann, 2008; Jacob and Morada, 2023).

Harm of Hate Speech

Communication theory offers insights into the detrimental effects of hate speech. According to the ritual model of communication, racist expressions categorize minorities with negative attributes, directly harming them. Research by Matsuda et al. further indicates that racist speech can induce direct physical and emotional changes in its recipients.[5] The repeated use of such expressions causes and reinforces the subordination of these minorities. This has been enough to sway the court in previous cases such as *Brown v. Board of Education* in the United States of America, in which the Court stated that segregation ''generates a feeling of inferiority as to their [African American's] status in the community that may affect their hearts and minds in a way unlikely ever to be undone." The idea that hate speech is a mechanism of subordination is supported by scholarly evidence.[6]

Systemic Hate Speech and Violence : While international human rights conventions obligate states to prohibit hate speech, these frameworks can be inadequate under specific circumstances. This is particularly true when hate speech is systematically and strategically deployed by a state or a state-like organization's leadership as part of a planned persecution against a specific religious, racial, or ethnic group. In such situations, the dangers of incitement to hatred and the profound responsibility of those who instigate such speech acts extend beyond mere human rights obligations, proving insufficient for preventing

---

5. Mari Matsuda, Charles R. Lawrence, III, et al., "Words That Wound: Critical Race Theory, Assaultive Speech, and the First Amendment" (Westview Press 1993).

6. Hate Speech and its Harms: A Communication Theory Perspective |journal of Communication, 1997, volume 47 P 4–19.

genocides and other ethnically motivated violence, or for bringing the true originators of these crimes to justice.

Hate Speech as Persecution and its Enforcement : International tribunals have recognized that hate speech, when certain conditions are met, can constitute the crime against humanity of persecution. This understanding of vicious hate propaganda's legal implications dates back to the Nuremberg trials. For instance, the Nuremberg Tribunal convicted Julius Streicher, the founder and editor of the anti-Semitic newspaper *Der Stürmer*, on the grounds that his incitement to murder and extermination, at a time when Jews were being systematically killed, clearly constituted persecution based on political and racial grounds, thus a Crime Against Humanity. Domestically, many national laws also criminalize such speech; for example, Section 29 of the Media Authority of the Republic of South Sudan explicitly defines hate speech and incitement to violence as offenses.[7] Furthermore, when addressing cases involving incitement to hatred and freedom of expression, the European Court of Human Rights[8] employs two distinct approaches under the European Convention on Human Rights:

---

7. Section 29 of the Media Authority of the Republic of South Sudan provides that hate speech and incitement to violence is an offence

8. When dealing with cases concerning incitement to hatred and freedom of expression, the European Court of Human Rights uses two approaches which are provided for by the European Convention on Human Rights: - the approach of exclusion from the protection of the Convention, provided for by Article 17 (prohibition of abuse of rights) where the comments in question amount to hate speech and negate the fundamental values of the Convention; and the other approach of setting restrictions on protection, provided for by Article 10, paragraph 2 of the Convention (this approach is adopted where the speech in question, although it is hate speech, it does not apt to destroy the fundamental values of the Convention).

- **Exclusion from Protection:** This approach is applied when comments amount to hate speech that negates the Convention's fundamental values, effectively excluding them from protection.

- **Setting Restrictions on Protection:** Free speech under Article 10, paragraph 2 of European Convention on Human Rights (ECHR) is used as protection mechanism at some point in essence where hate speech doesn't meet a threshold: This approach is used when speech, although constituting hate speech, does not aim to destroy the European Convention's fundamental values. In such instances, restrictions may be placed on the protection of that speech.

This legal precedence underscores the severe implications of systematic hate propaganda and highlights the need for robust legal frameworks and enforcement to prevent mass atrocities and ensure accountability for those who instigate them.[9]

The International Covenant on Civil and Political Rights states that *"any advocacy of national, racial or religious hatred that constitutes incitement to discrimination, hostility or violence shall be prohibited by law."*

On May 3, 2011, Michael O'Flaherty, on behalf of the United Nations Human Rights Committee, issued General Comment No. 34 on the International Covenant on Civil and Political Rights. This document expressed apprehension that many forms of hate speech do not meet the gravity threshold set forth in Article 20, a concern further

---

9. Restraining the heartless: racist speech and minority rights. Journal, Indiana Law-Journal, Summer/2009 | volume 84 | P. 963

elaborated in Paragraph 54 of the 'Draft General Comment No. 34,' published on the same date during the Committee's Hundredth and first session.

This perspective suggests that certain expressions of hatred, while potentially harmful, may not reach the stipulated threshold of incitement to discrimination, hostility, or violence as defined under Article 20 of the ICCPR (Fino, 2023). This crucial distinction differentiates between mere expressions of hatred and those crossing the legal threshold for prohibition, aligning with Article 20, paragraph 2, of the International Covenant on Civil and Political Rights (Liern, 2020)".[10]

The Convention on the Elimination of All Forms of Racial Discrimination (ICERD) prohibits all incitement of racism.[11]

On several occasions, debates on the use of internet to further hate speech and incitement violence have been held. This provides on the other hand a shrinking space for freedom of expression and how hate speech and other forms of unwanted communication can contribute negatively to the existence of such debates.

Concerning the debate over how freedom of speech applies to the Internet, conferences concerning such sites have been sponsored by the United Nations High Commissioner for Refugee.[12]

The 1994 Rwandan genocide tragically demonstrated the media's

---

10. Article 20 of the International Covenant on Civil and Political Rights.

11. Article 4 of the international Convention on the Elimination of All Forms of Racial Discrimination.

12. http://www.unhchr.ch Open Element "Report of the High Commissioner for Human Rights on the use of the Internet for purposes of incitement to racial hatred, racist propaganda and xenophobia.

role in inciting and preparing for mass violence. This event served as a critical lesson, prompting global efforts to sanction media outlets that propagate hate messaging, whether through new or conventional channels. Similar historical instances include the apartheid era in South Africa and recent rises in xenophobia across the African continent.

Countries approach hate speech differently in their legal frameworks:

South Africa: The Constitution explicitly excludes hate speech (along with incitement to violence and propaganda for war) from the protection of free speech. Furthermore, the Promotion of Equality and Prevention of Unfair Discrimination Act, 2000, states: *"No person may publish, propagate, advocate or communicate words based on one or more of the prohibited grounds, against any person, that could reasonably be construed to demonstrate a clear intention to be hurtful, harmful or to incite harm, and promote or propagate hatred"*.

Brazil: According to the 1988 Constitution, racism and other forms of race-related hate speech are classified as ''imprescriptible crimes'' or ''capital crimes,'' meaning they carry no right to bail for the accused.

Free Speech and Hate Speech

The intricate relationship between free expression and hate speech presents a complex challenge, requiring a delicate balance between individual rights and the necessity of preventing harm. While freedom of speech is fundamental for open dialogue, it is not without limits, especially when it directly incites illegal acts or causes harm. Hate speech differentiates itself from protected speech through its deliberate intention to spread hatred, cause harm, and provoke discrimination or violence against specific groups (Hassan et al., 2022). This distinction marks the crucial "thin line" where speech transitions from expressing an opinion to actively promoting hatred, discrimination, or violence. Consequently, international organizations such as the United Nations have developed strategies to counter hate speech while simultaneously upholding freedom of expression, acknowledging its severe consequences and its potential role as a precursor to human rights violations (Bilewicz et al., 2020; Schweppe and Perry, 2021; Rodríguez-Peral, Franco and Bustos, 2025).

Hate Speech: A Limiting Factor

Hate speech is commonly understood as a type of expression that does not typically receive free speech protections because its fundamental purpose is to inflict harm and potentially incite violence and discrimination. It is characterized as communication that targets and offends, threatens, or insults specific groups based on attributes such as race, color, religion, national origin, sexual orientation, or disability (Hassan et al., 2022; Fino, 2023). Its primary objective is to disseminate, provoke, advocate, or legitimize hatred rooted in intolerance, including but not limited to racial hatred, xenophobia, or prejudice against minority populations (Gajardo and Mata, 2023).

More than just offensive, hate speech is a dangerous form of discrimination that is intrinsically tied to psychological damage, the fostering of hostile environments, and the instigation of violence, and in severe cases, genocide (Schweppe and Perry, 2021). Historically, hate speech has frequently preceded public calls for violence and specific criminal acts, as evidenced by events like the Rwandan Genocide or attacks against the Rohingya community, illustrating its grave repercussions (Schweppe and Perry, 2021; Morada, 2023).

Free & Hate Speeches Distinction, & Legal Frameworks

The demarcation or thin line between free speech and hate speech is typically established by considering the communication's subject matter, its underlying intention, and its potential repercussions. While free speech safeguards the expression of diverse opinions, including those that are unpopular, hate speech crosses this boundary when it actively promotes animosity, discrimination, or violence against a protected group, rather than simply stating an opinion (Gaïni, 2022; Fino, 2023).

International legal frameworks, such as those formulated by the United Nations, designate incitement to genocide as a crime under international law (Fino, 2023). These frameworks aim to strike a balance between the right to freedom of expression and the critical need to safeguard individuals and communities from the severe psychological and physical damage that hate speech can cause. The UN has implemented a strategy and action plan on hate speech to assist states in countering these harmful narratives while simultaneously upholding freedom of expression (Rodríguez-Peral, Franco and Bustos, 2025). This proactive stance by international bodies highlights the serious implications of hate speech and the necessity of addressing it not merely as a matter of opinion, but as a potential precursor to severe human rights violations (Bilewicz et al., 2020; Schweppe and Perry, 2021).

Hate Speech Versus Defamation

While both hate speech and defamation involve harmful communication, their differences are significant and often involve complex legal and ethical considerations. Hate speech is primarily defined by expressions of animosity or incitement directed at groups based on protected characteristics like religion, ethnicity, gender, or sexual orientation, with the intention of promoting discrimination, hostility, or violence (Gaïni, 2022; Fino, 2023).

In contrast, defamation pertains to false factual statements that harm an individual's reputation, leading to public dishonor or detriment (Gaïni, 2022). The fundamental distinction lies in their main targets and legal objectives: hate speech aims to incite harm or discrimination against a collective identity, whereas defamation safeguards an individual's honor and good name from untrue claims. However, the boundary can blur if hate speech, by targeting a group, also implicitly damages the reputation of identifiable individuals within that group, thus occasionally obscuring this otherwise clear legal and ethical separation. The subtle distinctions between hate speech and defamation require meticulous legal interpretation, given that both concepts address different yet sometimes interconnected forms of communicative harm (Gaïni, 2022).

Defamation

Defamation encompasses false statements of fact that are communicated to a third party, made with a degree of fault, and cause damage to an individual's reputation by exposing them to hatred, ridicule, or contempt, or by causing them to be shunned or harming their profession or trade. This legal concept primarily protects an individual's honor and good name from untrue assertions, whether partially or entirely fabricated. It typically differentiates between libel, which is written or broadcast defamation, and slander, which is spoken. Despite these distinctions, the fundamental aim of defamation law across jurisdictions remains the redress of reputational harm caused by false statements (Gaïni, 2022).

Elements of Defamation

The legal burden in a defamation case rests upon the allegedly defamed individual, who must conclusively demonstrate that:

1. The statement was **false** and **defamatory**, meaning it was capable of harming the individual's reputation by exposing them to hatred, ridicule, or contempt, or by causing them to be shunned or harming their profession or trade.

2. The statement was **published** (communicated) to a third party.

3. The statement **identified** the individual, either directly or indirectly.

4. The statement was made with a requisite **degree of fault** (e.g., negligence, actual malice).

5. The statement caused, or was likely to cause, **serious harm** to the individual's reputation.

These elements are crucial in legal contexts not only to delineate what constitutes defamation from protected speech, such as opinions or truthful criticisms, but also to navigate the complex legal and ethical considerations that sometimes blur the lines between defamation and other forms of harmful communication, like hate speech (Gaïni, 2022).

Libel

Libel represents a specific type of defamation conveyed through enduring mediums, such as printed materials, written texts, images, symbols, or effigies. It inflicts harm upon an individual's reputation, exposing them to public disdain, scorn, or ridicule, or detrimentally affecting their professional or business standing, particularly when perpetrated with malicious intent. Instances of libel include defamatory caricatures, written narratives, or other published works that are inaccurate and designed to damage a person's good name.(Shao, 2024).

Criminality of Libel

Internationally, defamation is predominantly regarded as a civil wrong, falling under tort law. However, some countries, such as South Sudan, adopt a more stringent approach, treating libel as a criminal matter. This criminalization reflects a societal determination that certain defamatory publications pose a sufficiently grave threat to individual reputation and public order to warrant state intervention through the criminal justice system. Consequently, the injured party in these jurisdictions may pursue a case in either civil or criminal courts. Such criminalization typically applies to criminal libel, which, as a permanent form of defamatory material, often carries more severe penalties. Nevertheless, a common thread across all jurisdictions, irrespective of whether defamation is treated as a civil tort or a criminal offense, is the requirement for the claimant to prove that the published statement explicitly identified the aggrieved individual (Bermingham and Brennan, 2012). Beyond this, the evidentiary requirements for proving defamation vary. For instance, some jurisdictions recognize 'defamation per se' in cases of online defamation, where explicit evidence of harm to reputation is not required to establish a claim (Chiruvella and Guddati, 2021). Conversely, in the United Kingdom, the Defamation Act 2013 introduced a stricter mandate, requiring a defamation claimant to demonstrate that the publication of the allegedly defamatory statement 'caused, or is likely to cause serious harm' (Bogle and Lindsay, 2024). This requirement for demonstrating serious harm has since been integrated into the legal frameworks of several Australian jurisdictions and Scotland, while Ireland is currently evaluating its potential implementation.

Slander

Slander is a form of defamation consisting of a false and defamatory statement spoken aloud. Historically, this distinction from libel (written defamation) was crucial, particularly in ancient times when oral communication predominantly shaped public opinion and reputations.

Libel Versus Slander: Understanding Defamation Law

The terms libel, slander, and defamation are often confused, yet they all fall under the umbrella of defamation law, which concerns false statements that harm a person's reputation. Libel specifically refers to written defamatory statements, while slander denotes oral ones.

Historically, the legal distinction between libel and slander was significant, affecting litigation requirements and burden of proof, with libel generally regarded as the more serious offense. However, in many jurisdictions, such as Illinois, this bifurcated approach has evolved, and now both libel and slander are treated similarly under a single set of rules.

Types of Defamatory Statements

Defamation can be categorized into two main types:

1. Defamation Per Se: These statements are so inherently and obviously harmful to one's reputation that proof of actual injury is not required. Illinois law recognizes five categories as defamatory per se:

- Accusing a person of committing a crime.

- Imputing that a person has a loathsome communicable disease.

- Suggesting a person is unable to perform their employment duties or lacks integrity for the role.

- Imputing a lack of ability or prejudice against a person in their profession.

- Accusing a person of adultery or fornication.

A statement is only defamatory per se if its harmful effect is evident without needing additional context.

2. Defamation Per Quod: If a defamatory statement does not fit into a per se category or requires extrinsic facts to demonstrate its harmful nature, it is considered defamation per quod. In such cases, the plaintiff must allege and prove special damages, which means demonstrating a specific, quantifiable economic or pecuniary loss directly resulting from the defamation, such as lost income or sales.

Social Media and Accountability

Individuals and entities alike are accountable for their actions and statements on social media. This platform serves as a significant arena for accountability, where posts, shares, and engagements can profoundly impact reputation, relationships, and professional outcomes. Whether a business, non-profit, public figure, or private individual, responsibility for online content is paramount.

Conventional Media Accountability

Professional journalists and media organizations are held to strict standards of accountability, guided by codes of conduct and journalistic ethics. These guidelines serve as the benchmark for professionalism. Governments often issue licenses and accreditations to media outlets and journalists, reserving the right to withdraw them if professional standards are deemed to be violated. This raises questions about its potential impact on freedom of expression and access to information, even when practiced within legal boundaries.

Administrative Remedies

Administrative remedies involve filing complaints with supervisory authorities, which can lead to investigations and potential enforcement actions against non-compliant companies or media institutions. The doctrine of exhaustion of administrative remedies prevents litigants from immediately seeking redress in courts until all available administrative channels have been fully pursued. This doctrine, rooted in principles of comity, is widely applied in common countries, where many cases are initially handled by independent agencies responsible for specific statutes or regulations.

Press and Broadcast Council

The Press and Broadcast Council typically fulfills three key functions: receiving complaints, investigating the merits of these complaints, and resolving disputes through mediation and negotiation.[13]

Media Authority Board

The board of media authority is the highest administrative remedy for the matters arising from ethical or unethical practice of the media. When PBC is not able to resolve a matter, an appeal is allowed and or else the matter is transferred PBC transfers the case to the board of the Authority if the solution is not acceptable to the parties but only if it has merits.

---

13. In South Sudan, Press and Broadcast Council is empowered by section 29 subsection 3 of the Media Authority Act 2013 to receive complaints, investigate and resolve it amicably. This might be the same approach in other countries though it may have a different naming as the media council amongst others.

The board may dismiss and or admit for hearing and reach a resolution. The board has the power to forward the matter or else its decisions are appealable before a court of law as a final remedy.[14]

Administrative Sanctions

To safeguard the integrity of public discourse and maintain professional standards, journalistic entities and media organizations that violate established ethical codes are subject to oversight by designated regulatory bodies. These authorities are empowered to impose a range of sanctions commensurate with the nature and severity of the transgression. Operating either domestically or as international equivalents, these media regulatory authorities typically adjudicate administrative matters, often serving as a primary recourse before judicial intervention. Their legal mandate encompasses the imposition of various measures against implicated parties, including journalists, media organizations, and other involved third parties, which may entail:

1. Mandates for public retraction, dissemination of corrective information, or formal apologies.

2. Orders for monetary restitution to compensate directly for demonstrable harm.

3. Levying of significant punitive financial penalties.

4. Issuance of formal admonishments or censures.

5. Temporary suspension or permanent revocation of broadcasting licenses.

---

14. See section 29 subsection 4 of the Media Authority Act of the Republic of South Sudan 2013.

6. Prohibition of access to public or designated operational premises.

7. Seizure of operational equipment essential to media functions.

8. Mandates for the cessation of broadcasting operations or, in severe cases, dissolution of the offending entity.

9. For print media, directives to discontinue specific publications or cease all publishing activities.

10. Withdrawal of professional accreditation.

Court of Law

The primary and indispensable function of a court is to uphold the rule of law and facilitate the impartial administration of justice. This concept of a 'court' transcends its physical premises, embodying the entire judicial institution, as exemplified by eminent bodies such as the U.S. Supreme Court or the Supreme Court of the Republic of Sudan. Judicial systems are characteristically organized in hierarchical structures, ranging from local tribunals to national supreme courts. Each tier meticulously addresses cases according to its specific jurisdiction, which is rigorously defined by comprehensive civil and criminal procedural law. Consequently, once administrative recourse has been exhausted, individuals or media entities are empowered to initiate legal proceedings before a competent judicial authority.

This action seeks to secure a definitive resolution, culminating in a legally binding ruling or judgment that addresses the merits of the case.[15]

When admirative remedies have been exhausted, individuals and or media houses can litigate before a judge in a court of law[16] and can therefore reach a solution through a court decision mostly known as ruling or judgement[17].

Going to court to handle a matter is the last resort after all administrative remedies have failed with respect to any dispute involving journalists and media houses.

---

15. Article 13 of the European Convention on Human Rights enshrines that if people's rights are violated, they can access effective remedy. This means they can take their case to court to seek a judgment.

16. According to section 29 subsection 6 of the media authority act of the Republic of South Sudan Sudan; In serious cases where a malicious intent or recklessness is shown and damage is serious, a prison term of up to five years may be imposed by a competent court. Malice may be defined in this section as intent to cause hatred or discrimination because of religion, ethnic and gender or other reason recognized as discriminatory.

17. The 1948 Universal Declaration of Human Rights – states in Article 8: Everyone has the right to an effective remedy by the competent national tribunals for acts violating the fundamental rights granted him by the constitution or by law.

Chapter 16

New Media and Citizen Journalism

New Media encompasses digital forms of communication, including social networking platforms, software, and online content. These platforms enable individuals, groups, and companies to connect and share information such as text and images. Prominent examples include Facebook, Snapchat, and Instagram. New media also extensively features online journalism, including citizen journalism (also known as guerrilla journalism or participatory journalism). This form involves community members actively collecting, reporting, analyzing, and disseminating news and information, often without formal journalistic training or adherence to traditional professional ethics.

Citizen Journalism thrives on social media accounts like Facebook timelines, X/Twitter, YouTube, LinkedIn, Instagram, and TikTok. These platforms, often with live-streaming and broadcast capabilities, allow individuals to publicize information they find interesting, often bypassing conventional journalistic gatekeepers.

The integration of social media into the daily lives of individuals and the operations of news organizations has profoundly impacted how information is consumed and disseminated. This transformative tool presents a dual nature, offering numerous advantages while simultaneously introducing significant challenges, particularly for broadcast journalism.

The Impact of Social Media

Social media has profoundly reshaped the landscape of news, presenting broadcast journalism with both significant opportunities for expanded reach, audience engagement, and rapid dissemination, and complex challenges such as the proliferation of misinformation, concerns over credibility, and shifts in journalistic practices and consumption patterns. These platforms have become powerful tools for news distribution, enabling journalists to reach wider audiences and provide immediate updates, thereby enhancing interaction and offering new promotional avenues. However, the lack of rigorous fact-checking also makes social media a breeding ground for unverified information, raising serious credibility issues and impacting audience trust. This dual impact necessitates substantial adaptation in content creation, dissemination methods, and business models for news organizations (Mirabito, 2020; Li, 2023).

Advantages of Social Media

Social media offers numerous advantages that have been embraced by individuals and the news industry:

1. **Convenience and Ease of Access:** Social media platforms provide accessible means of communication and information. For journalists, they have become critical publishing tools and the main method for citizens to consume the latest news (Bondielli and Marcelloni, 2019). News spreads much faster on social networks than through traditional media, especially during crisis situations (Bondielli and Marcelloni, 2019). This immediacy allows for real-time reporting and engagement with breaking stories (Humeira and Ramadhan, 2022). The shift in communication patterns due to social media has led to increased global connectivity (Amelia and Balqis, 2023).

2. **Fosters Innovation and Learning:** Social media facilitates the exchange of ideas and knowledge. It has provided an environment for collective sense-making and the emergence of amateur content, which can sometimes fill gaps in traditional reporting (Caled and Silva, 2021). This fosters new approaches in storytelling and content creation within broadcast journalism, driving methodological and narrative innovation (Zhao, 2023).

3. **Provides Entertainment:** Broadcast journalists can leverage the entertaining aspects of social media to engage wider audiences, particularly younger demographics, by adapting content formats and delivery styles to align with platform trends (Albrechtslund and Albrechtslund, 2014).

4. **Platform for Societal Change:** social media enables collective action and advocacy, allowing individuals and groups to mobilize, disseminate information, and build collective identity for social movements and protests (Leong et al., 2020). It supports rapid information dissemination and micro-mobilization, influencing public opinion and policymakers (Milan, 2015), which broadcast journalists frequently cover and use as primary sources for understanding public sentiment.

5. **Professional Networking:** Social media serves as a powerful tool for professional networking, especially for journalists, PR professionals, and writers. Journalists actively use platforms like Twitter and Instagram to connect with colleagues, stay informed, and engage with their audiences, thereby expanding their professional roles and digital presence (Mellado and

Alfaro, 2020). These platforms are used not only for news construction and dissemination but also for branding and building professional relationships, even influencing editorial decisions in mainstream media (Cagé, Hervé and Mazoyer, 2020).

6. **Expanded Reach and Dissemination:** News organizations actively use multiple social media platforms (e.g., Facebook, X/Twitter, YouTube, Instagram) to distribute their content, reaching wider audiences and facilitating faster news spread (Guo and Chen, 2022; Hu, 2023). Social media serves as a critical publishing tool for journalists and a primary method for citizens to get the latest news (Bondielli and Marcelloni, 2019).

7. **Audience Engagement and Interaction:** social media enables greater interaction between news organizations and their audiences. Journalists can use these platforms to gauge public opinion on breaking news, discover new stories, and engage with viewers (Bondielli and Marcelloni, 2019). TV news organizations, for instance, utilize social media to distribute video and engage audiences in online settings, influencing content production decisions based on platform recommendations and metrics (García-Perdomo, 2021).

8. **Immediacy of News:** Social networks are highly effective in spreading breaking news much faster than traditional media, particularly during crisis situations (Bondielli and Marcelloni, 2019). This immediacy has become a key value in television news production, with social media facilitating real-time updates (Bivens, 2015).

9. **New Promotional Avenues:** Social media offers new promotional opportunities for news outlets, helping them adapt to changing news consumption habits, where people increasingly seek news from multiple platforms and online sources (Lestari et al., 2018; Omar, Al-Samarraie and Wright, 2020).

10. **Cultivating Relationships:** Media organizations are using social media to cultivate relationships with their audiences, encouraging consumption, comments, and sharing of news (Badham and Mykkänen, 2022).

Disadvantages of Social Media

Despite its undeniable benefits, social media also introduces a host of formidable disadvantages that pose ethical and practical challenges:

1. **Cyberbullying:** The anonymous or semi-anonymous nature of online interactions has contributed to the rise of cyberbullying and online harassment, which can have significant negative effects on individuals, including psychological and physical impacts such as increased depression, anxiety, and self-harm (Ray, McDermott and Nicho, 2024). This phenomenon also targets journalists, impacting their well-being and potentially chilling critical reporting, while also necessitating news organizations to manage hostile online discussion environments.

2. **Reduces Face-to-Face Communication:** The alteration of communication patterns due to social media has brought about shifts in interaction frequency and style compared to offline communication, potentially leading to a decrease in in-person

social interaction (Singh, 2022). For broadcast journalism, this shift can complicate traditional reporting methods that rely on direct community engagement, interviews, and on-the-ground presence, potentially mediating a journalist's understanding of events.

3. **Fake News and Misinformation:** social media has become a fertile ground for the rapid spread of unverified and false information, often referred to as "fake news" or misinformation (Caled and Silva, 2021). The absence of stringent fact-checking and control over user-generated content means that unverified posts can go viral quickly (Haschke, 2016). This challenges the credibility of journalism, as algorithms often favor emotionally charged or sensational stories over fact-based reporting (T., 2024). The spread of fake news is a significant global problem that requires understanding how content propagates online and how people process news (Lazer et al., 2018), forcing broadcast journalists to dedicate resources to verification and counter-narratives.

4. **Health Issues:** Excessive social media use has been linked to health consequences such as increasingly prevalent sedentary lifestyles, which negatively impact physical and mental well-being. Studies indicate that prolonged screen time can replace physical activity and contribute to conditions like obesity, diabetes, and hypertension (Hanna, You and El-Sherif, 2023). Excessive use can also have negative impacts on physical health, as seen in studies of university students (Hosen et al., 2021). While primarily an individual health concern, these widespread issues within the audience and among media

professionals underscore the societal impact that broadcast journalism is increasingly tasked with covering.

5. **Risk of Hacking:** Social media platforms are vital but also pose significant threats to security and privacy, as hackers aggressively exploit them for malicious intentions. Cyber threats include identity theft, phishing, malware distribution, data breaches, and unauthorized access to accounts (Herath, Khanna and Ahmed, 2022). For news organizations, this risk extends to compromising sensitive journalistic data, source protection, and the integrity of their digital broadcasting infrastructure.

6. **Addiction:** Social media addiction, characterized by compulsive and excessive engagement, particularly among teenagers, has detrimental effects on real-life relationships and responsibilities, driven by psychological factors like low self-esteem and fear of missing out (Ji et al., 2023). Consequences include increased anxiety, depression, and disrupted sleep patterns (Perez-Lozano and Espinosa, 2024). As a pervasive societal issue, addiction impacts audience engagement patterns and presents a critical topic for broadcast journalism to investigate and report on.

7. **Distraction in Daily Routines:** social media is a major source of distraction, with constant notifications and updates drawing individuals' attention away from important tasks and impeding focus and productivity (Shanmugasundaram and Tamilarasu, 2023). This can negatively affect academic performance and well-being (Barton et al., 2018). For broadcast journalism, this translates into challenges in maintaining audience attention

spans and competing for limited cognitive resources in a highly saturated media landscape.

8. **Spread of Misinformation and Disinformation:** The absence of rigorous control and fact-checking on social media platforms makes them fertile ground for the rapid spread of unverified or false information. Users often share posts without verifying sources or the validity of the information (Bondielli and Marcelloni, 2019; Hu, 2023).

9. **Credibility Concerns:** While social media is widely used for news, there are ongoing debates about its credibility as a news medium. Factors like the homophily of social media contacts and trust in alternative news sources can influence the perceived credibility of news consumed on these platforms (Cha, 2025). The increasing reliance on social media for news has also been linked to a decline in trust in news overall in some contexts (Fletcher et al., 2024).

10. **Pressure on Journalistic Practices:** The "digital-first" push has changed established journalistic practices, impacting content distribution methods and the nature of the content itself. Journalists often face a "love-hate relationship" with social media, balancing its utility with its demands (Mirabito, 2020).

11. **Shift in Consumption Patterns:** The innovation in social media and digital technology has profoundly transformed media user consumption patterns, requiring news organizations to adapt their content and dissemination methods to retain audiences (Li, 2023). Audiences tend to value immediacy over quality and favor spectatorship over investigation (Omar, Al-Samarraie and Wright, 2020).

12. **Impact on Newsroom Decisions:** Social media not only affects how news is consumed but also how it is produced, influencing newsroom production decisions in traditional media outlets (Cagé, Hervé and Mazoyer, 2020). The use of digital audience analytics can negatively impact the performance of journalistic roles like "watchdog" and "civic" functions, potentially leading to gaps between ideal journalistic standards and actual practice (Mothes et al., 2024).

13. **Decline in Trust and Subscriptions:** Given the continuous decrease in subscription rates and audience trust in news media, news organizations need to understand how their social media activity influences audience engagement and trust (Rath et al., 2018).

A significant correlation exists between social media usage and adverse sleep outcomes, including disturbances, reduced quality, and diminished duration, particularly in young adult populations (Hjetland et al., 2025). This pervasive issue negatively impacts the holistic well-being and cognitive functions of both news consumers and media professionals, thereby subtly influencing the creation and reception of journalistic content.

Within the journalistic sphere, the implications of social media are diverse. While it offers unparalleled opportunities for extensive reach and audience engagement, it concurrently exacerbates the ethical dilemmas confronting journalists. These challenges notably involve the tension between the swift dissemination of information and the crucial need for rigorous verification, alongside the ongoing battle against misinformation (Craig, 2021; Sonni et al., 2024).

Consequently, news organizations are compelled to continuously adapt their strategies to capitalize on the benefits afforded by social media while simultaneously mitigating its inherent risks and ethical complexities (Trattner et al., 2021).

Major Social Media Platforms

1. **Facebook:** A widely used social networking site that allows users to create profiles, connect with friends and colleagues, and share various content formats, including text, photos, videos, live streams, and stories. This versatility enables tailored content delivery.

2. **X (formerly Twitter):** A microblogging system enabling users to send and receive short posts (tweets) of up to 140 characters, often including images or links. Its primary purpose is to connect people and facilitate the sharing of thoughts with a broad audience. Users leverage it for news updates, brand promotions, communication, and following public figures. For businesses, X boosts brand recognition, facilitates customer engagement, drives website traffic, keeps them updated on industry trends, and helps build relationships with influencers.

3. **YouTube:** A free video-sharing platform where users can watch, like, share, and upload videos. Launched in 2005, it has become one of the most popular sites globally, with billions of hours of video consumed monthly. While accessible on various devices, video quality varies, and some content may contain misinformation or be pirated.

4. **Instagram:** Owned by Meta Platforms, Instagram is a photo and video sharing social networking service.

Users can upload media, apply filters, organize content with hashtags, and add geographical tags. Posts can be shared publicly or with pre-approved followers. However, it presents challenges such as image distortion, unrealistic beauty standards, privacy concerns, social comparison, addiction, cyberbullying, mental health impacts, algorithmic changes, and the prevalence of fake accounts and bots.

5. **LinkedIn:** The world's largest professional networking site, LinkedIn facilitates job searching, professional connections, skill development, and career advancement. It also offers blogging and article publishing. Employers frequently use the platform to research and evaluate potential candidates, emphasizing the importance of an established online professional presence.

6. **TikTok:** A social media platform dedicated to creating, sharing, and discovering short videos. Popular among younger demographics, it serves as an outlet for self-expression through singing, dancing, comedy, and lip-syncing. Unlike other platforms, TikTok focuses solely on short-form video content, making it ideal for entertainment and comedy, though it is increasingly used for infotainment and by influencers offering advice and self-promotion. Its use of trending topics and hashtags allows content creators to significantly increase viewership.

OTT and VOD

Over-the-Top and Video On Demand Media represent fundamental elements in contemporary digital media consumption, characterized by their distinct yet frequently convergent approaches to content distribution. Specifically, OTT services involve the direct transmission of content via the internet, thereby circumventing conventional broadcasting, cable, and satellite television infrastructures. Conversely, VOD systems provide users with the capability to access and view video content asynchronously, at their discretion, rather than adhering to predetermined broadcast schedules.

Over-the-Top (OTT)

These are Media Services that stream content directly to consumers via the internet, bypassing traditional content distributors such as cable, broadcast, and satellite television providers. Operating frequently on a subscription model, these platforms offer extensive libraries of on-demand content, granting viewers the autonomy to select what and when they watch, a distinct departure from fixed television schedules.

However, OTT services also come with several drawbacks, including substantial data consumption, ongoing subscription expenses, the risk of content addiction, privacy concerns, inconsistent service quality, and a notable lack of content regulation. Furthermore, their disruptive effect on conventional media outlets has fundamentally altered media consumption patterns, compelling traditional broadcasters to adapt their strategies to remain competitive (Parviz, 2024).

Video On Demand (VoD)

VoD refers to digital video content available to users upon their specific request. This typically encompasses a diverse array of media, including premium cinematic releases, extensive television program libraries, live sporting events, and concert recordings. Platforms like YouTube enable users to access content on demand or build personal digital archives.

Launched in 2017, TikTok exemplifies a VOD platform for short-form video, rapidly becoming one of the most downloaded applications globally with 1.1 billion monthly users (Chalaby, 2023). By 2018, its downloads had surpassed those of WhatsApp, Instagram, and YouTube, signaling its swift rise in the digital landscape (Chakraborty, Kapoor and Ilavarasan, 2020).

Distinction between OTT and VOD

Although interconnected, Over-the-Top services transmit streaming content directly via internet protocols, frequently employing private live broadcasting methodologies, thereby circumventing conventional distribution channels. In contrast, Video On Demand facilitates access to pre-recorded video material on an asynchronous basis, utilizing diverse transmission infrastructures, including cable networks, satellite systems, and the internet. Consequently, while all OTT services inherently encompass VOD offerings, the converse is not universally true; not all VOD content is exclusively mediated through an OTT framework, thereby underscoring a fundamental architectural divergence in their respective content distribution paradigms (Chakraborty, Kapoor and Ilavarasan, 2020).

CHAPTER 17

Data Protection

DATA PROTECTION IS THE essential process of safeguarding critical data from corruption, compromise, or loss. It also ensures the capability to restore this data to a functional state should it become inaccessible or unusable. In the realm of information, data misuse can lead to malpractice, hence everyone handling personal data must adhere to strict guidelines known as 'data protection principles'. These principles, which underpin comprehensive legal frameworks such as the General Data Protection Regulation, mandate that personal information must be used fairly, lawfully, and transparently.

Principles of Data Protection

Despite variations in national data protection regulations, a set of seven widely accepted principles, often forming the bedrock of comprehensive legal frameworks such as the General Data Protection Regulation, universally guiding the protection of personal information:

Lawfulness, Fairness, and Transparency : The principle of Lawfulness, Fairness, and Transparency dictates that all processing of personal data must be grounded on a legitimate legal basis, such as informed consent or a contractual necessity. This ensures that data handling is not only permissible under law but also conducted ethically and without causing undue detriment to individuals. Fairness requires that data processing aligns with the reasonable expectations of the data subject, avoiding any misleading or unexpected uses. Furthermore, transparency demands that individuals are fully and clearly informed about every aspect of data collection and processing including the purposes, methods, and recipients of their data from the very first interaction. This foundational principle is paramount for establishing trust and safeguarding individual rights within any data handling operation.

Data Minimization : Only collect data that is adequate, relevant, and limited to what is necessary for the intended purpose. This principle emphasizes the importance of collecting only the essential data required to fulfill the specified purpose, thereby avoiding excessive data collection. By limiting the volume and scope of personal data, organizations reduce the potential risks associated with data breaches and misuse, enhancing overall data security and privacy. It encourages a careful assessment of data needs, promoting a 'privacy-by-design' approach where data collection is inherently restrictive and focused.

Storage Limitation : Data should be kept for no longer than is necessary for the purposes for which it is processed. This principle mandates that personal data should not be retained indefinitely. Organizations must establish clear data retention policies, defining how long data will be stored based on legal, contractual, or business requirements. Once the purpose for which the data was collected has been fulfilled, the data should be securely deleted or anonymized. This practice minimizes the risk of data exposure over time and supports responsible data governance.

Purpose Limitation : The principle of Purpose Limitation mandates that personal data be collected exclusively for explicitly stated, legitimate, and specific purposes. Crucially, this data must not subsequently be processed in any manner incompatible with those initial defined intentions.

This tenet is fundamental for safeguarding individual trust and autonomy, as it ensures that data subjects retain control over how their personal information is utilized and prevents unauthorized or unexpected uses. To uphold this principle, individuals whose data is being processed must be clearly and comprehensively informed of these purposes. A general declaration of data collection and processing is insufficient; the precise intent driving the data collection must be communicated transparently and proactively from the outset. Failure to adhere to this principle can lead to significant breaches of privacy, erode public confidence, and result in legal and ethical repercussions.

For example, a general physician sharing a patient list with their spouse, who operates a travel agency, for the purpose of offering holiday deals, would violate this principle, as such disclosure would be incompatible with the initial reasons for which the patient information was obtained.

Accuracy : Personal data must be accurate and, where necessary, kept up to date. Maintaining the accuracy of personal data is crucial to ensure that decisions made based on this information are correct and fair. Outdated or inaccurate data can lead to significant issues, impacting individuals' rights and potentially causing harm. Organizations are therefore obliged to take reasonable steps to ensure data is correct, and individuals often have the right to request rectification of inaccurate data. Regular reviews and updates are integral to upholding this principle.

Integrity and confidentiality : Safeguarding personal data necessitates an unwavering commitment to the principles of confidentiality and integrity. This consequently mandates the implementation of robust security measures and stringent protocols designed to preclude unauthorized access, misuse, accidental loss, modification, or damage.

Such comprehensive protection is effectively achieved through advanced technical safeguards and well-defined organizational frameworks. Furthermore, as a fundamental tenet, confidentiality extends beyond sensitive personal data, encompassing critical information across diverse sectors, including finance, healthcare, and national security. Ultimately, this is paramount for ensuring data sovereignty within data-driven applications. Maintaining data integrity guarantees that any data modifications occur with explicit user awareness and permission, thereby preserving authenticity and preventing unauthorized alterations, tag forging, or data leakage attacks (Sobroza et al., 2020).

Accountability in Data Protection : The seventh principle of data protection is Accountability. This principle places the sole responsibility on the Data Controller to not only comply with all Data Protection Principles but also to be able to actively demonstrate that compliance. This involves taking full responsibility for personal data processing activities and maintaining appropriate records and measures to prove adherence to general data protection regulations (such as GDPR)[1] to the relevant data protection authority. Ultimately, accountability serves as the custodian for all other data protection principles, acting as the primary mechanism for their enforcement and ensuring the safeguarding of personal data.

---

1. The General Data Protection Regulation (GDPR) is an EU law on data privacy and security that governs how personal data of EU individuals is collected, processed, and stored. It grants individuals more control over their personal data and imposes strict obligations on organizations, including those outside the EU, that process the data of EU residents. The regulation emphasizes data security, requires lawful and transparent data processing, and provides for penalties for non-compliance.

Press Freedom and Data Protection : While freedom of the press grants individuals and organizations the right to express, publish, and share information, ideas, and opinions without censorship or government interference, this right is not absolute. It does not extend to activities such as defamation, hate speech, or incitement to violence. The legal frameworks that guarantee free speech also stipulate that this freedom must be exercised within the bounds of the law. This implies that media professionals, when exercising their right to free expression, must consider the right to privacy and the principles of data protection. The exercise of one's rights often concludes where the rights of others begin, meaning privacy rights, data protection principles, and the right to access information are crucial considerations that must be balanced within legal parameters.[2]

Access to Information versus Data Protection : The right to access information, frequently termed freedom of information, constitutes a foundational principle adopted by numerous national governments to uphold citizens' entitlements to freedom of opinion and expression, alongside fostering trust in public discourse, thereby promoting transparent, accountable, and open governance. It is defined as the fundamental right for both natural and legal persons to seek, receive, and impart information held by public bodies. This right is critical for fostering democratic participation by enabling scrutiny of governmental functions and ensuring public access to records (Shepherd, 2015).

---

2. Madison's version of the speech and press clauses, introduced in the House of Representatives on June 8, 1789, provided: "The people shall not be deprived or abridged of their right to speak, to write, or to publish their sentiments; and the freedom of the press, as one of the great bulwarks of liberty.

A distinct yet related concept is the right of subject access to data, commonly enshrined within data protection frameworks. This grants individuals the right to obtain a copy of their personal data, along with supplementary information regarding its processing. This right is crucial for empowering individuals to understand how and why organizations process their data, thereby enabling them to verify the lawfulness and fairness of such operations. The practical exercise of these rights typically necessitates a formal written request. The acceptance or denial of such requests is often contingent upon specific legal exemptions or proportionality considerations as defined by national laws and regulations.[3]

Classified information : Classified information, meticulously categorized as Top Secret, Secret, or Confidential, is exclusively reserved for matters critically affecting national interest. The Top-Secret designation is applied when unauthorized disclosure could foreseeably result in exceptionally severe detriment to national interests, potentially jeopardizing national security, foreign relations, or economic stability, with such an impact characterized by its profound magnitude, immediate consequence, and irreversible nature. This stringent criterion underscores the necessity for the highest level of protection. Each classification level is rigorously delineated by specific protocols and stringent security measures dictating information safeguarding practices. These comprehensive governance structures undergo continuous review and dynamic modification by states to proactively address evolving information management complexities and sustain the paramount efficacy of secrecy protocols in safeguarding vital

---

3. The Right of Access to Information Act, 2013 provides for modes used for access to information as well as information that is or is not accessible.

state interests (Heide and Villeneuve, 2020).[4]

Unclassified Information : Unclassified information refers to data that, while not classified as secret, still requires specific safeguarding or dissemination controls in accordance with applicable laws, regulations, and government policies. This category can include information that has never been classified, or declassified documents that previously contained classified information which has since been removed, redacted, or deemed no longer in need of protection.

A significant subset of unclassified information is Sensitive but Unclassified (SBU) data. This broad category encompasses material designated with labels such as For Official Use Only, Law Enforcement Sensitive, Sensitive National Security Information, Sensitive Security Information, and Critical Infrastructure Information, among others. This indicates that while not classified, its public disclosure could still pose risks or be inappropriate.

Integrity and Confidentiality : Safeguarding personal data necessitates an unwavering commitment to the principles of confidentiality and integrity. This mandates the implementation of robust security measures and stringent protocols designed to preclude unauthorized access, misuse, accidental loss, modification, or damage. Such comprehensive protection is effectively achieved through advanced technical safeguards and well-defined organizational

---

4. If a journalist or any other member of the public publishes, broadcasts and leak, and or view classified information posted in the public domain on your computer, either intentionally or inadvertently, then such a person must report a data spill, and the spill must be isolated and contained on the computer you used to view it. Select Top Secret, Secret, or Confidential for each statement. In most counties leaking classified information constitute an offence against the state and may lead to a capital punishment.

frameworks. Furthermore, as a fundamental tenet, confidentiality extends beyond sensitive personal data, encompassing critical information across diverse sectors, including finance, healthcare, and national security. Ultimately, this is paramount for ensuring data sovereignty within data-driven applications. Maintaining data integrity guarantees that any data modifications occur with explicit user awareness and permission, thereby preserving authenticity and preventing unauthorized alterations, tag forging, or data leakage attacks.

Privacy : Generally, Privacy refers to an individual's right to be left alone or freedom from interference and intrusion. More specifically, information privacy is the right to have some control over how one's personal information is collected, used, and disclosed. Protecting privacy is crucial for ensuring human dignity, safety, and self-determination, allowing individuals to freely develop their own personality.

Types of Privacy

Privacy is a complex and multifaceted concept, encompassing various dimensions of an individual's life and information. Understanding the distinct categories of privacy is crucial for grasping its different facets, which extend beyond personal data to include psychological, social, and physical aspects. These categories collectively describe privacy as an individual's control over access to themselves, aiming for a balance between disclosure and withdrawal in different contexts.

Individual Privacy : This refers to an individual's ability to maintain personal space, often facilitated by physical barriers such as doors, walls, blinds, curtains, or screens. It encompasses the right to control access to one's person and freedom from surveillance and unwanted intrusions (Heek, Maidhof and Ziefle, 2023).

This concept can also be understood as physical privacy, which focuses on preventing interference in a person's physical space or properties (Abdelaal, 2020).

Communications Privacy : This type of privacy concerns limitations on the interception, use, and disclosure of communications, as well as regulations governing what service providers can do with their customers' information. Its primary goal is to prevent the interception of communications and safeguard communication metadata (Sandeepa et al., 2022; Sasy and Goldberg, 2023). Regulations related to communications privacy are frequently compared across different regions to ensure robust protection against surveillance and unauthorized access (Qatawneh, Almobaideen and Qatawneh, 2022).

Information Privacy : Information privacy is concerned with the protection of individuals' personal data, specifically focusing on the control over 'personal facts a person does not want to reveal to others' (Abdelaal, 2020). This type of privacy is paramount because it directly addresses the collection and access to user data and personal information by various entities, including companies that routinely gather financial, family, credit, and educational details for their operations (Mols, Wang and Pridmore, 2021). Ensuring information privacy means preventing users' data from being automatically available and controlled by unauthorized individuals and organizations (Sandeepa et al., 2022).

The rapid development of big data and artificial intelligence has intensified concerns, as existing privacy laws often offer insufficient protection against the harm stemming from current data practices (McCoy et al., 2023). This has consequently led to increased regulatory scrutiny and the implementation of new guidelines governing the collection and processing of personal data (Kouchih and Mataa, 2024; OECD, 2024).

Private Citizen's Privacy : A private citizen is an individual who does not hold an official or professional role within a sovereign country, though the same person might hold an official role in another context.

For private citizens, the level of respect and confidentiality surrounding their data is exceptionally high. This includes robust protection for storing and sharing data about them, ensuring they are not subjected to unlawful state surveillance, and upholding their right to control the dissemination of information about their private life, including covertly taken photographs.[5]

Public Figure's Privacy : For constitutional post holders and other highly prominent individuals, the protection afforded to their personal data is inherently diminished. Their public status inevitably exposes a significant amount of personal information to public scrutiny. Consequently, aspects traditionally considered private, such as personal relationships or public appearance, transition from individual control to the public domain. This reduced expectation of privacy for public figures is fundamentally driven by a paramount societal interest in transparency regarding those who hold positions of substantial influence or public trust, especially concerning matters critical to national security or public safety. This inherent trade-off between individual privacy rights and the public's right to know underscores a complex balancing act that legal frameworks continuously seek to define and uphold, particularly as the distinction between publicly available and commercially available information becomes increasingly nuanced (Struensee, 2024).[6]

---

5. In a country like the Republic of South Sudan in East Africa, malicious use of a private citizen's data is prohibited by law meanwhile public officials or constitutional post holders do not benefit to claim protection under the law relating to defamation. See sections 28 and 29 of the Media Authority Act, 2013.

The pre-existing availability of certain personal data pertaining to prominent public figures within the public domain complicates the effective protection of such information.

Personal Data : Personal data encompasses any information that can directly or indirectly identify an individual. This is a broad category, including details such as a name, date of birth, address, license plate number, job application information, or even a picture of a tattoo. For clarity, this information is often further categorized into general personal information, sensitive personal information, and biometric data. It's important to note that the term 'personal data' applies to both natural (living individuals) and, in some contexts, legal persons. Essentially, personal data is defined as any information related to an identified or identifiable person that could be used to pinpoint an individual.

Sensitive Data : Sensitive personal data demands heightened protection and rigorous handling due to the profound implications of its misuse. Improper management of such data can lead to significant consequences, including ethical and legal liabilities, data breaches, unauthorized access, and widespread misuse (Benatti et al., 2022; Pina et al., 2024). The emergence of data breaches as a major challenge highlights the critical need for robust data privacy measures, as these incidents can result in confidential information being shared with unauthorized third parties (Ho, Ho-Dac and Huang, 2023). Risks are further amplified when highly sensitive data, such as biometrics, are compromised across multiple databases, potentially

---

6. Once, certain Hon. Awut Deng Achuil, A Foreign Minister of the Republic of South Sudan was criticized for her dress code and examined by the public as to how a public official should dress and be presentable. Unlike a private citizen whose dress code is not of a concern to any one in a country.

exposing individuals' genetic characteristics, medical conditions, or enabling unlawful activities (Arman et al., 2024). Therefore, it is crucial for anyone handling personal data to accurately identify these categories and exercise extra caution to minimize harm and ensure ethical data practices (McCoy et al., 2023). The types of data often considered sensitive include:

1. Racial or ethnic origin

2. Political, religious, or philosophical beliefs

3. Trade union membership

4. Genetic data or biometric data (e.g., fingerprints)

5. Health information

6. Sexual relationships or orientation

These categories align closely with what are often termed "special categories of personal data" in legal frameworks like the EU's General Data Protection Regulation (Georgiou and Lambrinoudakis, 2020; Aime et al., 2023). Originating in European Union data protection law, these sensitive data categories are singled out for extra protection globally due to their inherent nature, which, when processed, may put data subjects in jeopardy (Georgiou and Lambrinoudakis, 2020; Solove, 2023).

Enhanced Protection and Implications

The inherent nature of these special categories means their processing may put data subjects in jeopardy, necessitating enhanced protection and specific safeguards (Georgiou and Lambrinoudakis, 2020). For instance, the GDPR explicitly prohibits the processing of such sensitive personal data unless specific measures are taken under certain circumstances, such as when the data subject has given explicit consent or for research and public health purposes (Lysaght et al., 2023). The stricter handling requirements for sensitive data stem from the significant risks associated with its misuse or breach. Improperly managed sensitive data can lead to ethical and legal liabilities (Benatti et al., 2022; Pina et al., 2024). Data breaches, where confidential information is accessed by unauthorized parties, pose a major challenge, raising concerns about privacy and potentially severe consumer outcomes (Boustead and Herr, 2020; Ho, Ho-Dac and Huang, 2023). These risks are amplified when sensitive data like biometrics are used across multiple databases, as stolen biometric data could expose individuals' genetic characteristics or medical conditions, and even facilitate unlawful activities by compromising medical records (Arman et al., 2024).

Academic research highlights the ongoing challenge of balancing the versatile use of data with the protection of individual rights. The increasing availability and processing of data in digital formats have boosted interest in its use but also demand that data controllers remain mindful of ethical issues and legal liabilities (Benatti et al., 2022). While some legal frameworks, like GDPR, provide specific protection for these categories (Calvi, 2025), there can still be ambiguities or challenges in their application, especially with evolving technologies like AI. For example, in Europe, assessing whether an AI system discriminates based on ethnicity can be problematic because the GDPR generally bans the use of special categories of data like ethnicity, religion, and sexual preference (Bekkum and Borgesius, 2022).

In summary, the identification and stringent protection of sensitive personal data are critical in modern data privacy, demanding careful adherence to regulations and continuous ethical consideration to mitigate the risks of harm and ensure individual rights are upheld (McCoy et al., 2023; Pina et al., 2024).

Data Subject Rights

A **data subject** is any individual who can be identified, either directly or indirectly, through identifiers such as a name, ID number, location data, or factors specific to their physical, physiological, genetic, mental, economic, cultural, or social identity.

Data subjects are endowed with several fundamental rights concerning their personal information. These include the right to access, rectify, erase, restrict processing, and data portability. This means individuals can review their personal data at any time, correct inaccuracies, delete portions or all of it from a database, limit third-party access and processing, and even refuse access to their data (Abiteboul and Stoyanovich, 2019).

Right of Access to Data : Data subjects have the right to request and receive confirmation of whether their personal data is being held. If so, they are entitled to obtain a copy of that data, along with comprehensive information detailing the purpose of its processing, the categories of personal data involved, the recipients to whom the data has been or will be disclosed, the envisioned retention period, and the source of the data if not collected directly from them. This right is crucial for fostering transparency and empowering individuals to verify the lawfulness and accuracy of their data processing. This right, articulated in Article 15 and Recital 63 of the GDPR, acts as a foundational element for individuals to gain greater awareness and knowledge regarding how their data is processed (Antunes et al., 2023).

Right to Rectification of Data : This right enables data subjects to promptly obtain the correction of any inaccurate personal data concerning them from the data controller. It underpins the fundamental principle of data accuracy, ensuring that personal information used for processing is reliable and up-to-date. This safeguard prevents decisions from being based on faulty or incomplete data, thereby protecting individual interests and maintaining the integrity of their digital identity. Moreover, individuals have the right to have incomplete personal data completed, potentially by providing a supplementary statement to ensure its comprehensiveness (Colonna and Greenstein, 2022).

Right to Erasure of Data : This fundamental prerogative, often termed the 'right to be forgotten,' empowers individuals to demand the removal or deletion of their personal data or information. While its precise application and qualifying conditions may exhibit nuances across different legal frameworks, this right provides a crucial mechanism for data subjects to reclaim control over their digital footprint. This right is enshrined in Article 17 of the GDPR, allowing for the deletion of personal data under specific circumstances, such as when the data is no longer necessary for the purposes for which it was collected or when the data subject withdraws consent and there is no other legal ground for processing (Antunes et al., 2023) (Singh and Cobbe, 2019).

Right to Restrict Processing of Data : This right allows individuals to restrict an organization's processing of their personal data, serving as an alternative to complete data erasure by empowering data subjects to impose limitations for specific, legitimate reasons (Ausloos, Mahieu and Veale, 2019). It is especially relevant when the data's accuracy is disputed, processing is unlawful, or the data, though no longer needed by the controller, is required by the data subject for legal claims (Colonna and Greenstein, 2022).

Right to Portability of Data : The right to data portability, established by Article 20 of the GDPR, grants individuals the ability to obtain their personal data in a structured, commonly used, and machine-readable format, and to subsequently transmit this data to another controller without impediment (Aljeraisy et al., 2020). This right facilitates the secure and unhindered transfer, replication, or movement of personal data across diverse services and IT environments, thereby enabling data subjects to regain mastery over their information. The stipulation for a structured, commonly used, and machine-readable format" is vital for ensuring interoperability between services. This provision not only enhances individual awareness and control but also addresses the prevalent economic asymmetry between large corporations and data subjects. By simplifying transitions between service providers, data portability actively mitigates vendor lock-in and stimulates competition and innovation within the digital economy. Collectively, these rights constitute a robust framework for safeguarding personal data, obliging companies to manage consumer data securely while affording users mechanisms to access, control, update, and delete their information (Saltarella et al., 2024).

References

1. Canavilhas, J. and Fátima, B.D. (2024) "Decoding Journalism in the Digital Age: Self-Representation, News Quality, and Collaboration in Portuguese Newsrooms," *Journalism and Media*, 5(2), p. 515. doi:10.3390/journalmedia5020034.
2. Forja-Pena, T., Orosa, B.G. and García, X.L. (2024) "A Shift Amid the Transition: Towards Smarter, More Resilient Digital Journalism in the Age of AI and Disinformation," *Social Sciences*, 13(8), p. 403. doi:10.3390/socsci13080403.
3. Jacobson, S., Marino, J. and Gutsche, R. (2015) "The digital animation of literary journalism," *Journalism*, 17(4), p. 527. doi:10.1177/1464884914568079.
4. Krieken, K. van and Sanders, J. (2019) "What is narrative journalism? A systematic review and an empirical agenda," *Journalism*. SAGE Publishing, p. 1393. doi:10.1177/1464884919862056.
5. Nerone, J. (2008) "Journalism, History of," *The International Encyclopedia of Communication*. doi:10.1002/9781405186407.wbiecj005.
6. Weber, J. (2006) "Strassburg, 1605: The Origins of the Newspaper in Europe," *German History*, 24(3), p. 387. doi:10.1191/0266355406gh380oa.
7. Auzarmi, Z.K. (2024) "An Analysis of Afghan Broadcast Media News Orientation Based on Galtung's Theory: A Study of ToloNews Programs," 1(1), p. 53. doi:10.62810/jssh.v1i1.10.
8. Damgaard, M. (2018) "Car Wash, Crisis, and Political Cataclysm : Corruption Narratives in the Brazilian Mediascape," Research Portal Denmark, p. 231. Available at: https://local.forskningsportal.dk/local/dki-cgi/ws/cris-link?src=ku&id=ku-28827ec0-a446-4edb-a5cd 9d8aa67edf6b&ti=Car%20Wash%2C%20Crisis%2C%20and%20Political%20Cataclysm%20%3A%20Corruption%20Narratives%20in%20the%20Brazilian%20Mediascape (Accessed: July 2025).
9. Thorgeirsdóttir, H. (2005) "Introduction," in Brill | Nijhoff eBooks. Brill, p. 1. doi:10.1163/9789047415206_004.
10. Abdelraouf, E. (2024) "Examining AI Integration by Audio-Visual Media Platforms in Oman: A Qualitative Analysis of Media Professionals' Perspectives," *Arab Media and Society*. [Preprint], (37). doi:10.70090/es24eaii.
11. Alghazo, S. *et al.* (2024) "The construction of stance in English and Arabic newspaper editorials: a case study," *Humanities and Social Sciences Communications*, 11(1). doi:10.1057/s41599-024-03418-2.
12. Almeida, E.S. de, Ahmed, I. and Hoek, A. van der (2023) "Let's Go to the Whiteboard (Again): Perceptions From Software Architects on Whiteboard Architecture Meetings," *IEEE Transactions on Software Engineering*, 49(10), p. 4773. doi:10.1109/tse.2023.3314410.
13. Armona, L. *et al.* (2024) *What is Newsworthy? Theory and Evidence.* doi:10.3386/w32512.
14. Audette-Longo, P.H. *et al.* (2023) "Forced change: Pandemic pedagogy and journalism education," *Facts & Frictions Emerging Debates Pedagogies and Practices in Contemporary Journalism*, 3(1). doi:10.22215/ff/v3.i1.01.
15. Azeez, P.Z. (2020) "Investigating Editing and Proofreading Strategies used by Koya University Lecturers," *Evaluation Study of Three Diagnostic Methods for Helicobacter pylori Infection*, 7(3), p. 341. doi:10.24271/garmian.2070324.

16. Benson, C.H., Okolo, C.H. and Oke, O. (2024) "Automating Media Production Workflows: The Role of AI in Streamlining Post-Production, Editing, and Distribution," *International Journal of Scientific Research in Civil Engineering*, 8(5), p. 168. doi:10.32628/ijsrce248514.

17. Bernhard, J. and Rußmann, U. (2023) "Blurring Boundaries: A Longitudinal Analysis of Skills Required in Journalism, PR, and Marketing Job Ads," *Journalism & Mass Communication Quarterly*, 101(3), p. 612. doi:10.1177/10776990231181544.

18. Bojić, L., Prodanović, N. and Samala, A.D. (2024) "Maintaining Journalistic Integrity in the Digital Age: A Comprehensive NLP Framework for Evaluating Online News Content," *arXiv (Cornell University)* [Preprint]. doi:10.48550/arxiv.2401.03467.

19. Bolívar, A. (2002) "The structure of newspaper editorials," p. 290. doi:10.4324/9780203422656-21.

20. Booth, P., Solvoll, M.K. and Krumsvik, A.H. (2023) "Newspaper executives' positioning toward the evolving use of social media," *Newspaper Research Journal*, 45(1), p. 45. doi:10.1177/07395329231211866.

21. Brannon, W. *et al.* (2024) "AudienceView: AI-Assisted Interpretation of Audience Feedback in Journalism," *arXiv* [Preprint]. doi:10.48550/ARXIV.2407.12613.

22. Carlos, E. (2024) *Content Operations from Start to Scale: Perspectives from Industry Experts*, Virginia Tech Publishing eBooks. doi:10.21061/content_operations_evia.

23. Ekström, M., Ramsälv, A. and Westlund, O. (2021) "Data-driven news work culture: Reconciling tensions in epistemic values and practices of news journalism," *Journalism*, 23(4), p. 755. doi:10.1177/14648849211052419.

24. Espinosa, Dra.P.M. (2003) "Géneros para la persuasión en prensa: los editoriales del Diario El País," *Ámbitos Revista Internacional de Comunicación*, p. 225. doi:10.12795/ambitos.2003.i09-10.12.

25. Fontes, I. and Menegon, L.F. (2021) "The competences of the editor-in-chief of a scientific journal: gaps and trends," *Revista de Gestão*, 29(2), p. 199. doi:10.1108/rege-04-2021-0062.

26. Hagen, A.L., Tolstad, I.M. and Bygdås, A.L. (2021) "'Magic through many minor measures': How introducing a flowline production mode in six steps enables journalist team autonomy in local news organizations," *AI & Society*, 37(2), p. 745. doi:10.1007/s00146-021-01176-2.

27. Hashmi, K.A. (2024) "The Evolving Landscape of Medical Editing in Healthcare," *Pakistan Heart Journal*, 57(4), p. 268. doi:10.47144/phj.v57i4.2905.

28. Ibrahim, R.A., Hidayana, R.A. and Saefullah, R. (2024) "Broadcasting Adaptation in the Streaming Era: Industrial Transformation in the Digital Revolution," *International Journal of Linguistics Communication and Broadcasting*, 2(2), p. 53. doi:10.46336/ijlcb.v2i2.107.

29. "International Journal of New Developments in Education" (2022) *International Journal of New Developments in Education* [Preprint]. doi:10.25236/ijnde.

30. King, A., Zavesky, E. and Gonzales, M.J. (2021) "User Preferences for Automated Curation of Snackable Content," p. 270. doi:10.1145/3397481.3450690.

31. Koivunen, S., Olshannikova, E. and Olsson, T. (2021) "Understanding Matchmakers' Experiences, Principles and Practices of Assembling Innovation Teams," *Computer Supported Cooperative Work (CSCW)*, 30(4), p. 589. doi:10.1007/s10606-021-09413-4.

32. Kustermann, A. *et al.* (2022) "Facets of Journalistic Skills. Demand for traditional, digital, and tech skills in news professionals." doi:10.31235/osf.io/ydx6f.

33. Laor, T. (2022) "Radio on demand: New habits of consuming radio content," *Global Media and Communication*, 18(1), p. 25. doi:10.1177/17427665211073868.

34. Lima, I.R. *et al.* (2023) "ARTICONF decentralized social media platform for democratic crowd journalism," *Social Network Analysis and Mining*, 13(1). doi:10.1007/s13278-023-01110-y.

35. Lopez, M.G. *et al.* (2022) "Making newsworthy news: The integral role of creativity and verification in the human information behavior that drives news story creation," *Journal of the Association for Information Science and Technology,* 73(10), p. 1445. doi:10.1002/asi.24647.

36. Lourens, A. (2016) "The use of comments as a strategy in the accountable editing of academic texts," *Literator,* 37(1). doi:10.4102/lit.v37i2.1277.

37. Luk, G. *et al.* (2020) *Dialogue IO1 : Teaching constructive and dialogue-based journalism to B.A. students. A practitioner's report, Research Portal Denmark.* Technical University of Denmark, p. 39. Available at: https://local.forskningsportal.dk/local/dki-cgi/ws/cris-link?src=dmjx&id=dmjx-888f67da-a41d-4a5b-a941-48f8dea7d00e&ti=Dialogue%20IO1%20%3A%20Teaching%20constructive%20and%20dia logue-based%20journalism%20to%20B.A.%20students.%20A%20practitioner's%20report (Accessed: July 2025).

38. Merriam, S. *et al.* (2021) "Avoiding Death by Meeting: An Interactive Workshop for Academic Faculty Highlighting Strategies to Facilitate Effective Team Meetings," *MedEdPORTAL* [Preprint]. doi:10.15766/mep_2374-8265.11121.

39. Miranda, J. (2023) "Responsabilização e Qualidade do Jornalismo: Instrumentos e Práticas Digitais de Accountability dos Média Portugueses," *Comunicação e Sociedade,* 44. doi:10.17231/comsoc.44(2023).4750.

40. Mitrić, P. (2022) "Can the Audience Design method help youth content reach audiences? : The case of 'Efterskolen,'" *Research Portal Denmark* [Preprint]. Available at: https://local.forskningsportal.dk/local/dki-cgi/ws/cris-link?src=ku&id=ku-42d1dbc1-d66e-4825-a0c0-79f3014967fe&ti=Can%20the%20Audience%20Design%20method%20help%20youth%20 content%20reach%20audiences%3F%20%3A%20The%20case%20of%20'Efterskolen' (Accessed: August 2025).

41. Moher, D. *et al.* (2017) "Core competencies for scientific editors of biomedical journals: consensus statement," *BMC Medicine,* 15(1). doi:10.1186/s12916-017-0927-0.

42. Moulson, A. *et al.* (2024) "Practical Implementation of Automated Next Generation Audio Production for Live Sports," *Journal of the Audio Engineering Society,* 72, p. 517. doi:10.17743/jaes.2022.0151.

43. Nelson, J.L. (2019) "The next media regime: The pursuit of 'audience engagement' in journalism," *Journalism,* 22(9), p. 2350. doi:10.1177/1464884919862375.

44. Ngoma, C. and Adebisi, Y.A. (2023) "Exploring electronic cigarette portrayals: a content and thematic analysis of African online news coverage," *Substance Abuse Treatment Prevention and Policy,* 18(1). doi:10.1186/s13011-023-00559-6.

45. Nguyen, T.T., Veer, E. and Ballantine, P.W. (2025) "The drivers and boundaries of consumer switching from full-length to derivative condensed content," *Journal of Retailing and Consumer Services,* 86, p. 104341. doi:10.1016/j.jretconser.2025.104341.

46. Panagiotidis, K. *et al.* (2020) "A Participatory Journalism Management Platform: Design, Implementation and Evaluation," *Social Sciences,* 9(2), p. 21. doi:10.3390/socsci9020021.

47. Petelin, R. (2002) "Managing organisational writing to enhance corporate credibility," *Journal of Communication Management,* 7(2), p. 172. doi:10.1108/13632540310807304.

48. Rashid, A. (2024) *Untitled.* doi:10.55277/researchhub.vq5dnd6h.

49. Salvo, P.D. (2024) "A Typology of Digital Leaks as Journalistic Source Materials," in, p. 469. doi:10.1007/978-3-031-30438-5_26.

50. Sawi, I.A. and Alaa, A. (2024) "Navigating the impact: a study of editors' and proofreaders' perceptions of AI tools in editing and proofreading," *Discover Artificial Intelligence*, 4(1). doi:10.1007/s44163-024-00116-5.

51. Sharma, G.P. *et al.* (2021) "On Decomposition and Deployment of Virtualized Media Services," *IEEE Transactions on Broadcasting*, 67(3), p. 761. doi:10.1109/tbc.2021.3099740.

52. T., S.S. (2024) "THE CHALLENGES AND ROLE OF MODERN JOURNALISM IN DIGITAL MEDIA ENTERPRISES," *ShodhKosh Journal of Visual and Performing Arts*, 5(7). doi:10.29121/shodhkosh.v5.i7.2024.1921.

53. Telkmann, V. (2020) "Broadcasters' content distribution and programming decisions in multi-channel environments: a literature review," *Journal of Media Business Studies*. Taylor & Francis, p. 106. doi:10.1080/16522354.2020.1765669.

54. Veerbeek, J. and Diakopoulos, N. (2024a) "Using Generative Agents to Create Tip Sheets for Investigative Data Reporting," *arXiv (Cornell University)* [Preprint]. doi:10.48550/arxiv.2409.07286.

55. Veerbeek, J. and Diakopoulos, N. (2024b) "Using Generative Agents to Create Tip Sheets for Investigative Data Reporting." doi:10.48550/ARXIV.2409.07286.

56. Wright, C. *et al.* (2020) "AI IN PRODUCTION: VIDEO ANALYSIS AND MACHINE LEARNING FOR EXPANDED LIVE EVENTS COVERAGE," *SMPTE Motion Imaging Journal*, 129(2), p. 36. doi:10.5594/jmi.2020.2967204.

57. Zhang, H. (2024) "Strategic Analysis of Content Production for Broadcast Programs in a Multi-Platform Environment," in *Advances in economics, business and management research/Advances in Economics, Business and Management Research*. Atlantis Press, p. 234. doi:10.2991/978-94-6463-538-6_26.

58. Azeez, P.Z. (2020) "Investigating Editing and Proofreading Strategies used by Koya University Lecturers," *Evaluation Study of Three Diagnostic Methods for Helicobacter pylori Infection*, 7(3), p. 341. doi:10.24271/garmian.2070324.

59. Baron, I. *et al.* (2016) "European Identities : Centre and Periphey," *Research Portal Denmark*, p. 112. Available at: https://local.forskningsportal.dk/local/dki-cgi/ws/cris-link?src=cbs&id=cbs-95ee6f9d-5b42-4f19-9ea3-d567cbe1fe19&ti=European%20Identities%20%3A%20Centre%20and%20Periphey (Accessed: July 2025).

60. Beckers, K. (2017) "Vox pops in the news: The journalists' perspective," *Communications*, 43(1), p. 101. doi:10.1515/commun-2017-0040.

61. Beckers, K. (2019) "What Vox Pops Say and How That Matters: Effects of Vox Pops in Television News on Perceived Public Opinion and Personal Opinion," *Journalism & Mass Communication Quarterly*, 96(4), p. 980. doi:10.1177/1077699019843852.

62. Beckers, K. (2020) "The Voice of the People in the News: A Content Analysis of Public Opinion Displays in Routine and Election News," *Journalism Studies*, 21(15), p. 2078. doi:10.1080/1461670x.2020.1809498.

63. Beckers, K. (2021) "Power of the people or the expert? The influence of vox pop and expert statements on news-item evaluation, perceived public opinion, and personal opinion," *Communications*, 47(1), p. 114. doi:10.1515/commun-2019-0186.

64. Blum, I.H. (2024) "'Facebook is a bit like a lost cause' : Social Movement Actors' Perspectives on Social Media Affordances," *Research Portal Denmark*, p. 133. Available at: https://local.forskningsportal.dk/local/dki-cgi/ws/cris-link?src=cbs&id=cbs-1a7ae299-cac0-4b64-8487-24ac291663c0&ti=%201CFacebook%20is%20a%20bit%20like%20a%20lost%20cause%201

D%20%3A%20Social%20Movement%20Actors%2019%20Perspectives%20on%20Social%2
0Media%20Affordances (Accessed: July 2025).

65. Carlos, E. (2024) *Content Operations from Start to Scale: Perspectives from Industry
Experts, Virginia Tech Publishing eBooks*. doi:10.21061/content_operations_evia.

66. Cushion, S. (2018) "Using public opinion to serve journalistic narratives: Rethinking vox
pops and live two-way reporting in five UK election campaigns (2009–2017)," *European
Journal of Communication*, 33(6), p. 639. doi:10.1177/0267323118793779.

67. Ekström, M., Ramsälv, A. and Westlund, O. (2021) "Data-driven news work culture:
Reconciling tensions in epistemic values and practices of news journalism," *Journalism*,
23(4), p. 755. doi:10.1177/14648849211052419.

68. Higgins, K.C. (2021) "'Nobody feels safe': Vulnerability, fear and the micro-politics of
ordinary voice in crime news television," *Journalism*, 23(10), p. 2114.
doi:10.1177/14648849211001788.

69. Lourens, A. (2016) "The use of comments as a strategy in the accountable editing of
academic texts," *Literator*, 37(1). doi:10.4102/lit.v37i2.1277.

70. Mitrić, P. (2022) "Can the Audience Design method help youth content reach audiences? :
The case of 'Efterskolen,'" *Research Portal Denmark* [Preprint]. Available at:
https://local.forskningsportal.dk/local/dki-cgi/ws/cris-link?src=ku&id=ku-42d1dbc1-
d66e-4825-a0c0-
79f3014967fe&ti=Can%20the%20Audience%20Design%20method%20help%20youth%20
content%20reach%20audiences%3F%20%3A%20The%20case%20of%20'Efterskolen'
(Accessed: August 2025).

71. Moher, D. *et al.* (2017) "Core competencies for scientific editors of biomedical journals:
consensus statement," *BMC Medicine*, 15(1). doi:10.1186/s12916-017-0927-0.

72. Nagai, K. (2023) "The representation of public opinion in reporting poll results on
environment issues," *Frontiers in Communication*, 8. doi:10.3389/fcomm.2023.1225306.

73. O'Sullivan, P., Kuper, A. and Cleland, J. (2024) "Who should proof my paper?," *Advances
in Health Sciences Education*, 29(3), p. 721. doi:10.1007/s10459-024-10352-0.

74. Peter, C. (2019) "The People's Voice—The People's Choice? How Vox Pop Exemplars Shape
Audience Judgments as a Function of Populist Attitudes," *Journalism & Mass
Communication Quarterly*, 96(4), p. 1004. doi:10.1177/1077699019852323.

75. Sawi, I.A. and Alaa, A. (2024) "Navigating the impact: a study of editors' and proofreaders'
perceptions of AI tools in editing and proofreading," *Discover Artificial Intelligence*, 4(1).
doi:10.1007/s44163-024-00116-5.

76. Alhuntushi, A. and Lugo-Ocando, J. (2024) "Science journalism in the Kingdom of Saudi
Arabia: news sources engagement and [lack of] science accountability," *Journal of Science
Communication*, 23(5). doi:10.22323/2.23050204.

77. Andersen, N.B. (2017) "Framing perfect victims : The February 2015 Copenhagen shooting
in Danish newspapers," *Research Portal Denmark*, p. 289. Available at:
https://local.forskningsportal.dk/local/dki-cgi/ws/cris-link?src=kp&id=kp-85452760-
2a08-46e1-b3fa-
3143720e7e7e&ti=Framing%20perfect%20victims%20%3A%20The%20February%202015
%20Copenhagen%20shooting%20in%20Danish%20newspapers (Accessed: July 2025).

78. Audette-Longo, P.H. *et al.* (2023) "Forced change: Pandemic pedagogy and journalism
education," *Facts & Frictions Emerging Debates Pedagogies and Practices in Contemporary
Journalism*, 3(1). doi:10.22215/ff/v3.i1.01.

79. Azeez, P.Z. (2020) "Investigating Editing and Proofreading Strategies used by Koya University Lecturers," *Evaluation Study of Three Diagnostic Methods for Helicobacter pylori Infection*, 7(3), p. 341. doi:10.24271/garmian.2070324.

80. Bailey, G. (2022) *Investigating Tangible and Hybrid Interactions to Augment the Reading Experience.* doi:10.23889/suthesis.61288.

81. Barnett, C. (1998) "Guest Editorial," *Environment and Planning D Society and Space.* SAGE Publishing. doi:10.1068/d160631.

82. Bevilaqua, M.V.O. (2020) "Guide to image editing and production of figures for scientific publications with an emphasis on taxonomy Image editing for scientific publications," *Zoosystematics and Evolution*, 96(1), p. 139. doi:10.3897/zse.96.49225.

83. Bick, E. *et al.* (2024) "Man or machine : Evaluating Spelling Error Detection in Danish Newspaper Corpora," *Research Portal Denmark*, p. 204. Available at: https://local.forskningsportal.dk/local/dki-cgi/ws/cris-link?src=sdu&id=sdu-076a68fb-45c6-4fa2-bc23-49dd4f1f06f0&ti=Man%20or%20machine%20%3A%20Evaluating%20Spelling%20Error%20Detection%20in%20Danish%20Newspaper%20Corpora (Accessed: July 2025).

84. Bihan, F.L. *et al.* (2024) "Initiation à la fabrication additive pour l'électronique flexible : Réalisation de capteurs résistifs par sérigraphie," *J3eA*, 23, p. 1013. doi:10.1051/j3ea/20241013.

85. Bolívar, A. (2002) "The structure of newspaper editorials," p. 290. doi:10.4324/9780203422656-21.

86. Borkar, A. and Paul, B. (2023) "Misreporting biodiversity loss due to invasive species escalates social tension," *Research Square (Research Square)* [Preprint]. doi:10.21203/rs.3.rs-3738860/v1.

87. Brookes, P.S. (2025) "Misconduct Detection — Evolving Methods & Lessons from 15 Years of Scientific Image Sleuthing," *The Journal of Law Medicine & Ethics*, p. 1. doi:10.1017/jme.2025.32.

88. Dharavath, H.N. (2023) "Digital Color Output Conformity to ISO12647-7 Standards (GRACoL 2013 [CGATS21-2-CRPC6]) With the Use of Statistical Process Control (SPC)," *The Journal of Technology Management and Applied Engineering*, 39(4). doi:10.31274/jtmae.16104.

89. Enquist, A. (2000) "Substantive Editing Versus Technical Editing: How Law Review Editors Do Their Job," 30, p. 451. Available at: https://digitalcommons.law.seattleu.edu/faculty/502 (Accessed: November 2025).

90. Erwanda, Y.T. and Doli, E.R. (2024) "Comparative Study of Digital and Traditional Marketing Strategies in Increasing Product Sales," *Smart International Management Journal*, 1(3), p. 14. doi:10.70076/simj.v1i3.40.

91. Fotopoulos, S. (2023) "Traditional media versus new media: Between trust and use," *European View*, 22(2), p. 277. doi:10.1177/17816858231204738.

92. Froud, K. *et al.* (2024) "Middle-schoolers' reading and lexical-semantic processing depth in response to digital and print media: An N400 study," *PLoS ONE*, 19(5). doi:10.1371/journal.pone.0290807.

93. Gokce, Assoc.Prof.S. (2022) "Scientific Study Comparing Digital Advertising and Print Advertising," *Zenodo (CERN European Organization for Nuclear Research)* [Preprint]. doi:10.5281/zenodo.7587676.

94. Haddock, G. *et al.* (2019) "The medium can influence the message: Print-based versus digital reading influences how people process different types of written information," *British Journal of Psychology*, 111(3), p. 443. doi:10.1111/bjop.12415.

95. Hagen, A.L., Tolstad, I.M. and Bygdås, A.L. (2021) "'Magic through many minor measures': How introducing a flowline production mode in six steps enables journalist team autonomy in local news organizations," *AI & Society*, 37(2), p. 745. doi:10.1007/s00146-021-01176-2.

96. HORIMOTO, K. (2011) "The Advanced Printing Technologies," *Journal of the Japan Society of Colour Material*, 84(10), p. 358. doi:10.4011/shikizai.84.358.

97. "ISO 12647, GRACoL and SWOP for Separation, Proof and Print" (2008) in *X.media.publishing*. Springer Nature, p. 76. doi:10.1007/978-3-540-69377-2_4.

98. Kanchan, S. and Gaidhane, A. (2024) "Print Media Role and Its Impact on Public Health: A Narrative Review," *Cureus*. Cureus, Inc. doi:10.7759/cureus.59574.

99. Kucirkova, N. (2022) "The explanatory power of sensory reading for early childhood research: The role of hidden senses," *Contemporary Issues in Early Childhood*, 25(1), p. 93. doi:10.1177/14639491221116915.

100. LaBerge, J.M. and Andriole, K.P. (2003) "Digital Image Processing: A Primer for JVIR Authors and Readers," *Journal of Vascular and Interventional Radiology*, 14(12), p. 1481. doi:10.1097/01.rvi.0000106744.94154.b3.

101. Li, S. (2023) "The historical evolution of educational technology: from the printing press to online education," *OOO Zhurnal Voprosy Istorii*, 2023, p. 272. doi:10.31166/voprosyistorii202309statyi27.

102. Lopez, M.G. *et al.* (2022) "Making newsworthy news: The integral role of creativity and verification in the human information behavior that drives news story creation," *Journal of the Association for Information Science and Technology*, 73(10), p. 1445. doi:10.1002/asi.24647.

103. Lundström, J. and Verikas, A. (2012) "Assessing print quality by machine in offset colour printing," *Knowledge-Based Systems*, 37, p. 70. doi:10.1016/j.knosys.2012.07.022.

104. Mangold, F., Bachl, M. and Prochazka, F. (2022) "How News Audiences Allocate Trust in the Digital Age: A Figuration Perspective," *Journalism & Mass Communication Quarterly*, 101(4), p. 955. doi:10.1177/10776990221100515.

105. Masse, R.E. (1985) "Theory and practice of editing processes in technical communication," *IEEE Transactions on Professional Communication*, (1), p. 34. doi:10.1109/tpc.1985.6448866.

106. Maštrapa, S.B., John, R. and Brautović, M. (2020) "Accuracy in Online Media," *Medijske studije*, 11(21), p. 66. doi:10.20901/ms.11.21.4.

107. Meier, K. *et al.* (2022) "Examining the Most Relevant Journalism Innovations: A Comparative Analysis of Five European Countries from 2010 to 2020," *Journalism and Media*, 3(4), p. 698. doi:10.3390/journalmedia3040046.

108. O'Donnell, C. (2022) "An Analysis of the History and Development of the Printing Press as Critique of Technological Determinism," *Zenodo (CERN European Organization for Nuclear Research)* [Preprint]. doi:10.5281/zenodo.6874616.

109. Omar, B., Al-Samarraie, H. and Wright, B. (2020) "Immediacy as news experience: exploring its multiple dimensions in print and online contexts," *Online Information Review*, 45(2), p. 461. doi:10.1108/oir-12-2019-0388.

110. Pilmis, O. and Matthews, T. (2014) "Producing in Urgent Situations," *HAL (Le Centre pour la Communication Scientifique Directe)* [Preprint].

111. Pinem, M.S.U. (2023) "The Shift from Print to Digital Media and Its Effect on Users' Media Literacy in Critiquing the Depth of News: A Systematic Literature Review," *Edunity Kajian Ilmu Sosial dan Pendidikan*, 2(11), p. 1369. doi:10.57096/edunity.v2i11.179.

112. Ross, A.A. *et al.* (2023) "Shortcuts to trust: Relying on cues to judge online news from unfamiliar sources on digital platforms," *Journalism*, 25(6), p. 1207. doi:10.1177/14648849231194485.

113. Sawi, I.A. and Alaa, A. (2024) "Navigating the impact: a study of editors' and proofreaders' perceptions of AI tools in editing and proofreading," *Discover Artificial Intelligence*, 4(1). doi:10.1007/s44163-024-00116-5.

114. Shu, K. *et al.* (2020) "Combating disinformation in a social media age," *Wiley Interdisciplinary Reviews Data Mining and Knowledge Discovery*, 10(6). doi:10.1002/widm.1385.

115. Silva, P., Portillo, M.P. and Fernández-Quintela, A. (2022) "Resveratrol and Wine: An Overview of Thirty Years in the Digital News," *International Journal of Environmental Research and Public Health*, 19(23), p. 15815. doi:10.3390/ijerph192315815.

116. Spence, C. (2020) "The Multisensory Experience of Handling and Reading Books," *Multisensory Research*. Brill, p. 902. doi:10.1163/22134808-bja10015.

117. Suomalainen, K. *et al.* (2025) "Fact-Checking in Journalism: An Epistemological Framework," *Journalism Studies*, 26(10), p. 1129. doi:10.1080/1461670x.2025.2492729.

118. T., S.S. (2024) "THE CHALLENGES AND ROLE OF MODERN JOURNALISM IN DIGITAL MEDIA ENTERPRISES," *ShodhKosh Journal of Visual and Performing Arts*, 5(7). doi:10.29121/shodhkosh.v5.i7.2024.1921.

119. Thorgeirsdóttir, H. (2005) "Introduction," in *Brill | Nijhoff eBooks*. Brill, p. 1. doi:10.1163/9789047415206_004.

120. Tomassi, A., Falegnami, A. and Romano, E. (2025) "Disinformation in the Digital Age: Climate Change, Media Dynamics, and Strategies for Resilience," *Publications*, 13(2), p. 24. doi:10.3390/publications13020024.

121. Tulin, M. *et al.* (2024) "How Can Journalists Strengthen Their Fight Against Misinformation in a Changing Media Landscape?," *VIEW Journal of European Television History and Culture*, 13(25), p. 1. doi:10.18146/view.324.

122. Vandendaele, A., Cuypere, L.D. and Praet, E.V. (2015) "Beyond 'Trimming the Fat,'" *Written Communication*, 32(4), p. 368. doi:10.1177/0741088315599391.

123. Veleva, S. and Tsvetanova, A.I. (2020) "Characteristics of the digital marketing advantages and disadvantages," in *IOP Conference Series Materials Science and Engineering*. IOP Publishing, p. 12065. doi:10.1088/1757-899x/940/1/012065.

124. Venkatraman, V. *et al.* (2021) "Relative Effectiveness of Print and Digital Advertising: A Memory Perspective," *Journal of Marketing Research*, 58(5), p. 827. doi:10.1177/00222437211034438.

125. Wates, E. and Campbell, R.M. (2007) "Author's version vs. publisher's version: an analysis of the copy-editing function," *Learned Publishing*, 20(2), p. 121. doi:10.1087/174148507x185090.

126. Weidmüller, L. and Engesser, S. (2024) "Oldies but goldies? Comparing the trustworthiness and credibility of 'new' and 'old' information intermediaries," *Communications*, 50(2), p. 257. doi:10.1515/commun-2023-0020.

127. Zhang, X. *et al.* (2022) "Impact of News Overload on Social Media News Curation: Mediating Role of News Avoidance," *Frontiers in Psychology*, 13. doi:10.3389/fpsyg.2022.865246.

128. Zhao, B. and Liang, W. (2025) "Application of Intelligent Proofreading in Publishing Industry in the Era of Artificial Intelligence," in *Lecture notes in operations research*. Springer International Publishing, p. 1135. doi:10.1007/978-981-96-9697-0_86.

129. Aguar-Torres, J. (2025) "Spanish Journalists at the Epicentre of Power: From the Media to Institutions," *Journalism and Media*, 6(2), p. 57. doi:10.3390/journalmedia6020057.

130. Almirón, N. (2020) "The 'Animal-Based Food Taboo.' Climate Change Denial and Deontological Codes in Journalism," *Frontiers in Communication*, 5. doi:10.3389/fcomm.2020.512956.

131. Andersen, N.B. (2017) "Framing perfect victims: The February 2015 Copenhagen shooting in Danish newspapers," *Research Portal Denmark*, p. 289. Available at: https://local.forskningsportal.dk/local/dki-cgi/ws/cris-link?src=kp&id=kp-85452760-2a08-46e1-b3fa-3143720e7e7e&ti=Framing%20perfect%20victims%20%3A%20The%20February%202015%20Copenhagen%20shooting%20in%20Danish%20newspapers (Accessed: July 2025).

132. Buschow, C. (2020) "Practice-driven journalism research: Impulses for a dynamic understanding of journalism in the context of its reorganization," *Studies in Communication Sciences*, 20(2). doi:10.24434/j.scoms.2020.02.006.

133. Clifton, N., Füzi, A. and Loudon, G. (2019) "Coworking in the digital economy: Context, motivations, and outcomes," *Futures*, 135, p. 102439. doi:10.1016/j.futures.2019.102439.

134. Cohen-Almagor, R. (2023) "Toward Responsible Journalism: Code of Practice, Journalist Oath and Conscience Clause," *SSRN Electronic Journal* [Preprint]. doi:10.2139/ssrn.4511358.

135. Damgaard, M. (2018) "Car Wash, Crisis, and Political Cataclysm : Corruption Narratives in the Brazilian Mediascape," *Research Portal Denmark*, p. 231. Available at: https://local.forskningsportal.dk/local/dki-cgi/ws/cris-link?src=ku&id=ku-28827ec0-a446-4edb-a5cd-9d8aa67edf6b&ti=Car%20Wash%2C%20Crisis%2C%20and%20Political%20Cataclysm%20%3A%20Corruption%20Narratives%20in%20the%20Brazilian%20Mediascape (Accessed: July 2025).

136. Himma-Kadakas, M. and Mõttus, M. (2021) "Ready to Hire a Freelance Journalist: the Change in Estonian Newsrooms' Willingness to Outsource Journalistic Content Production," *Central European Journal of Communication*, 14, p. 27. doi:10.51480/1899-5101.14.1(28).2.

137. Jaakkola, M. (2018) "Journalistic Writing and Style," *Oxford Research Encyclopedia of Communication*. doi:10.1093/acrefore/9780190228613.013.884.

138. Josephi, B. and O'Donnell, P. (2022) "The blurring line between freelance journalists and self-employed media workers," *Journalism*, 24(1), p. 139. doi:10.1177/14648849221086806.

139. Kabel, L. (2016) "Danske nyhedsmediers dækning af tærskellande i forskellig udvikling : hvordan journalistiske valg og metoder i 2015 prægede dækningen af vækstøkonomierne og dermed mediernes verdensbilleder," *Research Portal Denmark*, p. 12. Available at: https://local.forskningsportal.dk/local/dki-cgi/ws/cris-link?src=dmjx&id=dmjx-4a36d654-ac48-4127-bd4b-0b420b62d2e0&ti=Danske%20nyhedsmediers%20d%E6kning%20af%20t%E6rskellande%20i%20forskellig%20udvikling%20%3A%20hvordan%20journalistiske%20valg%20og%20metoder%20i%202015%20pr%E6gede%20d%E6kningen%20af%20v%E6kst%F8konomierne%20og%20dermed%20mediernes%20verdensbilleder (Accessed: July 2025).

140. Komatsu, T. *et al.* (2020) "AI should embody our values: Investigating journalistic values to inform AI technology design," p. 1. doi:10.1145/3419249.3420105.

141. Maštrapa, S.B., John, R. and Brautović, M. (2020) "Accuracy in Online Media," *Medijske studije*, 11(21), p. 66. doi:10.20901/ms.11.21.4.

142. Matthews, J. and Onyemaobi, K. (2024) "Precarious Professionalism: Journalism and the Fragility of Professional Practice in the Global South," in *Routledge eBooks*. Informa, p. 242. doi:10.4324/9781003544517-14.

143. Oso, L., Adeniran, R. and Arowolo, O. (2024) "Journalism ethics: the dilemma, social and contextual constraints," *Cogent Social Sciences*, 10(1). doi:10.1080/23311886.2024.2328388.

144. Østergaard, T.G. (2021) *Popular music journalism in the digital age : a cross-national content analysis of popular music journalism in Danish and German news media*, Research Portal Denmark. Technical University of Denmark, p. 236. Available at: https://local.forskningsportal.dk/local/dki-cgi/ws/cris-link?src=dmjx&id=dmjx-75aa0b05-ccdc-4de4-ae70-9b79cb59a9c7&ti=Popular%20music%20journalism%20in%20the%20digital%20age%20%3A%20a%20cross-national%20content%20analysis%20of%20popular%20music%20journalism%20in%20Danish%20and%20German%20news%20media (Accessed: July 2025).

145. Reich, Z. and Godler, Y. (2017) "Being There? The Role of Journalistic Legwork Across New and Traditional Media," *Journalism & Mass Communication Quarterly*, 94(4), p. 1115. doi:10.1177/1077699016687723.

146. Rosenmeier, M. *et al.* (2021) *Festskrift til Jørgen Blomqvist*, Research Portal Denmark. Technical University of Denmark, p. 764. Available at: https://local.forskningsportal.dk/local/dki-cgi/ws/cris-link?src=ku&id=ku-c4d2d722-8f8e-4a2b-8136-05ae84f0b379&ti=Festskrift%20til%20J%F8rgen%20Blomqvist (Accessed: July 2025).

147. Skana, P. and Gjerazi, B. (2024) "Public perception of media social responsibility in developing countries: a case study of Albania," *Frontiers in Communication*, 9. doi:10.3389/fcomm.2024.1338587.

148. Sonni, A.F., Putri, V.C.C. and Irwanto, I. (2024) "Bibliometric and Content Analysis of the Scientific Work on Artificial Intelligence in Journalism," *Journalism and Media*, 5(2), p. 787. doi:10.3390/journalmedia5020051.

149. Sparre, K. (2017) "Journalists like the rest of them? A case study of journalistic work routines at a Danish free newspaper," *Studies in Communication Sciences*, 17(1). doi:10.24434/j.scoms.2017.01.007.

150. Steel, J.R. *et al.* (2025) "Journalism and Ethical Praxis: A Thematic Analysis of Journalism Ethics Across Five European Countries," *Journalism Practice*, p. 1. doi:10.1080/17512786.2025.2480746.

151. Sword, H. (2009) "Writing higher education differently: a manifesto on style," *Studies in Higher Education*, 34(3), p. 319. doi:10.1080/03075070802597101.

152. Syahri, Moch. (2020) "Journalism ethics in local newspaper," *Masyarakat Kebudayaan dan Politik*, 33(1), p. 1. doi:10.20473/mkp.v33i12020.1-14.

153. Abunales, D. (2016) "Peace Journalism: Preparing Aspiring Journalists to Value Culture of Peace," *Asia Pacific Media Educator*, 26(2), p. 252. doi:10.1177/1326365x16666851.

154. Ajetunmobi, U.O. (2023) "Media framing and construction of socio-political issues in Nigeria: (Dis)connection between theory and professional ethics?," *Mediterranean Journal of Social & Behavioral Research*, 7(2), p. 93. doi:10.30935/mjosbr/13053.

155. Alcântara, J. and Simões, R.B. (2023) "The Same or Worse? Juggling the Private and Professional Lives of Women Journalists during Pandemic Coverage," *Journalism Practice*, p. 1. doi:10.1080/17512786.2023.2298237.

156. Andersen, N.B. (2017) "Framing perfect victims : The February 2015 Copenhagen shooting in Danish newspapers," *Research Portal Denmark*, p. 289. Available at: https://local.forskningsportal.dk/local/dki-cgi/ws/cris-link?src=kp&id=kp-85452760-2a08-46e1-b3fa-3143720e7e7e&ti=Framing%20perfect%20victims%20%3A%20The%20February%202015%20Copenhagen%20shooting%20in%20Danish%20newspapers (Accessed: July 2025).

157. Auerbach, Y. and Bloch-Elkon, Y. (2004) "Media Framing and Foreign Policy: The Elite Press vis-à-vis US Policy in Bosnia, 1992–95," *Journal of Peace Research*, 42(1), p. 83. doi:10.1177/0022343305049668.

158. Bilder, R.B. (2010) "Kosovo and the 'New Interventionism': Promise or Peril?," *SSRN Electronic Journal* [Preprint]. Available at: https://papers.ssrn.com/sol3/papers.cfm?abstract_id=1551969 (Accessed: October 2025).

159. Bishop, R.L. (2006) "The Whole World Is Watching, But So What? A Frame Analysis of Newspaper Coverage of Antiwar Protest," in *Palgrave Macmillan US eBooks*. Palgrave Macmillan, p. 39. doi:10.1057/9781403977311_4.

160. Dahal, P. (2021) "Protection of Journalists in Armed Conflict: An Insight from the Perspective of International Humanitarian Law," *Zenodo (CERN European Organization for Nuclear Research)* [Preprint]. doi:10.5281/zenodo.6860198.

161. Damissah, H.E. *et al.* (2025) "Media independence and democratic accountability in modern governance systems and public administration frameworks," *GSC Advanced Research and Reviews*, 23(1), p. 12. doi:10.30574/gscarr.2025.23.1.0102.

162. Entman, R.M. (2010) "Media framing biases and political power: Explaining slant in news of Campaign 2008," *Journalism*, 11(4), p. 389. doi:10.1177/1464884910367587.

163. Galtung, J. and Fischer, D. (2013) "High Road, Low Road: Charting the Course for Peace Journalism," in *SpringerBriefs on pioneers in science and practice*. Springer International Publishing, p. 95. doi:10.1007/978-3-642-32481-9_8.

164. Galtung, J. and Ruge, M.H. (1965) "The Structure of Foreign News," *Journal of Peace Research*, 2(1), p. 64. doi:10.1177/002234336500200104.

165. Gavin, N.T. (2018) "Media definitely do matter: Brexit, immigration, climate change and beyond," *The British Journal of Politics and International Relations*, 20(4), p. 827. doi:10.1177/1369148118799260.

166. Givskov, C. (2015) "Exploring digital inequality in later life : An analysis of senior citizens' media repertoires," *Research Portal Denmark* [Preprint]. Available at: https://local.forskningsportal.dk/local/dki-cgi/ws/cris-link?src=ku&id=ku-859a1dd2-b6ab-4de0-b708-f9f249190290&ti=Exploring%20digital%20inequality%20in%20later%20life%20%3A%20An%20analysis%20of%20senior%20citizens%2019%20media%20repertoires (Accessed: July 2025).

167. Glogger, I. *et al.* (2022) "The world around us and the picture(s) in our heads: The effects of news media use on belief organization," *Communication Monographs*, 90(2), p. 159. doi:10.1080/03637751.2022.2149830.

168. Gómez, H.A., Sáez, M.T.M. and Álvarez-Villa, À. (2024) "Verifying a new historical stage in the ethics of communication: second generation ethics codes," *Frontiers in Communication*, 9. doi:10.3389/fcomm.2024.1495897.

169. Guo, Y., Duan, X. and Yang, X. (2025) "Valuing or devaluing nuclear weapons in the war journalism: a cross-national comparative content analysis of news coverage during the Russian war in Ukraine," *Humanities and Social Sciences Communications*, 12(1). doi:10.1057/s41599-025-05587-0.

170. Hamada, B.I. (2021) "Determinants of Journalists' Autonomy and Safety: Evidence from the Worlds of Journalism Study," *Journalism Practice*, 16(8), p. 1715. doi:10.1080/17512786.2021.1871861.

171. Hanitzsch, T. (2007) "Deconstructing Journalism Culture: Toward a Universal Theory," *Communication Theory*, 17(4), p. 367. doi:10.1111/j.1468-2885.2007.00303.x.

172. Hanitzsch, T., Hanusch, F., *et al.* (2010) "MAPPING JOURNALISM CULTURES ACROSS NATIONS," *Journalism Studies*, 12(3), p. 273. doi:10.1080/1461670x.2010.512502.

173. Hanitzsch, T., Anikina, M., *et al.* (2010) "Modeling Perceived Influences on Journalism: Evidence from a Cross-National Survey of Journalists," *Journalism & Mass Communication Quarterly*, 87(1), p. 5. doi:10.1177/107769901008700101.

174. Hanitzsch, T. and Mellado, C. (2011) "What Shapes the News around the World? How Journalists in Eighteen Countries Perceive Influences on Their Work," *The International Journal of Press/Politics*, 16(3), p. 404. doi:10.1177/1940161211407334.

175. Harcup, T. and O'Neill, D. (2001) "What Is News? Galtung and Ruge revisited," *Journalism Studies*, 2(2), p. 261. doi:10.1080/14616700118449.

176. Harcup, T. and O'Neill, D. (2016) "What is News?," *Journalism Studies*, 18(12), p. 1470. doi:10.1080/1461670x.2016.1150193.

177. Harrison, J. and Pukallus, S. (2022) "The civil norm building role of news journalism in post-civil war settings," *Journalism*, 24(1), p. 120. doi:10.1177/14648849211072947.

178. Husband, C. (2017) "Framing inclusive journalism: Between necessary idealism and essential realism," *Journal of Applied Journalism & Media Studies*, 6(3), p. 425. doi:10.1386/ajms.6.3.425_1.

179. İnceoğlu, Y.G., Cinarli, I. and Aral, S. (2006) "Weapons of Mass Destruction? Or, of Mass Deception? Media in Iraq War and After," *RePEc: Research Papers in Economics* [Preprint].

180. Isager, C. (2022) "The Passive-Responsive Journalist : An Offensive Case of Immersion in the Danish Film Industry," *Research Portal Denmark*, 14, p. 32. Available at: https://local.forskningsportal.dk/local/dki-cgi/ws/cris-link?src=ku&id=ku-c580d7e8-2f1f-47d9-bbad-796fe482d91b&ti=The%20Passive-Responsive%20Journalist%20%3A%20An%20Offensive%20Case%20of%20Immersion%20in%20the%20Danish%20Film%20Industry (Accessed: August 2025).

181. Jamaluddin, J., Khan, R.U.A. and Shahzad, M.A. (2020) "Framing Peace Process and Sharia: An Evidence of Peace Journalism during Violent Conflict in District Swat, Pakistan," *Global Legal Studies Review*, p. 29. doi:10.31703/glsr.2020(v-iv).04.

182. Joseph, T. (2014) "Mediating War and Peace: Mass Media and International Conflict," *India Quarterly A Journal of International Affairs*, 70(3), p. 225. doi:10.1177/0974928414535292.

183. Joye, S., Heinrich, A. and Wöhlert, R. (2016) "50 years of Galtung and Ruge: Reflections on their model of news values and its relevance for the study of journalism and communication today," *CM Communication and Media*, 11(38), p. 5. doi:10.5937/comman11-9514.

184. Kellow, C.L. and Steeves, H.L. (1998) "The Role of Radio in the Rwandan Genocide," *Journal of Communication*, 48(3), p. 107. doi:10.1111/j.1460-2466.1998.tb02762.x.

185. Konieczna, M. and Maria, E.S. (2023) "'I can't be neutral or centrist in a debate over my own humanity': A Study of Disagreements Between Journalists and Editors, and What They Tell Us About Objectivity," *Journalism Studies*, 24(15), p. 1839. doi:10.1080/1461670x.2023.2247487.

186. Kotišová, J. (2023) "The epistemic injustice in conflict reporting: Reporters and 'fixers' covering Ukraine, Israel, and Palestine," *Journalism*, 25(6), p. 1290. doi:10.1177/14648849231171019.

187. Kull, S., Ramsay, C. and Lewis, E. (2003) "Misperceptions, the Media, and the Iraq War," *Political Science Quarterly*, 118(4), p. 569. doi:10.1002/j.1538-165x.2003.tb00406.x.

188. Lam, Q.K.H. (2020) "Framing Theory for Higher Education Research," in *Theory and method in higher education research*. Emerald Publishing Limited, p. 167. doi:10.1108/s2056-375220200000006011.

189. Lynch, J. (2015) "Peace journalism: Theoretical and methodological developments," *Global Media and Communication*, 11(3), p. 193. doi:10.1177/1742766515606297.

190. Lynch, J. and Freear, M. (2023) "Why intervention in Afghan media failed to provide support for peace talks," *Frontiers in Communication*, 8. doi:10.3389/fcomm.2023.1118776.

191. Lynch, J. and Tiripelli, G. (2022) "Overcoming the peace journalism paradox: A case study in journalist training as media development aid," *Journal of Applied Journalism & Media Studies*, 11(2), p. 211. doi:10.1386/ajms_00091_1.

192. McLeod, D.M. (2009) "Derelict of Duty: The American News Media, Terrorism, and the War in Iraq," *Marquette law review*, 93(1), p. 113. Available at: https://epublications.marquette.edu/mulr/vol93/iss1/10/ (Accessed: September 2025).

193. McQuail, D. (2000) *McQuail's mass communication theory*. Available at: http://bvbr.bib-bvb.de:8991/F?func=service&doc_library=BVB01&local_base=BVB01&doc_number=018974946&sequence=000002&line_number=0001&func_code=DB_RECORDS&service_type=MEDIA (Accessed: November 2025).

194. Mitra, S. (2016) "Socio-cultural contexts and peace journalism: A case for meso-level comparative sociological investigation of journalistic cultures," *Journalism*, 19(11), p. 1517. doi:10.1177/1464884916657510.

195. Mitrić, P. (2022) "Can the Audience Design method help youth content reach audiences? : The case of 'Efterskolen,'" *Research Portal Denmark* [Preprint]. Available at: https://local.forskningsportal.dk/local/dki-cgi/ws/cris-link?src=ku&id=ku-42d1dbc1-d66e-4825-a0c0-79f3014967fe&ti=Can%20the%20Audience%20Design%20method%20help%20youth%20content%20reach%20audiences%3F%20%3A%20The%20case%20of%20'Efterskolen' (Accessed: August 2025).

196. Mohi-ud-Din, H., Rasul, S. and Munir, M.Z. (2021) "THE DISCOURSE OF CONFLICT AND MEDIA PROPAGANDA: AN ANALYSIS OF THE SELECTED US NEWSPAPER EDITORIALS," *ISSRA Papers*, 13, p. 57. doi:10.54690/issrap.v13ixiii.88.

197. Mont'Alverne, C., Athanásio, E. and Marques, F.P.J. (2018) "The Journalist between the Profession and the Newspaper's Interests: Values and Routines in the Production of Folha De S. Paulo's Editorials," *Brazilian Journalism Research*, 14(2), p. 384. doi:10.25200/bjr.v14n2.2018.1088.

198. Mosdell, N.A. et al. (2006) *Shoot First and Ask Questions Later: Media Coverage of the 2003 Iraq War*. Available at: http://ci.nii.ac.jp/ncid/BA79052941 (Accessed: September 2025).

199. Newbury, C. (1995) "Background To Genocide: Rwanda," *Issue*, 23(2), p. 12. doi:10.1017/s1548450500004741.

200. Nohrstedt, S.A. and Ottosen, R. (2015) "Peace journalism: A proposition for conceptual and methodological improvements," *Global Media and Communication*, 11(3), p. 219. doi:10.1177/1742766515606289.

201. Ntete, J.M. (2022) "Newspapers in Preparation of Genocide Committed against Tutsi in 1994 in Rwanda under Pretext of Freedom of Expression.," *SSRN Electronic Journal* [Preprint]. doi:10.2139/ssrn.4164550.

202. Olivera, C.A., Thomas, R. and Kilby, A. (2020) "Peace Journalism in Theory and Practice: Kenyan and Foreign Correspondent Perspectives," *Journalism Practice*, 16(7), p. 1383. doi:10.1080/17512786.2020.1856707.

203. Paasch-Colberg, S. and Strippel, C. (2021) "'The Boundaries are Blurry...': How Comment Moderators in Germany See and Respond to Hate Comments," *Journalism Studies*, 23(2), p. 224. doi:10.1080/1461670x.2021.2017793.

204. Prager, A. and Hameleers, M. (2018) "Disseminating information or advocating peace? Journalists' role perceptions in the face of conflict," *Journalism*, 22(2), p. 395. doi:10.1177/1464884918791788.

205. Provencher, J. (2000) *Is Scholarship Advancing?: An Analysis of Fifteen Years of Framing Research.* doi:10.15760/etd.2701.

206. Rawan, B. and Rahman, S.I. ur (2020) "Comparative Frame Analysis of Coverage of Kashmir Conflict in Indian and Pakistani Newspapers from War/Peace Journalism Perspective," *Sir Syed Journal of Education & Social Research (SJESR)*, 3(2), p. 338. doi:10.36902/sjesr-vol3-iss2-2020(338-345).

207. Reese, S.D. and Shoemaker, P.J. (2016) "A Media Sociology for the Networked Public Sphere: The Hierarchy of Influences Model," *Mass Communication & Society*, 19(4), p. 389. doi:10.1080/15205436.2016.1174268.

208. Reid, S.A., Giles, H. and Abrams, J.R. (2004) "A Social Identidy Model of Media Usage and Effects," *Zeitschrift für Medienpsychologie*, 16(1), p. 17. doi:10.1026/1617-6383.16.1.17.

209. Ristić, K. and Satjukow, E. (2022) "The 1999 NATO Intervention from a Comparative Perspective: An Introduction," *Comparative Southeast European Studies*, 70(2), p. 189. doi:10.1515/soeu-2022-0026.

210. Robinson, P. (2000) "Research Note: The News Media and Intervention," *European Journal of Communication*, 15(3), p. 405. doi:10.1177/0267323100015003008.

211. Salaudeen, M.A. (2021) "From Personal to Professional: Exploring the Influences on Journalists' Evaluation of Citizen Journalism Credibility," *Journalism Practice*, 16(10), p. 2040. doi:10.1080/17512786.2021.1892517.

212. Samsudin, D. (2019) "Understanding the Models of Framing Analyses Approaches in Media Framing Studies," p. 385. doi:10.5220/0009159503850389.

213. Shah, U.A. (2022) "Editorial Treatment of the Pulwama Attack in Indo-Pak Press: War and Peace Journalism Perspective," *Journal of Development and Social Sciences*, 3, p. 27. doi:10.47205/jdss.2022(3-i)03.

214. Shaw, I.S., Lynch, J. and Hackett, R.A. (2012) *Expanding peace journalism: comparative and critical approaches*, Sydney University Press eBooks. doi:10.30722/sup.9781920899707.

215. Shultziner, D. (2025) "Journalistic Interventionism: Types, Professional, and Normative Conceptions," *Mass Communication & Society*, p. 1. doi:10.1080/15205436.2025.2478892.

216. Slater, M.D. (2014) "Reinforcing Spirals Model: Conceptualizing the Relationship Between Media Content Exposure and the Development and Maintenance of Attitudes," *Media Psychology*, 18(3), p. 370. doi:10.1080/15213269.2014.897236.

217. Solnet, D. *et al.* (2022) "Tourism work, media & COVID-19: A changed narrative?," *Annals of Tourism Research*, 97, p. 103492. doi:10.1016/j.annals.2022.103492.

218. Steel, J.R. *et al.* (2025) "Journalism and Ethical Praxis: A Thematic Analysis of Journalism Ethics Across Five European Countries," *Journalism Practice*, p. 1.

doi:10.1080/17512786.2025.2480746.

219. Stupart, R. (2021) "Feeling responsible: Emotion and practical ethics in conflict journalism," *Media War & Conflict*, 14(3), p. 268. doi:10.1177/17506352211013461.

220. Szabo, A.S. (2013) "Social News Sites as Democratic Media : An evaluative study of Reddit's coverage of the 2012 US presidential election campaign," *Research Portal Denmark*, p. 256. Available at: https://local.forskningsportal.dk/local/dki-cgi/ws/cris-link?src=ku&id=ku-51607b8f-fb1c-4c9b-92b2-74f1612ecee3&ti=Social%20News%20Sites%20as%20Democratic%20Media%20%3A%20 An%20evaluative%20study%20of%20Reddit's%20coverage%20of%20the%202012%20US% 20presidential%20election%20campaign (Accessed: July 2025).

221. Alper, M. (2013). War on Instagram: Framing conflict photojournalism with mobile photography apps. *New Media & Society*, 16(8), 1233. https://doi.org/10.1177/1461444813504265

222. Barber, C. M. (2020). COVID-19 en portada: radiografía ética de la cobertura fotográfica de la pandemia en España. *REVISTA ESPAÑOLA DE COMUNICACIÓN EN SALUD*, 42. https://doi.org/10.20318/recs.2020.5435

223. Barcelos, J. D. (2014). Por um fotojornalismo que respeite a dignidade humana: a dimensão ética como questão fundamental na contemporaneidade. *Discursos Fotográficos*, 10(16), 111. https://doi.org/10.5433/1984-7939.2014v10n16p111

224. Beuran, R. (2015). *PROFESSIONAL PHOTOJOURNALISM IN THE AGE OF NEW MEDIA*. 60(2), 5. https://www.ceeol.com/search/article-detail?id=306893

225. Carlson, M. (2019). News Algorithms, Photojournalism and the Assumption of Mechanical Objectivity in Journalism. *Digital Journalism*, 7(8), 1117. https://doi.org/10.1080/21670811.2019.1601577

226. Ganapathy-Doré, G., Olinga, M., Crowley, C., Naumann, M., Boulicaut, Y. L., Coulardeau, J., Taouchichet, S., Zambo, C. É. O., Dosoruth, S., Vilar, F., & Griffin, P. R. (2013). IMAGES OF DECOLONIZATION / IMAGES DE LA DECOLONISATION. *HAL (Le Centre Pour La Communication Scientifique Directe)*. https://hal.science/hal-00821522

227. Gynnild, A., Nilsson, M., Simonsen, A. H., & Weselius, H. (2017). Introduction: Photojournalism and Editorial Processes. *Nordicom Review/NORDICOM Review*, 38, 1. https://doi.org/10.1515/nor-2017-0410

228. Hasemann, U., Maagaard, M. S., Makarov, E., Khamis, H. allah A. A., Kiviniemi, E., Hørlyck, M., Skjoldjensen, A. R., Bæk, A., Lau-Nielsen, M., Navntoft, N., Veilmark, S., Kragh, K. M., Gestsson, O. S., Øllgaard, J. W., Rinne, R., Pagter, S., Luk, G., & Greve, M. (2017). Life Exposed : DMJX Photojournalism 25. In *Research Portal Denmark* (p. 70). Technical University of Denmark. https://local.forskningsportal.dk/local/dki-cgi/ws/cris-link?src=dmjx&id=dmjx-da7ebe5e-ae82-40cf-a205-241051559570&ti=Life%20Exposed%20%3A%20DMJX%20Photojournalism%2025

229. Hrib, I. (2023). Photojournalism. Between Industry and Culture. *Culture Society Economy Politics*, 3(2), 92. https://doi.org/10.2478/csep-2023-0012

230. Iqbal, M., & Badar, M. B. (2022). Fotografer dan Dinamika Jurnalisme Positif perspektif Jurnalistik Islam: Studi Media Online Times Indonesia. *Moderasi Journal of Islamic Studies*, 2(1), 60. https://doi.org/10.54471/moderasi.v2i1.24

231. Kontos, I., & Galanopoulos-Papavasileiou, I. (2024). Photojournalism: Values and Constraints, Aestheticism, and Aftermath Photography. *European Journal of Fine and Visual Arts*, 2(1), 1. https://doi.org/10.24018/ejart.2024.2.1.20

232. Lavoie, V. (2010a). *Photojournalistic Integrity*. http://journals.openedition.org/etudesphotographiques/3462

233. Lavoie, V. (2010b). Photojournalistic Integrity. Codes of Conduct, Professional Ethics, and the Moral Definition of Press Photography. *Études Photographiques, 26.* https://journals.openedition.org/etudesphotographiques/pdf/3462

234. Mäenpää, J. (2014). Rethinking Photojournalism: The Changing Work Practices and Professionalism of Photojournalists in the Digital Age. *Nordicom Review/NORDICOM Review, 35*(2), 91. https://doi.org/10.2478/nor-2014-0017

235. Mäenpää, J. (2023a). Future directions of professional photographers: A case study of changing hats between journalism and humanitarian photography. *Nordicom Review/NORDICOM Review, 44*(1), 65. https://doi.org/10.2478/nor-2023-0004

236. Mäenpää, J. (2023b). The changing working life of photojournalism professionals in the contemporary media environment. *Journal of Visual Political Communication, 10*(1), 27. https://doi.org/10.1386/jvpc_00025_1

237. Maillot, F. A. (2019). *An Analysis of How the Internet has Changed Photography and the Profession of Photojournalism.* https://aquila.usm.edu/cgi/viewcontent.cgi?article=1675&context=honors_theses

238. Mapesa, H. (2016). Photojournalism as a Core Journalism Course Unit: Challenges and Solutions. A Survey of Some Universities in Rwanda. *International Journal of Science and Research (IJSR), 5*(1), 151. https://doi.org/10.21275/v5i1.nov152108

239. Mortensen, T. B., & Keshelashvili, A. (2013). If Everyone with a Camera Can Do This, Then What? Professional Photojournalists' Sense of Professional Threat in the Face of Citizen Photojournalism. *Visual Communication Quarterly, 20*(3), 144. https://doi.org/10.1080/15551393.2013.820587

240. Mraz, J. (2018). Analyzing Historical Photographs: Genres, Functions, and Methodologies. *Estudos Ibero-Americanos, 44*(1), 6. https://doi.org/10.15448/1980-864x.2018.1.27785

241. Palomo, B., & Guerrero-García, V. (1970). The crisis of photojournalism: rethinking the profession in a participatory media ecosystem. *Communication & Society, 28*(4), 33. https://doi.org/10.15581/003.28.35940

242. Prestianta, A. M. (2022). Mobile Journalism Practice in the Kompas.com Newsroom. *Komunikator, 14*(2), 137. https://doi.org/10.18196/jkm.15883

243. Ramos, J. C. L., & Marocco, B. (2017). Photojournalism: Diverse Concepts, Uniform Practices. *Brazilian Journalism Research, 13*(1), 132. https://doi.org/10.25200/bjr.v13n1.2017.914

244. Rehman, S. (2018). A camera never told the truth: An exploration of objectivity in photojournalism. *Annales Etyka w Życiu Gospodarczym, 21*(4), 45. https://doi.org/10.18778/1899-2226.21.4.05

245. Rodal, A. B., & Segarra, I. M. (2017). Sesenta años del premio de fotoperiodismo Word Press Photo of the Year: una visión con perspectiva de géneroSesenta años del premio de fotoperiodismo Word Press Photo of the Year: una visión con perspectiva de género. *CIC Cuadernos de Información y Comunicación, 22.* https://doi.org/10.5209/ciyc.55979

246. Silva, M. F. S., & Eldridge, S. A. (2020). *The Ethics of Photojournalism in the Digital Age.* https://doi.org/10.4324/9780429504686

247. Thomson, T. J., & Greenwood, K. (2016). Beyond Framing. *Journalism Practice, 11*(5), 625. https://doi.org/10.1080/17512786.2016.1152908

248. Thomson, T. J., & Sternberg, J. (2021). Journalism Employability in the Modern Newsroom: Insights From Applicant Resumes and Cover Letters. *Journalism & Mass Communication Educator, 77*(2), 157. https://doi.org/10.1177/1077695821103285

249. Urbonavičiūtė, L. (2015). The ethics of photojournalism in Lithuania: views of the news photographers. *Žurnalistikos Tyrimai, 8,* 70. https://doi.org/10.15388/zt/jr.2015.8.8843

250. Tayeebwa, W. (2017) "From Conventional Towards New Frames of Peace Journalism:," in *CODESRIA eBooks*, p. 209. doi:10.2307/j.ctvgc60jf.13.

251. Thomas, P., Alhassan, A.-R.K. and Lie, A.L.K. (2020) "Bunad, minorities and belonging in Norway," *National Identities*, 24(2), p. 165. doi:10.1080/14608944.2020.1851669.

252. Thomas, S. (2024) "Echoes of peace: media's challenges and opportunities in shaping societal narratives," *International Journal of Science and Research Archive*, 12(1), p. 2695. doi:10.30574/ijsra.2024.12.1.1085.

253. Valdez, J.E.P. *et al.* (2023) "Equity, diversity, and inclusion in the construction of journalistic and training agendas for peace in Colombia," *Frontiers in Education*, 8. doi:10.3389/feduc.2023.1083050.

254. Zaklama, S. (2025) "Exploring the Foundations of Media Framing Theory," *European Modern Studies Journal*, 9(1), p. 75. doi:10.59573/emsj.9(1).2025.7.

255. Ajaegbu, O.O. and Ajaegbu, C. (2024) "The new democratisation: social media impact on the political process in Sub-Saharan Africa," *Frontiers in Communication*, 9. doi:10.3389/fcomm.2024.1394949.

256. Amodu, L., Usaini, S. and Ige, O. (2016) "The Media as Fourth Estate of the Realm." doi:10.13140/rg.2.2.19311.02720.

257. Bruns, A. (2009) "From Reader to Writer: Citizen Journalism as News Produsage," in *Springer eBooks*. Springer Nature, p. 119. doi:10.1007/978-1-4020-9789-8_6.

258. Bucy, E.P. and Groshek, J. (2017) "Empirical support for the media participation hypothesis: Trends across presidential elections, 1992–2012," *New Media & Society*, 20(5), p. 1889. doi:10.1177/1461444817709281.

259. Chitanana, T. and Mutsvairo, B. (2019) "The Deferred 'Democracy Dividend' of Citizen Journalism and Social Media: Perils, Promises and Prospects from the Zimbabwean Experience," *Westminster Papers in Communication and Culture*, 14(1). doi:10.16997/wpcc.305.

260. Damissah, H.E. *et al.* (2025) "Media independence and democratic accountability in modern governance systems and public administration frameworks," *GSC Advanced Research and Reviews*, 23(1), p. 12. doi:10.30574/gscarr.2025.23.1.0102.

261. Danso, S. (2025) "Media and politics: investigating government interests, ownership influence and media independence in combating corruption in Ghana," *Cogent Social Sciences*, 11(1). doi:10.1080/23311886.2025.2483391.

262. Esser, F. and Neuberger, C. (2018) "Realizing the democratic functions of journalism in the digital age: New alliances and a return to old values," *Journalism*, 20(1), p. 194. doi:10.1177/1464884918807067.

263. Hamada, B.I. (2021) "Determinants of Journalists' Autonomy and Safety: Evidence from the Worlds of Journalism Study," *Journalism Practice*, 16(8), p. 1715. doi:10.1080/17512786.2021.1871861.

264. Hanitzsch, T. and Mellado, C. (2011) "What Shapes the News around the World? How Journalists in Eighteen Countries Perceive Influences on Their Work," *The International Journal of Press/Politics*, 16(3), p. 404. doi:10.1177/1940161211407334.

265. Hanitzsch, T. and Vos, T.P. (2016) "Journalism beyond democracy: A new look into journalistic roles in political and everyday life," *Journalism*, 19(2), p. 146. doi:10.1177/1464884916673386.

266. Kalogeropoulos, A., Toff, B. and Fletcher, R. (2022) "The Watchdog Press in the Doghouse: A Comparative Study of Attitudes about Accountability Journalism, Trust in News, and News Avoidance," *The International Journal of Press/Politics*, 29(2), p. 485. doi:10.1177/19401612221112572.

REECH MALUAL

267. Maniou, T.A. (2022) "The Dynamics of Influence on Press Freedom in Different Media Systems: A Comparative Study," *Journalism Practice*, 17(9), p. 1937. doi:10.1080/17512786.2022.2030246.

268. Marsili, M. (2021) "The Press: Fourth Power or Counter-power?," *DOAJ (DOAJ: Directory of Open Access Journals)* [Preprint]. doi:10.25770/artc.18415.

269. McNair, B. (2010) *Journalism and Democracy, Routledge eBooks*. Informa. doi:10.4324/9780203021286.

270. Nielsen, R.K., Cornia, A. and Kalogeropoulos, A. (2016) "Challenges and opportunities for news media and journalism in an increasingly digital, mobile and social media environment," *SSRN Electronic Journal* [Preprint]. Available at: https://apo.org.au/node/71071 (Accessed: August 2025).

271. Østergaard, T.G. (2021) *Popular music journalism in the digital age : a cross-national content analysis of popular music journalism in Danish and German news media, Research Portal Denmark*. Technical University of Denmark, p. 236. Available at: https://local.forskningsportal.dk/local/dki-cgi/ws/cris-link?src=dmjx&id=dmjx-75aa0b05-ccdc-4de4-ae70-9b79cb59a9c7&ti=Popular%20music%20journalism%20in%20the%20digital%20age%20%3A%20a%20cross-national%20content%20analysis%20of%20popular%20music%20journalism%20in%20Danish%20and%20German%20news%20media (Accessed: July 2025).

272. Ots, M., Berglez, P. and Nord, L. (2023) "Who Watches the Watchdog? Understanding Media Systems as Information Regimes," *Media and Communication*, 12(2024). doi:10.17645/mac.7216.

273. Riedl, A. (2018) "Which Journalists for Which Democracy?," *Journalism Studies*, 20(10), p. 1377. doi:10.1080/1461670x.2018.1519638.

274. Scherman, A., Fierro, P. and Shan, Y. (2025) "Democracy, Deliberation, and Media: The Role of Incidental Exposure and News Consumption," *Media and Communication*, 13. doi:10.17645/mac.9959.

275. Szabo, A.S. (2013) "Social News Sites as Democratic Media : An evaluative study of Reddit's coverage of the 2012 US presidential election campaign," *Research Portal Denmark*, p. 256. Available at: https://local.forskningsportal.dk/local/dki-cgi/ws/cris-link?src=ku&id=ku-51607b8f-fb1c-4c9b-92b2-74f1612ecee3&ti=Social%20News%20Sites%20as%20Democratic%20Media%20%3A%20An%20evaluative%20study%20of%20Reddit's%20coverage%20of%20the%202012%20US%20presidential%20election%20campaign (Accessed: July 2025).

276. Vestergaard, M. (2022) "Digital threats to democracy : studies in digital politics and digitalization policy-making," *Research Portal Denmark*, p. 219. Available at: https://local.forskningsportal.dk/local/dki-cgi/ws/cris-link?src=ku&id=ku-d2a866b5-5520-40dd-9d4d-06e90d5da28d&ti=Digital%20threats%20to%20democracy%20%3A%20studies%20in%20digital%20politics%20and%20digitalization%20policy-making (Accessed: August 2025).

277. Audette-Longo, P.H. *et al.* (2023) "Forced change: Pandemic pedagogy and journalism education," *Facts & Frictions Emerging Debates Pedagogies and Practices in Contemporary Journalism*, 3(1). doi:10.22215/ff/v3.i1.01.

278. Bartliff, Z. *et al.* (2020) "Leveraging digital forensics and data exploration to understand the creative work of a filmmaker: A case study of Stephen Dwoskin's digital archive," *Information Processing & Management*, 57(6), p. 102339. doi:10.1016/j.ipm.2020.102339.

279. Bhatti, S.A. (2025) "AI in our Justice System."

280. Birnbauer, W. (2017) "Non-profit investigative reporting in American journalism, 2007-2015." Available at: https://oatd.org/oatd/record?record=handle\:1959.3\%2F450265 (Accessed: October 2025).

281. Biscop, M. and Décary-Hétu, D. (2022) "Anonymity Technologies in Investigative Journalism: A Tool for Inspiring Trust in Sources," *Journalism Practice*, 18(6), p. 1420. doi:10.1080/17512786.2022.2113740.

282. Bjerknes, F. (2020) "Inventive Factfinders: Investigative Journalism as Professional Self-representation, Marker of Identity and Boundary Work," *Journalism Practice*, 16(6), p. 1037. doi:10.1080/17512786.2020.1845780.

283. Bravo, A.A. and Tellería, A.S. (2020) "Data Journalism: From Social Science Techniques to Data Science Skills," *Hipertext net Revista Académica sobre Documentación Digital y Comunicación Interactiva*, (20), p. 41. doi:10.31009/hipertext.net.2020.i20.04.

284. Buschow, C. and Suhr, M. (2023) "Organizations as Innovations: Examining Changes in Journalism Through the Lens of Newly-Emerging Organizations," *Media and Communication*, 12. doi:10.17645/mac.7399.

285. Cancela, P., Gerber, D.J. and Dubied, A. (2021) "'To Me, It's Normal Journalism' Professional Perceptions of Investigative Journalism and Evaluations of Personal Commitment," *Journalism Practice*, 15(6), p. 878. doi:10.1080/17512786.2021.1876525.

286. Carson, A. (2019) "What Is Investigative Journalism?," in *Routledge eBooks*. Informa, p. 53. doi:10.4324/9781315514291-3.

287. Chandel, P. (2024) "Can privacy and foreign affiliations thwart academic research? Empirical challenges in the Indian mediascape," *Media Asia*, p. 1. doi:10.1080/01296612.2024.2370123.

288. Chouliaraki, L. and Al-Ghazzi, O. (2021) "Beyond verification: Flesh witnessing and the significance of embodiment in conflict news," *Journalism*, 23(3), p. 649. doi:10.1177/14648849211060628.

289. Cifliku, B. and Heuer, H. (2025) "'This could save us months of work' -- Use Cases of AI and Automation Support in Investigative Journalism," *arXiv* [Preprint]. doi:10.48550/ARXIV.2503.16011.

290. Danso, S. (2025) "Media and politics: investigating government interests, ownership influence and media independence in combating corruption in Ghana," *Cogent Social Sciences*, 11(1). doi:10.1080/23311886.2025.2483391.

291. Dean, S.E. *et al.* (2024) "Djinn—Data Journalism Interface for Newsgathering and Notifications," in *Lecture notes in computer science*. Springer Science+Business Media, p. 147. doi:10.1007/978-3-031-77918-3_11.

292. Fierens, M. *et al.* (2023) "SLAPPs against journalists in Europe: Exploring the role of self-regulatory bodies," *European Journal of Communication*, 39(2), p. 161. doi:10.1177/02673231231213539.

293. Freedman, E. (2020) "In the crosshairs: The perils of environmental journalism," *Journal of Human Rights*, 19(3), p. 275. doi:10.1080/14754835.2020.1746180.

294. Hauter, J. (2021) "Forensic conflict studies: Making sense of war in the social media age," *Media War & Conflict*, 16(2), p. 153. doi:10.1177/17506352211037325.

295. Horan, C. and Saiedian, H. (2021) "Cyber Crime Investigation: Landscape, Challenges, and Future Research Directions," *Journal of Cybersecurity and Privacy*, 1(4), p. 580. doi:10.3390/jcp1040029.

296. Horsman, G. (2019) "Formalising investigative decision making in digital forensics: Proposing the Digital Evidence Reporting and Decision Support (DERDS) framework," *Digital Investigation*, 28, p. 146. doi:10.1016/j.diin.2019.01.007.

297. Hutchinson, B., Dekker, S. and Rae, A. (2024) "How audits fail according to accident investigations: A counterfactual logic analysis," *Process Safety Progress*, 43(3), p. 441. doi:10.1002/prs.12579.

298. Ismail, A.H., Ahmad, M.K. and Mustaffa, C.S. (2014) "Conceptualization of Investigative Journalism: The Perspectives of Malaysian Media Practitioners," *Procedia - Social and Behavioral Sciences*, 155, p. 165. doi:10.1016/j.sbspro.2014.10.274.

299. Jamil, H.M. and Rubaiat, S.Y. (2024) "Online Digital Investigative Journalism using SociaLens," *arXiv (Cornell University)* [Preprint]. doi:10.48550/arxiv.2410.11890.

300. Khan, S.A. *et al.* (2023) "Visual User-Generated Content Verification in Journalism: An Overview," *IEEE Access*, 11, p. 6748. doi:10.1109/access.2023.3236993.

301. Kibarabara, J., Cheruiyot, D. and Muindi, B. (2022) "Missionaries of Excellence? Post-award Role Orientations of Journalism Prize Winners," *Journalism Studies*, 24(1), p. 45. doi:10.1080/1461670x.2022.2142647.

302. Konow-Lund, M. (2020) "Reconstructing investigative journalism at emerging organisations," *The Journal of Media Innovations*, 6(1), p. 9. doi:10.5617/jomi.7830.

303. Leimbach, T. *et al.* (2015) "Assessing Big Data : Results and experiences from Germany," *Research Portal Denmark*, p. 243. Available at: https://local.forskningsportal.dk/local/dki-cgi/ws/cris-link?src=au&id=au-1aae740c-c95a-4e53-85c5-ebef6878becb&ti=Assessing%20Big%20Data%20%3A%20Results%20and%20experiences%20from%20Germany (Accessed: July 2025).

304. Louis-Sidois, C. and Mougin, E. (2020) "Silence the Media or the Story? Theory and Evidence of Media Capture," *SSRN Electronic Journal* [Preprint]. doi:10.2139/ssrn.3561443.

305. Lovell, R. *et al.* (2023) "Using machine learning to assess rape reports: Sentiment analysis detection of officers' 'signaling' about victims' credibility," *Journal of Criminal Justice*, 88, p. 102106. doi:10.1016/j.jcrimjus.2023.102106.

306. Maniou, T.A. and Ketteni, E. (2020) "The impact of the economic crisis on media corruption: A comparative study in South and North Europe," *International Communication Gazette*, 84(1), p. 66. doi:10.1177/1748048520942751.

307. Medina, M., Sánchez-Tabernero, A. and Breiner, J. (2021) "Some viable models for digital public-interest journalism," *El Profesional de la Informacion* [Preprint]. doi:10.3145/epi.2021.ene.18.

308. Meier, K. *et al.* (2022) "Examining the Most Relevant Journalism Innovations: A Comparative Analysis of Five European Countries from 2010 to 2020," *Journalism and Media*, 3(4), p. 698. doi:10.3390/journalmedia3040046.

309. Mills, A.R. (2018) "Now You See Me – Now You Don't: Journalists' Experiences With Surveillance," *Journalism Practice*, 13(6), p. 690. doi:10.1080/17512786.2018.1555006.

310. NeCastro, M. (2014) "Muckrakers vs. Public Relations: Analytical Case Studies." Available at: https://digitalcommons.library.umaine.edu/cgi/viewcontent.cgi?article=1143&context=honors (Accessed: December 2024).

311. Nurhadiyati, N. (2024) "Revolutionizing Newsgathering: The Impact of Digital Media and New Technologies," in *Asian Conference on Media & Mass Communication official conference proceedings*, p. 85. doi:10.22492/issn.2186-5906.2024.7.

312. Pandey, B. *et al.* (2024) "Efficient usage of web forensics, disk forensics and email forensics in successful investigation of cyber crime," *International Journal of Information Technology*, 16(6), p. 3815. doi:10.1007/s41870-024-02014-6.

313. Papadopoulou, L. and Maniou, T.A. (2024) "'SLAPPed' and censored? Legal threats and challenges to press freedom and investigative reporting," *Journalism* [Preprint]. doi:10.1177/14648849241242181.

314. Salvo, P.D. (2021) "'We Have to act Like our Devices are Already Infected': Investigative Journalists and Internet Surveillance," *Journalism Practice*, 16(9), p. 1849. doi:10.1080/17512786.2021.2014346.

315. Şen, A.F. (2021) "Watchdog Journalism during the Coronavirus Crisis in Turkey," *Advances in Applied Sociology*, 11(10), p. 500. doi:10.4236/aasoci.2021.1110044.

316. Sennewald, C.A. and Tsukayama, J.K. (2015) "Report Writing and Note Taking," in *Elsevier eBooks*. Elsevier BV, p. 181. doi:10.1016/b978-0-12-800166-0.00014-0.

317. Shah, A.K. (2021) "Reform Lessons From Investigative Journalism. Review Essay of 'Beancounters' by Richard Brooks," *The British Accounting Review*, 54(3), p. 101069. doi:10.1016/j.bar.2021.101069.

318. Steel, J.R. *et al.* (2025) "Journalism and Ethical Praxis: A Thematic Analysis of Journalism Ethics Across Five European Countries," *Journalism Practice*, p. 1. doi:10.1080/17512786.2025.2480746.

319. Steensen, S. *et al.* (2022) "Journalism and Source Criticism. Revised Approaches to Assessing Truth-Claims," *Journalism Studies*, 23(16), p. 2119. doi:10.1080/1461670x.2022.2140446.

320. Stray, J. (2019) "Making Artificial Intelligence Work for Investigative Journalism," *Digital Journalism*, 7(8), p. 1076. doi:10.1080/21670811.2019.1630289.

321. T., S.S. (2024) "THE CHALLENGES AND ROLE OF MODERN JOURNALISM IN DIGITAL MEDIA ENTERPRISES," *ShodhKosh Journal of Visual and Performing Arts*, 5(7). doi:10.29121/shodhkosh.v5.i7.2024.1921.

322. Turkel, E. *et al.* (2021) "A method for measuring investigative journalism in local newspapers," *Proceedings of the National Academy of Sciences*, 118(30). doi:10.1073/pnas.2105155118.

323. Veerbeek, J. and Diakopoulos, N. (2024) "Using Generative Agents to Create Tip Sheets for Investigative Data Reporting." doi:10.48550/ARXIV.2409.07286.

324. Verhovnik, M. (2018) "Trauma journalism and disaster resilience. German journalists' coping strategies when reporting about crime, violence, accidents, crises and natural disasters," *Studies in Communication Sciences*, 17(2). doi:10.24434/j.scoms.2017.02.006.

325. Walulya, G. and Nassanga, G.L. (2020) "Democracy at Stake: Self-Censorship as a Self-Defence Strategy for Journalists," *Media and Communication*, 8(1), p. 5. doi:10.17645/mac.v8i1.2512.

326. Woude, M. van der, Dodds, T. and Torres, G. (2024) "The ethics of open source investigations: Navigating privacy challenges in a gray zone information landscape," *Journalism* [Preprint]. doi:10.1177/14648849241274104.

327. Wuergler, L. *et al.* (2023) "Identifying Investigative Pieces," *Journalism Studies*, 24(14), p. 1754. doi:10.1080/1461670x.2023.2209814.

328. Yisrael, R.-Z. (2010) "Report Writing and Field Notes," in *Elsevier eBooks*. Elsevier BV, p. 427. doi:10.1016/b978-1-85617-746-7.00035-3.

329. Zákopčanová, K. *et al.* (2020) "Visilant: Visual Support for the Exploration and Analytical Process Tracking in Criminal Investigations," *IEEE Transactions on Visualization and Computer Graphics*, 27(2), p. 881. doi:10.1109/tvcg.2020.3030356.

330. Zhao, K. (2023) "A Study on the Application of New Media in Broadcast Newscasting and Writing under the Perspective of Media Integration," *World Journal of Educational Research*, 10(6). doi:10.22158/wjer.v10n6p25.

331. Anastasiou, A. (2016) "Dynamics of news selection in different socio-cultural contexts: Theoretical and methodological issues," for(e)dialogue, 1(1), p. 95. doi:10.29311/for(e)dialogue.v1i1.535.

332. Barboutis, C. (2013) "The birth of radio broadcasting: The matrix of science, technology and communication in the western world," Radio Journal International Studies in Broadcast & Audio Media, 11(2), p. 155. doi:10.1386/rjao.11.2.155_1.

333. Bateman, J. and Tseng, C.-I. (2023) "Multimodal discourse analysis as a method for revealing narrative strategies in news videos," Multimodal Communication, 12(3), p. 261. doi:10.1515/mc-2023-0029.

334. Bivens, R. (2015) "Affording Immediacy in Television News Production: Comparing Adoption Trajectories of Social Media and Satellite Technologies," International journal of communication, 9(1), p. 19. Available at: https://ir.library.carleton.ca/pub/10561/1001-14081-1-PB.pdf (Accessed: October 2025).

335. Black, J.R. (1998) "Journalism Nethics," Convergence The International Journal of Research into New Media Technologies, 4(4), p. 10. doi:10.1177/135485659800400402.

336. Bogdanić, A. (2020) "Theorizing News: Toward a Constitutive Model of Journalistic Discourse," Journalism & Mass Communication Quarterly, 99(2), p. 487. doi:10.1177/1077699020966755.

337. Bro, P., Hansen, K.R. and Andersson, R. (2015) "IMPROVING PRODUCTIVITY IN THE NEWSROOM?," Journalism Practice, 10(8), p. 1005. doi:10.1080/17512786.2015.1090883.

338. Bro, P. and Wallberg, F. (2014) "Digital Gatekeeping," Digital Journalism, 2(3), p. 446. doi:10.1080/21670811.2014.895507.

339. "Broadcasting" (2022) in The MIT Press eBooks. The MIT Press, p. 105. doi:10.7551/mitpress/11281.003.0010.

340. Budak, C. et al. (2023) "The Stability of Cable and Broadcast News Intermedia Agenda Setting Across the COVID-19 Issue Attention Cycle," Political Communication, 40(6), p. 827. doi:10.1080/10584609.2023.2222382.

341. Buschow, C. (2020) "Practice-driven journalism research: Impulses for a dynamic understanding of journalism in the context of its reorganization," Studies in Communication Sciences, 20(2). doi:10.24434/j.scoms.2020.02.006.

342. Canavilhas, J. and Fátima, B.D. (2024) "Decoding Journalism in the Digital Age: Self-Representation, News Quality, and Collaboration in Portuguese Newsrooms," Journalism and Media, 5(2), p. 515. doi:10.3390/journalmedia5020034.

343. Chen, L. (2024) "Digital Transformation and Innovation of the News Media," International Journal of Education and Humanities, 17(1), p. 154. doi:10.54097/j5w0kb62.

344. Chin-Fook, L. and Simmonds, H. (2013) "Redefining Gatekeeping Theory For A Digital Generation," The McMaster Journal of Communication, 8. doi:10.15173/mjc.v8i0.259.

345. Chivers, T. and Allan, S. (2022) "A public value typology for public service broadcasting in the UK," Cultural Trends, 33(2), p. 205. doi:10.1080/09548963.2022.2151340.

346. Cottle, S. and Ashton, M.S. (1999) "From BBC Newsroom to BBC Newscentre : On Changing Technology and Journalist Practices," Convergence The International Journal of Research into New Media Technologies, 5(3), p. 22. doi:10.1177/135485659900500304.

347. Dan, V. (2018) "A Methodological Approach for Integrative Framing Analysis of Television News," in, p. 191. doi:10.4324/9781315642239-9.

348. Dhiman, B. (2023) "Unleashing the Power of Television Broadcasting in the Digital Age: A Critical Review." doi:10.36227/techrxiv.24329260.v1.

349. Ding, X., Horning, M. and Rho, E.H.R. (2023) "Same Words, Different Meanings: Semantic Polarization in Broadcast Media Language Forecasts Polarity in Online Public Discourse," Proceedings of the International AAAI Conference on Web and Social Media, 17, p. 161. doi:10.1609/icwsm.v17i1.22135.

350. Ding, X., Horning, M.G. and Rho, E.H.R. (2023) "Same Words, Different Meanings: Semantic Polarization in Broadcast Media Language Forecasts Polarization on Social Media Discourse," arXiv (Cornell University) [Preprint]. doi:10.48550/arxiv.2301.08832.

351. Dongre, R. and Nehulkar, R. (2019) "Paradigm Shift in TV and Radio Broadcasting in Digital Age," SSRN Electronic Journal [Preprint]. doi:10.2139/ssrn.3393903.

352. Eilders, C. (2006) "News factors and news decisions. Theoretical and methodological advances in Germany," Communications, 31(1), p. 5. doi:10.1515/commun.2006.002.

353. Eskiadi, I.G. and Panagiotou, N. (2024) "Embracing Immersive Journalism: Adoption and Integration by News Media Producers," Journalism and Media, 5(4), p. 1494. doi:10.3390/journalmedia5040093.

354. Fick, R. (2024) "Digital Readiness in a Digital Revolution: How is community radio responding to digital transformation in the changing broadcast environment of South Africa?," in EPiC series in education science, p. 149. doi:10.29007/vzzf.

355. Flensburg, S. et al. (2023) "Who controls the internet in Myanmar?," Research Portal Denmark, p. 26. Available at: https://local.forskningsportal.dk/local/dki-cgi/ws/cris-link?src=ku&id=ku-ea03adcb-cd09-4e14-84ea-45c8fd9dc6e6&ti=Who%20controls%20the%20internet%20in%20Myanmar%3F (Accessed: July 2025).

356. Fraile, M. and Hernández, E. (2024) "What is political and what is not? Illustrating how the salience of abortion in the media shapes public perceptions about its political nature," Acta Politica [Preprint]. doi:10.1057/s41269-024-00347-5.

357. Givskov, C. (2015) "Exploring digital inequality in later life : An analysis of senior citizens' media repertoires," Research Portal Denmark [Preprint]. Available at: https://local.forskningsportal.dk/local/dki-cgi/ws/cris-link?src=ku&id=ku-859a1dd2-b6ab-4de0-b708-f9f249190290&ti=Exploring%20digital%20inequality%20in%20later%20life%20%3A%20An%20analysis%20of%20senior%20citizens%2019%20media%20repertoires (Accessed: July 2025).

358. Gutiérrez-Caneda, B., Lindén, C. and Vázquez-Herrero, J. (2024) "Ethics and journalistic challenges in the age of artificial intelligence: talking with professionals and experts," Frontiers in Communication, 9. doi:10.3389/fcomm.2024.1465178.

359. Hamilton, J.W. (2018) "Excavating Concepts of Broadcasting," Digital Journalism, 6(9), p. 1136. doi:10.1080/21670811.2018.1481762.

360. Henkel, I. et al. (2020) "Do Online, Offline, and Multiplatform Journalists Differ in their Professional Principles and Practices? Findings from a Multinational Study," Journalism Studies, 21(10), p. 1363. doi:10.1080/1461670x.2020.1749111.

361. Hosseinmardi, H. et al. (2025) "Unpacking media bias in the growing divide between cable and network news," Scientific Reports, 15(1), p. 17607. doi:10.1038/s41598-025-01046-7.

362. Ilan, J. (2019) "Saving some news for later: The making and gatekeeping process of the national TV news filler," The Communication Review, 22(1), p. 26. doi:10.1080/10714421.2018.1564503.

363. Ilan, J. (2021) "We Now Go Live: Digital Live-News Technologies and the 'Reinvention of Live' in Professional TV News Broadcasting," Digital Journalism, 9(4), p. 481. doi:10.1080/21670811.2021.1886862.

364. Kriyantono, R. (2020) "QAULAN SADIDAN PRINCIPLES AND FACTUALITY IN PUBLIC BROADCASTING INSTITUTION NEWS," Profetik Jurnal Komunikasi, 12(2), p. 275. doi:10.14421/pjk.v12i2.1680.

365. Kroon, Å. and Eriksson, G. (2019) "The Impact of the Digital Transformation on Sports Journalism Talk Online," Journalism Practice, 13(7), p. 834. doi:10.1080/17512786.2019.1577695.

366. Laor, T. (2022) "Radio on demand: New habits of consuming radio content," Global Media and Communication, 18(1), p. 25. doi:10.1177/17427665211073868.

367. Mathis, W. and Titze, A. (2021) "100 Years of Wireless Telephony in Germany: Experimental Radio Transmission from Eberswalde and Königs Wusterhausen," Advances in radio science, 19, p. 93. doi:10.5194/ars-19-93-2021.

368. Ollikainen, V. et al. (2011) "Comparing Media Types and Delivery Methods on Mobile Terminals," International Journal of Multimedia Technology, 1(2), p. 64. doi:10.5963/ijmt0102001.

369. Otmakhova, Y. and Frermann, L. (2025) "Narrative Media Framing in Political Discourse," in Findings of the Association for Computational Linguistics: ACL 2022, p. 9167. doi:10.18653/v1/2025.findings-acl.477.

370. Parks, P. (2018) "Textbook News Values: Stable Concepts, Changing Choices," Journalism & Mass Communication Quarterly, 96(3), p. 784. doi:10.1177/1077699018805212.

371. Pepple, I.I. and Acholonu, I.J. (2018) "Media Ethics as Key to Sound Professionalism in Nigerian Journalism Practice," Journalism and mass communication, 8(2). doi:10.17265/2160-6579/2018.02.002.

372. Sambrook, R. and Nielsen, R.K. (2016) "What is happening to television news," SSRN Electronic Journal [Preprint]. Available at: https://papers.ssrn.com/sol3/Delivery.cfm/SSRN_ID2771080_code2070733.pdf?abstract id=2771080&mirid=5 (Accessed: February 2025).

373. Scacco, J.M., Curry, A.L. and Stroud, N.J. (2015) "Digital Divisions: Organizational Gatekeeping Practices in the Context of Online News," 5(1), p. 106. Available at: https://digitalcommons.usf.edu/spe_facpub/932/ (Accessed: August 2025).

374. Shabir, G. et al. (2015) "Process of Gate Keeping in Media: From Old Trend to New," Mediterranean Journal of Social Sciences [Preprint]. doi:10.5901/mjss.2015.v6n1s1p588.

375. Shahid, A. (2023) "Ethical Challenges in Journalism: Balancing Objectivity and Sensitivity in Reporting." doi:10.31219/osf.io/xebmv.

376. Sharma, G.P. et al. (2021) "On Decomposition and Deployment of Virtualized Media Services," IEEE Transactions on Broadcasting, 67(3), p. 761. doi:10.1109/tbc.2021.3099740.

377. Simmons, J.C. and Winograd, J.M. (2024) "Interoperable Provenance Authentication of Broadcast Media using Open Standards-based Metadata, Watermarking and Cryptography," arXiv (Cornell University) [Preprint]. doi:10.48550/arxiv.2405.12336.

378. Singer, J.B., Lewis, S.C. and Wahl-Jorgensen, K. (2023) "Journalism in the Quarterly: A Century of Change in the Industry and the Academy," Journalism & Mass Communication Quarterly, 100(4), p. 773. doi:10.1177/10776990231189455.

379. Solvoll, M.K. and Høiby, M. (2023) "Framing of the COVID-19 pandemic:," MedieKultur Journal of media and communication research, 38(73), p. 6. doi:10.7146/mk.v38i73.131934.

380. Steel, J.R. et al. (2025) "Journalism and Ethical Praxis: A Thematic Analysis of Journalism Ethics Across Five European Countries," Journalism Practice, p. 1. doi:10.1080/17512786.2025.2480746.

381. Sterne, J. (1999) "Television under construction: American television and the problem of distribution, 1926-62," Media Culture & Society, 21(4), p. 503. doi:10.1177/016344399021004004.

382. Tewksbury, D. and Scheufele, D.A. (2009) "NEWS FRAMING THEORY AND RESEARCH," in Routledge eBooks. Informa, p. 33. doi:10.4324/9780203877111-8.

383. "'Towers In The Sky': Satellites And Emerging Global Media Infrastructures" (2023) in The MIT Press eBooks. The MIT Press, p. 19. doi:10.7551/mitpress/13771.003.0004.

384. Wallace, J. (2017) "Modelling Contemporary Gatekeeping," Digital Journalism, 6(3), p. 274. doi:10.1080/21670811.2017.1343648.

385. Yevdokymova, N. et al. (2025) "The Ethical Labyrinth of Journalistic Genres: Navigating Media Problems Through the Lens of Work and Text Theory." doi:10.2139/ssrn.5225919.

386. Zare, J., Abbaspour, E. and Nia, M.R. (2012) "Presupposition Trigger-A Comparative Analysis of Broadcast News Discourse," International Journal of Linguistics, 4(3). doi:10.5296/ijl.v4i3.2002.

387. Albrechtslund, A.B. and Albrechtslund, A. (2014) "Social media as leisure culture," First Monday [Preprint]. doi:10.5210/fm.v19i4.4877.

388. Amelia, L.T.D. and Balqis, N.R. (2023) "Changes in Communication Patterns in the Digital Age," ARRUS Journal of Social Sciences and Humanities, 3(4), p. 544. doi:10.35877/soshum1992.

389. Barton, B.A. et al. (2018) "The effects of social media usage on attention, motivation, and academic performance," Active Learning in Higher Education, 22(1), p. 11. doi:10.1177/1469787418782817.

390. Bondielli, A. and Marcelloni, F. (2019) "A survey on fake news and rumour detection techniques," Information Sciences, 497, p. 38. doi:10.1016/j.ins.2019.05.035.

391. Cagé, J., Hervé, N. and Mazoyer, B. (2020) "Social Media and Newsroom Production Decisions," SSRN Electronic Journal [Preprint]. doi:10.2139/ssrn.3663899.

392. Caled, D. and Silva, M.J. (2021) "Digital media and misinformation: An outlook on multidisciplinary strategies against manipulation," Journal of Computational Social Science, 5(1), p. 123. doi:10.1007/s42001-021-00118-8.

393. Craig, D.A. (2021) "Global Social Media Ethics and the Responsibility of Journalism," Oxford Research Encyclopedia of Communication. doi:10.1093/acrefore/9780190228613.013.917.

394. Hanna, F., You, E. and El-Sherif, M.W. (2023) "Editorial: The impact of sedentary behavior and virtual lifestyle on physical and mental wellbeing: social distancing from healthy living," Frontiers in Public Health, 11. doi:10.3389/fpubh.2023.1265814.

395. Haschke, P. (2016) "The media, the elites and the army in Egypt from the early 2000s to today," HAL (Le Centre pour la Communication Scientifique Directe) [Preprint]. Available at: https://hal-sciencespo.archives-ouvertes.fr/tel-03471888 (Accessed: January 2025).

396. Herath, T.B.G., Khanna, P. and Ahmed, M. (2022) "Cybersecurity Practices for Social Media Users: A Systematic Literature Review," Journal of Cybersecurity and Privacy, 2(1), p. 1. doi:10.3390/jcp2010001.

397. Hjetland, G.J. et al. (2025) "How and when screens are used: comparing different screen activities and sleep in Norwegian university students," Frontiers in Psychiatry, 16. doi:10.3389/fpsyt.2025.1548273.

398. Hosen, M.J. et al. (2021) "Health impacts of excessive use of Facebook among university students in Bangladesh," Heliyon, 7(6). doi:10.1016/j.heliyon.2021.e07271.

399. Humeira, B. and Ramadhan, A. (2022) "The Uses of Social Media in Journalism Practices: The Reversed-Agenda Setting on Television News Production," Jurnal Studi Jurnalistik, 4(2), p. 19. doi:10.15408/jsj.v4i2.28964.

400. Ji, Y. et al. (2023) "The Causes, Effects, and Interventions of Social Media Addiction," Journal of Education Humanities and Social Sciences, 8, p. 897. doi:10.54097/ehss.v8i.4378.

401. Lazer, D. et al. (2018) "The science of fake news," Science, 359(6380), p. 1094. doi:10.1126/science.aao2998.

402. Leong, C. et al. (2020) "Digital organizing of a global social movement: From connective to collective action," Information and Organization, 30(4), p. 100324. doi:10.1016/j.infoandorg.2020.100324.

403. Mellado, C. and Alfaro, A. (2020) "Platforms, Journalists and Their Digital Selves," Digital Journalism, 8(10), p. 1258. doi:10.1080/21670811.2020.1817763.

404. Milan, S. (2015) "From social movements to cloud protesting: the evolution of collective identity," Information Communication & Society, 18(8), p. 887. doi:10.1080/1369118x.2015.1043135.

405. Perez-Lozano, D. and Espinosa, F.S. (2024) "Social Media Addiction: Challenges and Strategies to Promote Media Literacy," in IntechOpen eBooks. IntechOpen. doi:10.5772/intechopen.1006166.

406. Ray, G.H., McDermott, C.D. and Nicho, M. (2024) "Cyberbullying on Social Media: Definitions, Prevalence, and Impact Challenges," Journal of Cybersecurity, 10(1). doi:10.1093/cybsec/tyae026.

407. Shanmugasundaram, M. and Tamilarasu, A. (2023) "The impact of digital technology, social media, and artificial intelligence on cognitive functions: a review," Frontiers in Cognition. Frontiers Media. doi:10.3389/fcogn.2023.1203077.

408. Singh, H. (2022) "Impact of social media on interpersonal communication," International Journal of Communication and Information Technology, 3(2), p. 26. doi:10.33545/2707661x.2022.v3.i2a.69.

409. Sonni, A.F. et al. (2024) "Digital Newsroom Transformation: A Systematic Review of the Impact of Artificial Intelligence on Journalistic Practices, News Narratives, and Ethical Challenges," Journalism and Media. Multidisciplinary Digital Publishing Institute, p. 1554. doi:10.3390/journalmedia5040097.

410. T., S.S. (2024) "THE CHALLENGES AND ROLE OF MODERN JOURNALISM IN DIGITAL MEDIA ENTERPRISES," ShodhKosh Journal of Visual and Performing Arts, 5(7). doi:10.29121/shodhkosh.v5.i7.2024.1921.

411. Trattner, C. et al. (2021) "Responsible media technology and AI: challenges and research directions," AI and Ethics, 2(4), p. 585. doi:10.1007/s43681-021-00126-4.

412. Zhao, K. (2023) "A Study on the Application of New Media in Broadcast Newscasting and Writing under the Perspective of Media Integration," World Journal of Educational Research, 10(6). doi:10.22158/wjer.v10n6p25.

413. García, J.S., Vázquez, A.I.R. and García, X.L. (2021) "Sistemas de verificación en medios nativos digitales e implicación de la audiencia en la lucha contra la desinformación en el modelo ibérico," Revista de Comunicación de la SEECI, (54), p. 41. doi:10.15198/seeci.2021.54.e738.

414. Lima, I.R. et al. (2023) "ARTICONF decentralized social media platform for democratic crowd journalism," Social Network Analysis and Mining, 13(1). doi:10.1007/s13278-023-01110-y.

415. Hagen, A.L., Tolstad, I.M. and Bygdås, A.L. (2021) "'Magic through many minor measures': How introducing a flowline production mode in six steps enables journalist team autonomy in local news organizations," AI & Society, 37(2), p. 745. doi:10.1007/s00146-021-01176-2.

416. Kanchan, S. and Gaidhane, A. (2024) "Print Media Role and Its Impact on Public Health: A Narrative Review," Cureus. Cureus, Inc. doi:10.7759/cureus.59574.

417. Miranda, J. (2023) "Responsabilização e Qualidade do Jornalismo: Instrumentos e Práticas Digitais de Accountability dos Média Portugueses," Comunicação e Sociedade, 44. doi:10.17231/comsoc.44(2023).4750.

418. Gokce, Assoc.Prof.S. (2022) "Scientific Study Comparing Digital Advertising and Print Advertising," Zenodo (CERN European Organization for Nuclear Research) [Preprint]. doi:10.5281/zenodo.7587676.

419. Venkatraman, V. *et al.* (2021) "Relative Effectiveness of Print and Digital Advertising: A Memory Perspective," *Journal of Marketing Research*, 58(5), p. 827. doi:10.1177/00222437211034438.

420. Christensen, B. and Khalil, A. (2021) "Reporting Conflict from Afar: Journalists, Social Media, Communication Technologies, and War," *Journalism Practice*, 17(2), p. 300. doi:10.1080/17512786.2021.1908839.

421. Eilders, C. (2005) "Media under fire: Fact and fiction in conditions of war," *International Review of the Red Cross*, 87(860), p. 639. doi:10.1017/s1816383100184474.

422. Panagiotidis, K. *et al.* (2020) "A Participatory Journalism Management Platform: Design, Implementation and Evaluation," *Social Sciences*, 9(2), p. 21. doi:10.3390/socsci9020021.

423. Bell, M. (1998) 'The Truth is our Currency', The Harvard International Journal of Press/Politics 3(1).

424. Dente R. (2007). Peace Journalism: constructive Media in a Global Community. Global Media Journal. Mediterranean Edition, 2(2)

425. Jowett & O'Donnell (1999), cited in Lynch, J. & McGoldrick, A. (2010). "A global standard for reporting conflict and peace", in Keeble R, Tulloch J, Zollmann F. (2010), Peace Journalism, War and Conflict Resolution, New York: Peter Lang Publishing,

426. Galtung, J. (1986). On the Role of the Media for Worldwide Security and Peace. In Tapio Varis (ed). Communication and Peace. San Jose: Universidad para la Paz.

427. Galtung, J. & Ruge, M. (1965) "The structure of foreign news: the presentation of the Congo, Cuba and Cyprus crises in four Norwegian newspapers", Journal of International Peace Research (1).

428. Gitlin T. (1980), The whole world is watching: mass media in the making and unmaking of the new left, Berkeley: University of California Press.

429. Hackett, R. (2006). Is Peace Journalism Possible? Three Frameworks for Assessing Structure and Agency in News Media. Conflict & Communication online, 5(2).

430. Hanitzsch, T., & Mellado, C. (2011). What Shapes the News around the World? How Journalists in Eighteen Countries Perceive Influences on Their Work. The International Journal of Press/Politics, 16(3).

431. Hanitzsch, T. (2007). Situating peace journalism in Journalism Studies: A critical appraisal. Conflict & Communication online, 6(2).

432. Hanitzsch T, Anikina M, Berganza R, Cangoz I, Coman M, Hamada B, Hanusch F, et al. (2010). "Modeling Perceived Influences on Journalism: Evidence from a Cross-National Survey of Journalists." Journalism & Mass Communication Quarterly.

433. Harcup, T., & O'Neill, D. (2001). What Is News? Galtung and Ruge revisited. Journalism Studies, 2(2).

434. Loyn, D. (2007). Good journalism or peace journalism? Conflict & Communication online, 6(2).

435. Lynch J. (2014), A Global Standard for Reporting Conflict, Routledge, New York and London.

436. Hanitzsch, T. *et al.* (2010) "Modeling Perceived Influences on Journalism: Evidence from a Cross-National Survey of Journalists," *Journalism & Mass Communication Quarterly,* 87(1), p. 5. doi:10.1177/107769901008700101.

437. Nohrstedt, S.A. and Ottosen, R. (2015) "Peace journalism: A proposition for conceptual and methodological improvements," *Global Media and Communication,* 11(3), p. 219. doi:10.1177/1742766515606289.

438. Nielsen, R.K., Cornia, A. and Kalogeropoulos, A. (2016) "Challenges and opportunities for news media and journalism in an increasingly digital, mobile and social media environment," *SSRN Electronic Journal* [Preprint]. Available at: https://apo.org.au/node/71071 (Accessed: August 2025).

439. *Handbook on Gender-responsive Police Services for Women and Girls Subject to Violence* (2021) *United Nations eBooks.* United Nations. doi:10.18356/9789216040710.

440. Bibi, M., Mallal, Z. and Ali, S. (2025) "Psychological Impact of Gender-Based Violence: A Study on Trauma, Coping Mechanisms, and Mental Health Outcomes," 4(3), p. 4203. doi:10.63056/acad.004.03.0696.

441. *Breaking the Cycle of Gender-based Violence* (2023). doi:10.1787/b133e75c-en.

442. Daalen, K.R. van *et al.* (2022) "Extreme events and gender-based violence: a mixed-methods systematic review," *The Lancet Planetary Health.* Elsevier BV. doi:10.1016/s2542-5196(22)00088-2.

443. Kiasalar, M. *et al.* (2022) "Media codes of ethics for health professionals and media professionals: a qualitative study," *Journal of Medical Ethics and History of Medicine* [Preprint]. doi:10.18502/jmehm.v15i2.9036.

444. Koutra, K. *et al.* (2022) "Trauma Recovery Rubric: A Mixed-Method Analysis of Trauma Recovery Pathways in Four Countries," *International Journal of Environmental Research and Public Health,* 19(16), p. 10310. doi:10.3390/ijerph191610310.

445. Nwabueze, R.N. (2024) "Posthumous Photographic Images," in *Routledge eBooks.* Informa, p. 276. doi:10.4324/9781003304593-24.

446. Skana, P. and Gjerazi, B. (2024) "Public perception of media social responsibility in developing countries: a case study of Albania," *Frontiers in Communication,* 9. doi:10.3389/fcomm.2024.1338587.

447. Agunlejika, T. (2025) "AI-Driven Fact-Checking in Journalism: Enhancing Information Veracity and Combating Misinformation: A Systematic Review." doi:10.2139/ssrn.5122225.

448. Borkar, A. and Paul, B. (2023) "Misreporting biodiversity loss due to invasive species escalates social tension," *Research Square (Research Square)* [Preprint]. doi:10.21203/rs.3.rs-3738860/v1.

449. Domenico, G.D. and Visentin, M. (2020) "Fake news or true lies? Reflections about problematic contents in marketing," *International Journal of Market Research,* 62(4), p. 409. doi:10.1177/1470785320934719.

450. Harro-Loit, H. and Eberwein, T. (2023) "News Media Monitoring Capabilities in 14 European Countries: Problems and Best Practices," *Media and Communication,* 12. doi:10.17645/mac.7199.

451. Shahid, A. (2023) "Ethical Challenges in Journalism: Balancing Objectivity and Sensitivity in Reporting." doi:10.31219/osf.io/xebmv.

452. Comfort, S.E. (2020) "Journalism as an Advocacy Tool: Negotiating Boundaries of Professionalism in the 20th-Century American Environmental Movement," *Journalism & Mass Communication Quarterly*, 97(4), p. 1080. doi:10.1177/1077699020911076.

453. Daou, K.N. *et al.*(2018) "Public health journals' requirements for authors to disclose funding and conflicts of interest: a cross-sectional study," *BMC Public Health*, 18(1). doi:10.1186/s12889-018-5456-z.

454. Ehrlich, O. *et al.*(2019) "When patient advocacy organizations meet industry: a novel approach to dealing with financial conflicts of interest," *BMC Medical Ethics*, 20(1). doi:10.1186/s12910-019-0435-1.

455. Westlund, O., Krumsvik, A.H. and Lewis, S.C. (2020) "Competition, Change, and Coordination and Collaboration: Tracing News Executives' Perceptions About Participation in Media Innovation," *Journalism Studies*, 22(1), p. 1. doi:10.1080/1461670x.2020.1835526.

456. Cover, R. and Reid, J. (2010) "The Art of War Reporting: Embedded Journalism as Public Discourse," 10(4). Available at: https://research-repository.uwa.edu.au/en/publications/the-art-of-war-reporting-embedded-journalism-as-public-discourse(bc572813-f316-411d-8f00-bebc4549484d)/export.html (Accessed: December 2024).

457. Paul, C. and Kim, J.J. (2005) "Reporters on the battlefield: the embedded press system in historical context," *Choice Reviews Online*, 42(11), p. 42. doi:10.5860/choice.42-6314.

458. Mooney, M. (2004) "Live from the Battlefield: An Examination of Embedded War Correspondents' Reporting during Operation Iraqi Freedom (21 March-14 April 2003)." Available at: https://apps.dtic.mil/dtic/tr/fulltext/u2/a424638.pdf (Accessed: October 2025).

459. Brandenburg, H. (2007) "'SECURITY AT THE SOURCE,'" *Journalism Studies*, 8(6), p. 948. doi:10.1080/14616700701556120.

460. Clonan, T. (2008) "Truth and War Reporting: Journalism in Hostile Environments." doi:10.21427/d7b48q.

461. Brandenburg, H. (2007) "'SECURITY AT THE SOURCE,'" *Journalism Studies*, 8(6), p. 948. doi:10.1080/14616700701556120.

462. Lynch, J. & McGoldrick, A. (2010). 'A global standard for reporting conflict and peace',

463. in Peace Journalism, War and Conflict Resolution ed. by Johan Tulloch, Richard Lance

464. Keeble and Florian Zollmann (New York: Peter Lang Publishing 2010).

465. Lynch, J. & McGoldrick, A. (2005), Peace Journalism, Stroud, UK: Hawthorn Press.

466. McQuail D, (1994), Mass Communication Theory, An Introduction, (ed 3), Sage Publications.

467. Myers, G., Klak, T., & Koehl, T. (1996). The inscription of difference: news coverage of the conflicts in Rwanda and Bosnia. Political Geography, 15(1).

468. Richard Folk R. (2008) Foreword, in Lynch J. Debates in Peace Journalism, ix, University of Sydney, Australia: Sydney University Press.

469. Scheufele, D. A. (1999). Framing as a Theory of Media Effects. Journal of Communication (Winter 1999).

470. Ruigrok, N. (2010). From Journalism of Activism towards Journalism of Accountability. International Communication Gazette, 72(1).

471. Shoemaker, Pamela J., and Stephen D. Reese. 1996. Mediating the Message: Theories of Influence on Mass Media Content. White Plains, NY: Longman.

472. Tuchman G. (1978), Making news: A study in the construction of reality, New York: Free Press.

473. See Lynch, J. & McGoldrick, A. (2005), Peace Journalism, Hawthorn Press, Stroud, UK.

474. Lynch J. (2014), A Global Standard for Reporting Conflict, Routledge, New York and London, p. 36.

475. Richard Falk R. (2008) Foreword, in Lynch J. Debates in Peace Journalism, ix, Sydney University Press, University of Sydney, Australia.

476. Lynch, J. & McGoldrick, A. (2005), p6.

477. Lynch, J. "What is peace journalism?" (1) in Transcend Media: https://www.transcend.org/tms/about-peace-journalism/1-what-is-peace-journalism/

478. Peace Journalism: A growing Global Debate in www.peacejournalism.org.

479. Lynch J. (2008), Debates in Peace Journalism.

480. Galtung & Ruge (1965) and Harcup & O'Neill (2001) in Lynch J. (2014), p. 35.

481. Altay, S. et al. (2023) "A survey of expert views on misinformation: Definitions, determinants, solutions, and future of the field," Harvard Kennedy School Misinformation Review [Preprint]. doi:10.37016/mr-2020-119. Antunes, H.S. et al. (2023) Multidisciplinary Perspectives on Artificial Intelligence and the Law, Law, governance and technology series. Springer International Publishing. doi:10.1007/978-3-031-41264-6.

482. Bastos, M. and Tuters, M. (2023) "Meaningful disinformation: Narrative rituals and affective folktales," Big Data & Society, 10(2). doi:10.1177/20539517231215361.

483. Bhatti, S.A. (2025) "AI in our Justice System."

484. Calo, R. et al. (2021) "How do you solve a problem like misinformation?," Science Advances, 7(50). doi:10.1126/sciadv.abn0481.

485. Ferrara, E. (2024) "Charting the Landscape of Nefarious Uses of Generative Artificial Intelligence for Online Election Interference," arXiv (Cornell University) [Preprint]. doi:10.48550/arxiv.2406.01862.

486. Gondwe, G. (2025) "Can AI Outsmart Fake News? Detecting Misinformation With AI Models in Real-Time," Emerging Media [Preprint]. doi:10.1177/27523543251325902.

487. Hameleers, M. (2022) "Disinformation as a context-bound phenomenon: toward a conceptual clarification integrating actors, intentions and techniques of creation and dissemination," Communication Theory, 33(1), p. 1. doi:10.1093/ct/qtac021.

488. Jahn, L. (2023) "Curbing Amplifiation Online : Towards Improving the Quality of Information Spread on Social Media Using Agent-Based Models and Twitter Data," Research Portal Denmark, p. 150. Available at: https://local.forskningsportal.dk/local/dki-cgi/ws/cris-link?src=ku&id=ku-ef61aeed-56f5-4d78-b171-a00a80798d1a&ti=Curbing%20Amplifiation%20Online%20%3A%20Towards%20Improving%20the%20Quality%20of%20Information%20Spread%20on%20Social%20Media%20Using%20Agent-Based%20Models%20and%20Twitter%20Data (Accessed: July 2025).

489. Jaidka, K. *et al.* (2024) "Misinformation, Disinformation, and Generative AI: Implications for Perception and Policy," *Digital Government Research and Practice* [Preprint]. doi:10.1145/3689372.

490. Kauk, J. *et al.* (2024) "Large-scale analysis of online social data on the long-term sentiment and content dynamics of online (mis)information," *Computers in Human Behavior*, p. 108546. doi:10.1016/j.chb.2024.108546.

491. Lasser, J. *et al.* (2023) "From alternative conceptions of honesty to alternative facts in communications by US politicians," *Nature Human Behaviour*, 7(12), p. 2140. doi:10.1038/s41562-023-01691-w.

492. Lazer, D. *et al.* (2018) "The science of fake news," *Science*, 359(6380), p. 1094. doi:10.1126/science.aao2998.

493. López, A.B., Pastor-Galindo, J. and Ruipérez-Valiente, J.A. (2024) "Frameworks, Modeling and Simulations of Misinformation and Disinformation: A Systematic Literature Review," *arXiv (Cornell University)* [Preprint]. doi:10.48550/arxiv.2406.09343.

494. Mouratidis, D., Kanavos, A. and Kermanidis, K.L. (2025) "From Misinformation to Insight: Machine Learning Strategies for Fake News Detection," *Information*, 16(3), p. 189. doi:10.3390/info16030189.

495. Nault, K. and Ruhi, U. (2023) "User experience with disinformation-countering tools: usability challenges and suggestions for improvement," *Frontiers in Computer Science*, 5. doi:10.3389/fcomp.2023.1253166.

496. Pantazi, M., Hale, S.A. and Klein, O. (2021) "Social and Cognitive Aspects of the Vulnerability to Political Misinformation," *Political Psychology*, 42, p. 267. doi:10.1111/pops.12797.

497. Puska, A., Baroni, L.A. and Pereira, R. (2024) "Decoding the Sociotechnical Dimensions of Digital Misinformation: A Comprehensive Literature Review," *arXiv (Cornell University)* [Preprint]. doi:10.48550/arxiv.2406.11853.

498. Ripoll, L. and Matos, J.C.M. (2020) "Information reliability: criteria to identify misinformation in the digital environment," *Investigación Bibliotecológica Archivonomía Bibliotecología e Información*, 34(84), p. 79. doi:10.22201/iibi.24488321xe.2020.84.58115.

499. Schaewitz, L. *et al.* (2020) "When is Disinformation (In)Credible? Experimental Findings on Message Characteristics and Individual Differences," *Mass Communication & Society*, 23(4), p. 484. doi:10.1080/15205436.2020.1716983.

500. Søe, S.O. (2016) "The Urge to Detect, the Need to Clarify : Gricean Perspectives on Information, Misinformation and Disinformation," *Research Portal Denmark*, p. 194. Available at: https://local.forskningsportal.dk/local/dki-cgi/ws/cris-link?src=ku&id=ku-3ec2a23c-cac9-45de-8689-8a7e51b53998&ti=The%20Urge%20to%20Detect%2C%20the%20Need%20to%20Clarify%20%3A%20Gricean%20Perspectives%20on%20Information%2C%20Misinformation%20and%20Disinformation (Accessed: July 2025).

501. Tomassi, A., Falegnami, A. and Romano, E. (2024) "Mapping automatic social media information disorder. The role of bots and AI in spreading misleading information in society," *PLoS ONE*, 19(5). doi:10.1371/journal.pone.0303183.

502. Zeng, J. and Brennen, S.B. (2023) "Misinformation," *Internet Policy Review*, 12(4). doi:10.14763/2023.4.1725.

503. Zhang, J. *et al.* (2023) "Infodemic: Challenges and solutions in topic discovery and data process," *Archives of Public Health*, 81(1). doi:10.1186/s13690-023-01179-z.

504. McQuail D, (1994), Mass Communication Theory, An Introduction, Sage Publications, p. 270.

505. Harcup, T., & O'Neill, D. (2001). What Is News? Galtung and Ruge revisited. *Journalism Studies*, 2(2), pp. 264- 267.

506. Lynch, J. & McGoldrick, A. (2010). A global standard for reporting conflict and peace. In R.L. Keeble, J. Tulloch & F. Zollmann (eds.). Peace Journalism, War and Conflict Resolution. Peter Lang: New York, p.91

507. Jowett and O'Donnell (1999), cited in Lynch, J. & McGoldrick, A. (2010). A global standard for reporting conflict and peace, p.91.

508. Ruigrok, N. (2010). From Journalism of Activism towards Journalism of Accountability. *International Communication Gazette*, 72(1), p89.

509. See Lyon D. (2007), Good journalism or peace journalism? p, 9

510. Hanitzsch, T. (2007), Situating Peace Journalism in Journalism Studies: A critical appraisal. *Conflict & Communication online*, 6(2), pp. 1.

511. Myers, G., Klak, T., & Koehl, T. (1996). The inscription of difference: news coverage of the conflicts in Rwanda and Bosnia. *Political Geography*, 15(1), pp. 22.

512. Fiki, M. and Idi, S. (2025) "Ethical Issues in Online News Reporting in Nigeria," *Asian Journal of Science Technology Engineering and Art*, 3(4), p. 1147. doi:10.58578/ajstea.v3i4.6536.

513. Rahman, H.U. (2023) "Media Ethics in the Era of Clickbait Journalism: Ethical Dilemmas and Solutions in Online Media," *journal of social sciences review*, 3(4), p. 11. doi:10.54183/jssr.v3i4.392.

514. Real, D.D. and Menjívar, C. (2024) "The Tools of Autocracy Worldwide: Authoritarian Networks, the Façade of Democracy, and Neo-Repression," *American Behavioral Scientist*, 68(12), p. 1559. doi:10.1177/00027642241267926.

515. Hamborg, F. *et al.* (2021) "Newsalyze: Effective Communication of Person-Targeting Biases in News Articles," p. 130. doi:10.1109/jcdl52503.2021.00025.

516. Ordaz, L.V. (2023) "Research on selective media exposure in Spain: a critical review of its findings, application phases, and blind spots," *El Profesional de la Informacion*. Ediciones Profesionales de la Informacion SL. doi:10.3145/epi.2023.sep.07.

517. Rodrigo-Ginés, F.-J., Carrillo-de-Albornoz, J. and Plaza, L. (2023) "A systematic review on media bias detection: What is media bias, how it is expressed, and how to detect it," *Expert Systems with Applications*. Elsevier BV, p. 121641. doi:10.1016/j.eswa.2023.121641.

518. Sude, D., Sharon, G. and Dvir-Gvirsman, S. (2023) "True, justified, belief? Partisanship weakens the positive effect of news media literacy on fake news detection," *Frontiers in Psychology*, 14. doi:10.3389/fpsyg.2023.1242865.

519. Temmerman, M. *et al.* (2018) "Post-truth and the political: Constructions and distortions in representing political facts," *Discourse Context & Media*, 27, p. 1. doi:10.1016/j.dcm.2018.10.002.

520. Tomassi, A., Falegnami, A. and Romano, E. (2024) "Mapping automatic social media information disorder. The role of bots and AI in spreading misleading information in society," *PLoS ONE*, 19(5). doi:10.1371/journal.pone.0303183.

521. Zavolokina, L. *et al.* (2025) "Biased by Design: Leveraging Inherent AI Biases to Enhance Critical Thinking of News Readers." doi:10.48550/ARXIV.2504.14522.

522. Aissing, A. (2024) "Detecting and Debunking Disinformation: The Role of University Libraries in Promoting Information Literacy," *Contemporary Mediterranean*, 3(1), p. 35. doi:10.17818/sm/2024/1.3.

523. Akhtar, M.M. *et al.* (2023) "False Information, Bots and Malicious Campaigns: Demystifying Elements of Social Media Manipulations," *arXiv (Cornell University)* [Preprint]. doi:10.48550/arxiv.2308.12497.

524. Alam, F., Hasnat, A., Ahmed, F., Hasan, Md.A., *et al.* (2024) "ArMeme: Propagandistic Content in Arabic Memes," *arXiv (Cornell University)* [Preprint]. doi:10.48550/arxiv.2406.03916.

525. Alam, F., Hasnat, A., Ahmed, F., Hasan, M.A., *et al.* (2024) "ArMeme: Propagandistic Content in Arabic Memes." doi:10.48550/ARXIV.2406.03916.

526. Alghamdi, J., Luo, S. and Lin, Y. (2023) "A comprehensive survey on machine learning approaches for fake news detection," *Multimedia Tools and Applications*, 83(17), p. 51009. doi:10.1007/s11042-023-17470-8.

527. Altay, S., Berriche, M. and Acerbi, A. (2021) "Misinformation on Misinformation: Conceptual and Methodological Challenges." doi:10.31234/osf.io/edqc8.

528. Berrondo-Otermin, M. and Cabezuelo, A.S. (2023) "Application of Artificial Intelligence Techniques to Detect Fake News: A Review," *Electronics*. Multidisciplinary Digital Publishing Institute, p. 5041. doi:10.3390/electronics12245041.

529. Cavedon-Taylor, D. (2024) "Deepfakes: a survey and introduction to the topical collection," *Synthese*, 204(1). doi:10.1007/s11229-024-04634-8.

530. Croitoru, F.-A. *et al.* (2024) "Deepfake Media Generation and Detection in the Generative AI Era: A Survey and Outlook," *arXiv (Cornell University)* [Preprint]. doi:10.48550/arxiv.2411.19537.

531. Farid, H. (2022) "Creating, Using, Misusing, and Detecting Deep Fakes," *Journal of Online Trust and Safety*, 1(4). doi:10.54501/jots.v1i4.56.

532. Gambín, Á.F. *et al.* (2024) "Deepfakes: current and future trends," *Artificial Intelligence Review*, 57(3). doi:10.1007/s10462-023-10679-x.

533. Hoseini, M. *et al.* (2024) "Characterizing Information Propagation in Fringe Communities on Telegram," *Proceedings of the International AAAI Conference on Web and Social Media*, 18, p. 583. doi:10.1609/icwsm.v18i1.31336.

534. Kapoor, P.S. and Behl, A. (2024) "Those 'funny' internet memes: a study of misinformation retransmission and vaccine hesitancy," *Behaviour and Information Technology*, 43(16), p. 4079. doi:10.1080/0144929x.2024.2303582.

535. Lundberg, E. and Mozelius, P. (2024) "The potential effects of deepfakes on news media and entertainment," *AI & Society* [Preprint]. doi:10.1007/s00146-024-02072-1.

536. Melo, P. *et al.* (2024) "Don't Break the Chain: Measuring Message Forwarding on WhatsApp," *Proceedings of the International AAAI Conference on Web and Social Media*, 18, p. 1054. doi:10.1609/icwsm.v18i1.31372.

537. Mustak, M. *et al.* (2022) "Deepfakes: Deceptions, mitigations, and opportunities," *Journal of Business Research*, 154, p. 113368. doi:10.1016/j.jbusres.2022.113368.

538. Pröllochs, N. and Feuerriegel, S. (2023) "Mechanisms of True and False Rumor Sharing in Social Media: Collective Intelligence or Herd Behavior?," *Proceedings of the ACM on Human-Computer Interaction*, 7, p. 1. doi:10.1145/3610078.

539. Rahmanian, E. (2022) "Fake news: a classification proposal and a future research agenda," *Spanish Journal of Marketing - ESIC*, 27(1), p. 60. doi:10.1108/sjme-09-2021-0170.

540. Singh, S. (2025) "A Comprehensive Review on Deepfake Generation, Detection, Challenges, and Future Directions," *International Journal for Research in Applied Science*

and Engineering Technology. International Journal for Research in Applied Science and Engineering Technology (IJRASET), p. 6566. doi:10.22214/ijraset.2025.71713.

541. Surjatmodjo, D. *et al.* (2024) "Information Pandemic: A Critical Review of Disinformation Spread on Social Media and Its Implications for State Resilience," *Social Sciences.* Multidisciplinary Digital Publishing Institute, p. 418. doi:10.3390/socsci13080418.

542. Wu, H. *et al.* (2024) "Combating Deepfakes: An Entropy-Aware Framework for Detecting Forged Visual and Textual Information," *Research Square (Research Square)* [Preprint]. doi:10.21203/rs.3.rs-5380506/v1.

543. Zubiaga, A. and Jiang, A. (2020) "Early Detection of Social Media Hoaxes at Scale," *ACM Transactions on the Web,* 14(4), p. 1. doi:10.1145/3407194.

544. Ahmed, A.M.A. and Othman, A.K. (2024a) "False advertising and consumer online purchase behaviour," *Journal of Emerging Economies and Islamic Research,* 12(2), p. 1521. doi:10.24191/jeeir.v12i2.1521.

545. Ahmed, A.M.A. and Othman, A.K. (2024b) "The Effect of False Advertising on Consumer Online Purchase Behavior with the Mediating Effect of e-WOM: Consumers in Malaysia," *Information Management and Business Review,* 16, p. 115. doi:10.22610/imbr.v16i2(i)s.3774.

546. Chrysanthou, A., Pantis, Y. and Patsakis, C. (2023) "The Anatomy of Deception: Technical and Human Perspectives on a Large-scale Phishing Campaign," *arXiv (Cornell University)* [Preprint]. doi:10.48550/arxiv.2310.03498.

547. Fong, J., Guo, T. and Rao, A. (2021) "Debunking Misinformation in Advertising," *SSRN Electronic Journal* [Preprint]. doi:10.2139/ssrn.3875665.

548. Ghazi-Tehrani, A.K. and Pontell, H.N. (2021) "Phishing Evolves: Analyzing the Enduring Cybercrime," *Victims & Offenders,* 16(3), p. 316. doi:10.1080/15564886.2020.1829224.

549. Gorichanaz, T. (2025) "Data selves and identity theft in the age of AI." doi:10.48550/ARXIV.2509.12383.

550. Guedes, I., Martins, M.L. and Cardoso, C. (2022) "Exploring the determinants of victimization and fear of online identity theft: an empirical study," *Security Journal,* 36(3), p. 472. doi:10.1057/s41284-022-00350-5.

551. Hasibuan, J. and Syam, S. (2023) "A Legal Analysis on Online Fraud Using Fake Identity," *Indonesian Journal of Multidisciplinary Science,* 2(10), p. 3308. doi:10.55324/ijoms.v2i10.574.

552. Houtti, M. *et al.* (2024) "A Survey of Scam Exposure, Victimization, Types, Vectors, and Reporting in 12 Countries," *Journal of Online Trust and Safety,* 2(4). doi:10.54501/jots.v2i4.204.

553. Kayser, C.S., Back, S. and Toro-Alvarez, M.M. (2024) "Identity Theft: The Importance of Prosecuting on Behalf of Victims," *Laws,* 13(6), p. 68. doi:10.3390/laws13060068.

554. Kipngetich, A. (2025) "A review of online scams and financial frauds in the digital age," *GSC Advanced Research and Reviews,* p. 302. doi:10.30574/gscarr.2025.22.1.0025.

555. Lauder, C. and March, E. (2022) "Catching the catfish: Exploring gender and the Dark Tetrad of personality as predictors of catfishing perpetration," *Computers in Human Behavior,* 140, p. 107599. doi:10.1016/j.chb.2022.107599.

556. Liu, E. *et al.* (2024) "Give and Take: An End-To-End Investigation of Giveaway Scam Conversion Rates," p. 704. doi:10.1145/3646547.3689005.

557. Mistry, K. *et al.* (2024) "Fraudulent Participation in Online Qualitative Studies: Practical Recommendations on an Emerging Phenomenon," *Qualitative Health Research* [Preprint]. doi:10.1177/10497323241288181.

558. Ryan, S. and Taylor, J. (2024) "An exploration of the motivations of catfish perpetrators and the emotions and feelings expressed by catfish victims using automated linguistic analysis and thematic analysis," *Discover Data*, 2(1). doi:10.1007/s44248-024-00011-5.

559. Schmitt, M. and Fléchais, I. (2024) "Digital deception: generative artificial intelligence in social engineering and phishing," *Artificial Intelligence Review*, 57(12). doi:10.1007/s10462-024-10973-2.

560. Virmani, C. (2020) "Analysis of cyber attacks and security intelligence: Identity theft," *Indian Journal of Science and Technology*, 13(25), p. 2529. doi:10.17485/ijst/v13i25.580.

561. Wang, C., Zhu, H. and Yang, B. (2021) "Composite Behavioral Modeling for Identity Theft Detection in Online Social Networks," *IEEE Transactions on Computational Social Systems*, 9(2), p. 428. doi:10.1109/tcss.2021.3092007.

562. Wang, F. and Topalli, V. (2024) "The cyber-industrialization of catfishing and romance fraud," *Computers in Human Behavior*, 154, p. 108133. doi:10.1016/j.chb.2023.108133.

563. Wu, Y. and Geylani, T. (2020) "Regulating Deceptive Advertising: False Claims and Skeptical Consumers," *Marketing Science*, 39(4), p. 788. doi:10.1287/mksc.2020.1221.

564. Zulham, Z. (2023) "A Critical Review of Consumer Protection Online Shopping, False Advertising, and Legal Protection," *Journal of Law and Sustainable Development*. doi:10.55908/sdgs.v11i5.740.

565. Antunes, H.S. et al. (2023) Multidisciplinary Perspectives on Artificial Intelligence and the Law, Law, governance and technology series. Springer International Publishing. doi:10.1007/978-3-031-41264-6.

566. Aribarg, A. and Schwartz, E.M. (2019) "Native Advertising in Online News: Trade-Offs Among Clicks, Brand Recognition, and Website Trustworthiness," Journal of Marketing Research, 57(1), p. 20. doi:10.1177/0022243719879711.

567. Beckert, J. (2022) "A threat to journalism? How journalists and advertising sales managers in news organizations perceive and cope with native advertising," Journalism, 24(8), p. 1733. doi:10.1177/14648849211067584.

568. Christensen, L.H. (2017) "Danske medier inddrager Facebook i alle dele af journalistikken," Research Portal Denmark, p. 125. Available at: https://local.forskningsportal.dk/local/dki-cgi/ws/cris-link?src=aau&id=aau-f7df2d11-0419-40e2-a78c-ed68f80ab394&ti=Danske%20medier%20inddrager%20Facebook%20i%20alle%20dele%20af%20journalistikken (Accessed: July 2025).

569. Eberl, J., Boomgaarden, H.G. and Wagner, M. (2015) "One Bias Fits All? Three Types of Media Bias and Their Effects on Party Preferences," Communication Research, 44(8), p. 1125. doi:10.1177/0093650215614364.

570. Forja-Pena, T., Orosa, B.G. and García, X.L. (2024) "The Ethical Revolution: Challenges and Reflections in the Face of the Integration of Artificial Intelligence in Digital Journalism," Communication & Society, p. 237. doi:10.15581/003.37.3.237-254.

571. Gutiérrez-Caneda, B., Lindén, C. and Vázquez-Herrero, J. (2024) "Ethics and journalistic challenges in the age of artificial intelligence: talking with professionals and experts," Frontiers in Communication, 9. doi:10.3389/fcomm.2024.1465178.

572. Hagelstein, J., Einwiller, S. and Zerfaß, A. (2021) "The ethical dimension of public relations in Europe: Digital channels, moral challenges, resources, and training," Public Relations Review, 47(4), p. 102063. doi:10.1016/j.pubrev.2021.102063.

573. Hanitzsch, T. and Vos, T.P. (2016) "Journalism beyond democracy: A new look into journalistic roles in political and everyday life," Journalism, 19(2), p. 146. doi:10.1177/1464884916673386.

574. Krouwer, S., Poels, K. and Paulussen, S. (2019) "Moving Towards Transparency for Native Advertisements on News Websites: A Test of More Detailed Disclosures," International Journal of Advertising, 39(1), p. 51. doi:10.1080/02650487.2019.1575107.

575. Levi, L. (2015) "A 'Faustian Pact'?: Native Advertising and the Future of the Press," SSRN Electronic Journal [Preprint]. doi:10.2139/ssrn.2579341.

576. Naderer, B. et al. (2020) "Native and embedded advertising formats: Tensions between a lucrative marketing strategy and consumer fairness," Communications, 45(3), p. 273. doi:10.1515/commun-2019-0143.

577. Pansanella, V. et al. (2023) "Mass media impact on opinion evolution in biased digital environments: a bounded confidence model," Scientific Reports, 13(1), p. 14600. doi:10.1038/s41598-023-39725-y.

578. Patil, P. et al. (2021) "Study of Detecting the Political Bias in News Articles," International Journal of Scientific Research in Science and Technology, p. 57. doi:10.32628/ijsrst218315.

579. Poutanen, P., Luoma-aho, V. and Suhanko, E. (2016) "Ethical Challenges of Hybrid Editors," The International Journal on Media Management, 18(2), p. 99. doi:10.1080/14241277.2016.1157805.

580. Rodrigo-Ginés, F.-J., Carrillo-de-Albornoz, J. and Plaza, L. (2023) "A systematic review on media bias detection: What is media bias, how it is expressed, and how to detect it," Expert Systems with Applications. Elsevier BV, p. 121641. doi:10.1016/j.eswa.2023.121641.

581. Singh, S. (2025) "A Comprehensive Review on Deepfake Generation, Detection, Challenges, and Future Directions," International Journal for Research in Applied Science and Engineering Technology. International Journal for Research in Applied Science and Engineering Technology (IJRASET), p. 6566. doi:10.22214/ijraset.2025.71713.

582. Spinde, T. et al. (2023) "The Media Bias Taxonomy: A Systematic Literature Review on the Forms and Automated Detection of Media Bias," arXiv (Cornell University) [Preprint]. doi:10.48550/arxiv.2312.16148.

583. T., S.S. (2024) "THE CHALLENGES AND ROLE OF MODERN JOURNALISM IN DIGITAL MEDIA ENTERPRISES," ShodhKosh Journal of Visual and Performing Arts, 5(7). doi:10.29121/shodhkosh.v5.i7.2024.1921.

584. Wang, H. and Sparks, C. (2018) "Marketing Credibility," Journalism Studies, 20(9), p. 1301. doi:10.1080/1461670x.2018.1513815.

585. Yang, J. (2023) "How Mass Media Influences U.S. Political Polarization— A Comparison Study of CNN and Fox News," SHS Web of Conferences, 178, p. 2005. doi:10.1051/shsconf/202317802005.

586. Agarwal, V. and Puppala, V.N. (2024) "NAVIGATING THE SOCIAL MEDIA MAZE: ASSESSING THE EVOLVING RELEVANCE OF PUBLIC RELATIONS IN A DIGITAL LANDSCAPE," *PUBLIC ADMINISTRATION AND LAW REVIEW*, p. 34. doi:10.36690/2674-5216-2024-2-34-41.

587. Awoyemi, O. et al. (2023) "Strategic integration of media and public relations to address communication barriers in organizational reputation management," *Open Access Research Journal of Multidisciplinary Studies*, 6(1), p. 76. doi:10.53022/oarjms.2023.6.1.0035.

588. Babatunde, K.A. (2022) "Public Relations and Social Media for Effective Crisis Communication Management," *Jurnal Bina Praja*, 14(3), p. 543. doi:10.21787/jbp.14.2022.543-553.

589. Benthaus, J., Risius, M. and Beck, R. (2016) "Social media management strategies for organizational impression management and their effect on public perception," *The Journal of Strategic Information Systems*, 25(2), p. 127. doi:10.1016/j.jsis.2015.12.001.

590. Cosa, M. (2023) "Business digital transformation: strategy adaptation, communication and future agenda," *Journal of strategy and management*, 17(2), p. 244. doi:10.1108/jsma-09-2023-0233.

591. Cullerton, K. and Patay, D. (2024) "Inside a corporate affairs conference: the race for a social license," *Frontiers in Communication*, 9. doi:10.3389/fcomm.2024.1419959.

592. Elrod, J.K. and Fortenberry, J.L. (2020) "Public relations in health and medicine: using publicity and other unpaid promotional methods to engage audiences," *BMC Health Services Research*, 20. doi:10.1186/s12913-020-05602-x.

593. Eteki, B. (2024) "Impact of Social Media Engagement on Brand Image Perception in Cameroon," *American journal of public relations.*, 3(1), p. 12. doi:10.47672/ajpr.2054.

594. Fitzpatrick, K.R. and Weissman, P.L. (2021) "Public relations in the age of data: corporate perspectives on social media analytics (SMA)," *Journal of Communication Management*, 25(4), p. 401. doi:10.1108/jcom-09-2020-0092.

595. Floreddu, P.B., Cabiddu, F. and Evaristo, R. (2014) "Inside your social media ring: How to optimize online corporate reputation," *Business Horizons*, 57(6), p. 737. doi:10.1016/j.bushor.2014.07.007.

596. Hadeed, A.Y.A. *et al.* (2024) "Role of public relations practices in content management: the mediating role of new media platforms," *Frontiers in Sociology*, 8. doi:10.3389/fsoc.2023.1273371.

597. Jiang, Y. (2022) "Social Media Platforms and Public Relations for Brand Promotion," *BCP Business & Management*, 34, p. 769. doi:10.54691/bcpbm.v34i.3095.

598. Madupati, B. (2022) "Data Science in Public Relations Software Development," *Journal of Mathematical & Computer Applications*, p. 1. doi:10.47363/jmca/2022(1)e118.

599. Mohamed, K. and Bayraktar, Ü.A. (2022) "Analyzing the role of Sentiment Analysis in Public Relations: Brand Monitoring and Crisis Management," *International Journal of Humanities and Social Science*, 9(3), p. 116. doi:10.14445/23942703/ijhss-v9i3p116.

600. Nsibande, O., Dinath, W. and Niemand, C.J.P. (2025) "CI Practices to Gain Competitive Advantage through Social Media in the PR Industry," *South African journal of information management*, 27(1). doi:10.4102/sajim.v27i1.1996.

601. Olukemi, A., Broklyn, P. and Bell, C. (2024) "Social Media Sentiment Analysis for Brand Reputation Management," *SSRN Electronic Journal* [Preprint]. doi:10.2139/ssrn.4906218.

602. Smith, R.D. (2004) *Strategic Planning for Public Relations, Routledge eBooks*. Informa. doi:10.4324/9781410611468.

603. Søilen, K.S. (2024) "The Evolution of PR and Communications in the Digital Age," in *Springer texts in business and economics*. Springer International Publishing, p. 365. doi:10.1007/978-3-031-69518-6_35.

604. Soleymani, M., Rousta, A. and Asayesh, F. (2024) "Presenting a content marketing process model in Iran's banking industry (Case Study:Bank mellat)," 4(1), p. 56. doi:10.61838/kman.ijimob.4.1.7.

605. Tække, J. (2017) "Crisis Communication and Social Media. A Systems- and Medium-Theoretical Perspective," *Systems Research and Behavioral Science*, 34(2), p. 182. doi:10.1002/sres.2451.

606. Taherdoost, H. and Madanchian, M. (2023) "Artificial Intelligence and Sentiment Analysis: A Review in Competitive Research," *Computers*. Multidisciplinary Digital Publishing Institute, p. 37. doi:10.3390/computers12020037.

607. Ugoani, J. (2020) "Public Relations Practice and Its Impact on Strategy Effectiveness," *SSRN Electronic Journal* [Preprint]. Available at: https://papers.ssrn.com/sol3/papers.cfm?abstract_id=3598110 (Accessed: January 2025).

608. Umezurike, S.A. *et al.* (2025) "Advanced Sentiment Analysis Models for Crisis-Time Brand Trust Monitoring and Recovery," *International Journal of Social Science Exceptional Research*, 4(3), p. 232. doi:10.54660/ijsser.2025.4.3.232-242.

609. Vasudevan, A. (2025) "ARTIFICIAL INTELLIGENCE IN PUBLIC RELATIONS ANALYTICS: A FRAMEWORK FOR ENHANCED DECISION-MAKING AND STRATEGIC INSIGHTS," *INTERNATIONAL JOURNAL OF COMPUTER ENGINEERING & TECHNOLOGY*, 16(1), p. 1191. doi:10.34218/ijcet_16_01_091.

610. Vieira, E.T. (2018) *Public Relations Planning, Routledge eBooks*. Informa. doi:10.4324/9781315101880.

611. Wojciechowski, Ł. and Skrzypek-Ahmed, S. (2022) "Economic and social conditions of launching a new product on the martket.," *Journal of Modern Science*, 49(2), p. 482. doi:10.13166/jms/156420.

612. Захарченко, A. (2022) "PR-Message Analysis as a New Method for the Quantitative and Qualitative Communication Campaign Study," *Information & Media*, 93, p. 42. doi:10.15388/im.2022.93.60.

613. Awoyemi, O. *et al.* (2023) "Strategic integration of media and public relations to address communication barriers in organizational reputation management," *Open Access Research Journal of Multidisciplinary Studies*, 6(1), p. 76. doi:10.53022/oarjms.2023.6.1.0035.

614. Chukwu, O.J. (2023) "Understanding Event Management through Public Relations Prisms: The Implications and the Emerged Paradigms," *Integration Journal Of Social Sciences And Culture*, 1(2), p. 120. doi:10.38142/ijssc.v1i2.104.

615. Turk, J.V. (1985) "Information subsidies and influence," *Public Relations Review*, 11(3), p. 10. doi:10.1016/s0363-8111(85)80078-3.

616. Hallahan, K. *et al.* (2007) "Defining Strategic Communication," *International Journal of Strategic Communication*, 1(1), p. 3. doi:10.1080/15531180701285244.

617. Thomas, G.F. and Stephens, K.J. (2014) "An Introduction to Strategic Communication," *International Journal of Business Communication*, 52(1), p. 3. doi:10.1177/2329488414560469.

618. Zerfaß, A. *et al.* (2018) "Strategic Communication: Defining the Field and its Contribution to Research and Practice," *International Journal of Strategic Communication*, 12(4), p. 487. doi:10.1080/1553118x.2018.1493485.

619. Abdullah, A. *et al.* (2017) "Corporate engagement with the community: building relationships through CSR." Available at: http://psasir.upm.edu.my/id/eprint/61236/ (Accessed: September 2025).

620. Dike, H.W. (2025) "Public Relations Strategies and Reputation Management: Mastering Stakeholder Engagement and Community Building," *International Journal of Latest Technology in Engineering Management & Applied Science*, 14(3), p. 52. doi:10.51583/ijltemas.2025.14030008.

621. Gawroński, S. *et al.* (2021) "Communication Management within Community Relations by Local Governments in Poland," *EUROPEAN RESEARCH STUDIES JOURNAL*, p. 395. doi:10.35808/ersj/1969.

622. Singh, A. (2024) "Sustainability Practices in Business Operations," *International Journal for Research Publication and Seminars*, 15(3), p. 18. doi:10.36676/jrps.v15.i3.1424.

623. Thyagaraju, N. (2020) "CSR AS A STRATEGIC TOOL FOR BUILDING COMMUNITY RELATIONS," in. doi:10.25215/9389476526.08.

624. Dong, C., Zheng, Q. and Morehouse, J. (2023) "What do we know about government public relations (GPR)? A systematic review of GPR in public relations literature," *Public Relations Review*. Elsevier BV, p. 102284. doi:10.1016/j.pubrev.2022.102284.

625. Gawroński, S. *et al.* (2021) "Communication Management within Community Relations by Local Governments in Poland," *EUROPEAN RESEARCH STUDIES JOURNAL*, p. 395. doi:10.35808/ersj/1969.

626. Rozgonyi, K. (2023) "Accountability and platforms' governance: the case of online prominence of public service media content," *Internet Policy Review*, 12(4). doi:10.14763/2023.4.1723.

627. Henderson, J. and Christ, W.G. (2014) "Benchmarking ACEJMC Competencies," *Journalism & Mass Communication Educator*, 69(3), p. 229. doi:10.1177/1077695814525407.

628. Solkin, L. (2020) "Journalism Education in the 21st century: A thematic analysis of the research literature," *Journalism*, 23(2), p. 444. doi:10.1177/1464884920977299.

629. Pandiani, D.S.M., Sang, E.T.K. and Ceolin, D. (2024) "Toxic Memes: A Survey of Computational Perspectives on the Detection and Explanation of Meme Toxicities," *arXiv (Cornell University)* [Preprint]. doi:10.48550/arxiv.2406.07353.

630. Fino, A. (2023) "A critique of the UN Strategy and Guidance on 'Hate Speech': Some Legal Considerations," *Netherlands Quarterly of Human Rights*, 41(4), p. 190. doi:10.1177/09240519231211815.

631. Liern, G.R. (2020) "Redes sociales y discurso del odio: perspectiva internacional," *IDP Revista de Internet Derecho y Política* [Preprint], (31). doi:10.7238/idp.v0i31.3233.

632. Bermingham, V. and Brennan, C. (2012) "Elements of defamation," in *Oxford University Press eBooks*. Oxford University Press, p. 241. doi:10.1093/he/9780199639564.003.0015.

633. Bogle, S.J. and Lindsay, B. (2024) "How serious is the serious harm threshold?," *SSRN Electronic Journal* [Preprint]. doi:10.2139/ssrn.4769366.

634. Chiruvella, V. and Guddati, A.K. (2021) "Cyberspace and Libel: A Dangerous Balance for Physicians," *Interactive Journal of Medical Research*, 10(2). doi:10.2196/22271.

635. Shao, J. (2024) "Analysis on the Behavior Characteristics and Application of the Crime of Network Insult and Libel," *International Law Research*, 13(1), p. 11. doi:10.5539/ilr.v13n1p11.

636. Chakraborty, I., Kapoor, U. and Ilavarasan, P.V. (2020) "There Is Nothing Real! A Study of Nonuse of TikTok in India," in *IFIP advances in information and communication technology*. Springer Science+Business Media, p. 287. doi:10.1007/978-3-030-64861-9_26.

637. Chalaby, J.K. (2023) "The streaming industry and the platform economy: An analysis," *Media Culture & Society*, 46(3), p. 552. doi:10.1177/01634437231210439.

638. Parviz, M. (2024) "Global perspectives of COVID-19 pandemic on health, education, and the role of media," *Media Practice and Education*, p. 1. doi:10.1080/25741136.2024.2437489.

639. Abed, B. (2025) "Exploring Public Relation Campaigns Research from 2019 to 2024: A Systematic Review," *Open Journal of Business and Management*. Scientific Research Publishing, p. 3254. doi:10.4236/ojbm.2025.135172.

640. Anuar, A.Z.A. *et al.* (2025) "Optimizing Strategic Communication Through Social Media: The Roles of Public Relations Leaders and Multidisciplinary Team," in *Atlantis highlights in social sciences, education and humanities/Atlantis Highlights in Social Sciences, Education and Humanities*. Atlantis Press, p. 28. doi:10.2991/978-94-6463-756-4_4.

641. Aronoff, C.E. (1976) "Predictors of success in placing releases in newspapers," *Public Relations Review*, 2(4), p. 43. doi:10.1016/s0363-8111(76)80023-9.

642. Bentele, G. (2008) *Public Relations Research, VS Verlag für Sozialwissenschaften eBooks*. Springer VS. doi:10.1007/978-3-531-90918-9.

643. Chukwu, O.J. (2023) "Understanding Event Management through Public Relations Prisms: The Implications and the Emerged Paradigms," *Integration Journal Of Social Sciences And Culture*, 1(2), p. 120. doi:10.38142/ijssc.v1i2.104.

644. Cowan, K. and Guzmán, F. (2018) "How CSR reputation, sustainability signals, and country-of-origin sustainability reputation contribute to corporate brand performance: An exploratory study," *Journal of Business Research*, 117, p. 683. doi:10.1016/j.jbusres.2018.11.017.

645. Dike, H.W. (2025) "Public Relations Strategies and Reputation Management: Mastering Stakeholder Engagement and Community Building," *International Journal of Latest Technology in Engineering Management & Applied Science*, 14(3), p. 52. doi:10.51583/ijltemas.2025.14030008.

646. Elrod, J.K. and Fortenberry, J.L. (2020) "Public relations in health and medicine: using publicity and other unpaid promotional methods to engage audiences," *BMC Health Services Research*, 20. doi:10.1186/s12913-020-05602-x.

647. Farhi, F. *et al.* (2023) "Towards Communication in Achieving Sustainable Economic Development Goals: The Role of Communication in UAE Media Institutions," *Sustainability*, 15(10), p. 7933. doi:10.3390/su15107933.

648. Gasana, K. ((2024) "Crisis Communication and Reputation Management in the Age of Fake News," *Journal of Public Relations*, 3(1), p. 28. doi:10.47941/jpr.1773.

649. Gottschalk, P. (2024) "Content analysis of press releases from the Norwegian serious fraud office: what do the messages say about focal concerns?," *Policing An International Journal*, 47(6), p. 913. doi:10.1108/pijpsm-03-2024-0031.

650. Gregory, A. and Fawkes, J. (2019) "A global capability framework: Reframing public relations for a changing world," *Public Relations Review*, 45(3), p. 101781. doi:10.1016/j.pubrev.2019.05.002.

651. Gregory, A. and Macnamara, J. (2019) "An evaluation u-turn: From narrow organisational objectives to broad accountability," *Public Relations Review*, 45(5), p. 101838. doi:10.1016/j.pubrev.2019.101838.

652. Hadeed, A.Y.A. *et al.* (2024) "Role of public relations practices in content management: the mediating role of new media platforms," *Frontiers in Sociology*, 8. doi:10.3389/fsoc.2023.1273371.

653. Madupati, B. (2022) "Data Science in Public Relations Software Development," *Journal of Mathematical & Computer Applications*, p. 1. doi:10.47363/jmca/2022(1)e118.

654. Mitrić, P. (2022) "Can the Audience Design method help youth content reach audiences? : The case of 'Efterskolen,'" *Research Portal Denmark* [Preprint]. Available at: https://local.forskningsportal.dk/local/dki-cgi/ws/cris-link?src=ku&id=ku-42d1dbc1-d66e-4825-a0c0-79f3014967fe&ti=Can%20the%20Audience%20Design%20method%20help%20youth%20content%20reach%20audiences%3F%20%3A%20The%20case%20of%20'Efterskolen' (Accessed: August 2025).

655. Rijmenam, M. van *et al.* (2018) "Avoid being the Turkey: How big data analytics changes the game of strategy in times of ambiguity and uncertainty," *Long Range Planning*, 52(5), p. 101841. doi:10.1016/j.lrp.2018.05.007.

656. Santos, J. (2022) "Advocacy and the role of human rights organizations in the Brazilian legislative branch: Rede Justiça Criminal campaigns," *Journal of Communication Management*, 27(2), p. 155. doi:10.1108/jcom-04-2022-0040.

657. Shahid, A. (2023) "Ethical Challenges in Journalism: Balancing Objectivity and Sensitivity in Reporting." doi:10.31219/osf.io/xebmv.

658. Søilen, K.S. (2024) "The Evolution of PR and Communications in the Digital Age," in *Springer texts in business and economics*. Springer International Publishing, p. 365. doi:10.1007/978-3-031-69518-6_35.

659. Ugoani, J. (2020) "Public Relations Practice and Its Impact on Strategy Effectiveness," *SSRN Electronic Journal* [Preprint]. Available at: https://papers.ssrn.com/sol3/papers.cfm?abstract_id=3598110 (Accessed: January 2025).

660. White, J. and Hobsbawm, J. (2007) "PUBLIC RELATIONS AND JOURNALISM," *Journalism Practice*, 1(2), p. 283. doi:10.1080/17512780701275606.

661. Wojciechowski, Ł. and Skrzypek-Ahmed, S. (2022) "Economic and social conditions of launching a new product on the martket.," *Journal of Modern Science*, 49(2), p. 482. doi:10.13166/jms/156420.

662. Ahmad, P.N., Shah, A.M. and Lee, K.Y. (2025) "Enhanced Propaganda Detection in Public Social Media Discussions Using a Fine-Tuned Deep Learning Model: A Diffusion of Innovation Perspective," *Future Internet*, 17(5), p. 212. doi:10.3390/fi17050212.

663. Antunes, H.S. *et al.* (2023) *Multidisciplinary Perspectives on Artificial Intelligence and the Law, Law, governance and technology series*. Springer International Publishing. doi:10.1007/978-3-031-41264-6.

664. Chang, R.-C. *et al.* (2021) "Dataset of Propaganda Techniques of the State-Sponsored Information Operation of the People's Republic of China," *arXiv (Cornell University)* [Preprint]. doi:10.48550/arxiv.2106.07544.

665. Guarino, S. *et al.* (2020) "Characterizing networks of propaganda on twitter: a case study," *Applied Network Science*, 5(1). doi:10.1007/s41109-020-00286-y.

666. Krishnamurthy, G., Gupta, R.K. and Yang, Y. (2020) "SocCogCom at SemEval-2020 Task 11: Characterizing and Detecting Propaganda Using Sentence-Level Emotional Salience Features," p. 1793. doi:10.18653/v1/2020.semeval-1.235.

667. Marigliano, R., Ng, L.H.X. and Carley, K.M. (2024) "Analyzing digital propaganda and conflict rhetoric: a study on Russia's bot-driven campaigns and counter-narratives during the Ukraine crisis," *Social Network Analysis and Mining*, 14(1). doi:10.1007/s13278-024-01322-w.

668. Martino, G.D.S., Cresci, S., et al. (2020) "A Survey on Computational Propaganda Detection," p. 4826. doi:10.24963/ijcai.2020/672.

669. Martino, G.D.S., Shaar, S., et al. (2020) "Prta: A System to Support the Analysis of Propaganda Techniques in the News." doi:10.18653/v1/2020.acl-demos.32.

670. Mitrić, P. (2022) "Can the Audience Design method help youth content reach audiences? : The case of 'Efterskolen,'" *Research Portal Denmark* [Preprint]. Available at: https://local.forskningsportal.dk/local/dki-cgi/ws/cris-link?src=ku&id=ku-42d1dbc1-d66e-4825-a0c0-79f3014967fe&ti=Can%20the%20Audience%20Design%20method%20help%20youth%20content%20reach%20audiences%3F%20%3A%20The%20case%20of%20'Efterskolen' (Accessed: August 2025).

671. Mosiichuk, V. (2024) "The Neuropsychology of Narratives in Propaganda Justifying Military Aggression: An Examination," *SSRN Electronic Journal* [Preprint]. doi:10.2139/ssrn.4723195.

672. Pandiani, D.S.M., Sang, E.T.K. and Ceolin, D. (2024) "Toxic Memes: A Survey of Computational Perspectives on the Detection and Explanation of Meme Toxicities," *arXiv (Cornell University)* [Preprint]. doi:10.48550/arxiv.2406.07353.

673. Toursinov, A.A. (2024) "The Coercive Power of Manipulation in Propagandistic Discourses," *SSRN Electronic Journal* [Preprint]. doi:10.2139/ssrn.4911248.

674. Woolley, S. (2022) "Digital Propaganda: The Power of Influencers," *Journal of democracy*, 33(3), p. 115. doi:10.1353/jod.2022.0027.

675. Alkhamsi, N.N. and Alqahtani, S.S. (2024) "Compliance Framework for Personal Data Protection Law Standards," *International Journal of Advanced Computer Science and Applications*, 15(7). doi:10.14569/ijacsa.2024.0150751.

676. Cawthra, J. et al. (2020) *Data Integrity: Identifying and Protecting Assets Against Ransomware and Other Destructive Events*. doi:10.6028/nist.sp.1800-25.

677. Compagnucci, M.C., Dahi, A. and Davis, P. (2023) "Conducting a Data Protection Impact Assessment in Health Science: A Comprehensive Guide," *SSRN Electronic Journal* [Preprint]. doi:10.2139/ssrn.4651993.

678. Covert, Q. et al. (2020) "Towards a Triad for Data Privacy," in *Proceedings of the ... Annual Hawaii International Conference on System Sciences/Proceedings of the Annual Hawaii International Conference on System Sciences*. doi:10.24251/hicss.2020.535.

679. Gokulakrishnan, D.S.P. and Venkataraman, S. (2024) "ENSURING DATA INTEGRITY: BEST PRACTICES AND STRATEGIES IN PHARMACEUTICAL INDUSTRY," *Intelligent Pharmacy* [Preprint]. doi:10.1016/j.ipha.2024.09.010.

680. Marjanov, T. et al. (2023) "Data Security on the Ground: Investigating Technical and Legal Requirements under the GDPR," *Proceedings on Privacy Enhancing Technologies*, 2023(3), p. 405. doi:10.56553/popets-2023-0088.

681. Pant, A.R.M. (2023) "Importance of Data Security and Privacy Compliance," *International Journal for Research in Applied Science and Engineering Technology*, 11(11), p. 1561. doi:10.22214/ijraset.2023.56862.

682. Re, E.D. (2024) "Technologies of Data Protection and Institutional Decisions for Data Sovereignty," *Information*, 15(8), p. 444. doi:10.3390/info15080444.

683. Roy, P. *et al.* (2023) "A Survey of Data Security: Practices from Cybersecurity and Challenges of Machine Learning," *arXiv (Cornell University)* [Preprint]. doi:10.48550/arxiv.2310.04513.

684. Sobroza, T.V. *et al.* (2020) "Parapatric pied and red-handed tamarin responses to congeneric and conspecific calls," *Acta Oecologica*, 110, p. 103688. doi:10.1016/j.actao.2020.103688.

685. Shepherd, E. (2015) "Freedom of Information, Right to Access Information, Open Data: Who is at the Table?," *The Round Table*, 104(6), p. 715. doi:10.1080/00358533.2015.1112101.

686. Heide, M. and Villeneuve, J. (2020) "From secrecy privilege to information management: A comparative analysis of classification reforms," *Government Information Quarterly*, 37(4), p. 101500. doi:10.1016/j.giq.2020.101500.

687. _ (1999) "Preliminary Material," in *Brill / Nijhoff eBooks*. Brill. doi:10.1163/9789004640641_001.

688. Struensee, S. von (2024) "Safeguarding Data: Government Handling of Publicly Available Information (PAI) and Commercially Available Information (CAI)," *SSRN Electronic Journal* [Preprint]. doi:10.2139/ssrn.4794184.

689. Abiteboul, S. and Stoyanovich, J. (2019) "Transparency, Fairness, Data Protection, Neutrality," *Journal of Data and Information Quality*, 11(3), p. 1. doi:10.1145/3310231.

690. Antunes, H.S. *et al.* (2023) *Multidisciplinary Perspectives on Artificial Intelligence and the Law*, *Law, governance and technology series*. Springer International Publishing. doi:10.1007/978-3-031-41264-6.

691. Ausloos, J., Mahieu, R. and Veale, M. (2019) "Getting Data Subject Rights Right." doi:10.31228/osf.io/e2thg.

692. Bigo, D., Isin, E.F. and Ruppert, E. (2019) "Data Politics. Worlds, Subjects, Rights," *HAL (Le Centre pour la Communication Scientifique Directe)* [Preprint]. Available at: https://hal-sciencespo.archives-ouvertes.fr/hal-03385170 (Accessed: August 2025).

693. Bormida, M.D. (2021) "The Big Data World: Benefits, Threats and Ethical Challenges," in *Advances in research ethics and integrity*. Emerald Publishing Limited, p. 71. doi:10.1108/s2398-601820210000008007.

694. Colonna, L. and Greenstein, S. (2022) "Nordic Yearbook of Law and Informatics 2020–2021 Law in the Era of Artificial Intelligence."

695. Laje, A. and Schmidt, K. (2024) "The Right to Data Portability as a Personal Right," *Laws*, 13(4), p. 47. doi:10.3390/laws13040047.

696. Lam, W.M.W. and Liu, X. (2019) "Does data portability facilitate entry?," *International Journal of Industrial Organization*, 69, p. 102564. doi:10.1016/j.ijindorg.2019.102564.

697. Lienemann, G. (2023) "Global Perspectives on the Right to Personal Data Portability: Surveying Legislative Progress and Propositions for User-Led Data Transfers," *SSRN Electronic Journal* [Preprint]. doi:10.2139/ssrn.4427736.

698. Nebbiai, M. (2022) "Intermediaries do matter: voluntary standards and the Right to Data Portability," *Internet Policy Review*, 11(2). doi:10.14763/2022.2.1639.

699. Noya, A. (2021) "Mapping data portability initiatives, opportunities and challenges," *OECD digital economy papers* [Preprint]. doi:10.1787/a6edfab2-en.

700. Savin, A. (2013) *Interoperability : The Impact of Commission's Proposed Data Protection Regulation: Appendix to Deliverable D5.1, Research Portal Denmark.* Technical University of Denmark, p. 10. Available at: https://local.forskningsportal.dk/local/dki-cgi/ws/crislink?src=cbs&id=cbs-fb89873b-22d0-44d2-b9aa-8588c42b2a3f&ti=Interoperability%20%3A%20The%20Impact%20of%20Commission%2019s%20Proposed%20Data%20Protection%20Regulation%3A%20Appendix%20to%20Deliverable%20D5.1 (Accessed: July 2025).

701. Singh, J. and Cobbe, J. (2019) "The Security Implications of Data Subject Rights," *IEEE Security & Privacy*, 17(6), p. 21. doi:10.1109/msec.2019.2914614.

702. Aljeraisy, A. *et al.* (2020) "Privacy Laws and Privacy by Design Schemes for the Internet of Things: A Developer's Perspective," *HAL (Le Centre pour la Communication Scientifique Directe)* [Preprint]. Available at: https://hal.science/hal-02567959 (Accessed: July 2025).

703. Abdelaal, abdelnasser (2020) "The Religious Calculus of Privacy." Available at: https://aisel.aisnet.org/cgi/viewcontent.cgi?article=1074&context=treos_amcis2020 (Accessed: December 2024).

704. Aime, F. *et al.* (2023) "Forensic Databases (Part I)," in *Springer eBooks.* Springer Nature, p. 195. doi:10.1007/978-3-031-42944-6_22.

705. Anttila, S. and Domínguez-Armas, Á. (2025) "Argumentative Exclusion and the Case of Online Hate Speech," *Topoi* [Preprint]. doi:10.1007/s11245-025-10165-9.

706. Arman, S.M. *et al.* (2024) "A Comprehensive Survey for Privacy-Preserving Biometrics: Recent Approaches, Challenges, and Future Directions," *Computers, materials & continua/Computers, materials & continua (Print)*, 78(2), p. 2087. doi:10.32604/cmc.2024.047870.

707. Badham, M. and Mykkänen, M. (2022) "A Relational Approach to How Media Engage With Their Audiences on Social Media," *Media and Communication*, 10(1), p. 54. doi:10.17645/mac.v10i1.4409.

708. Baumgarten, N. *et al.* (2019) "Towards Balance and Boundaries in Public Discourse : Expressing and Perceiving Online Hate Speech (XPEROHS)," *Research Portal Denmark*, 50, p. 87. Available at: https://local.forskningsportal.dk/local/dki-cgi/ws/crislink?src=sdu&id=sdu-975529ca-681c-4c22-b4ba-c16809806db3&ti=Towards%20Balance%20and%20Boundaries%20in%20Public%20Discourse%20%3A%20Expressing%20and%20Perceiving%20Online%20Hate%20Speech%20(XPEROHS) (Accessed: August 2025).

709. Becker, H. (1949) "The Nature and Consequences of Black Propaganda," *American Sociological Review*, 14(2), p. 221. doi:10.2307/2086855.

710. Bekkum, M. van and Borgesius, F.Z. (2022) "Using sensitive data to prevent discrimination by artificial intelligence: Does the GDPR need a new exception?," *Computer Law & Security Review*, 48, p. 105770. doi:10.1016/j.clsr.2022.105770.

711. Benatti, R.M. *et al.* (2022) "Should I disclose my dataset? Caveats between reproducibility and individual data rights," *arXiv (Cornell University)* [Preprint]. doi:10.48550/arxiv.2211.00498.

712. Bilewicz, M. *et al.* (2020) "Hate Speech Epidemic. The Dynamic Effects of Derogatory Language on Intergroup Relations and Political Radicalization," *Political Psychology*, 41, p. 3. doi:10.1111/pops.12670.

713. Bivens, R. (2015) "Affording Immediacy in Television News Production: Comparing Adoption Trajectories of Social Media and Satellite Technologies," *International journal of communication*, 9(1), p. 19. Available at: https://ir.library.carleton.ca/pub/10561/1001-14081-1-PB.pdf (Accessed: October 2025).

714. Bondielli, A. and Marcelloni, F. (2019) "A survey on fake news and rumour detection techniques," *Information Sciences*, 497, p. 38. doi:10.1016/j.ins.2019.05.035.

715. Boustead, A.E. and Herr, T. (2020) "Analyzing the Ethical Implications of Research Using Leaked Data," *PS Political Science & Politics*, 53(3), p. 505. doi:10.1017/s1049096520000323.

716. Cagé, J., Hervé, N. and Mazoyer, B. (2020) "Social Media and Newsroom Production Decisions," *SSRN Electronic Journal* [Preprint]. doi:10.2139/ssrn.3663899.

717. Calvi, A. (2025) "Exploring the Synergies between Non-Discrimination and Data Protection: What Role for EU Data Protection Law to Address Intersectional Discrimination?," *SSRN Electronic Journal* [Preprint]. doi:10.2139/ssrn.5236999.

718. Cha, J. (2025) "Predictors of the Credibility of Social Media as a News Outlet: An Examination of the Influences of Social Media Contacts, Source Perceptions, and Media Use," *The International Journal on Media Management*, p. 1. doi:10.1080/14241277.2025.2481826.

719. DeDominicis, B.E. (2019) "Propagating the Image with Plausible Deniability: Covert Media Political Campaigns in the Context of Postwar Postmodernity," *The Global Journal of Business Research*, 13(1). Available at: http://connections-qj.org/article/propagating-image-plausible-deniability-covert-media-political-campaigns-context-postwar (Accessed: January 2025).

720. Deffenbaugh, N. (2024) "De-dehumanization: Practicing humanity," *International Review of the Red Cross*, 106(925), p. 56. doi:10.1017/s1816383124000079.

721. Fernández, L.R. (2023) "'Desinformación y relaciones públicas. Aproximación a los términos Black PR y Dark PR,'" *Revista ICONO14*, 21(1). doi:10.7195/ri14.v21i1.1920.

722. Fino, A. (2023) "A critique of the UN Strategy and Guidance on 'Hate Speech': Some Legal Considerations," *Netherlands Quarterly of Human Rights*, 41(4), p. 190. doi:10.1177/09240519231211815.

723. Fletcher, R. *et al.* (2024) "The link between changing news use and trust: longitudinal analysis of 46 countries," *Journal of Communication*, 75(1), p. 1. doi:10.1093/joc/jqae044.

724. Gaïni, S.M. (2022) "The Individual Consequences of Hate Speech : A Comparison of Defamation and Hate Speech/Group Libel," *Research Portal Denmark*, (1), p. 114. Available at: https://local.forskningsportal.dk/local/dki-cgi/ws/cris-link?src=ruc&id=ruc-7a1f63e4-69a6-40f9-8915-8910ef77f351&ti=The%20Individual%20Consequences%20of%20Hate%20Speech%20%3A%20A%20Comparison%20of%20Defamation%20and%20Hate%20Speech%2FGroup%20Libel (Accessed: August 2025).

725. Gajardo, J.M. *et al.* (2022) "Hate Speech and the Gender Perspective: A Problem from the Teaching of Social Sciences in School," *European Journal of Educational Research*, p. 133. doi:10.12973/eu-jer.12.1.133.

726. Gajardo, J.M. and Mata, J.C. (2023) "Transform hate speech in education from gender perspectives. Conceptions of Chilean teachers through a case study," *Frontiers in Education*, 8. doi:10.3389/feduc.2023.1267690.

727. García-Perdomo, V. (2021) "How Social Media Influence TV Newsrooms Online Engagement and Video Distribution," *Journalism & Mass Communication Quarterly*, 101(4), p. 911. doi:10.1177/10776990211027864.

728. Georgiou, D. and Lambrinoudakis, C. (2020) "Compatibility of a Security Policy for a Cloud-Based Healthcare System with the EU General Data Protection Regulation (GDPR)," *Information*, 11(12), p. 586. doi:10.3390/info11120586.

729. Guo, J. and Chen, H. (2022) "How Does Multi-Platform Social Media Use Lead to Biased News Engagement? Examining the Role of Counter-Attitudinal Incidental Exposure, Cognitive Elaboration, and Network Homogeneity," *Social Media + Society*, 8(4). doi:10.1177/20563051221129140.

730. Guyatt, G. *et al.* (2012) "Executive Summary," *CHEST Journal*, 141(2). doi:10.1378/chest.1412s3.

731. Hassan, G. *et al.* (2022) "PROTOCOL: Hate online and in traditional media: A systematic review of the evidence for associations or impacts on individuals, audiences, and communities," *Campbell Systematic Reviews*. The Campbell Collaboration. doi:10.1002/cl2.1245.

732. Heek, J.O., Maidhof, C. and Ziefle, M. (2023) "Somebody is watching me? Analyzing privacy preferences in using visual AAL technology considering human-, technology-, and context-related factors," *Universal Access in the Information Society* [Preprint]. doi:10.1007/s10209-023-01070-2.

733. Ho, F.N., Ho-Dac, N.N. and Huang, J.S. (2023) "The Effects of Privacy and Data Breaches on Consumers' Online Self-Disclosure, Protection Behavior, and Message Valence," *SAGE Open*, 13(3). doi:10.1177/21582440231181395.

734. Hobbs, R. (2020) "Propaganda in an Age of Algorithmic Personalization: Expanding Literacy Research and Practice," *Reading Research Quarterly*, 55(3), p. 521. doi:10.1002/rrq.301.

735. Holvoet, M. (2022) "International Criminal Liability for Spreading Disinformation in the Context of Mass Atrocity," *Journal of International Criminal Justice*, 20(1), p. 223. doi:10.1093/jicj/mqac014.

736. Hu, Y. (2023) "The Impact of Social Media on News Dissemination: Taking Weibo and Twitter as Examples," in *Advances in Social Science, Education and Humanities Research/Advances in social science, education and humanities research*, p. 176. doi:10.2991/978-2-38476-178-4_22.

737. Jacob, C. and Morada, N.M. (2023) "Hate Speech and Atrocity Prevention in Asia: Patterns, Trends and Strategies," *Global Responsibility to Protect*, 15, p. 93. doi:10.1163/1875984x-20230001.

738. Kouchih, A. and Mataa, H. (2024) "Consumer Empowerment and Privacy: The Case of Morocco," in *Springer proceedings in business and economics*. Springer International Publishing, p. 345. doi:10.1007/978-981-97-5400-7_19.

739. Kteily, N. and Bruneau, E. (2017) "Darker Demons of Our Nature: The Need to (Re)Focus Attention on Blatant Forms of Dehumanization," *Current Directions in Psychological Science*, 26(6), p. 487. doi:10.1177/0963721417708230.

740. Lestari, A.P. *et al.* (2018) "The new system for promoting news through social media," *International Journal of Data and Network Science*, p. 57. doi:10.5267/j.ijdns.2018.7.002.

741. Li, Z. (2023) "Shaping the Media Landscape: Exploring Media User Consumption in the Age of Social Media," *Journal of innovation and development*, 4(3), p. 68. doi:10.54097/jid.v4i3.13233.

742. Lysaght, T. *et al.* (2023) "An ethical code for collecting, using and transferring sensitive health data: outcomes of a modified Policy Delphi process in Singapore," *BMC Medical Ethics*, 24(1). doi:10.1186/s12910-023-00952-7.

743. Martino, G.D.S. *et al.* (2020) "A Survey on Computational Propaganda Detection," p. 4826. doi:10.24963/ijcai.2020/672.

744. McCoy, M.S. *et al.* (2023) "Ethical Responsibilities for Companies That Process Personal Data," *The American Journal of Bioethics*, 23(11), p. 11. doi:10.1080/15265161.2023.2209535.

745. Mchangama, J. and Alkiviadou, N. (2022) "Editorial Introduction," *International Journal for the Semiotics of Law - Revue internationale de Sémiotique juridique*, 35(6), p. 2187. doi:10.1007/s11196-022-09953-y.

746. Mirabito, T. (2020) "Digital First: The Push to Move Traditional Content Online," *Journal of sports media*, 15(2), p. 71. doi:10.1353/jsm.2020.0011.

747. Mitrić, P. (2022) "Can the Audience Design method help youth content reach audiences? : The case of 'Efterskolen,'" *Research Portal Denmark* [Preprint]. Available at: https://local.forskningsportal.dk/local/dki-cgi/ws/cris-link?src=ku&id=ku-42d1dbc1-d66e-4825-a0c0-79f3014967fe&ti=Can%20the%20Audience%20Design%20method%20help%20youth%20content%20reach%20audiences%3F%20%3A%20The%20case%20of%20'Efterskolen' (Accessed: August 2025).

748. Mols, A., Wang, Y. and Pridmore, J. (2021) "Household intelligent personal assistants in the Netherlands: Exploring privacy concerns around surveillance, security, and platforms," *Convergence The International Journal of Research into New Media Technologies*, 28(6), p. 1841. doi:10.1177/13548565211042234.

749. Morada, N.M. (2023) "Hate Speech and Incitement in Myanmar before and after the February 2021 Coup," *Global Responsibility to Protect*, 15, p. 107. doi:10.1163/1875984x-20230003.

750. Mothes, C. *et al.* (2024) "Spurring or Blurring Professional Standards? The Role of Digital Technology in Implementing Journalistic Role Ideals in Contemporary Newsrooms," *Journalism & Mass Communication Quarterly*, 102(1), p. 88. doi:10.1177/10776990241246692.

751. Neilsen, R. (2015) "'Toxification' as a More Precise Early Warning Sign for Genocide Than Dehumanization? An Emerging Research Agenda," *Genocide Studies and Prevention*, 9(1), p. 83. doi:10.5038/1911-9933.9.1.1277.

752. Norén, F. (2018) "H-Day 1967 – An alternative perspective on 'propaganda' in the historiography of public relation," *Public Relations Review*, 45(2), p. 236. doi:10.1016/j.pubrev.2018.10.004.

753. OECD (2024) *AI, data governance and privacy, OECD artificial intelligence papers.* doi:10.1787/2476b1a4-en.

754. Omar, B., Al-Samarraie, H. and Wright, B. (2020) "Immediacy as news experience: exploring its multiple dimensions in print and online contexts," *Online Information Review*, 45(2), p. 461. doi:10.1108/oir-12-2019-0388.

755. Pandiani, D.S.M., Sang, E.T.K. and Ceolin, D. (2024) "Toxic Memes: A Survey of Computational Perspectives on the Detection and Explanation of Meme Toxicities," *arXiv (Cornell University)* [Preprint]. doi:10.48550/arxiv.2406.07353.

756. Pérez, J.M. *et al.* (2023) "Assessing the Impact of Contextual Information in Hate Speech Detection," *IEEE Access*, 11, p. 30575. doi:10.1109/access.2023.3258973.

757. Pina, E. *et al.* (2024) "Data Privacy and Ethical Considerations in Database Management," *Journal of Cybersecurity and Privacy*, 4(3), p. 494. doi:10.3390/jcp4030024.

758. Pluta, A. *et al.* (2023) "Exposure to hate speech deteriorates neurocognitive mechanisms of the ability to understand others' pain," *Scientific Reports*, 13(1). doi:10.1038/s41598-023-31146-1.

759. Qatawneh, I.S.A., Almobaideen, W. and Qatawneh, M. (2022) "A comparative study on surveillance and privacy regulations (the UAE vs. the USA and the EU)," *Journal of Governance and Regulation*, 11(1), p. 20. doi:10.22495/jgrv11i1art2.

760. Rath, B. *et al.* (2018) "Impact of News Organizations' Trustworthiness and Social Media Activity on Audience Engagement," *arXiv (Cornell University)* [Preprint]. doi:10.48550/arxiv.1808.09561.

761. Rodríguez-Peral, E.M., Franco, T.G. and Bustos, D.R.-P. (2025) "Propagation of Hate Speech on Social Network X: Trends and Approaches," *Social Inclusion*, 13. doi:10.17645/si.9317.

762. Sandeepa, C. *et al.* (2022) "A survey on privacy for B5G/6G: New privacy challenges, and research directions," *Journal of Industrial Information Integration*, 30, p. 100405. doi:10.1016/j.jii.2022.100405.

763. Sasy, S. and Goldberg, I. (2023) "SoK: Metadata-Protecting Communication Systems," *Proceedings on Privacy Enhancing Technologies*, 2024(1), p. 509. doi:10.56553/popets-2024-0030.

764. Schweppe, J. and Perry, B. (2021) "A continuum of hate: delimiting the field of hate studies," *Crime Law and Social Change*, 77(5), p. 503. doi:10.1007/s10611-021-09978-7.

765. Solove, D.J. (2023) "Data Is What Data Does: Regulating Use, Harm, and Risk Instead of Sensitive Data," *SSRN Electronic Journal* [Preprint]. doi:10.2139/ssrn.4322198.

766. Timmermann, W.K. (2008) "Counteracting Hate Speech as a Way of Preventing Genocidal Violence," *Genocide Studies and Prevention*, 3(3), p. 353. doi:10.3138/gsp.3.3.353.

767. Toursinov, A.A. (2024) "The Coercive Power of Manipulation in Propagandistic Discourses," *SSRN Electronic Journal* [Preprint]. doi:10.2139/ssrn.4911248.

768. Vlăduțescu, Ștefan (2014) "Communicational Types of Propaganda," *International Letters of Social and Humanistic Sciences*, 33, p. 41. doi:10.18052/www.scipress.com/ilshs.33.41.

769. Yu, S. *et al.* (2021) "Interpretable Propaganda Detection in News Articles," p. 1597. doi:10.26615/978-954-452-072-4_179.

770. Тенева, Е.B. (2023) "Digital Pseudo-Identification in the Post-Truth Era: Exploring Logical Fallacies in the Mainstream Media Coverage of the COVID-19 Vaccines," *Social Sciences*, 12(8), p. 457. doi:10.3390/socsci12080457.

771. Transcend media: https://www.transcend.org/tms/about-peace-journalism

772. Peace Journalism: www.Peacejournalism.org

773. BBC Editorial Guidelines:
   http://www.bbc.co.uk/guidelines/editorialguidelines/guidelines/

774. The Los Angeles Times Ethics Guidelines:
   http://latimesblogs.latimes.com/readers/2011/02/la-times-ethics-guidelines.html

775. https://www.britannica.com/topic/journalism

776. https://www.spj.org/ethicscode.asp

777. https://www.nimcj.org/blog-detail/exploring

778. http://www.bbc.co.uk/guidelines/editorialguidelines/guidelines/

779. http://latimesblogs.latimes.com/readers/2011/

780. https://www.ncbi.nlm.nih.gov/pmc/

About the Author

REECH MALUAL STANDS AS a distinguished South Sudanese legal and media luminary, whose impactful career has encompassed a diverse range of pivotal roles including print and broadcast journalist, correspondent, managing editor, and television station manager with UN Radio Miraya, Citizen Television, and The Business Focus Newspaper.

His expertise has also been extensively sought as a media consultant for numerous organizations throughout the Republic of South Sudan, significantly contributing to media development in the region with Media Authority of South Sudan, Journalist for Human Rights, Juba Monitor, Catholic Radio Network and others. Internationally, Malual has earned prestigious fellowships such as the highly competitive Generation Change Fellowship with the United States Institute of Peace and the Mandela Washington Fellowship for Young African Leaders, underscoring his global recognition.

He is also a distinguished recipient of the Spirit of Detroit Leadership Award, Michigan, and the revered Poet Award from Wayne State University, United States of America, testaments to his profound leadership and creative influence.

Beyond these significant achievements, Malual's indelible impact is most profoundly felt through his pivotal contributions to peace journalism within South Sudan, where his pioneering efforts have been instrumental in navigating the complexities of protracted conflicts and surmounting the formidable challenges of media civil war reporting in a post-independence landscape. His groundbreaking work not only forcefully illuminates the intricate dance between journalistic ethics, media advancement, and the unwavering pursuit of press freedom but actively shapes a more responsible and independent media environment amidst the pervasive political and socio-economic hurdles prevalent in Africa's youngest nation, South Sudan. Specifically, his work profoundly elucidates how media can either exacerbate or mitigate tensions during periods of civil unrest, thereby advocating for robust strategies that actively promote conflict reduction and sustainable peacebuilding.

His extensive background in peace journalism, particularly within post-conflict South Sudan, offers an indispensable lens through which to critically analyze the intricate nexus between media influence, societal stability, and the pervasive issue of illicit practices as a unique perspective underscoring the vital role of transparent and responsible media in addressing underlying causes of conflicts.